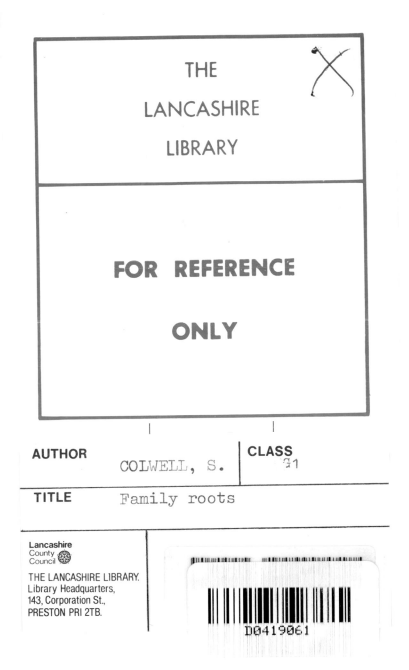

Family Roots

Discovering the Past in the Public Record Office

To all to whome this present writing shall Come Wee Richard Winston, John Winston and Robert Winston sonnes of Richard Winston of the parish of St Stephens Walbrooke London Confectioner deceased, Mary Underwood Widow late wife of Richard Underwood deceased one of the daughters of the said Richard Winston deceased, William Smith Citizen and Gouldsmith of London and Dorothy Smith my wife another daughter of the said Richard Winston deceased, Dorothy Winston and Elizabeth Winston, two other of the daughters of the said Richard Winston deceased, send greetinge. Whereas the said Richard Winston deceased, did in his life time pay and Adventure upon the proposicions for Land in Ireland, the some of Two hundred pounds. As by Lower severall receipts, two dated the 30th of Aprill 1642. for fifty pounds a peece and two others dated the 19th of July 1642. for fifty pounds apeece, may appeere And whereas the said Richard Winston in and by his Last will and testament bearing date the Seaven and twentieth day of February 1646. did give the residue of all his goods Chattells mony and debts to and amongst his Children: As by the same Will may more playnely appeare. Nowe knowe yee that wee the said Richard Winston, John Winston, Robert Winston, Mary Underwood, William Smith Dorothy Smith, Dorothy Winston and Elizabeth Winston. To the end that the last will and testament of the said Richard Winston deceased may be performed according to the intent and true meaninge thereof, doe hereby declare, That wee and every one of vs are Contented and Agreed That all such Land as shalbe allotted for the aforesaid some of Two hundred pounds, Shalbe devided and allotted to pe the said Richard Winston, John Winston, Robert Winston Mary Underwood Dorothy Smith, Dorothy Winston and Elizabeth Winston. and our heirds for ever, and to none other person, intent or purpose whatsoever In witnes whereof wee have hereunto sett our hands and Seales Given the Ffourth day of July In the yeere of our Lord: One Thousand Six hundred fifty and Three.

Richard Winston

Sealed and delivered by the said Richard Winston,
John Winston, William Smith, Anne Smith, Dorothy
Winston and Elizabeth Winston in the presence
of vs

Wm Sills
Henr: Cocke
James Walley his Serv'

And Sealed and delivered by the said Robert
Winston and Mary Underwood in the presence
of vs William Buckingham
Robt Rogers

John Winston
Robert Winston

will Smith Ann Smith

Dorothy Winston D W her marke
Elizabeth Winston E W her marke

Mary Underwood

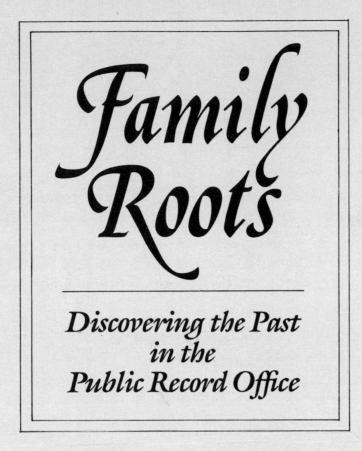

Family Roots

Discovering the Past
in the
Public Record Office

STELLA COLWELL

Weidenfeld and Nicolson   London

05174926

For Stanley

First published in 1991 by George Weidenfeld & Nicolson Ltd,
91 Clapham High Street, London SW4 7TA

British Library Cataloguing in Publication Data available

Designed by Martin Richards

Set in Galliard by Butler & Tanner Ltd

Printed and bound in England by Butler & Tanner Ltd, Frome
and London

*The signed agreement of 4 July 1653 of the three sons and
four daughters of the late Richard Winston of St Stephens
Walbrook, London, confectioner, an adventurer for lands
in Ireland in 1642. His allotted lands were to be divided
equally amongst them under the terms of his will, made
on 27 February 1646/7. SP63/289*

CONTENTS

Introduction 6

Acknowledgements 8

I   Understanding the Sources

1   The Legal System 11

2   The Holding and Transfer of Land 32

3   Tax and Other Sources of Revenue 49

4   Strangers and Settlers 73

II   The Sources at Work

5   The Turner and Plenderleath Families 102

6   The Gainsborough Family 118

7   The Walter Family 125

8   The Statham Family 140

9   The Fardon Family 150

10   The Wordsworth Family 160

11   The Garrick and Marx Families 169

12   The Dyer, Brenton and Walker Families 184

13   The Lyons, Evans, Massy and Atkinson Families 196

Notes 207

Bibliography 217

Index 223

INTRODUCTION

I first discovered the Public Record Office in June 1965 when I worked as a vacation student at the Society of Genealogists. Day after day, for three months, I pounded the hot pavements, past the street barrows spilling over with ripe strawberries and other luscious fruits, as I tried to pay for my Greek holiday, courtesy of my searches in the Probate Literary Department and the General Register Office in Somerset House, and the Public Record Office in Chancery Lane.

My only brief was to search for birth, marriage and death entries and the occasional will in the former repositories, and to examine the available Census Returns of 1841, 1851 and 1861 in the Long Room of the PRO. All the other treasures there were unknown and forbidden territory. I was introduced to an elderly professional searcher who was enlisted to keep an eye on me when things got tough, as they often did. I simply would not accept that if I was told to look at a certain place for a certain person at a certain date he might not be there. On one memorable and hot occasion I searched the whole of the 1851 Census of Maidstone for one elusive individual without success and searched it again in the belief that he must be lurking there somewhere. It was wonderful discipline for the mind, concentrating on very few sources and learning to know and manipulate them.

The worst part was the uncertainty that even if I arrived at opening time, 9.30 am, I was not assured of a seat, such was the crush for space. Without a seat I could not order any documents; the next worst part was sorting out the three references to the boxes or books I wished to scan. There were no street indexes and sometimes it was by process of elimination that a particular street in a large town was located. There was a wait of perhaps one and a half hours for a requisitioned box to be produced, five minutes spent flicking through its contents, and a short journey back to the counter to return it and collect the next one. Sometimes I ordered three

boxes, waited the prescribed period, found what I wanted in the first box and had to return the rest unopened and start the whole process again. Occasionally it was embarrassing when I realized to my horror that I had ordered the wrong references, confusing the 1841 for the 1851 Census which were listed together. All that waiting for nothing, and there was the slow march back to the production counter to be met by raised eyebrows at a search completed so quickly.

Time was of the essence, so the day was punctuated by forays outside into the fresh air to crunch my way through a bag of crisps or a bar of chocolate. Breakfast in a boarding-house on the busy Warwick Road, at Earls Court, was the highlight of the day. I was too tired in the evening to do anything other than buy a bag of those lovely ripe strawberries or a pound of cherries and spit out the bits from my bed in a room the size of a broom-cupboard onto the garden three storeys below. But I had my Greek holiday and I even volunteered myself the following year.

Then, when I embarked on a 'proper job' as my father called it, the full wealth of the PRO's records were at my disposal. This time, though, there was no-one to lead me through the maze. I was on my own to sink or swim in the welter of documentation arranged in files, bundled up or strung in boxes. Working as a genealogist at the College of Arms I had a wide range of cases to work on, some medieval, some firmly stuck in the eighteenth century, and others, most in fact, beginning with the clients' personal knowledge. During the first seven years at the College I discovered much of what was useful (and useless) at the PRO, but I had to teach myself, and I am aware that there are still yawning gaps in my knowledge, especially in relation to the more modern records of the twentieth century. I learnt according to the circumstances of each case.

There were no genealogical handbooks, no classes in genealogy to advise and educate, and no pool of experience to dip into to find out where to look next. The knowledge I accrued was in my head, an experience repeated I am sure by countless other professional and amateur genealogists tracking the same path through the sources. After that period of apprenticeship I began to feel confident enough to pass on some of the information to others by teaching.

This book is a culmination of those years of hard labour, excitement and experience, designed by a genealogist for other genealogists, and therefore unique. As I found it difficult to trace the background to and the purpose of many of the records in the PRO in a language I could understand, and as I regard an understanding of them as crucial to their proper usage, I have set down some introductory matter on the more elusive aspects of the major material on deposit, to try and make more sense of it and to make it more accessible to the genealogical reader. I have chosen the legal system, and land transfers because of the diverse records they have generated and because of the fictions employed in creating them; taxation was selected because I have nowhere seen an adequate analysis of the assessments and returns with the genealogist in mind; migration is included because it confronts all genealogists at some stage in their research. Finally there are chapters showing a selection of the various sources at work, illustrated by families whose profiles extend from the fifteenth to the late nineteenth centuries. Some of the information has had to be amplified by sources outside the PRO, but they are readily available in print or transcript, and this is indicated in the text, but I deliberately confined the studies as much as possible to demonstrate what a treasure house of records for the genealogist the PRO really is, covering all aspects of a person's life from birth to death and beyond.

The genealogist initially must establish filiations between one generation and the next and in relation to collateral branches of his family, generally by means of birth, baptism and marriage records, and by looking at documents where a family unit is seen such as in the Census, wills and monumental inscriptions. Sometimes these are defective, unavailable or ambiguous, are of a different period to the one required, or the people cannot be found, and so other sources have to be considered which are less obviously appropriate. But what are they? Where are they? What will they contain?

Once the skeleton has been put together the flesh can be added by the careful reconstruction of ancestors' lives from birth to death, using clues from personal recollection, tangible family ephemera kept as reminders of people's personalities and achieve-

ments, or from what was contained in the documents already consulted about abode, mobility, occupation and behaviour. The family historian seeks to answer questions of why a person came to be in a certain place at a certain time, and how he got there; why he pursued a certain occupation, how and where he trained for it, his income and responsibilities once employed, his achievements or failures; why a person came to be involved in legal proceedings, what was the outcome and how it affected himself and the rest of his family. As we ask these questions the genealogist should remember that human nature does not change: his predisposition to be shocked becomes anaesthetized and a growing fascination develops for the lifestyles of his forebears, eked out against different social, economic and religious backdrops to his own. The basic motives for certain actions remain constant: movement for better education, employment opportunities, promotion or travel; the eventual return to the family home or an environment geographically reminiscent of youth, to inherited property or business, to care for or be cared for by kinsfolk; or to take up a challenge or inducement proffered by relatives, business partners, employers, central or overseas government, or to escape from unhappy circumstances, relationships or behaviour. All these factors contribute to the hope of obtaining security and fulfilment, and were so in past times as much as today.

By finding at least some of the answers the family historian makes his own unique contribution to social history. A clutch of such histories of families living in a particular locality is, I maintain, much more conducive to the proper study of a nation's history than any set of statistics manipulated by demographers could ever hope to be. People are more important than figures.

How many genealogists have used printed transcripts or calendars of PRO material without first reading the essential introductory matter; how many indexes have been compiled without any explanation of the material being indexed? Floundering about among the first sources that come into his head, without thinking about their relevance, or appropriateness of period to his particular problem, is the genealogist really getting the best out of his valuable time and spending his energy (and his money) wisely? Family history has no academic requirements as a pursuit, but desk-top publishing has spawned a crop of cheap works of uneven quality purporting to help the researcher, often vying with each other for the same market and covering the same ground as if pre-nineteenth-century records did not exist. Fewer publications, of higher quality, on new topics, would be of far greater value. Like a sport, it can be approached in one of two ways: by rushing in head-long in a burst of enthusiasm which is quickly extinguished as the finer points of palaeography, dating schemes and choice of source present themselves and where the messing about produces only random success (the flounderer's approach), or by acquiring the techniques and skills necessary to harness and best apply a talent or interest, and take the subject seriously, respecting the documents he uses. After the first flurry, I am certain it is the second approach which becomes paramount in the genealogist's thinking.

This book will not rehearse what can be found in other works, but the bibliography at the end will refer the reader to what is already published; nor will it explain the procedure to be followed in requisitioning material for it has all been said before. What it will do, is point the genealogist in new directions, and send him along new paths of thought about the records he uses in his pursuit of ancestors, and, I hope, add immensely to his pleasure and appreciation of what the nation's archives hold for him. In short, this is the book I wish I had had myself in the summer of 1965. It would have saved a lot of aggravation and repository assistants' shoe leather.

Acknowledgements

I should like to thank the following members of staff at the Public Record Office, although I am sure there are more, to whom I apologize if I have omitted them: Susan Lumas (who went far beyond the call of duty to help), and Melvyn Stainton, both of Early Modern Records, Noel Amoordon, the foreman, and especially Jean Smith, both of Repository Section, Shirley Orjih and Roger Kershaw, both of Reprographic Section, all at Chancery Lane, and Eric O'Dell, the foreman, Mike Rogers, the Line Manager, and Marie Marshall and Dan Bowden, of Repository Section, and Mrs Bamrah, Mrs Allen and Tony Hammond of Reprographic Section, all at Kew. They smoothed my path by processing the many bulk (and bulky) orders of a wide range of bundles, boxes and files. Thanks for help of various kinds go to David Gurling of Lavenham, Hugh Belsey of Gainsbor-ough's House Museum, Sudbury, and Jenny Wilson at Weidenfeld for her valiant contribution to the typing. I want particularly to thank the following friends and supporters: Julian Duffus, Andrea Duncan, David House, Jude Howells, 'Duncan Kyle', Vivienne Lawrie, Sandra, Sarah and Stan Newens, Alf and Maureen Smeeth, Vanessa Thompson–Royds, Stanley West, and Oenone Wright. They checked that I was still alive, propped me up, undertook research, made me laugh, housed and fed me at moments of doubt and drama, and generally kept me going. Without the services of the Polstead Community Shop I could not have had my regular intake of jam doughnuts, chocolate bars and treacle toffee, and without my patient, trusting and encouraging editor, Emma Way, this book would never have been completed.

I
Understanding the Sources

Diagram 1: The structure of the Courts of common law and equity

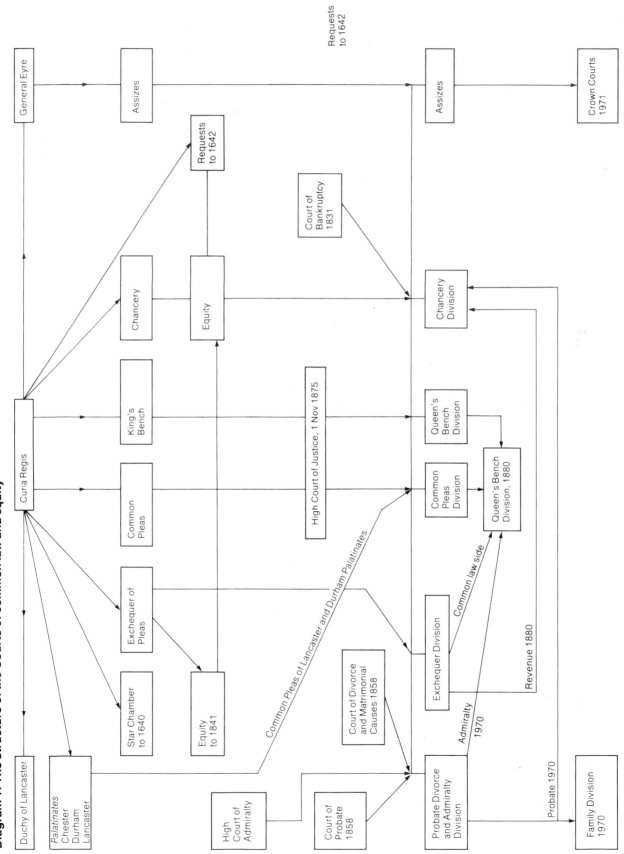

THE LEGAL SYSTEM

Justice in England was early administered by local custom. The medieval shire, hundredal and feudal courts constituted a rich source of revenue to the barons and landowners who ran them. Their virtual autonomy was only gradually eroded by the Crown as the King came to assume control over the law through his own commissioned judges and justices of the peace, and created a centralized system of courts known as 'common law'. The local courts decayed, but were never abolished.

The Common Law Courts

The fount of justice at common law was the King, operating through his Council (the Curia Regis). This also functioned as an executive and legislative body, until broadened in the thirteenth century to an 'elected' Parliament of knights of the shire and burgesses, and of barons and spiritual lords summoned there by writ. In time it hived off much of the business of the Council and reinforced its decisions by public and private statutes, for which the sovereign's subjects petitioned to obtain privileges, correct grievances, effect a divorce, change of name, naturalization, land enclosure, and alterations to settlements for the descent of land. The House of Lords scrutinized peerage claims, was the ultimate Court of Appeal from the lower courts, and like the House of Commons had the power of impeachment over and dealt with breaches of privilege by its members. Since 1876 judicial appeals to the House of Lords have been heard by salaried life peers. The monarch continued to consult a smaller circle of advisers drawn from the chief officers of State, and from the fourteenth century it came to be called the Privy Council, acting as a judicial tribunal where the common law was lacking in a remedy. Through its judicial committees it hears appeals in the Admiralty jurisdiction, and civil and criminal appeals from the Commonwealth and Dominions.

The three main common law courts, of the Exchequer, Common Pleas, and King's Bench, broke away from the Council for the hearing of civil disputes and major criminal cases, either in Westminster or on Circuit. Later, courts of equity were set up to remedy the procedural defects, limitations and restrictions of the common law courts. They were reunited under the High Court of Justice by the Supreme Court of Judicature Act 1873.

– The Court of Exchequer –

The Exchequer became a separate department in the early twelfth century during the reign of Henry I. It supervised the collection and oversight of royal revenue. By mid-century, in the reign of Henry II, it had also developed a judicial function and was known as the Exchequer of Pleas. Its judges were Exchequer Barons, headed by the Chief Baron of the Court. After the fourteenth century he was always a professional lawyer. Originally its business was confined to disputes between the Crown and its subjects concerning revenue. Later this was widened by means of a fiction to include disputes between subjects rendering the plaintiff less able (*quo minus*) to pay debts owed to the Crown because of the debts owed to him by the defendant. It also dealt with tithe disputes between the clergy and the laity. The records of the cases are filed on the Court's Plea Rolls[1] and include the judgments, and there is a printed Calendar of tithe suits between the fifteenth and eighteenth centuries.[2]

The Court was abolished in 1875 and its jurisdiction passed to the High Court; from 1880 the common law side has been exercised through the Queen's Bench Division, and the revenue through the Chancery Division. This Court had also evolved an equity jurisdiction by the mid-sixteenth century.

> *and ninety eight Between Thomas Trout of West Dowlish in the County of Somerset yeoman of the first part John Staple now or late of Chard in the same County Gentleman and Henry Conway of Milton in the County of Dorset Gentleman Executors in Trust of the last Will and Testament of Robert Matthers late of Crewkerne in the said County of Somerset Currier since deceased of the second part and John Vincent of Knowle Saint Giles in the said County of Somerset Gentleman of the third part Whereas by a certain Bond or Obligation in writing under the hands and Seals of the said Robert Matthers deceased and Alexander Wade of Bridport in the County of Dorset Esqr bearing date on or about the eighth day of November one Thousand seven hundred and eighty nine they the said Robert Matthers and Alexander Wade became bound unto Thomas Jeffery of Crewkerne aforesaid officer of Excise in the Sum of one Thousand two hundred pounds with Condition thereunder written for making the same void on payment unto the said Thomas Jeffery his Exors Admors or assigns of the Sum of Six hundred pounds and lawful Interest for the same on the eighth day of August then next And Whereas by a certain Indenture of three parts bearing even date with*

Part of the pleadings of a suit brought before the Court of Exchequer of Pleas in Michaelmas Term 39 George III (1798), by Thomas Jeffery, of Crewkerne, Somerset, Officer of Excise, against the executors of the late Robert Matthers, of Crewkerne, Currier, in connection with a loan. E13/1159

– The Court of Common Pleas –

The Court of Common Pleas was the second court to split away from the Curia Regis. When the King heard civil disputes in Council, suitors were forced to follow the Court wherever it travelled, causing great inconvenience. In 1215, Magna Carta provided that common pleas should be heard in 'a certain place', which was fixed at Westminster. The Court had a monopoly over actions for recovery of land (real actions), and settled disputes between subjects where the King was not involved, for example in personal actions of debt, detinue (where goods have been wrongfully detained), covenant (a breach of an obligation made in writing under the seal of the defendant), and account (where a bailiff or business partner could be compelled to account to the plaintiff for moneys received on his behalf), and also in cases of ejectment and trespass where a title to land was concerned. The Court's Plea Rolls, Placita de Banco (or De Banco) Rolls[3] are the main source for tracing cases, together with the Recovery Rolls,[4] while Posteas[5] also record the final judgments.

The judges were full-time lawyers chosen from the serjeants-at-law, senior advocates who had an exclusive right of audience in this Court, and they were presided over by the Chief Justice of the Court. They were highly paid and the excessive formality of the pleadings made proceedings protracted and expensive.

In 1875 the Court was absorbed into the High Court of Justice, and from 1880 it became part of the Queen's Bench Division.

– The Court of King's Bench –

The Court of King's Bench was the last of the three to break away, towards the end of the thirteenth century, during the reign of Henry III. It was closest to the King, who, even as late as the eighteenth century, was present during its deliberations. During the Commonwealth it was known as the Upper Bench. The Court was headed by the Lord Chief Justice of England, and run by judges of the Bench, and followed the King's person, although it usually met at Westminster. Its original jurisdiction was mainly in civil matters (the Plea side) covering most actions in tort (infringements of legal rights) which derived from the writ of trespass, and included forgery, deceit and fraud committed against a person or his property, but in the late sixteenth century it began to deal with actions in contract under the writ of *assumpsit* (breach of promise). The Court's sphere was widened to take in writs of debt using the fictitious Bill of Middlesex. By this the Sheriff of Middlesex was directed to arrest the defendant for a trespass '*vi et armis*' (by force and arms) which resulted in a breach of the King's peace. He was taken into custody and committed to the King's Bench Prison to await trial. The real cause of action was then heard and the trespass dropped. If he was not to be found in Middlesex the bill was marked '*non est inventus*' (he has not been found), and a writ of '*latitat*' was sent to the sheriff of the county in which he lurked and ran about ('*latitat et discurrit*'). The Bill was abolished in 1832. The proceedings of the Court are recorded to 1701 on the Placita Coram Rege Rolls,[6] and thereafter on the Plea (or Judgment) Rolls[7] and in the Entry Books of Rules[8] of the Court.

The Court had power to issue prerogative writs (orders) of mandamus, prohibition, and certiorari, restraining excesses and abuses of jurisdiction by inferior courts, corporations and public officials. It also issued writs of quo warranto (to test the authority by which a person claimed an office, franchise or liberty) and from 1679 writs of habeas corpus (to test the legality of an imprisonment). It also reinforced decisions taken in ecclesiastical courts.

Besides having a civil function, the Court of King's Bench was the principal court of criminal jurisdiction, before which informations were laid and indictments presented (the Crown side). It heard cases ranging from breaches of the peace to high treason and it was to this Court that the Jacobites were brought for trial after the Rebellions of 1715 and 1745. The main records of cases are on the Coram Rege Rolls to 1701, continued on the Crown Rolls.[9] The very earliest enrolments, up to 1271, are on the Curia Regis Rolls.[10] Another useful series are the Controlment Rolls,[11] noting the progress of trials.

The Court was also appellate, dealing with cases from the inferior courts by means of a writ of error. Until 1875, appeal from here was either to the Courts of Exchequer Chamber, or directly to the House of Lords; thereafter it was to the Court of Appeal.

In 1875 the Court was amalgamated into the High Court, and from 1880 has functioned as part of the Queen's Bench Division.

– The Court of Chancery –

From the late thirteenth century the Court of Chancery also had a common law jurisdiction, and its business covered repeals of letters patent, co parceny and dower, inquisitions post mortem, lunacy and idiocy, and recognizances. The records of its proceedings are filed in the Petty Bag Office,[12] and the pleadings in the Tower[13] and the Rolls Chapel Series.[14]

– The Court of Exchequer Chamber –

The Court of Exchequer Chamber was the title used by four different appellate courts: the first, set up in 1357, acted solely as a court of error from the Exchequer, and met in any nearby council room, with the Chancellor, Treasurer and judges of the common law courts as assessors; the second originally met informally to allow the bench of judges to consider difficult points of law arising from cases in the common law courts, and by the fifteenth century their judgments were regarded as binding; the third was established under statute in 1585, and was a court of error from the Court of King's Bench presided over by any six judges from the other two common law courts; the last was created in 1830 as a court of error from all three of the common law courts and was composed, like the third, of judges drawn from the two courts other than the one where the case originated. Appeal beyond this lay with the House of Lords. In 1875 it was replaced by the Court of Appeal. Records of appeals are found among the Plea Rolls of the Court of King's Bench (Plea side),[15] King's Bench Rule Books (Court of Appeal),[16] and in Final and Interlocutory Appeals, Motions,[17] and Final Interlocutory Orders, Order Books[18] of the Supreme Court of Judicature.

The Criminal Law Courts

– The Courts of Assize –

The General Eyre was the precursor of the Courts of Assize on Circuit. From the late twelfth century, itinerant justices were sent at intervals of several years from Westminster into the shires to safeguard royal interests of all kinds and to hear common pleas arising since their last visit and to try more serious offences. Once every seven years they held an inquisition into the administration of justice within each county, during which the shire courts were suspended. Surviving records, dating from 1194 until its effective abolition in 1294, are contained on the Curia Regis Rolls and Eyre Rolls,[19] and include the quo warranto proceedings of the reign of Edward I.

The Eyre was unpopular for it was seen as an intrusion into local affairs and posed a threat to the magnates' authority in the shires, but it was an early attempt at standardization and improved efficacy of justice. It was superseded about 1340 by the Assize Courts, following the same pattern of regular visits by justices from London; the burgeoning influence of meetings of Parliament in different parts of the realm also contributed to its eclipse.

In the twelfth century, Henry II set up a Grand Assize to try questions of seisin (possession) and title to land by enquiry of sixteen men sworn to speak the truth. Magna Carta provided that assizes of novel desseisin (for the recovery of land of which a person had recently been dispossessed), *mort d'ancestor* (for the restoration of land of which a person had been deprived on the death of an ancestor) and darrein presentment (where the advowson of a living had been disturbed by the intervention of a stranger making a presentation to a vacant benefice), should take place only in the counties where the land was situated. Pairs of justices were dispatched up to three

times a year under the Statute of Westminster 1285 to determine the disputes at petty (or possessory) assizes, which would normally have come before the justices itinerant in eyre, but which had suffered lengthy delays and inconvenience because of the relative infrequency of their tours. Gradually it became impossible to administer criminal law by trial in London, so justices were sent out into the country to hold assizes (sittings) of the Royal courts. The judges were from the common law courts, or were serjeants-at-law or prominent laymen, acting on Royal commissions of 'oyer and terminer' (to hear and determine), and of gaol delivery (to try prisoners delivered up from prison). In the early fourteenth century, Edward I organized groups of contiguous counties into four Assize Circuits (later increased to six, and re-formed in 1875), which were visited several times a year by his judges, presiding in pairs in the various county towns within their circuit. Originally its business was purely criminal, but the 1285 Statute extended its scope to certain civil actions, to relieve the burden of transporting local juries to Westmins-

Diagram 2: The Assize Circuits

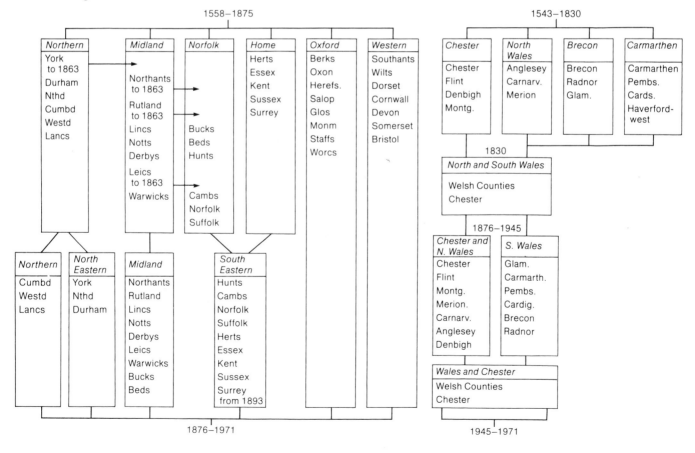

ter. A writ of *nisi prius* was sent to the county sheriff to secure the jury's attendance at Westminster '*nisi prius*' (unless before) the case had been heard locally at an assize, which it generally was. In the fourteenth and fifteenth centuries its ambit was widened to embrace all types of civil action, but because only issues of fact were tried locally and the jury's verdict returned to Westminster, its main business concentrated on criminal cases, the defendants being brought for trial in the county of apprehension. From 1842, cases of treason, murder and felonies punishable by life imprisonment were referred on to the Assizes by the local magistrates sitting in the county Quarter Sessions.

Possessory assizes were abolished in 1833, as were the Assize Courts and Quarter Sessions under the Courts Act 1971, being replaced by Crown Courts.

The records of the Assize Circuits are the Minute Books detailing for each sitting the defendants' names, charges, verdicts and sentences, the indictments setting out details of the offence, and the plea, verdict and sentence, the depositions of witnesses, and Gaol Books listing inmates, their abode, occupation and date when committed.[20] Posteas, the records of the *nisi prius* proceedings returned to the Court of King's Bench, are filed with that Court.[21] Cases held before the possessory assizes form part of the Assize Rolls of the Justices Itinerant.[22]

– The Old Bailey Sessions –

The Old Bailey Sessions, superseded by the Central Criminal Court in November 1834, had jurisdiction over the metropolitan and adjacent areas.[23] It usually met twelve times a year and its business matched that of the Assize Circuit. The Central Criminal Court also hears cases relating to crimes on the high seas or abroad, and those which have been transferred from other courts to ensure a fair trial where local prejudice might be an issue, and to avoid delay. Many of the proceedings have been published.[24]

The Annual Criminal Registers, for Middlesex from 1791 to 1849,[25] and for England and Wales between 1805 and 1892[26] and including Middlesex from 1850, are arranged alphabetically by county and list each indictable defendant appearing before Quarter Sessions or Assizes, for what offence, the verdict and sentence. There is a similar Calendar of Prisoners running up to 1909,[27] both classes being amongst the records of the Home Office. These are immensely helpful in tracking down the date and place of trial.

The Courts in Action

– Civil Procedure –

The basic principle in common law was that a common law right only existed if there was a procedure for enforcing it. Thus, if there was no existing writ to fit the alleged facts, the aggrieved party had no redress. Civil actions ran in three stages, initiated by the issue of a writ appropriate to the allegations and which was purchased from Chancery, followed by formal pleadings, and finally the trial. Real actions were for the recovery of land, and personal actions for damages, and where both were concerned the causes were known as mixed actions. Real actions were almost entirely abolished under the Real Property Limitation Act 1833, and finally by the Common Law Procedure Acts between 1852 and 1860.

The earliest pleadings were delivered orally in open court and written up by a clerk of the record, but by the fifteenth century they were separated from the trial and were submitted in writing. The parties became able to fix the dispute at issue between them and debate it at the trial. But only one issue and only one defence could be argued. A defence on a point of law was called a demurrer, and a defence on the facts a special plea, or of general issue (a straightforward denial of the allegations). The latter created difficulties for the plaintiffs so the Civil Procedure Act 1833 gave power to the judges to make rules of procedure requiring defendants to plead specific defences. The writ system, whereby a specific writ had to be applied for, was abolished in 1852. The Supreme Court of Judicature Acts, 1873–5, put a final gloss on what was already developing by establishing the modern system of pleading, commencing with a statement of claim, followed by a defence or counterclaim, and further pleadings, each filed with the Court within prescribed time limits. The most important series of records are the Judgment Books,[28] which superseded the Plea Rolls of the various common law courts, and the means of reference to them is through the Cause Books of the different Divisions,[29] setting out the date and usually the number of the judgment of each case, of which only samples remain.

Trials of right were by combat (not abolished until 1819), those of debt and detinue by wager of law (compurgation) under which the oaths of a number of persons, usually twelve, testified to the defendant's good character and the ill-foundation of the claim

Part of a list of actual and suspected Papists, Non-Jurors and Quakers refusing to take the oaths prescribed by the statute passed in 1714 (of allegiance, rejection of the Pope's authority and abjuration of the Pretender). Those named had been summoned by the Quarter Sessions held in Newcastle-upon-Tyne, Northumberland, on 11 April 1716, to take the oaths, but had neglected to appear. Such refusal carried the penalty of being judged a Popish recusant convict and two-thirds of the recusant's estates became forfeit. C203/6

against him. If insufficient numbers could be found, or they wavered in taking the oath, then guilt was presumed. Compurgation was abolished in 1833. All other actions were tried before a judge and jury of twelve good and lawful men. Where an issue of law was at stake the parties argued before the judge; where it was an issue of fact the outcome was decided by a jury. Until the fifteenth century the jurors were witnesses rather than judges of fact, so other witnesses were rarely called.

Trials at assize took place in two stages: the issue of fact was tried at *nisi prius* before the judge and jury and its verdict returned to Westminster, where judgment was entered on the record of the Court of King's Bench.[30] By the fifteenth century, when the justices were all legally trained, the whole process was dealt with at local level, although as a formality the judgments continued to be entered at Westminster.

To 1830 appeal was by writ of error to the King's Bench or Court of Exchequer Chamber, or direct to the House of Lords, and thereafter to the second of these, until supplanted by the Court of Appeal in 1875. This writ alleged there was an error on the record and only extended to points of law, such as a defect in the pleadings. However, in the seventeenth century it became possible for a litigant to move for a new trial in civil actions.

– Criminal Procedure –

The conduct of criminal prosecution was divided into four parts: the arrest of the alleged offender and his custody, the presentation for trial, the trial itself, and finally the verdict and sentence. Offences of murder, manslaughter, rape, burglary and larceny were felonies; offences created by later statutes or by the Court of Star Chamber were classified as misdemeanours, and on this distinction depended the mode of trial and sentence.

The three principal methods of prosecution were by an appeal of felony, on indictment, or by summary trial. Trial on indictment was the most important means of prosecution and used a jury. The evolution of the jury system led to a decline of the appeal of felony, which in the case of murder was hampered by the fact that a year and a day had to elapse before the alleged offender could be tried, whereas the accused could be immediately tried on indictment. Summary trials were the province of petty sessions, and the manorial courts leet, whose records were retained by their own officers.

The earliest means by which an offender was apprehended was by frankpledge. A collective responsibility was placed on the community by making every person without substantial property a member of a group of ten, known as a tithing. If one member committed a crime the rest were expected to bring him to justice. The records of the manorial courts are the prime example of this procedure at work. The Assize of Clarendon 1166 promulgated that hundredal juries should present suspects for trial by the visiting justices itinerant in eyre. These were known as juries of

Part of the report on the inquisition held at the Bush Inn, Longtown, Cumberland on 25 and 27 June 1851, on the body of Thomas Plenderleath, by the coroner and twelve jurors. Their verdict was one of murder, and William Kirkpatrick, the assailant, was sent for trial at the Cumberland Summer Assizes, held at Carlisle in August, where he was found guilty of manslaughter and sentenced to six months in gaol with hard labour. ASSI44/168 Part I

EXAMINATION

Of a CANDIDATE for the Situation of a Police Constable.

QUESTIONS.	ANSWERS.
Name	Edward Kilburn
Age	22 years; born 24th day of January 1866
Height	5 feet 9½ inches.
Weight	10 stones 6 lbs.
Chest measurement	35 inches.
Complexion	Fresh.
Eyes	Brown.
Hair	Brown.
Particular Marks	None.
Where Born — In the Parish	Fylham.
In or near the Town of	London.
In the County of	Middx.
Trade or Calling	Musician
Single or Married	Single.
Number of Children	—
Residence	22 Bloomsbury Sq. W.C.
What Public Services	Army.
Police, Regiment, Corps, &c.	1st Shropshire.
Length of Service	6 yrs. 309 days.
When discharged	23 August 1866. 18 Jan. 1887.
With whom last employed	Mr R.B. Jones.
And where	2. Hare Court. Temple.
If ever in the Metropolitan Police Service	No.
Whether belonging to any illegal Secret Society	No.

Date 29 January 1889   Brown
                              Examining Clerk.

SURGEON'S CERTIFICATE.

I HEREBY CERTIFY that I have examined the above Candidate, as to his health and bodily strength, and that I consider him fit for the Police Duty.

Surgeon in Chief.

Certificate of Service records of the Metropolitan Police Force, relating to the successful medical examination of a candidate, Edward Kilburn, on 29 January 1889. He previously was a soldier, discharged on 18 January 1887 and was last employed at Hare Court, in the Temple, presumably by a barrister. MEP04/361

presentment. From the fourteenth century parishes began to appoint their own annually elected constables for the maintenance of law and order and they were given powers of arrest. At the same time administration of justice within the counties was beginning to shift away from the sheriffs to being the responsibility of a nominated body of justices of the peace, acting under Crown Commissions, and who from the late fourteenth century began to hold Quarter Sessions for judicial and administrative purposes, although the sheriff remained the major vehicle through whom the Crown acted in sending out writs and commands. The justices of the peace scrutinized and approved the parochial nominees as constables. Under the Metropolitan Police Act 1829, and the County Police Act 1839, parish constables were gradually replaced by a paid professional force. Names and warrant numbers of joiners and leavers in the Metropolitan Police Force, service records, deaths while in service, pensions and gratuities of personnel are open for inspection.[31]

The Grand Jury was the earliest type of jury used at Assizes and Quarter Sessions. It consisted of twenty-four county freeholders and succeeded the jury of presentment. At first it presented suspects for trial, often on the basis of personal knowledge, but its later role was to enquire into the allegations to decide whether a bill of indictment should be preferred; from 1554 its duty was limited to certifying indictments as 'True Bills', the justices of the peace having previously examined whether the actions alleged constituted an offence. The Grand Jury was abolished by the Criminal Justice Act 1948. From 1352 the petty jury of twelve lesser freeholders served to give its verdict at the end of the trial. Until 1670 its members could be fined or gaoled if the judge considered a verdict perverse. The names of both sets of jurors often survive among the Assize Indictments and Miscellanea.[32]

Originally, trial was by ordeal, by wager of law, or by jury. While no person could be compelled to submit to a jury trial without his consent, torture was often employed to encourage it. This was only abolished in 1772, thereafter silence was treated as a plea of guilty, a position not reversed until 1827. Until 1898, the defendant was not allowed to give evidence on his own behalf, though he was permitted to make an unsworn statement from the dock on which he could not be cross-examined. Evidence was given by sworn witnesses present in the Court. In cases where a coroner's inquest had been held, a copy of the report would be produced. An example of a trial where this was done is in chapter 5, when William

Kirkpatrick was indicted at the Summer Assizes for Cumberland in 1851 for the unlawful killing of Thomas Plenderleath.

If found guilty as a felon the sentence was capital punishment or maiming, with forfeiture of the offender's goods and lands to the Crown, in the latter case on the same terms under which he had held them (for life, a term of years or as a freehold). For a misdemeanour, the penalty was a fine or imprisonment.

Mitigation was possible and by the late eighteenth century only about one person in eight condemned to death was actually executed.[33] The Royal prerogative of mercy was used in the form of a pardon conditional on transportation for life or term of years to the American and (after 1787 and up to 1868) the Australian colonies, or the juries fictitiously assessed the value of stolen property at less than a shilling, thus converting a capital offence into the misdemeanour of petty larceny. The third mitigating plea was 'benefit of clergy'. Dating from the reign of Henry II, in the twelfth century, criminous clerks were tried in ecclesiastical courts where the punishments were less severe and where there was no jury. Compurgation was available to them so convictions were rare. After 1352 secular clerks could claim benefit of clergy. The test to determine status as a clerk was whether a person could read. As evidence of this he was required to recite a verse of a Latin psalm. Benefit of clergy could be claimed after conviction and before sentence, but the guilty party was not exempt from forfeiture even if his plea succeeded. A statute of 1490 limited the privilege to first offenders, but they were still subjected to branding as a mark of conviction, and from the reign of Henry VIII the plea was no longer open to murderers with malice aforethought. In 1576 criminous clerks were ordered to be released without being handed over to the Church, and the Court was given a discretionary power of imprisonment for up to a year. Eventually it applied only to certain common law felonies and was abolished in 1827. Forfeiture for felony was not ended until the Forfeiture Act 1870.

Prison Records

Originally gaols were places of confinement for persons awaiting trial. Each county had its own houses of correction close to the places of trial, which were the responsibility of the county to sustain.

Part of a petition for an early release made by Oscar Wilde in Reading Gaol, 13 November 1896. He was convicted at the Central Criminal Court on 20 May 1895, of gross indecency, and sentenced to two years with hard labour. The petition gives a graphic description of the effect on him of prison life. He was not released till 19 May 1897 and died in 1900.
HO45/24514/A56887/19a

89

Easter Term in the Fifth year of the Reign of King George the Fourth.

Middlesex. William Pole Tilney Long Wellesley late of Wanstead in the County of Essex Esquire Outlawed in London at the suit of William Jackson in a certain plea of trespass on the case to the damage of the said William Jackson of Three hundred and Fifty pounds

By Inquisition indented taken at the house known by the name of the Sheriffs Office Red Lion Square in the County of Middlesex on the twelfth day of January in the fourth year of the reign of his present Majesty before George Byrom Whittaker Esquire and Peter Laurie Esquire Sheriff of the said County by virtue of the Kings Writ to the said Sheriff directed and to the said Inquisition annexed It is found on the Oath of James Vrall and others lawful men of his Bailiwick That William Pole Tilney Long Wellesley in the said Writ to this Inquisition annexed named on the twenty first day of July One thousand eight hundred and twenty three on which day he was Outlawed in London at the suit of William Jackson in a certain plea of Trespass on the case was and yet is possessed of and entitled unto as of his own goods and chattels of and in a certain Box in the Theatre Royal Drury Lane in the said County situate and being on the ground tier or Circle on the south side of the said Theatre and numbered 5 and the free and exclusive use and enjoyment thereof and of every part thereof respectively together with the full and free liberty of Ingress Egress and Regress way and passage into and from the said Theatre and to and from the said Box every Evening and Night upon which any public

William Pole Tilney Long Wellesley, outlawed on 21 July 1823 at the suit of William Jackson, in a plea of trespass with £350 damages, has his box in the Theatre Royal, Drury Lane, seized by the sheriffs, reckoned by them to be worth £600. Born in 1788, he succeeded his father as the Earl of Mornington, and was nephew to the first Duke of Wellington. E173/3

Gradually they became centres for punishment. Transportation to the colonies dried up in 1868, giving rise to grave shortages of prison housing. Even before this many convicts had languished and died on board the severely overcrowded and insanitary prison hulks moored in estuaries for the long wait for transportation. In 1877 a concerted national system was set up under the Prison Commission. Lists of prisoners are to be found among Home Office papers, arranged by county,[34] while prisons, such as Newgate,[35] Millbank and Pentonville, merit their own series.[36] There are lists of prisoners confined in hulks,[37] and transported to the colonies, in the Home Office records,[38] with occasional censuses of them, and pardons granted,[39] while overseas. Some of the convicts transported before 1787 are named in Treasury records,[40] chiefly from Middlesex and the Home Counties, and much work has been done in extracting and publishing the names of transportees.[41] There is also a series of applications made for wives and families of convicts to be allowed to join them among the records of the Home Office and elsewhere.[42]

Defendants who failed to appear in Court to submit themselves to civil or criminal suits were put outside its protection by having judgments of outlawry made against them. This rendered them liable to imprisonment or capital punishment, and to forfeiture of goods and escheat of land. Outlawry proceedings were finally extinguished in 1938, though they were defunct long before this. Records of them can be perused among those of the three common law courts,[43] and an outline of the lands and goods involved is noted in the Outlawry Books of the Exchequer, dating from 1639 and running to 1884. The two Walter brothers, Sir William and David, of Oxfordshire, were declared outlaws in the 1640s and orders for the seizure of their goods and lands sent to the sheriff (see chapter 7).

425	William Oldham or Holding	16	4	9¾	L? Brown	do	Fresh — Small scar on right eye & scar on left knee	do	no residence being a tramp	Mother Mary Tramp, Syamstiekes Magull or Liverpool	Laborer	Imp
430	George Watts	16	4 / 4	8¼ / 9½	Brown / Brown		Fresh — much freckled 2 scars inside of right thigh projection of flesh inside of under lip — cut on forefinger left hand	Buxton Norfolk	Buxton	Mother Drusina Watts, Weaver Buxton	Laborer	Imp
432	John Sheban	14	4	3	do grey		Fresh — Stout small scar on second finger of right hand	Holborn London	London	Mother Anne Sheban, Irish woman 3 Fennis Court Middlesex Holborn London	None	Rates
433	George Barnes	16	5 / 5	2¾ / 3½	Brown	do	Fresh — Stout scar on bridge of nose — cut on under lip — cut on left cheek bone	(London) Westminster	Westminster	Father Edward Barnes, Messiah 23 Quist St Martin Lane London	None	Roads

Prison Register of Parkhurst. Entry number 430 shows George Watts aged 16 and 4 feet 9½ inches tall with his physical characteristics. He was both born and resident at Buxton in Norfolk, where his mother was living as a weaver. He was committed at Aylsham in Norfolk on 7 August 1851 and convicted of arson at Norwich Assizes on 15 March 1852, receiving a sentence of seven years. He was released on a licence on 8 April 1856. The clerk notes that his father, uncle and cousin had been transported. PCOM2/59 f22d

The Courts of Equity

The common law partly overcame its own rigidity by the use of fictions extending the scope of the original writs, assuming jurisdiction, or using the plea of benefit of clergy, but these were insufficient to remedy all its defects. Legislation, the main agency of law reform, was not widely available in the Middle Ages. The Courts of Equity: Chancery (dating from the late fourteenth century), Exchequer (from the mid-sixteenth century) and Requests (from the late fifteenth century) evolved to help dissatisfied litigants who were unable to fit the facts of their case into any existing writ, or who had been defeated by compurgation.

The guiding principle of equity was to ensure that no wrong was suffered without there being a remedy; often cases brought to these courts referred to previous suits dismissed by the common law courts. Their business was to act on a person's rights as against another's, rather than on the property itself, and related chiefly to breaches of trust (for example, mortgages, wills, settlements and business agreements), prevention of fraud, enforcement or variation of contracts (for instance marriage settlements and

trusts), and gave effect to a person's intentions where the common law or ecclesiastical courts could not (such as wills concerning realty over which the Church had no jurisdiction, and in tithe matters). The Court of Chancery also exercised protective custody over infants, with the power to appoint guardians, and also over persons of unsound mind.

– The Court of Chancery –

The procedure in the Court of Chancery was that as there was no writ, rights and remedies could be created as required. The means by which a remedy was achieved was through interlocutory orders and injunctions compelling or forbidding certain actions by the parties, and finally by decree setting out the Court's decision after a hearing of the suit and it summarized each side's case and their respective rights. The suit commenced with a bill of complaint (called an English bill, because unlike the Latin pleadings in the common law courts before Easter Term 1733, proceedings in the Courts of Equity were in English) filed by the plaintiff in the Court, disclosing a reason for the monarch or Chancellor to intervene and issue a writ of subpoena (under a penalty) to the defendant compelling him to attend and answer the petition. The plaintiff was described as the orator, for originally the cases were conducted orally in court. The defendant was required to enter an appearance acknowledging the suit, and then to return an answer or demurrer within a prescribed time limit. The answer might make a counterclaim to which the petitioner might respond with a replication, the defendant with a rejoinder, the petitioner a rebutter, the defendant a surrebutter, until either party became exhausted (financially or otherwise) or was ready to proceed to the next stage. The demurrer alleged that no good cause of action had arisen or challenged the

ceedings, and signed written answers to them (depositions) obtained from sworn witnesses either in the provinces[46] or in London.[47] These were prefaced by the name, age, residence and occupation of the Country or Town deponent, while the body of his answers may reveal incidental autobiographical information about him as well as details about the suitors not mentioned in the Proceedings themselves.

Proceedings before the Chancellor were confined to legal argument. Where further testimony was needed it was supplied on affidavit. Sometimes exhibits[48] were called for to support the evidence given, such as pedigrees, deeds, letters, business and estate papers, and even material objects, and many of these were left with the Court. An example of the variety of ephemera lodged as exhibits can be seen in the welter of documents relating to the Oxfordshire family of Walter covering the years from the end of the seventeenth century to the mid-eighteenth (see chapter 7). Finally the Court issued a decree giving its judgment.[49]

Unfortunately the Court of Chancery eventually became the victim of its own good intentions, for its system was bogged down in paperwork and officialdom, and its procedure grew increasingly dilatory and expensive. Whereas plaintiffs had originally petitioned the King to exercise his prerogative, he delegated this to his Lord Chancellor, as custodian of the Great Seal; in the sixteenth century he appointed Masters in Chancery, headed by the Master of the Rolls, to hear the cases, delivering only the judgments himself. In 1813 Vice-Chancellors were engaged to off-set the mounting stockpile of arrears, but even this was not enough. By the sixteenth and seventeenth centuries the Court was possessed of a formidable hierarchy of officers: there were the Six Clerks, and their assistants 'the clerks in court' or 'sworn clerks', collectively known as the Sixty Clerks, who received the bills and entered memoranda of them under the name of the plaintiff and Six Clerk in a Bill Book. Once an appearance had been entered by the defendant the sworn clerk removed the bill, drafted a copy for the defendant, and when his answer was received it was annexed to the bill which was then returned to the appropriate Six Clerk office. The bills were kept there for six clear legal terms for reference purposes before being sorted alphabetically under the surnames of the plaintiffs and arranged in bundles. The clerks also received and filed the replications, rejoinders and other counterclaims, and the Country depositions forwarded by local Commissioners. These subsequent documents were filed with the records of the term in which they were received, and were detached from the bills to which

Part of a draft bill of complaint to the Court of Chancery on behalf of Lady Elizabeth Walter, widow of Sir John Walter, Bt, of Sarsden in Oxfordshire, and his half-brother, Sir Robert Walter, Bt, 9 July 1722. The defendants were Sir John's sister Mary and her husband Sir Robert Rich, Bt, who had challenged the validity of Sir John's last will. Sir Robert is described as the son of Sir William Walter by his second wife Lady Mary Bruce. The box of Chancery Master's Exhibits revealed an array of family and estate papers. C110/135

appropriateness of the court, and asked for the bill to be thrown out and costs awarded to the defendant for his vexation and charges and expenses. These documents were known collectively as Chancery Proceedings,[44] from 1842 called pleadings.[45] A series of interrogatories (questions) was then drawn up on each side relating to all the alleged facts in the Pro-

they referred; the Country depositions were stored in the sworn clerks' office for two years before being arranged with the records of the relevant Six Clerk. The examiners in Chancery interviewed the London witnesses and took down their depositions in writing. The registrar's job was to take the Court minutes and draft the various decrees, dismissions and orders. The Masters in Chancery had custody of whatever exhibits had been produced, and made reports on matters of practice and legal interpretation when called upon by the Court, and on any action taken by them in the execution of court orders. This chaotic state of affairs was an open scandal and long ripe for reform.

It is little wonder that bills and answers were very often not joined together or reunited. A bill taken out for amendments to be made to it might be refiled as a fresh one and be filed later than the answer; some answers were removed for copying by the plaintiff's clerk and not returned for many years afterwards,

again in a different place; sometimes the bill and answer were filed with different Six Clerks because the bill had been removed by a clerk in another office to await the answer from a co-defendant; subsequent counterclaims were not necessarily filed with the original bill and answer; if there were several plantiffs and co-defendants in a suit, only the first few were listed, yet each might produce an answer or counterclaim which when filed might make them seem to be quite unconnected litigants; not all the plaintiffs to a suit

A plan of the Six Clerks (or Prothonotaries) and Inrolment Offices of the High Court of Chancery, July 1829, showing the storage facilities for the equity pleadings and memoranda books. The Record Room was where they were eventually housed after being kept in the studies of the Six Clerks for six terms to allow free access. (removed from C113/259/8 and 9) MPA10

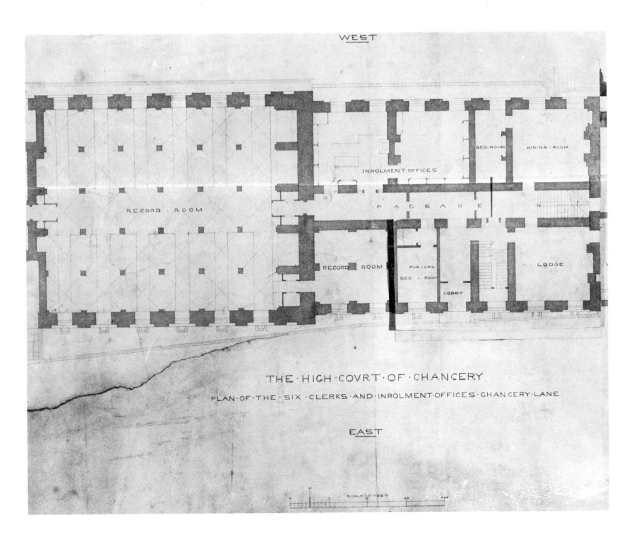

were entered in the Bill Book which added to the difficulties of matching up later papers; when a plaintiff died and the action was taken over by a successor any future answers would be addressed to him, again suggesting an independent case; as clerks died, so their papers were gathered up and returned to their Six Clerks and filed under 'pleadings', and thus were organized out of order. 'Single bills' were also arranged separately when defendants failed to enter an appearance. This might seem to pose an almost intractable problem for the genealogist or historian trying to piece together the various stages of a suit. The Entry Books of decrees and orders, called A and B Books, dating from 1544 and 1547[50] respectively, list the various instructions given by the Court during the course of the case, by legal term and initial letter of the plaintiff's surname, and these can help to track down an individual case. But these might go on for a long time before the final decree (if any) was issued, and years might elapse after the commencement of the action, so it is to the original list of plaintiffs[51]

that the searcher must always turn, and from the reign of James I to the Six Clerks' Series,[52] to make the search complete, bearing in mind also that many cases never even went as far as the Court for any order to be issued. From the reign of Elizabeth the Country depositions and Town depositions were filed apart from the bills and answers, listed under the names of the plaintiffs and defendants, until united with them in 1714. Charles Bernau compiled an index of Town deponents to 1800, and of Country deponents up to

---

Part of the bill of complaint presented to the Court of Exchequer (Equity Side) in Easter Term 10 James I (1612), by George Owen of Godstow, Oxfordshire, concerning the deeds of certain chantries at Chipping Norton and the Oxford suburbs granted to his grandfather by letters patent on 25 March 3 Edward VI (1549) and now in the hands of the defendants, leaving him without a remedy. E112/115 no 141

the end of the reign of Charles I, plus eight percent of the rest to 1800. A microfilm of the index is held at the library of the Society of Genealogists, in London.

Appeal from the Court lay to the Lord Chancellor for a rehearing, or directly to the House of Lords. The Court of Appeal in Chancery was established in 1851, and was abolished in 1875 to make way for the Court of Appeal applicable to all civil cases.

The Court of Chancery was merged into the High Court in 1875 and continues as the Chancery Division.

– The Court of Exchequer –

The equity side of the Court of Exchequer followed the pattern of procedure set in the Court of Chancery, but also heard suits relating to debts, tithes, mineral rights, and other matters which ultimately might affect the Crown's revenue interests. Bills in matters relating to the King were brought by the Attorney General and were called informations. In 1841 it was abolished and later cases came before the Court of Chancery. The Bill Books are arranged by reign and then by county,[53] and are the main means of reference to the pleadings.[54] The Bernau Index described above also contains a list of defendants and deponents between 1558 and 1695; a further manuscript list running to 1800 is in the library of the Society of Genealogists.

– The Court of Requests –

The Court of Requests was set up about the year 1483 to grant relief to poor litigants and to the King's servants. Its jurisdiction and procedure were the same as for the other two courts, but was the usual resort of cases of minor importance, which could be dealt with expeditiously and cheaply. It was presided over by the Lord Privy Seal, assisted by Masters of Requests. On the outbreak of the Civil War in 1642, the Court was suspended and was never revived. All the documentation relevant to each suit is filed together,[55] and there are excellent nominal indexes to the suitors, and topographical indexes to the places involved. The latter can be a clue as to whether an antecedent who was known to be an inhabitant might have been a witness and left a signed deposition giving personal details about himself as well as the suitors. An example can be seen in the Statham case in the middle of the sixteenth century (see chapter 8).

Other Courts

– The Court of Star Chamber –

The Court of Star Chamber retained close links with the King's Council, where it had its origins. It was established in 1487, exercising the Royal prerogative through members of the Council, the Lord Chancellor, Treasurer and Privy Seal, and common law judges. It had a civil jurisdiction over matters outside the common law, such as mercantile and ecclesiastical disputes, but its later encroachment into areas of common law attracted great hostility, and it was abolished in 1642. Its criminal jurisdiction extended from misdemeanours of a public nature (riot, unlawful assembly and conspiracy), the perversion of justice (including perjury, and abuse of powers by public officials), municipal and trade disputes, to crimes of violence and against property (extortion, forgery and fraud) and the State (contempt of Royal Proclamations, offences against the statutes especially by Roman Catholics, and the creation and sale of seditious literature). Enclosure and tithe disputes, problems between landlord and tenant, and testamentary cases also found their way to this court. There are nominal and place-name indexes to the cases. Bills and answers, and surviving records include depositions and other proceedings, though not the decrees and orders.[56]

The plaintiffs were mainly gentry, reflecting the cost of litigation. Its civil procedure was similar to that of the Equity Courts, but criminal proceedings were instituted by an 'information' laid by the Attorney General, followed by an interrogation of the defendant, while evidence from witnesses was often by affidavit, thus curtailing any opportunity for cross-examination. There was no jury, and the verdict was reached by the members of the Court.

– The High Court of Admiralty –

The High Court of Admiralty is said to have been established in the early fourteenth century during the reign of Edward III, and had a jurisdiction over maritime cases. Its business was administered by doctors in civil law in the courts of Doctors' Commons. It was divided into the Instance Court which heard cases relating to seamen's wages, damage to ships, salvage and piracy, while at the Old Bailey in the session of oyer and terminer and gaol delivery

List of interrogatories to be put to George Wisham, gentleman, defendant in a case brought to the Court of Star Chamber by John Statham, gentleman, concerning moneys paid to John Callowhill on security of lands in Worcestershire, now in the defendant's possession. The answer was taken on 17 June 1577. STAC5/S28/523

for the Admiralty of England the judge and jury on the criminal side heard trials for murder and piracy on the high seas. After November 1834 the criminal jurisdiction passed to the Central Criminal Court. The second and third courts were the Prize Court and the Court of Appeal for Prizes, concerning captures from wartime enemies. Vice-Admiralty Courts also sat in the maritime counties of England and Wales and in the Crown's dominions to hear similar cases, and appeal lay from there to the King in Council.

In 1875 the High Court of Admiralty was absorbed into the High Court, and from then until 1969 was part of the Probate, Divorce and Admiralty Division. Since 1970 its business has been conducted in the Queen's Bench Division. The Oyer and Terminer

Books record brief notes of proceedings,[57] which are also entered in the Assignation Books of the three Courts,[58] and the Court Minute Books,[59] and Instance Papers,[60] while the Vice-Admiralty Court Proceedings relate chiefly to colonial cases.[61]

– *The High Court of Delegates* –

The High Court of Delegates was instituted by Henry VIII in 1533 to supersede Papal jurisdiction in appeals from the ecclesiastical courts and the Instance Court of the High Court of Admiralty. It handled questions of marriage, legitimacy, testaments, tithes, fees and offences of a moral and behavioural nature such as slander. The Court was abolished in 1832 and its powers transferred to the Privy Council, which in 1834 set up a permanent Judicial Committee made up of Privy Council members; its first registrar had previously serviced both the High Court of Admiralty and the High Court of Delegates. Processes,[62], Acts,[63] Assignation Books[64] and Case Books[65] contain notes of the proceedings until 1833, and from 1834 these are in Privy Council Appeals records.[66]

– The Prerogative Court of Canterbury –

Law suits concerning wills and administrations were also conducted in the Prerogative Court of Canterbury, to determine the authenticity of a testament, to identify the administrator of an intestate's property, or 'in inventory and account' where an executor was suspected of having committed a fraud on the beneficiaries, and to obtain 'proofs in solemn form' when an executor, suspecting that the testament's validity might be challenged, asked for it to be authenticated by sworn witnesses. The Court's decision was by decree or sentence, after procedure similar to that in the Courts of Equity. Often there was a concurrent case in the Court of Chancery dealing with the validity of the will (which related to realty, whereas the testament was concerned with personalty, although for convenience the two were combined in one document). The Acts of Court Books[67] and Acts of Court[68] are the keys to the Prerogative Court suits, the former being indexed under the plaintiffs' names, and the latter under the names of the deceased. The Probate[69] and Administration Act Books[70] will contain marginal notes referring to suits, while the registered copy will and administration grant indexes[71] should indicate whether litigation was commenced. The pleadings,[72] depositions,[73] exhibits,[74] and Processes,[75] together with the Cause Papers,[76] form a wide range of sources available to the genealogist, and many of these are indexed under the names of the deceased and the plaintiffs, making the task of identifying a particular case relatively straightforward.

Appeal lay from this Court to the Court of Arches, whose records are at Lambeth Palace Library, in London, and there is a printed index of cases from 1660 until 1858;[77] or to the High Court of Delegates, which was the superior ecclesiastical court of the two provinces. There is a printed list of wills produced to this Court running from 1651 until 1858.[78]

The Prerogative Courts were abolished in 1857[79] and their business taken over by the Court of Probate. In 1875 it was superseded by the Probate, Divorce and Admiralty Division of the High Court. When this was renamed the Family Division in 1970 contentious probate matters were transferred to the Chancery Division.

– The Court of Augmentations and Revenues of the Crown –

Another of the Courts founded by Henry VIII was that of Augmentations of the Revenues of the Crown, set up in 1535 to manage lands and revenues confiscated during the Dissolution of the Monasteries. In 1541 the Court of the General Surveyors of the King's Lands was given custody of all lands falling to the Crown by attainder, escheat and forfeit. Both were abolished in 1547/8 to make way for the Court of Augmentations and Revenues of the King's Crown, which continued to flourish until dissolved in 1554/5 and its business annexed by the Court of Exchequer. The bills, answers and other related matters to the suits are filed in the Court of Augmentations Proceedings[80] and Miscellaneous Books,[81] the latter of which contain decrees and orders.

– Duchy, Palatinate and other Courts –

In the Court of Duchy Chamber of the Duchy of Lancaster equity causes were heard, while the Duchy Bench dealt with common law suits; in the Palatinate of Chester, the Exchequer Court was the recourse for debt cases and the Chancery Court for equity matters. Pleas of the Crown and at common law were tried at the Court of Great Sessions, formed in 1543, and which took in the Welsh counties, until it was abolished in 1830 and its jurisdiction transferred to the North and South Wales Circuit. Diagram 2 shows its composition and later division. The Palatinate of Lancaster had its own equity court of Chancery and of Common Pleas as well as Assizes. In 1875 the common law jurisdiction was merged into the High Court of Justice, together with that of the Court of Pleas of the Palatinate of Durham. The two equity courts of Chancery of the Palatinates of Lancaster and of Durham were abolished in 1971. The records of these courts are filed accordingly. Most of the records of the Principality of Wales, however, are now in the National Library of Wales, at Aberystwyth, and relate to both common law and equity suits.

The Palace Court was created in 1630 to try actions for the recovery of small debts within twelve miles of the Palace of Westminster which fell outside the jurisdiction of the City of London or other Liberties, until abolished in 1849. Cases could be removed from here on a writ of habeas corpus to a superior court where the damages involved exceeded £5.

The Court of the Honour of Peveril's records of proceedings between 1662 and 1850 are also extant.[82]

Bankruptcy

Under a statute of 1543 the Privy Council administered the estates of bankrupts, but in 1571 bankruptcy matters were placed under the authority of the Lord Chancellor. He commissioned proceedings, sought legal advice and delivered judgments on unresolved legal issues, and was the final arbiter between a debtor and his creditors. In 1813 a Vice-Chancellor of the Court of Chancery was assigned to help. The Court of Bankruptcy was set up in 1831, with a Court of Review, from which appeal lay to the Lord Chancellor or to the House of Lords. The Court of Review was abolished in 1847 and its jurisdiction transferred to a Vice-Chancellor in Chancery. The central Court of Bankruptcy was in London, but County Courts (created by statute in 1846) were empowered to act where the debts were below a certain figure. Since 1876 bankruptcy proceedings have been dealt with in the Chancery Division of the High Court, and in County Courts, to identify, quantify and distribute a proven bankrupt's assets among his creditors and to relieve him of the unpaid balance of his debts.

Until 1860 only traders could be made bankrupt. The term was defined in the mid-nineteenth century as relating to anyone who sought a living by workmanship of goods or commodities. Since 1861, however, all debtors may be made the subject of proceedings, although before 1935, married women could only be adjudicated bankrupt when trading.

A creditor or creditors petitioned the Lord Chancellor, declaring an intention to render a debtor bankrupt, by striking a docket. An individual creditor had to prove he was owed £100, which increased in multiples of £50 for every creditor joining with him, and each was required to enter a bond with the Lord Chancellor as security against false claims. The Lord Chancellor then issued a Commission of Bankruptcy (a fiat from 1832, an adjudication from 1849) citing the debtor and summoning him to surrender himself and his possessions to a nominated Commissioner or his assignee. The Commission was announced in *The London Gazette* to alert potential creditors and give notice of the three meetings called by the Commissioner which the debtor was obliged to attend to face his creditors. At the first or second meeting the creditors elected their assignee, who was sworn in by the Commissioner, and given the task of collecting in moneys owed to the debtor and of inventorying, and valuing his estate, which might later form the

basis of any sale. After 1831 an official assignee was usually appointed to help the creditors' nominee and prevent any fraud. At the last meeting, not more than forty-two days after the advertisement, a business account was produced by the debtor setting out a statement of his affairs. Often this period was extended on adjournment to give more time to prepare the accounts. The Commissioner collected sworn depositions and affidavits from the creditors proving the moneys owed to them, and from relatives and business associates of the debtor, to determine whether he met the statutory requirements of a bankrupt (that he was a trader and had committed an act of bankruptcy such as fleeing abroad, hiding from his creditors, or transferring his assets to someone else in order to defeat their claims). Either side could petition the Lord Chancellor about aspects of the bankruptcy, which might be referred by him to a Master in Chancery for advice, or he might recommend a trial of issue at law in the Court of King's Bench. The Lord Chancellor also made an adjudication over disputed debts.

Proceedings could be terminated at this stage if the debtor proved he was not bankrupt, paid his debts in full, or came to some arrangement with his creditors. There is an example of a suspended Commission in chapter 6, where John Gainsborough, a Suffolk clothier, had bankruptcy proceedings stayed against him in October 1733.

Next, a certificate of conformity was issued, discharging the debtor, on the petition of the creditors if a large majority of them and the Commissioner were satisfied by the bankrupt's statement of affairs, and a small allowance made to him representing a percentage of the sale proceeds beyond so many pence in the pound. The valued estate was sold off by the assignee in stages. After each sale the Commissioner met with the creditors to examine, audit and approve the accounts of realization and costs. If there was a credit balance a dividend was paid out to the creditors. The first dividend was normally paid within four months and the last at eighteen months, making the settlement of debts a long drawn out business, so in the 1840s attempts were made to streamline the process by putting the estate in the Court's hands if the debts fell below £300, and the Court oversaw the sale and distribution of the proceeds. Alternatively, the bankrupt might make a 'proposal' for paying off his debts by instalments, and if approved by the Court and his creditors the scheme was implemented.

The Court of Bankruptcy Docket Books[83] contain originating and subsequent petitions between 1710 and 1849, the Enrolment Books[84] the commissions, fiats and adjudications, assignments and certificates of conformity from the same date, and include examinations and depositions, while Files[85] similarly hold a number of examinations, depositions, business accounts and other proceedings. The Order Books [86] incorporate the decisions of the Lord Chancellor, the Court of Review, and of the Vice-Chancellor up to 1861, and the orders on appeal by the Lord Chancellor and other Lords Justices, and these are integrally indexed. Lastly, the Registers,[87] running from 1733, include certificates of conformity, commissions, fiats, sub-assignments, prisoners' petitions, petitions of bankrupts and creditors, and the Docket Books of the London, Country and County Courts.

Since 1876 the application of creditors or insolvent debtor to the Court for a Commission for an act of bankruptcy is followed by a petition for a receiving order to protect the estate. The property vests in an official receiver, who calls a creditors' meeting. The debtor is obliged to furnish him with a statement of his financial affairs, while the creditors also have to provide evidence of the moneys owed to them. The debtor is publicly examined by the registrar of the Court and if no composition or scheme of arrangement with his creditors is offered or accepted, he is declared bankrupt and his property passes to a trustee in bankruptcy and is divisible among his creditors after its valuation and sale. Since 1914 if the real estate is viewed by the trustee as more of a financial burden than an asset it escheats to the Crown. A bankruptcy can be annulled by an order of discharge. The Cause Papers[88] and Entry Books of Decrees and Orders of the Chancery Division[89] set out details of bankruptcies since 1876.

The debtors' prisons were the Marshalsea of the Court of King's Bench, the Marshalsea of His Majesty's Household, and the Fleet, the last of which also housed bankrupts. They also had custody of persons in contempt of court. They were abolished in 1842, the Marshalsea of the Court of Queen's Bench being renamed the Queen's Prison and continuing to be used for the detention of debtors and bankrupts until its closure in 1862.

The Supreme Court of Judicature

The Judicature Acts of 1873 and 1875 served to fuse the common law courts and those of Equity under the Supreme Court of Judicature, which was divided into the High Court of Justice and the Court of Appeal, to which were added the Crown Courts in 1971. The High Court can meet anywhere in England and Wales. Since 1 November 1875 it has been the umbrella for the common law courts, Chancery, probate, divorce and matrimonial causes, the High Court of Admiralty, the Courts of Common Pleas of the Palatinates of Lancaster and of Durham, for those courts created by commissions of oyer and terminer, gaol delivery and assize, and from 1883, the London Court of Bankruptcy. Until 1933 it also had authority to hear appeals from the County Courts. Later appeals were transferred to the Court of Appeal, which since 1966 has also had a criminal jurisdiction, formerly exercised from 1848 by the Court for Crown Cases Reserved, succeeded in 1907 by the Court of Criminal Appeal. Their records too can be inspected.[90]

The High Court was divided into five Divisions, using a uniform set of pleadings. The Chancery Division deals with administration of estates, the execution of trusts, redemption and foreclosures of mortgages, rectification and cancellation of deeds, enforcement of contracts for sale of land, business partnership disputes, winding-up of companies in liquidation, bankruptcies, Revenue matters, town and country planning, and landlord and tenant disputes. Since 1959 it has been a Court of Protection in the management of the property and affairs of mental patients, and from 1970 has dealt with probate disputes.

The Queen's Bench Division is much wider in scope, for in 1880 two of the other Divisions, the Common Pleas and Exchequer, were merged with it. It handles mainly actions in tort and contract, commercial disputes, and Admiralty cases. The High Court's criminal and appellate jurisdiction also lie with this Division, and it has a supervisory role over the inferior courts and Tribunals. The other Division, of Probate, Divorce and Admiralty, was renamed the Family Division in 1970. Probate cases were transferred to the Chancery Division and Admiralty matters to the Queen's Bench. The Family Division has jurisdiction over matrimonial causes and children. Divorce by judicial decree became possible under the Matrimonial Causes Act 1857, and ecclesiastical authority over marriages of non-Anglicans thus ceased. The new Court for Divorce and Matrimonial Causes was merged in 1875 with the High Court. There are indexes[91] and registers of decrees of divorce,[92] but not all of these are open for inspection because of their confidential nature.

Each of the Divisions has equal competence and a judge from one may sit in another; cases may be similarly transferred to or initiated in more than one Division. Their procedure is governed by the Rules of the Supreme Court giving them much more flexibility.

The consequent effect of the legislation on record-keeping was profound. The Plea Rolls of the individual common law courts were replaced by the 'Judgment Papers', summarizing court judgments enrolled in Judgment Books,[93] although Chancery enrolments continued to be made in the Entry Books of Decrees and Orders.[94] The means of reference to the Judgment Books is by the Divisional Cause Books,[95] which give details of the date and judgment number of each case, as well as the date when pleadings were filed. In 1880 a Central Office was established and from this date union series of pleadings,[96] depositions[97] and affidavits[98] were kept, whereas between 1875 and 1879 the first two were filed together for the common law courts,[99] and those of the Chancery Division in an independent series,[100] while the affidavits were organized by Division.[101]

The Problems of Legal Records

The major stumbling block for the genealogist wishing to use records of the central law courts is the lack of adequate personal name indexes of the suitors and defendants appearing before them. The common law courts are deficient in printed calendars and lists of litigants, a problem magnified by the use of Latin as the legal language up to 1733, with the exception of the Commonwealth period, which for many searchers will render the documents inaccessible. The court rolls are often physically enormous, written in a tight abbreviated hand, generally with marginal notes of the counties where the disputes arose. Many will relate only to one of the four legal terms of a regnal year, making a speculative search time-consuming, with no certainty of finding what you seek.

My first experience of the Crown Rolls of the Court of King's Bench was a daunting one, having heaved the numerous flattened, boarded and strung-up membranes onto my desk, but a little perseverance produced a gem of a dispute concerning the refusal in 1733 of the Bishop of Lichfield to grant a schoolmaster's licence to a local parson, John Rushworth of Fillongley, Warwickshire, after a writ of mandamus had been issued by the Court at the priest's request.[102] The grounds for the Bishop's refusal were the parson's drunken and debauched way of life, his verbal harangues from the pulpit of his hapless congregation in general, and some in particular, and his quarrelsome nature which were not traits conducive to good schoolmastering in Coventry, where his reputation was so well known that parents preferred to keep their children at home. This was the same bishop who intervened with his Regimental Colonel to bring David Garrick's father home from Gibraltar (see chapter 11).

The same Crown Roll included a complaint against two overseers of the poor for withholding from their successors public books relating to their office, the blockage of the King's Highway by two orange boxes, breaking and entering with assault, the publication of seditious and libellous books against the King and Queen, impersonation of a public official to obtain money, and outlined various cases of incest, rape, defamation, adultery, non-payment of tithes, and of Church rates, and there was an action brought against an administrator for having failed to produce accounts of an intestate's property, a testacy case brought by a beneficiary against an executor, and a divorce on the grounds of cruelty. A look at the Controlment Rolls revealed the enrolment of the writ of mandamus addressed to the Bishop on 6 November 1733.[103] To find out what became of the parson a glance at the Bishops' Certificates of Institutions to Benefices showed that he remained in his parish until his resignation in 1758, when the King, as patron, nominated his successor.[104] Any alteration to the size, nature and forbearance of his congregation is not recorded.

If the above are the contents of one Roll, for one legal term, what other treasures await the genealogist in the rest of them?

Another problem is the uncomprehensive and chaotic nature of the lists compiled in the courts of record themselves, chiefly the Court of Chancery. If an antecedent was joined as a fourth or fifth party it is unlikely that his name will appear in any list, unless he produced documents on his own behalf, nor is there any cross-indexing under the names of defendants. The early proceedings up to the end of the reign of Elizabeth are undated, and abstracts of them arranged in bundles under the names of the Chancellors to whom the petitions were addressed. Subsequent ones must be garnered by searching the Six Clerks' Series, the lists of which are of variable quality, by far the worst being the published indexes of Reynardson's Series to 1714. Yet amongst these records lie the very stuff of genealogical research, for the suits are by their nature retrospective, provide information on migration including overseas, close and remote kinships, family behaviour and health, and amplify relationships ambiguous or unstated elsewhere. The Masters' exhibits lodged in Court are a microcosm of a family's activities, being hoarded collections of bills and receipts, letters and diaries, leases and title deeds, marriage settlements and wills, which might otherwise have been destroyed and lost forever if it were not for the litigation.

Until the fifteenth century, unfree tenants had no status in a court of law. The extensive genealogies of litigants constructed in order to establish right of access to the courts display collateral networks and kinships by marriage. A number of the early ones were extracted and printed in *Pedigrees from the Plea Rolls, 1200–1500*, edited by Major General The Honourable G. Wrottesley (no date), again affording insight into the veritable wealth of family historical information these Rolls contain.

The cases put by each party to a suit are at variance with each other for obvious reasons, and not even the sworn depositions and affidavits are totally reliable. Human memory tends also to vagueness in recollection of people and events many years ago, so not all the genealogical details may be accurate, unintentionally or otherwise. But because the records predate parish registers, and perhaps refer to people who never made or featured in wills, they offer a potentially rich harvest for the researcher.

Even if a person was not party to a suit he might well have been requested to give information material to the allegations by deposition or in an affidavit. Unfortunately the main means of access to the majority of these has to be by consulting the papers of cases involving places where they were known to have lived. The abstracts and lists of Chancery Proceedings to 1714 do at least record topographical details, and the place-name indexes of the other two Courts of Equity, and of Star Chamber, can be used to extract references to cases appropriate to the area. Otherwise the searcher may refer to compilations such as the Bernau Index to discover whether a particular ancestor was ever a deponent in these Courts.

Writ of mandamus from the Court of Kings Bench (Crown Side) addressed to Richard [Smalbroke] Bishop of Lichfield and Coventry ordering him to grant a schoolmaster's licence to John Rushworth, elected Usher at the free Grammar School, Coventry, or show cause to the contrary, 6 November 7 George II (1733). KB29/393

In the case of Assize records, the Minute Books prove helpful in identifying individual defendants because each covers a reasonable time span for all the counties within a particular Circuit, and once found the charges can be read in more detail in the Indictments. Alas, the records' survival rate is patchy and uneven between one class and another. From the early nineteenth century, the Annual Criminal Registers are an important adjunct to these, and lists of transportees to the colonies have attracted much attention, the printed indexes of which often include references to the date and place of trial and the convict ship on which an individual sailed.

In short, the records of the courts are not for the faint-hearted, but well reward patient perusal once a particular class and approximate period can be identified as relevant. Even if you fail to find your forebear, by reading through other suits you learn to appreciate that life in past times was not all that different from today, our ancestors' problems were much the same in their dealings with their relatives, friends, neighbours, landlords, business partners and customers.

[2]

THE HOLDING AND TRANSFER OF LAND

After his conquest of England, King William I rewarded his chief retainers with gifts of land seized from Anglo-Saxons who had resisted him, been put to flight, or died. In return, these tenants-in-chief, holding their lands directly from the King, rendered him certain services, which ran with the land. As the land was passed to another owner, so were the services. The services were known as tenures and were usually of a military or agricultural nature. The Domesday Survey of 1086 informed the King about his tenants-in-chief, and the extent, state of cultivation and value of the land possessed by them a generation after the Conquest.

Some of the tenants-in-chief granted parts of their lands to other tenants in return for similar services. The land retained by the lords for themselves was their demesne. The process of sub-granting was subinfeudation. This deprived the King and the chain of intermediate lords of certain rights, called incidents of tenure, which were exacted by the immediate lords from their tenants, so the Statute Quia Emptores 1290 brought subinfeudation to an end. Thereafter only grants of land by substitution of one tenant by another were possible, except for grants made by the King himself or for a person's lifetime.

Feudal Tenure

Tenure was the basis of the feudal structure of land-ownership and was classified according to the type of service rendered, be it in chivalry (grand serjeanty — where offices of an honourable nature were performed, or knight service — where a specified number of armed horsemen had to be provided, although by the mid-twelfth century this was commuted to a fixed money payment called scutage), or spiritual (the saying of masses or other services, almsgiving, or frankalmoign — where prayers were offered for the soul of the lord), or socage (petty serjeanty — where specific duties were carried out, or common socage — where the nature and amount of the service were fixed, usually related to the cultivation of the land). In towns the usual form of common socage was money (burgage tenure) and by the fifteenth century the practice of commutation was widespread. Finally, there was villein tenure, where the amount, though not the nature, of the service was fixed, and again this was normally agricultural. Unlike common socage tenure, these tenants were not free and to the fifteenth century had no status in a court of law. They held their land at the will of their lord and if ousted by him had no redress. In the fourteenth century epidemics like the Black Death and wars abroad seriously decimated the population on the land, resulting in a shortage of labour to till it, decreased pressure for land space, and ultimately led to agricultural expansion, thus increasing the villeins' bargaining power. The customs of the manors in which their strips of land lay gradually became paramount, and by the late fifteenth century were binding at common law. They became known as customary tenants, holding their land by copy of the manorial court roll (copyholders).

Knight service and most forms of serjeanty were extinguished and converted into common socage under the Tenures Abolition Act 1660; frankalmoign by the Administration of Estates Act 1925, and copyhold tenure was abolished in the same year under the Law of Property Act 1922, which compulsorily converted it to freehold. The only tenure today is common socage.

The land also attracted other obligations and rights, the incidents of tenure. The tenures in chivalry imposed a duty on tenants to attend the lord's court and assist in its deliberations, and they owed him homage and fealty by which a spiritual and temporal bond was created. The lord had a right to levy aids on certain occasions (reduced by Magna Carta 1215 to three, to pay his ransom, for the knighting of

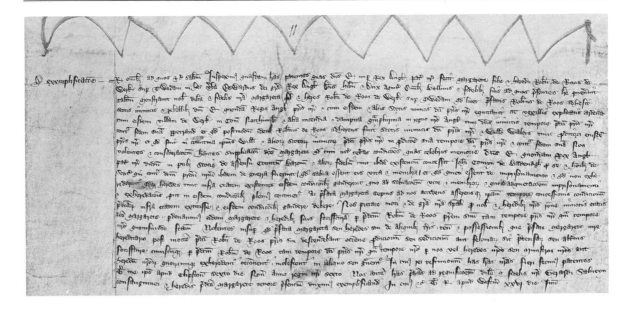

Enrolment of an exemplification dated at Westminster, 26 June [1367] of the letters patent of 6 November 6 Edward II (1312) granting a pardon to Margaret, the daughter and heiress of Robert de Roos of Wark-upon-Tweed, Northumberland, of his forfeitures to Edward I and Edward II for his adherence to the Scots rebels, at the request of her son Gerard Salveyn. He died on 1 August 1369 and an inquisition post mortem was taken on his lands held as a tenant-in-chief of the Crown in 1373. C66/275/11

his eldest son, and the first marriage of his eldest daughter), to distress and forfeiture, by which the lord could seize (distrain) a tenant's goods for non-performance of services, and if expressly given the right to do so, could take his land. On a tenant's death, if the next heir was twenty-one, the lord seized the land and took a fine (relief) before it was restored; if he was under age the lord had a right of wardship and marriage over him. During the period of minority the lord managed the land, extracted its profits and issues and used them to maintain and educate the heir. He could also select a wife for him and should the choice be refused, a penalty was imposed. Often these two rights were sold to the highest bidder, making the heir and his lands vulnerable to the unscrupulous. If a tenant died without any heir, the land escheated (reverted) to the lord.

The incidents accruing to socage tenure were as for chivalry, but excluding homage, wardship and marriage.

Manorial Tenants

Under the incidents of villein tenure copyhold tenants owed suit of court, fealty, custom (for instance rights over mines and minerals, sports, markets and fairs, commons, and obligations to maintain bridges and ditches), fines (payable on every transfer of land between tenants), forfeiture, heriots (the best beast or other chattel taken by the lord on a tenant's death), relief and escheat. Until the Forfeiture Act 1870, escheat occurred also when a tenant was convicted of a capital felony.

A tenant wishing to transfer land first surrendered it to his lord at the yearly or biannual manorial Court Baron, and nominated his successor. The lord (or his steward) admitted the new tenant and took an entry fine. When a tenant died this was reported to the next meeting of the Court and the customary heir, or a new tenant, was admitted depending on the nature of the tenancy. The lord took a heriot from the deceased and a fine from the newcomer. The transactions were recorded on the manorial court roll and a copy of the entry was given to the new tenant as his proof of title. The Court Baron and Halmote rolls of surrenders and admittances of successive tenants of Crown manors and those of the Duchy of Lancaster, the Palatinates and the Honour of Peveril,[1] together with rentals, extents, surveys and minutes of the presentments made at the Views of Frankpledge and Courts Leet (which dealt with administrative and judicial matters) form an important archive for the genealogist from early medieval times, although the records are often sporadic, and are in Latin to 1733 with the exception of the Commonwealth years, and are prefaced by regnal year (running from the date of accession of each monarch, the new year commencing on each anniversary). Mostly they are contained in Special Collections,[2] the records of the Crown Estate Commissioners,[3] the Land Revenue Office of the Exchequer,[4] and the Duchy and Palatinates series.[5] When the manors passed out of Crown hands the new lords maintained records of their tenants' activities. Many of these have been deposited in county record offices, but a number remain in private hands.

Incidents of Tenure Today

Only two incidents of tenure survive today: those expressly preserved by the act abolishing the tenures themselves, and secondly those relating to common socage which have not been extinguished by any statute, although some of these are merely vestigial. In 1926 copyhold land was compulsorily enlarged into fee simple by enfranchisement under the Law of Property Act 1922, although it had been possible under a sequence of Copyhold Acts from 1841. Enfranchisement to 1925 was achieved by voluntary agreement between lord and tenant, at a price representing the value to the lord of lost rights, paid as a lump sum or an annual rentcharge, and was evidenced by a deed of conveyance. It could also be made mandatory on application by either side without the consent of the other to the Board of Agriculture for an Award, but compensation was still payable to the lord. The records of awards to 1925 are filed with records of the Ministry of Agriculture Fisheries and Food.[6] Under the 1922 legislation, certain copyhold incidents were allowed to prevail another ten years from January 1926. During this time lords and tenants were to reach agreement as before on compensation for lost rights, failing which an approach could be made to the Board of Agriculture for a decision. A five-year extension was given to allow uncompleted negotiations to be concluded or referred to the Board. Because of the War the provision was suspended from 1939 until 1949 and the final deadline set at 31 October 1950. The records relating to these are found, like the earlier enfranchisements, in the Ministry of Agriculture Fisheries and Food.[7]

The Inheritance of Land

Historically, a person's next heir, or heir at law, was deemed to be his nearest blood relative, commencing with his issue, then his collaterals (males first). After the Inheritance Act 1833 ancestors were preferred before collaterals, the father and grandfather ranking before the mother and grandmother. A female was heiress only if there was no-one of the male blood of the same degree as herself, and any other female in that grade was joined with her as co-heiress. They held the land either by co-parceny (tenancy in common, whereby each share passed on the co-parcenor's death to her heir), or by joint tenancy with a *jus accrescendi* (the right of the surviving tenant to all the land on the deaths of the others). Since the Law of Property Act 1925 co-ownership can only exist behind a trust for sale, the trustees being joint tenants, but the co-owners may be either joint tenants or tenants in common.

The Administration of Estates Act 1925 established the next of kin's right to an intestate's land in place of the heir at law. Previously the next of kin's only right was to the personal estate whereas the heir at law was entitled to the real estate. The next of kin is fixed in order of seniority as the deceased's spouse, children, grandchildren, parents, siblings, half-brothers and half-sisters, grandparents, uncles and aunts, half-uncles and half-aunts, and failing these, the land escheats to the Crown as '*bona vacantia*'. Those kin of the same degree are equally entitled, and who is deemed to be the next of kin can be immensely useful to the genealogist seeking to know the closest living relatives of a deceased person.

It was a common law rule that husband and wife were one person. On marriage a husband had a right to all his wife's possessions and to a life interest in her inheritable estates, but any land conveyed to trustees for her own use by a marriage or other settlement was hers alone. The Matrimonial Causes Act 1857 protected any land acquired by a wife while living apart from her husband under a decree of judicial separation or protection order, but it was not until the Married Women's Property Act 1882 that a wife's real estate was regarded as her own outright. The legislation only applied to women married on or after 1 January 1883, and until 1893[8] if her land was devised by will it still had to be re-executed on her husband's death for he retained his right to a life interest in it. Since the Law of Property Act 1925 husband and wife can act independently in the pur-

The grant of letters of administration of the goods and chattels of James Christie, made to his son James Christie, the widow, Jane, having renounced, 26 November 1803. The estate was valued under £10,000, and probate accounts required by November 1804. The auctioneer lived next door to Thomas Gainsborough and was a friend of David Garrick. PROB1/179 f793

chase of property, though they will often buy as joint tenants because of the favourable probate rules of taxation.

Estates in Land

The duration of a tenancy is termed an estate. The types of estate in the land are for life, in fee simple, fee tail and for term of years. Up to 1925, the first three were classed as freeholds. Since then[9] only fee simple estates are freehold.

– Life Estate –

Where a life estate is held the tenant is described as tenant for life, because when he dies his interest in the land ceases and his heir has no right to it. He can transfer the land to someone else, but only for his own lifetime, which might be short or long, and therefore of indefinite duration; the new tenant is called the tenant for life *pur autre vie*. A life estate may also be made conditional or determinable (ended) on the occurrence of a specific situation or event declared in the original grant. Life estates were created by charters, deeds and by will, and the early ones are in Latin, but by the sixteenth century English had largely supervened. There are numerous examples of grants

of life estates in private collections of deeds, Ancient and Modern Deeds,[10] and in the wills proved in the Prerogative Court of Canterbury.[11]

At the end of the life estate the land reverts to the grantor, who in the meantime is known as the owner of the fee simple in reversion. Before the life estate was set up and after it is restored to him, he is known as the owner of the fee simple in possession. He might create a string of life estates to take effect one after the other. This is known as a settlement. The second life tenant, while he waits, is called the remainderman, and he has a right to future enjoyment of the land and its profits. The creator of the life estate might sell or gift his reversion in the fee simple to someone else, who is also known as the remainderman. If he dies before the tenant for life the fee simple reversioner can will his future interest to another person, and if he does not do so or dies intestate, it will in due course vest in his heir (to 1925) or next of kin (from 1926).

– Fee Simple Estate –

Life held for the fee simple estate is capable of being inherited. The person holding it is said to be seised (possessed) of the land in fee simple. From early times it was possible to transfer it by gift or sale during the owner's lifetime (*inter vivos*). It can be made conditional or determinable in the same way as the life estate. Otherwise it is a fee simple absolute.

The transfers were accomplished by charters and deeds, custody of which authorized a person's legal title to the land. The most ancient form was the deed of feoffment, endorsed with the date on which the new owner actually came into physical possession of the land 'by livery of seisin'. The King made grants of land by royal deeds and charters, letters patent or letters close, office copies of which were enrolled on the appropriate rolls[12] in his Chancery. Until 1733

The enrolment of a Royal Charter dated at Westminster, 5 November [1363], granting and confirming to Gerard Salvayn kinsman and heir of Gerard Salvayn the right to hold a weekly market and a three-day fair at Duffield in Yorkshire, and to have the right of free warren there and in his other manors of Millington-juxta-Givendale, Sandhall and Harswell, all in the same county. These privileges had previously been extended to Gerard Salvayn, the son of Sibyl Salvayn, by the King's grandfather. Other evidence suggests that the first Gerard was the grantee's grandfather. C53/147/11/6

they were written in Latin, thereafter and during the Commonwealth period in English. Similar registers of deeds were kept in the Duchy of Lancaster and in the Palatinates.[13]

Until 1660 tenants-in-chief of the Crown required licences to sell (alienate) their lands. From the early thirteenth century, inquisitions *ad quod damnum* were taken by the King's escheators to ascertain whether the grant of a licence would prejudice his or others' interests, and the results were filed in Chancery.[14] Copies of the licences were enrolled on the Patent Rolls;[15] the fines levied for them or for pardons for alienation without a licence were entered on the Fine Rolls.[16] Both series are in Latin and are dated by regnal year, but translated abstracts of them are available in printed Calendars up to the sixteenth century.[17] From 1576 the collection of these and

other fines was farmed out to the Earl of Leicester on a ten-year lease, renewed in 1586. He was responsible for valuing the lands and extracting the fines, a proportion of which he paid to the Queen.[18] The Alienation Office was set up to administer the work and continued after his death, coming eventually under the care of the Treasury Commissioners. In 1660 the revenue drawn from fines for alienation was severed with the abolition of feudal tenure, but its other business remained until the Office was finally closed in 1835.

Before 1540 if the owner died seised in fee simple his estate passed to his next heir. The Statute of Wills 1540 allowed him to devise all land held by common socage and up to two thirds by knight service, the remaining third being reserved for the heir to enable the Crown to claim feudal dues on the tenant-in-chief's death. Henceforward, the next heir only inherited the whole of the fee simple if the owner died still in possession of it and had not willed it to anyone else, or died intestate.

All fetters on the transfer of fee simple estates were removed in 1660 with the abolition of feudal tenure.

On the death of a tenant-in-chief of the Crown, a writ was issued out of Chancery for the taking of an inquisition post mortem by the King's escheators in each of the counties where his lands lay. A jury of local gentry was empanelled to enquire under oath into the estates of which he was seised on the day of his demise, the rents and services related to them, with the names of any tenants, and to ascertain the name, age and relationship of the next heir, so that the King could be informed of any right he might have of wardship, marriage or escheat. The inquisitions often recite exactly how and when the tenant came by his lands, his subsequent actions in connection with them, for instance provision made in his will for their disposal, or any settlement which he might have created, and in the absence of any extant original deeds, these are of immense value to the genealogist, especially if they had passed to him by descent. The adult heir then came before the King to do homage and fealty and pay relief, in return for which he was granted livery of seisin of his lands. If the heir was under age, he was made a ward of the Crown, which also had a right of wardship over heirs who were idiots or lunatics. The issues of their lands were managed by the Court of Exchequer. In 1541, Henry VIII set up a special court to deal with wardships and liveries, which functioned until 1660, when inquisitions also officially came to an end, although they were obsolete by the latter stages of the reign of Charles I.

Inquisitions post mortem stem from the reign of Henry III in the early thirteenth century, and are filed in Chancery,[19] with duplicates of many of them in the records of the Exchequer.[20] This is because the escheators were obliged to account to the Exchequer for the profits of the lands while in their custody, and the inquisitions were used as their vouchers. There are also additional inquisitions here, not found in Chancery, and where one may be in poor physical condition or illegible, the other may be substituted. They are in Latin, dated by regnal year, but translated Calendars of them run up to 1405[21] and for the reign of Henry VII (1485–1509).[22] Files of inquisitions taken in the Duchies of Lancaster and Cornwall and the Palatinates are kept among their records.[23]

Purchases of wardship and marriage were recorded on the Fine Rolls,[24] along with the writs connected with the inquisition process. On attaining his majority the heir took out a writ *de aetate probanda*. Under this witnesses were examined by the escheators to establish his date of birth and present age, and their depositions were returned to Chancery and filed with the inquisitions. The heir then performed his obligations of homage and fealty to the King before receiving livery of seisin. The witnesses' accounts contain vivid descriptions of the birth and baptism and the ensuing celebrations, as well as other events happening on the same day to them or their neighbours. They supply their names, ages, residences and occupations and often snippets of autobiography about people of varying social backgrounds.

Entry of a pardon for alienation of lands held directly from the Crown, Trinity Term 9 Charles I (1633), by Edmund Shillingford alias Izard, gentleman, and his wife Grisell, concerning a grant made by them on 21 January 2 Charles I (1626/7) to his son and heir apparent John Shillingford alias Izard of the Rectory and attendant lands and hereditaments at Beckley in Oxfordshire forever, the couple retaining the use of half for their lives. A fine of 100s was fixed on 6 July. A4/17

From about the fourteenth century it became possible for an owner to leave an interest in his fee simple estate on his death to someone other than his heir, by means of 'uses' (later called trusts), authorizing the nominee to take the rents and profits from it. A deed of feoffment conveyed the estate to one or more feoffees to hold it to the 'use' of the feoffor (owner). It was then granted back to him by a further deed subject to specified uses (in the case of the Statham deed of 1453 in chapter 8, for the feoffor's life and then to his sons and their male heirs in turn), or his will gave the feoffees directions about its disposal. The Court of Chancery recognized the feoffees, as

A commission, by way of a writ of mandamus sent from Westminster on 6 July 47 Edward III (1373) for an inquisition post mortem to be held into the lands held in chief in Yorkshire from the King by Gerard Salvayn, Knight, and Robert Salvayn, his son, at the days of their deaths. The inquisition was held at York on 9 August and revealed that the manor of Millington was subject to an entail, and after the lifetime of himself and his wife Agnes, was to be divided into two halves, one for their son Richard and his heirs and the other for another son Robert and his heirs. Gerard Salvayn died on 1 August 1369, leaving Gerard, the son of his eldest son John, as the heir to other manors, but Robert Salvayn was still alive and had inherited all of the manor of Millington when Richard died without issue. C135/235 no 66

the vendors, as the legal owners, so when the feoffor died, the heir at law's claim was defeated, and the superior lord was denied his feudal dues because the feoffees were still alive. They were then able to convey the land to the new owner, who similarly could carry out an enfeoffment of his own, creating new 'uses', provided that the original one had not established a sequence of them which he could not break.

The Statute of Uses 1535 provided that from 1 May 1536 whoever had the 'use' should be treated as the legal owner; the Stature of Enrolments 1536 put an end to the secret bargains and sales of inherited and freehold land which had caused trouble for purchasers owing to the uncertainty as to who actually owned it should any dispute arise, by enacting that from 31 July 1536 no such sale was to be valid unless

evidenced by a deed and the deed enrolled within six months in a central court of record at Westminster, or locally with the clerk of the peace of the county. Exemption was given to cities, boroughs and corporate towns where a lawful system of enrolment was already in force, and in 1563 the Statute was extended to take in the Palatinates. However there were loopholes in both Acts. The lawyers soon found a way round the first by creating the 'double use', the first use bestowed the legal ownership, but the second was enforceable in the Courts of Equity. The second Statute did not cover copyhold or leasehold land, so the lawyers manipulated this lacuna to evolve the device of the lease and release, under which the freeholder vendor leased the land for a year to the intending purchaser, by an indenture of lease. The following day a further indenture between the parties released the reversion of the freehold at the end of the term to the lessee purchaser, thus avoiding enrolment. From 1841 the need for two documents was dispensed with, the release being sufficient on its own. Many of these have found their way into county record offices and some were enrolled centrally.[25]

At Westminster the enrolments were made on the dorse of the Close Rolls,[26] continued from 1903 in the Enrolment Books (Indentures) of the High Court.[27] They are in English, and give full particulars of the names, residences and status of the parties, the date of the transaction, the nature, extent and value of the land and the price paid for it, together with other conditions of the sale. Up to 1648 the indexes of grantors are by initial letter under regnal year, thereafter by calendar year. There is also a counterpart index of grantees running to 1837. The Statutes were repealed by the Law of Property Act 1925, but until then this was the nearest approach to a national registration scheme of land transfers. After this the Land Registration Acts, 1925–71, introduced the system which we know today, but even now parts of the country do not have compulsory registration so purchasers have to rely on the vendors' title deeds showing proof of ownership of the land for a period of fifteen years.

The Close Rolls also recorded earlier private land transfers, from 1571 enrolled grants of bankrupts' estates which had escheated to the Crown (since 1914 the trustee in bankruptcy has had the option of including them among the person's assets unless considered a financial liability to the detriment of the creditors), during the Commonwealth the grants and sales of land sequestrated from the supporters of Charles I (called delinquents), and between 1715 and 1791 the registration of many of the lands held by Roman Catholics. The Rolls therefore set out details of landownership which may not be available to the searcher elsewhere.

– The Fee Tail Estate –

The Statute De Donis Conditionalibus 1285 established the third type of freehold estate, the fee tail. Until then a landowner could express a wish for the devolution of his land after his death, but could not be certain that it would be implemented. What the Statute did was to ensure that land granted to a person and to the heirs of his body descended in the way it was intended. The fee tail estate was created by a deed of entail or set up by a will, and took effect on the day the deed was executed (signed, sealed and witnessed), or on the day of the testator's death. The grantor could thus determine the descent of his land over many generations to keep it in his family's hands and the fee tail was enforceable at common law. Once all the lines specified in the entail were extinct, the grant provided for the land's reversion back to the grantor (or some other person) and his rightful heirs and assigns in fee simple. This might occur hundreds of years later, when the names of the grantor and other descendants were long forgotten or untraceable. If the original deed disappeared or could not be retrieved it became difficult for remoter kinsmen to enforce their rights over the land should they become entitled to it. Copies of the deeds were therefore often enrolled in monastic cartularies or in one of the central courts of record at Westminster such as the Court of Common Pleas[28] for safekeeping and future reference.

During the course of the entail the person actually seised of the land is called the tenant in tail in possession, while the next in line is the tenant in tail in remainder, and the others further down the chain retain merely a '*spes successionis*' (a hope of succession) which may or may not eventually vest in them. The grantor and his heirs retain an interest in the fee simple in reversion.

Contingent remainders occur when the identity of the future beneficiary is unknown (for example, an unborn second child), or as long as any condition set out in the grant remains unfulfilled (a beneficiary's marriage for instance), otherwise the remainder is said to be vested. Contingent interests are also subject to the rule against perpetuities to prevent the land being tied up in a family forever waiting for the contingent interests to vest and which would be against the public interest. At common law this means each interest must vest within a life or lives in being (including those *en ventre sa mère*) on the date the deed was made or at the death of the testator, plus twenty-one years from the expiry of the last life in being plus any later relevant gestation period. Under the Perpetuities and Accumulations Act 1964 the grantor may alternatively expressly fix a perpetuity period of not more than eighty years during which the interest must vest.

The types of fee tail are tail male (male heirs of the body), tail general (male issue followed by female), tail female, or tail special (for example, the issue of a specific marriage). Since 1925[29] a fee tail can only exist behind a trust as 'entailed interests', and any legal action comes before the Chancery Division of the High Court.

The tenant in tail in possession was originally limited to selling or gifting the land for his lifetime only, after which it passed to the remainderman. This made it difficult for the tenant in tail to raise money should he need it, and prospective purchasers did not consider a life interest of uncertain duration a particularly good investment. Under a statute of 1540[30] the tenant in tail was permitted to grant leases of up to twenty-one years determinable on three specified lives. This meant that the lease ended with the death of the last of these named people if it happened before the term was up. He could not charge a lump sum for the lease but was able to collect a fixed rent, which protected his successor against any temptation the tenant in tail might feel to impose a high entry fine and a low immutable rent, which might in time become totally uneconomic. In the fifteenth century, therefore, ways were found of frustrating the entail by adapting existing devices of fines and common recoveries.

A common recovery of 20 acres of land in Warehorne, Kent, suffered by William Darcy against Thomas Gregory, having claimed he was originally deprived of it by 'Hugh Hunt'. Thomas defends the defective title by calling on two vouchees to warrant it. They would fail to turn up, so judgment would be awarded in default to William. Later the land would probably be conveyed by him to Thomas as a fee simple estate. CP43/760

In 1472 it became possible through the willing connivance of the Court of Common Pleas for the fee tail to be destroyed (barred) and converted into a fee simple estate. The collaborating purchaser (demandant) brought a fictitious suit against the vendor tenant in tail in possession. He alleged in a writ of *praecipe quod reddat* that he had previously wrongfully been dispossessed of the land by 'Hugh Hunt', and queried the tenant in tail's title to it. He asked that the tenant in tail should warrant (defend) it. The tenant in tail called on the 'common vouchee' (usually the court crier or some other man of straw) to guarantee it for him. This the vouchee did, and denied that Hugh Hunt had evicted the demandant. The demandant asked for a court adjournment so that he could imparl (confer) with the vouchee. When they reconvened, the vouchee defaulted in contempt of court and judgment was awarded to the demandant, who was given the tenant in tail's land free of any restrictions as his title was held to be void. The demandant was said to have 'suffered a common

recovery'. The tenant in tail, meanwhile, was nominally recompensed with lands of equal value belonging to the vouchee. The fee simple estate was subsequently conveyed to the tenant in tail by the demandant by a deed of bargain and sale.

Usually common recovery was by double voucher. Whereas the single voucher described above freed the land from any actual rights and interests which the tenant in tail in possession might have in it at the time of the action, the double voucher applied to any latent and future interests which might arise and therefore was much more effective. In a double voucher, the land was previously conveyed as a life estate to a stranger by the tenant in tail in possession, or by the remainderman with his consent. The writ was brought against the life tenant, who cited the tenant in tail as vouchee, who called on the court crier, with the same outcome as before.

The fine was more limited in scope. It did not require the consent of the tenant in tail in possession, but it resulted in a base fee under which the entail was barred only for the tenant in tail breaking it and his own descendants. Once his line was extinct, the fee tail re-activated and the land passed to the next remainderman. Its use became established by 1540, though the 'levying of a fine' to convey land was of much earlier origin, and can be traced back at least to 1182. The co-operating purchaser (querient) initiated proceedings by bringing a writ of covenant against the vendor (deforciant) alleging that he had deprived him of his land. A pre-fine representing a tenth of the land's annual value was paid to the King. When the Court gave leave to the parties to agree, a post-fine or King's Silver, amounting to $\frac{3}{20}$ of the annual value, was levied. The action was settled by a final concord or agreement. The deforciant accepted that the querient had a right to the land by his gift. In return for a specified sum paid to him by the querient he now renounced all present and future claim which he, his heirs and assigns might have to the land and its issues. Three copies were made of the indenture, the chirograph or 'foot of fine' was filed among the court records, endorsed with the proclamations of the agreement made in open court in the four legal terms afterwards. The other two copies were given to the parties. The land was then usually conveyed to the tenant in tail deforciant by a deed of bargain and sale. The base fee could be further enlarged to a fee simple by a common recovery once the tenant in tail in remainder came into possession, or if he obtained permission from the existing tenant in tail in possession. Otherwise he could sell or gift his interest only for the duration of his own line.

Feet of Fines[31] and Common Recoveries[32] are written in Latin to Hilary term 1733; during the Commonwealth and thereafter they are in English. They are arranged by legal term and regnal year and subdivided into county bundles, and the manuscript indexes to them are similarly organized. The pre-fines are recorded in the Court of Common Pleas[33] and from 1576 in the Alienation Office,[34] while the post-fines are entered in the Court records to 1758[35] and thereafter in the latter Office.[36]

Both the fines and recoveries required further deeds to give full effect to the barring of the fee tail. These were expressed in the Court enrolments as a 'deed to lead the uses' if it had been executed prior to the fine or recovery, or as a 'deed to declare the uses' if it was executed afterwards. These signified the tenant in tail's real intentions when barring the entail and were binding on the querient or demandant and their assigns. The deeds themselves were not generally enrolled unless by choice and this was normally done within six months. The abstract of Walter deeds includes a deed to declare the uses executed on 29 June 1695 between Sir John Walter, Baronet, and John Clapham and Edward Tregenna, after the levying of a fine in Trinity Term to make the latter couple tenants of the freehold so that a writ of entry could be brought against them as a preliminary to a common recovery by Sir John under which he was given the fee simple of certain Oxfordshire manors (see chapter 7).

The Fines and Recoveries Act 1833 abolished these archaic and expensive methods of destroying fee tail estates and substituted a deed of disentailing assurance in their place. Under this, the tenant in tail

Foot of Fine enrolled in the Court of Common Pleas on the morrow of the Purification of The Blessed Virgin Mary 8 Edward I (1280) recording the final agreement between William de Preston and Agnes his wife, and Robert Salveyn and Sibill his wife, querients (purchasers), and Cecily, once wife of John le Chamberleyn, deforciant (vendor), by which she recognizes the right of the wives to a third of a third of the manor of North Duffield in Yorkshire forever, for which they pay her two and a half marks a year for life, after which they are discharged. CP25(1)/266/59 m56

in possession could retain the land for himself by conveying it to a trustee to hold for him; if he wished to dispose of it he made a disentailing assurance in favour of a named beneficiary. The tenant in tail in remainder barring the entail was required to have the consent of the tenant in tail in possession and to nominate a 'protector of the settlement', usually the latter person, or sometimes the Court of Chancery. Enrolment of disentailing assurances was mandatory within six months, on the Close Rolls to 1903,[37] and then in the Enrolment Books (Indentures) of the High Court.[38] Since 1925, enrolment has no longer been necessary. Disentailing assurances effected by will were allowed under certain conditions by the Law of Property Act 1925.

– The Strict Settlement –

To counter the damage the creation and barring of entails could cause to the prospects of future

Part of the tripartite indenture of 18 January 1723/4 made between the widow of Sir John Walter, Baronet, the first party, Sir Robert Walter, Baronet, his half-brother, the second party, and Abraham Bulley and Samuel Rock, the third parties, by which the last were declared trustees of 100- and 200-year trusts for the benefit of the first two parties, and to enable Sir Robert to have an income more befitting his status while Sir John's widow was in possession of the estate left to her for her widowhood under his will made on 30 October 1718. C110/136

generations of a family another legal device emerged. This was the strict settlement. The term appears to have been coined in 1710, but they were being set up from at least 1660. It was a method by which a string of alternating life interests and entails could be fixed by the settlor and was a way of avoiding there ever being any tenant in tail in possession to bar the entail. The settlement had to include entails as life interests could only be given to people alive at the time it was made. The interests could be created by a deed of conveyance, a marriage settlement, or by will, provided that the settlor was of full age, was solvent, sane, unconvicted and a native, and, before 1883, not a married woman. A settlement could also be effected by a Private Act of Parliament.

The documents tend to be long and convoluted and were a source of much revenue for the drafting lawyers, who, until 1881, were paid according to the number of words they employed.

The usual occasions giving rise to strict settlements were the coming of age of the landowner's heir, marriage, the making of his will, or some other event. They were favoured by Roman Catholics because they could settle the land on Protestant relations and avoid the rigours of double taxation, confiscation for non-attendance at church, and attainder after the 1715 Jacobite rebellion.

The settlor normally vested the estate in himself for life, and then in his eldest son for life with the eldest (unborn) grandson as the tenant in tail. If the settlor had no children of his own he would often select a younger son of a relative to benefit, as the eldest son was likely to be already provided for. For instance, Sir Robert Walter's will, made in 1731, set up a life interest after his own death for the second son of his sister Isabella Charlotte Rolle. Often there were conditions imposed, such as the requirement to take up and use the surname and coat of arms of the settlor, with a 'shifting use' passing the land to the person next entitled for non-compliance. This con-

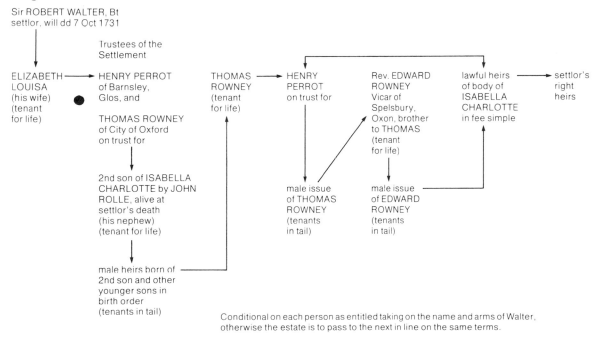

The abstract of Sir Robert Walter's title to his manors of Sarsden, Lyneham Merriscourt, Lyneham Finescourt and Churchill, all in Oxfordshire, beginning with details of the 1670 marriage settlement of William Walter, son and heir apparent of Sir William Walter, Baronet, and his intended bride, Lady Mary Tufton. In consideration of this marriage taking place, and the bride's portion of £5,000 and in order to provide her with a jointure, the manors were conveyed to trustees to hold for certain specified purposes. The couple were parents to Sir Robert's half-brother John; Robert was son by a second marriage. C110/136

Diagram 3: The Strict Settlement of the Oxfordshire manors of Sir Robert Walter, set up 1731

Sir ROBERT WALTER, Bt
settlor, will dd 7 Oct 1731

Trustees of the Settlement

ELIZABETH LOUISA (his wife) (tenant for life)

HENRY PERROT of Barnsley, Glos, and

THOMAS ROWNEY of City of Oxford on trust for

2nd son of ISABELLA CHARLOTTE by JOHN ROLLE, alive at settlor's death (his nephew) (tenant for life)

male heirs born of 2nd son and other younger sons in birth order (tenants in tail)

THOMAS ROWNEY (tenant for life)

HENRY PERROT on trust for

Rev. EDWARD ROWNEY Vicar of Spelsbury, Oxon, brother to THOMAS (tenant for life)

lawful heirs of body of ISABELLA CHARLOTTE in fee simple

settlor's right heirs

male issue of THOMAS ROWNEY (tenants in tail)

male issue of EDWARD ROWNEY (tenants in tail)

Conditional on each person as entitled taking on the name and arms of Walter, otherwise the estate is to pass to the next in line on the same terms.

dition was set in Sir Robert's strict settlement above (see chapter 7).

Enrolment of changes of name by deeds poll are found on the Close Rolls to 1903,[39] and from 1904 in the Enrolment Books of the Supreme Court,[40] whereas changes of name by royal licence which were popular in the eighteenth century and were generally used where arms were involved were registered at the College of Arms in London, and entered in the State Papers Domestic, Entry Books to 1781,[41] and thereafter in the Warrant Books of the Home Office.[42] Both were often, though not always, published in *The London Gazette*.[43]

Protection was given to the contingent interests by the implementation of a trust to prevent the life tenant from destroying the entail. The trustees were conveyed the fee simple estate or a term of years (in the Walter settlement of 1723/4 it was for 100 and 200 years; the settlement of 1731 appointed trustees for the lifetime of his sister's second son only). The common law rule against perpetuities stopped the land from being tied up forever, and any unreasonable terms, modifications and actions against abuses of the settlement could be referred to the Court of Chancery by the remainderman for decree.

When the tenant in tail came of age, he was frequently persuaded by the current holder and/or trustees to consent to a barring of the entail in exchange for an annuity providing him with an income until he inherited the land. A resettlement would then follow under which he was given a life estate and his as yet unborn eldest son was made tenant in tail. A succession of barred entails and resettlements was commonplace every time a tenant in tail reached his majority. If there was no consensus, then the tenant in tail might eventually come into possession of the land and destroy the settlement by enlarging it into a fee simple estate by means of a common recovery. A fee simple could also be created by a Private Act of Parliament or by decree from the Court of Chancery.

The appointed trustees had a duty to oversee the payment of the heir's annuity, of any pin-money (pocket money) for the settlor's wife, her jointure (widow's pension), and any compensatory portions to younger children as prescribed in the settlement. These were mostly drawn from the rents and profits of the whole or part of the land. The trustees had a power of re-entry to the land for non-payment or arrears. The trustees and the beneficiaries were given powers to lease, sell, exchange and mortgage the land, normally with the exclusion of the principal mansion house and its parkland. The money raised might then be used to boost the estate's income to pay the jointures and portions of different generations, to settle debts and legacies left by the previous life tenant, to cover the costs of enclosure or to purchase other land to expand and improve the profitability of the estate. Heirlooms might also be designated to run with the mansion, such as books, paintings and furniture. After the Settled Land Act 1882 the life tenant was able to sell all the land and convert it into capital which was paid over to trustees and invested for his benefit and that of his successors, provided the trustees' consent was obtained and unless the settlement stated otherwise.

The jointures were normally a percentage, say ten per cent, of the dowry brought by a bride on her marriage, but it could come out of the estate rents and profits, with the settlement fixing an upper ceiling, or it could be part of the land itself in lieu of money, set aside for her widowhood. The jointure terminated either at remarriage or on death and was payable as an annual rentcharge. The children's portions were usually payable either at eighteen or on marriage, whichever happened first, with provision for a small percentage of interest, such as four percent, to be paid out each year for their maintenance, education, apprenticeship or purchase of a commission in the interim. The portions were not always the same for all offspring. There might also be a 'hotchpot' clause allowing an early advance of capital which was then deducted from the portion when it eventually fell due. Often the portions were set up long before marriage was likely, so families eagerly compared settlements to find ones of prospective future partners whose terms were compatible with their own.

Evidence of strict settlements is to be found in wills and private muniments, while others found their way into the Court of Chancery as exhibits in cases relating to their creation and content.[44] They were always written in English and contain much useful genealogical information about close and remoter relatives of the settlor chosen to benefit and the financial arrangements made for them. The Death Duty Registers, 1796–1903,[45] extract details relevant for taxation purposes from settlements created by will, and it is a sobering thought to know that much of the business in the Court of Chancery in the nineteenth century was in connection with strict settlements. Unfortunately for us, there was no obligatory registration of them.

Since the Settled Land Act 1925 strict settlements can only operate behind a trust. Trusts are only enforceable in the Courts of Equity. They were usually established to give or bequeath property for charitable purposes (defined under the Statute for

Charitable Uses in 1601), to favour a daughter at marriage by bestowing her with land for her own use but often restricting her use and disposal of its income, and have also been created to avoid estate duty, for as in the case of the earlier 'feoffees' the trustees never die, being replaced in turn as they do so but ensuring that at least one always survives. Many of the educational and religious trusts are enrolled on the Close Rolls to 1903, and afterwards in the Enrolment Books of the High Court. There is a pasted-up index of places running from 1735 until 1870, otherwise the indexes are arranged as for other Close Roll enrolments.

The Leasehold Estate

All the above three estates were of indefinite duration, but the fourth type, for term of years (also called a lease) was for a fixed period as set out in the indenture of lease. The person granting the lease is the lessor and the person to whom it is granted is the lessee. As long as the lease endures the lessor retains the leasehold reversion. The lessee may himself grant a sub-lease of a shorter term than his own; conversely the lessor may grant a lease of a longer period to someone else, subject to the one already in being. The term of years was often tied to a number of nominated lives, not exceeding three, and the lease ended on the expiry of the last of these if it came before the term was up. This type of lease was

Part of the enrolment of an indenture of 16 January 1723/4 relating to the trust set up in 1626 to provide salaries for the parson of Sarsden and lecturer at Churchill, Oxfordshire. This section recites the events leading up to an earlier indenture of 23 July 1693 when new trustees were appointed, and chronicles the genealogy of Sir Robert Walter, Baronet, one of the new trustees, back to his great-grandfather, Sir John Walter, Knight. C54/5242 m40 no 8

common in the West Country, and we have an example in the chapter on the Walter family of Sarsden in Oxfordshire.

The lease defined the boundaries, extent and nature of the land giving names of any tenants, and for the want of any accompanying map, recorded field-names and abutments on adjacent properties. It set the lump sum to be paid and the annual rent on certain due days (usually Lady Day and Michaelmas) in default of which the lessor had a right of distress and re-entry. Other rights and obligations might be incorporated into the lease, which was then countersigned and dated, one copy being given to each party bearing the signature of the other. Any later assignments of the term were engrossed on the back. They are invariably in English.

Leases of land for more than twenty-one years in Yorkshire and Middlesex were registered in Deeds Registries established by statute in the West Riding in 1705, the East Riding in 1708, the North Riding in 1739 and in Middlesex from 1709, to serve as a protection from fraud. Since 1926 all grants of long leases and certain assignments of them are registrable in Local Land Charges Registers, or with the Land Registry in areas covered by the Land Registration Acts, 1925–71.

A lease is treated as personal rather than real estate because it is a contract made between the lessor and lessee. On a person's death therefore it passes into his personal estate and prior to 1926 would have gone on intestacy to the next of kin.

Leases presented an attractive opportunity for raising money for the fee simple or fee tail owner, for without totally relinquishing control over the land he could let it out for a fixed term, collect a regular income from the lessee, and if a fine was payable, receive a lump sum on execution of the agreement. In the event of arrears or non-payment, he could recover the land early, and at the falling in of the lease he could review the rent and renew or create a new lease or retain it for himself.

The Crown realized the advantage of granting short-term leases at the time of the Dissolution of the Monasteries between 1536 and 1539. The Court of Augmentations was set up to deal with confiscated ecclesiastical estates and to retrieve their muniments and charters. Many of the lands were conferred on royal favourites and officials. One of the beneficiaries was Sir John Walter, Baronet, a distinguished lawyer who died in 1630, who held land once belonging to the dissolved monasteries of Bruern and Godstow in Oxfordshire (see chapter 7). The fee-farm rents (a form of perpetual rent charge or annuity) were

enrolled in the registers of the Augmentation Office until it was superseded by the Court of Exchequer to which it was annexed in 1554/5. Subsequent leases and grants are enrolled in the Land Revenue Office of the Exchequer[46] along with grants of leases on lands sequestrated from delinquents supporting Charles I. Leases of lands lying within the Duchy of Lancaster and the Palatinates are filed among their archives.[47] Other leases may be located as Court exhibits, in county record offices and in private collections, occasionally wrapped round lampshade frames.

Mortgages and Annuities

The lease was one means of procuring capital, but sometimes low land values made this undesirable, the landowner's powers of leasing were restricted, the money raised might be insufficient for his needs, or the land was already under lease, so another option was to take out a mortgage, using the land as security for the loan. The mortgage deed was similar to an indenture of lease. The borrower was the mortgagor and he conveyed the fee simple estate or term of years to the lender, the mortgagee, determinable if he repaid the loan with interest by a certain agreed date, usually six months or a year after the deed's execution. Meanwhile the mortgagee enjoyed the profits and issues of the land as a kind of interest. If the loan was repaid by the due date the land was reconveyed to the mortgagor and the land was said to be redeemed, but sometimes the mortgagee was reluctant to do so, and because he had also got custody of the title deeds, it was very difficult for the borrower to obtain a remedy. If the loan was not repaid in time the land was forfeit to the mortgagee, but the rents and profits from it might far exceed the actual debt, so the Court of Chancery's remedy was the 'equity of redemption', by which the legal estate was vested in the mortgagee on a type of trust for the benefit of the mortgagor, who was entitled to the rents and profits. The mortgagee's only recourse was to apply to the same Court for a decree to foreclose the mortgage and confirm his right to the fee simple, or to sell it, extract the debt, interest and his costs, and pay the balance over to the borrower mortgagor. The records of this Court abound with cases involving abuses of mortgages. One of the reasons why the Yorkshire and Middlesex Registries of Deeds were set up in the early eighteenth century was to protect both parties from further secret mortgages and from the fraud of one upon the other, so along with leases of over twenty-one years, sales and gifts and wills of freehold land, memorials of mortgages were recorded there and can be inspected in the appropriate Deeds Registries. After the Law of Property Act 1925, legal mortgages take effect by a demise for term of years terminable on repayment of the loan by a certain earlier date, or spread over the period in question by a series of regular instalments including interest, or secondly as a charge on the land in a deed expressed as a legal mortgage. In either event the title deeds are lodged with the lender as security for the loan, returned on its repayment.

Another way of acquiring capital was to grant a rent charge or life annuity from the fee simple estate and its rents and profits. A lump sum was paid to the landowner's agent or creditor in return for a fixed annuity guaranteed for their lives, and payable out of the estate which was then leased out on a long term to a fourth party subject to the annuity. The guarantees were given by way of penal bonds usually of double the amount of the lump sum, and activated if the annuity failed to be paid. Warrants of attorney confessing judgment allowed the annuitant to obtain judgment against them should the bonds fail to be fulfilled. In the example of Carrington Garrick (see chapter 11), he granted a piece of land, formerly or presently rented out, on a lease of 500 years to commence in 1778 and subject to this tenancy and a life annuity of £50 a year secured by a third party on payment to Garrick's associate of £300. The annuity was to terminate on the deaths of Garrick and the associate, and both entered penal bonds totalling £600 should the annuity not be paid.

The Enclosure of Land

One of the features of the Middle Ages was the enclosure of common pasture and wasteland by land-owners to consolidate strips of land from the open fields, to expand their holdings, and to change their use from arable to grazing land. It gathered momentum under the Tudors, but the peak period was in the mid-eighteenth and nineteenth centuries when a series of enabling statutes made the procedure easier, and went in tandem with agricultural improvements. Early enclosure was either done privately on agreement between a lord and his tenants, or by Chancery or Exchequer decree, with subsequent enrolment in the appropriate court records.[48] By the late eighteenth

century enclosure by Private Act of Parliament was more common, after presentation of a petition, the receipt and investigation of any objections to it, and a survey of the affected land by an *ad hoc* commission. The resulting awards were enrolled locally with the county clerks of the peace or with the incumbent of the parish, or in one of the courts of record at Westminster.[49] The first of the General Enclosure Acts was passed in 1801 and subsequent awards were enrolled as before, though between 1836 and 1845 any enclosure by agreement and without an Act of Parliament merely required local enrolment. Awards made after 1845 are filed among the records of the Ministry of Agriculture Fisheries and Food.[50] The statutes are among the records of Parliament in the House of Lords Record Office, London.

The Enclosure Awards detail the allotments made to affected landowners in compensation for their loss of enjoyment of the commons, and there is often an accompanying map showing the new boundaries. Sometimes too they were combined with a com-mutation of the tithe payable to the incumbent and any lay impropriators.

The Problems of Using Land Records

It has to be said that searching and understanding records of land transfer is a complex business. There are a variety of reasons for this. First, there is no central composite index of names of grantors or grantees or affected land, so you can never be sure that all the transactions that took place were ever recorded or are traceable. The transfers are scattered over a myriad collection of sources, some far more accessible to the searcher than others, either because they are in English (like the Close Roll enrolments after 1536), have been translated and calendared (for instance the inquisitions post mortem to 1405 and for the reign of Henry VII), and have good indexes to them, have been listed (for example the partially listed Ancient Deeds), or are indexed nominally or topographically, albeit by regnal year, by county and then initial letter of the grantor's name as in the case of the Feet of Fines. The handwriting, and terminology (much of it abbreviated because it was repetitive and formulaic in character, but nonetheless necessary to the effectiveness of the transaction), and the language being mostly in Latin to 1733, pose problems for the reader, as well as the variety of schemes used to date the documents. Generally this is by regnal year, then by one of the four legal terms, but some are attached to Church festivals and saints' days. These problems can be overcome by scanning translated and printed examples to discover the layout of a particular type of transfer (this is particularly effective with Feet of Fines many of which have been translated and published by local historical societies) to learn how to predict where the names of the parties and the essential information will occur. Time spent deciphering a range of handwriting styles will prepare the reader for the task of using sources written in differing court hands over a long time span, while ample reference to a textbook such as C.R. Cheney's *Handbook of Dates for Students of English History* (various editions) will render the dates intelligible.

Tracing the history of a family almost invariably means working back from the known to the unknown, using clues from examined sources as the key to new ones. For instance, the Census may reveal that a person was an annuitant or a landowner or farmer. He would almost certainly have been paying rent to someone, but on what terms and since what date and on what land? The tithe maps[51] and apportionments[52] plotted between 1836 and 1842 may show an antecedent's status as owner or occupier of his property, as may the Land Tax assessments of 1798 and at other dates.[53] His will might allude to a marriage settlement, to a purchase, lease, mortgage or inheritance of land and express a wish for its ownership or occupancy after his death. It might mention tenants or people in his debt for mortgages granted by him, and of course he might create a strict settlement tying up his land for many generations after him. The Death Duty Registers from 1796 may also provide extra particulars of landownership and tenancy. All of these alert the searcher to other records, many of which lie in the Public Record Office.

Landownership was long the key to power, privilege and public responsibility, besides offering a good yield in rents and profits to the investor. On the value of his land was based a person's qualification to vote, to serve as a juror at the Quarter Sessions and Assizes, and for public office by Commission from the Crown perhaps as a justice of the peace or commissioner for taxes and provided him with income sufficient to purchase commissions for military service, or to pay for an education leading to advancement in one of the professions. Conversely it also rendered a person liable to taxation. Aliens born and Roman Catholics were special categories attracting punitive tax levies.

Bankrupts, heirs who were minors or lunatics, outlaws and attainted persons all merited special registration of their estates.

A person's change of name may well be explained by his inheritance of land. Patterns of succession to land will also be discerned from land transfer records in the generation of the ancestor in question and in those before and after his time. If it was entailed then his or other tenants in tail's actions may feature in the Feet of Fines and Common Recoveries and in any legal proceedings instituted in connection with them. Court actions often relate to mortgages, and the circumstances of these and their creation come to light among the pleadings and exhibits and depositions produced in the prosecution of a case.[54]

Although private, many conveyances were enrolled centrally because it was mandatory, or because private collections have come into government hands, or because it was felt desirable to have a permanent record of a sale or gift stored centrally to protect the parties and their successors.

The vendor was once a purchaser or grantee himself, so each transfer is the key to the next stage. In the case of the manorial court rolls the date of admittance of the tenant now surrendering it immediately refers the searcher back to the meeting of the earlier Court Baron, cutting out valuable time spent scanning intervening minutes of the Court. The content of the record will reveal the venue, field-name, nature, extent and annual value of the property together with the names of any sub-tenants and the conditions under which it was to be held. However, early deeds often describe the land in a perfunctory way, which is insufficient to be able positively to identify where it lay. The purchase price might also be fictitious, if it was a preliminary transaction to some other deed between the parties who were acting in collaboration (for example in the case of Feet of Fines). Similarly, a deed may not actually be the end of a particular transaction, but was necessary to give the vendor's intentions full effect.

The succession of land in a family and its length of stay within it, what was done with it to expand it, increase its income, enclose it, mortgage it or raise annuities from it, exchange it or gift it to others than the next heir, and the final alienation or partition of it can add greatly to our knowledge about our ancestors' lives. It can reveal aspects of their behaviour such as their ability to manage their affairs, the prevailing economic and financial climates in which they lived, and takes the pursuit of a family's history into the wider realms of local, social, political and economic history.

48

Tax and other Sources of Revenue

The records of the various courts of law may be tapped to trace perhaps several generations instigating, caught up or mentioned in litigation and to build up profiles of their activities and lifestyles; the sources relating to land transfer tell us something of the nature, devolution and continuity of land-ownership and occupation. The next major collection of records, those of taxation, can be used to locate people of a certain status in place and time.

Early Means of Raising Money

Until the abolition of feudal tenure in 1660, the monarch's main income stemmed from his position as supreme landlord, as nominal head of the judiciary, and grantor of rights, offices and privileges. A foreign policy increasingly enmeshed in Continental alliances and dynastic wars meant frequent monetary exigencies, partially relieved by diversion of papal dues from the clergy to finance the Crusades, but for the rest the King had to rely on heavy borrowing and the levying of aids (restricted by Magna Carta, 1215, to paying off his ransom, on the occasion of the knighting of his eldest son, and on the first marriage of his eldest daughter), and the exacting of scutage from his knights in lieu of military service when called on campaign, tallage from his tenants on the royal demesne and demesne boroughs and cities, and hidage and carucage (which were types of land tax) on property not subject to knight service. The need for a more disparate source of income was fulfilled in 1166 when Henry II ordered an impost on movables (goods and chattels) to pay for the recapture of the Holy Land. Each man was left to his own conscience to value his possessions and to place his contribution in the parish chest. A further self-assessed tax, based on a tenth of land rents and goods and chattels, was levied in 1188, to underwrite the cost of recovering Jerusalem. The Saladin Tithe, as it was called, was the prototype for proportional taxation, as similar subsidies, of a seventh in 1203 and a thirteenth in 1207, brought in such huge sums that their potential was realized for quickly raising revenue. However, the Kings were always careful to secure the formal consent of the Council, and later of Parliament, whose statutes lent more weight and gravity to the impositions and in return for whose goodwill charters of liberties for their subjects were confirmed. The request for a subsidy was never in relation to normal administrative business but rather for the defence of the realm, to safeguard the borders, repel insurrections, support foreign campaigns and protect commerce, the final justification being that it was for the common 'weal'.

From 1290 assessment and collection was placed directly under the control of the Exchequer rather than the King's Cofferer. The shire was the unit of taxation, divided into geographic areas called hundreds, wapentakes or sokes, further broken down into the vills, townships and boroughs of which they were constituted. The larger boroughs and cities were organized into wards and parishes. The sheriff superintended the valuations undertaken by sworn local inhabitants before each levy taking care not to reduce below subsistence level a person's ability to maintain his present livelihood. In 1294 a distinction was drawn between the boroughs and shires in recognition of the greater concentration and value of movables in urban areas, so a fraction of a sixth was mulcted from the capital value of movables in cities and towns, and a tenth from the shires. The proportions later varied, but the distinction continued.

Lay Subsidies

Between 1290 and 1332 Parliament voted sixteen subsidies on the laity (see Table 1), but because of

Table 1 *List of Lay Subsidies*

Date of Statute		Nature of Levy
9 Richard I or 1 John	1197 or 1199	Carucage
2 Henry III	1217–18	Scutage
4	1219–20	Carucage
10	1225–6	Tallage
19	1234–5	Aid for marriage of King's sister
21	1236–7	30th
44	1259–60	Tallage
11 Edward I	1282–3	30th
18	1289–90	Aid for marriage of King's daughter
19	1290–1	15th
21	1292–3	15th (Welsh Marchers)
22	1293–4	10th
23	1294–5	11th and 7th
25	1296–7	8th and 5th, 12th and 8th, 9th
28	1299–1300	Scutage
29	1300–1	15th
31	1302–3	Scutage
32	1303–4	Tallage
34	1305–6	Scutage, Aid for knighting of King's son, 20th and 30th
1 Edward II	1307–8	20th and 15th
2	1308–9	25th
4	1310–11	Scutage
6	1312–13	15th and 10th
7	1313–14	20th and 15th
8	1314–15	Scutage
9	1315–16	15th
10	1316–17	16th
12	1318–19	18th and 12th
16	1322–3	10th and 6th
17–18	1323–5	Scutage
1 Edward III	1327–8	Scutage, 20th
6	1332–3	15th and 10th
8	1333–4	15th and 10th (standard quotas)
11	1337–8	Voluntary gift
12	1338–9	Grant of wool
14–15	1340–2	9th and 15th
15	1341–2	Grants of wool
20	1346–7	Aid to knight King's eldest son
21	1347–8	Grant of wool
22	1348–9	15th and 10th (for three years)
45	1371–2	Subsidy (£50,000)
51	1377	Poll Tax
2 Richard II	1379	Poll Tax
4	1381	Poll Tax
21	1397–8	Voluntary Aid (Essex and Herts.)
3 Henry IV	1401–2	Aid to marry King's daughter
6	1404–5	Subsidy on estates worth 500 marks p.a.
13	1411–12	Subsidy (half a mark on holders of 20 librates of land)
6 Henry VI	1427–8	Subsidy (on Knights' Fees and householders)
9	1430–1	Subsidy (20s on Knights' Fees)
14	1435–6	Subsidy (on freeholds of £5 and more)
18	1439–40	Subsidy on aliens (triennial)
20	1441–2	Subsidy on aliens (biennial)
27	1448–9	Subsidy on aliens (for four years)
28	1449–50	Subsidy (6d on every 20s freehold)
31	1452–3	Subsidy on aliens (for King's lifetime)
3 Edward IV	1463–4	Subsidy (£37,000)
22	1482–3	Subsidy on aliens
3 Henry VII	1487–8	Subsidy on aliens
4	1488–9	Subsidy (10th on income from land: revoked)
12	1496–7	Aid
19	1503–4	Subsidy (£40,000 in lieu of Aid)
3 and 4 Henry VIII	1511–13	Subsidy (from the nobility)
5	1513–14	Subsidy (£160,000)
6	1514–15	Subsidy (£110,000)
6 and 7	1514–16	Subsidy (6d in the pound on movables)
14 and 15	1522–4	Subsidy (four years, on income from land, capital value of goods, wages)
26	1534–5	Subsidy (two years)
32	1540–1	Loan
34 and 35	1542–4	Subsidy (three years)
35	1543–4	Benevolence
36	1544–5	Benevolence
37	1545–6	Subsidy (two years)
38	1546–7	Freewill Contribution (five monthly payments)
2 and 3 Edward VI	1548–50	Relief (for three years)
3 and 4	1549–51	Relief
2 and 3 Philip and Mary	1555–6	Subsidy (2) and 15th and 10th
4 and 5	1557–8	Subsidy and 15th and 10th
1 Elizabeth	1558–9	Subsidy and 15th and 10th
5	1562–3	Subsidy and 15th and 10th
8	1565–6	Subsidy and 15th and 10th
13	1570–1	Subsidy and 15th and 10th
18	1575–6	Subsidy and 15th and 10th
23	1580–1	Subsidy and 15th and 10th
27	1584–5	Subsidy and 15th and 10th
29	1586–7	Subsidy and 15th and 10th
31	1588–9	Subsidy (2) and 15th and 10th
35	1592–3	Subsidy (3) and 15th and 10th
39	1596–7	Subsidy and 15th and 10th
43	1600–1	Subsidy (8) and 15th and 10th
1 James I	1603–4	Subsidy (3) and 15th and 10th
3	1605–6	Subsidy (4) and 15th and 10th
5	1607–8	Subsidy and 15th and 10th
10	1612–13	Aid to marry King's daughter, Loan
18	1620–1	Subsidy (2) and 15th and 10th
20	1622–3	Freewill Contribution
21	1623–4	Subsidy (3) and 15th and 10th
1 Charles I	1625–6	Subsidy (2) and 15th and 10th
2	1626–7	Voluntary Loan
3	1627–8	Subsidy (5) and 15th and 10th
4	1628–9	Subsidy (4) and 15th and 10th
10–15	1634–40	Ship Money
16	1640–1	Subsidy (4) and 15th and 10th, Poll Tax, Grant (£400,000)
17	1641–2	Relief of Ireland
18	1642–3	Subsidy (2) and 15th and 10th
12 Charles II	1660–1	Poll Tax, 4 Grants (£140,000, £70,000, £420,000 and £70,000)
13	1661–2	Free and Voluntary Present, 15th
14	1662–3	Hearth Tax
15	1663–4	Subsidy (4) and 15th and 10th, Hearth Tax
16 and 17	1664–6	Grants (2), Hearth Tax
18 and 19	1665–6	Poll Tax, Hearth Tax, Grant
21–26	1669–74	Hearth Tax
22 and 23	1670–2	Grant
25	1673–4	Grant
29	1677–8	Grant
29 and 30	1677–9	Poll Tax
30	1678–9	Grant
31	1679–80	Grant
1 William and Mary	1689–90	Grant and Aid (2), Hearth Tax
2	1690–1	Poll Tax
3	1691–2	Grant
4	1692–3	Grant
5	1693–4	Grant
6 and 7 William III	1694–6	Grant
8	1696–7	Subsidy
10	1698–9	Poll Tax

widespread evasion, undervaluation and embezzlement, anticipated receipts were never achieved. In 1334, therefore, fixed shire and borough quotas were set, based on what had been collected in 1332. This quota continued to be levied until 1624, usually of a fifteenth coming from the shires and a tenth from towns and cities. After 1334, the Exchequer was concerned only with amounts rather than with how they had been apportioned out among the populace, so no nominal lists were produced. The problem of this device was that it did not properly reflect the changing prosperity or size of a community or region, though the statutes excluded areas such as the border counties which were constantly under threat, or laid waste, and regions and boroughs which were impoverished because of other factors like land erosion, flood, fire or epidemic. Communities under economic stress were able to apply for relief and reassessment, and from 1433 a deduction was invariably set aside for distribution among poor towns.[1] The Cinque Ports and other coastal ports were also given immunity as they already paid significant sums towards the construction of the King's ships, and, similarly, men absent on active military service were exempt.

A number of nominal 'rolls of particulars' of taxpayers, outlining their assessed or actual contributions, survive up to 1332 among the records of the Exchequer in county and date order, but there is no complete set for any county, and some are in poor or fragmentary condition.[2] The lists are filed under the original arrangement, the parchment membranes being stitched together sequentially top to tail, or all attached at the top, before being rolled up, and are frequently written on both sides, in Latin, the assessments and totals rendered in Roman numerals. Because stitching was the final act before committing the rolls to storage, what appears on the back of an individual membrane may be a continuation from the front, so the searcher must always assiduously check the dorse of every membrane in turn.

The preface for each hundred describes the nature and date of the subsidy, gives the names of the county commissioners appointed the task of assessment and collection, states whether the subsequent roll is an assessment or list of receipts, and provides the date of the compilation. The date is the regnal year, which commenced on the day of the monarch's accession, and its numbered anniversaries. Under a sub-heading or marginal note of the vill or borough is a string of names of liable inhabitants and what they were to pay. The total amount collected from each place appears at the bottom, and an overall hundredal sum

calculated at the end. A person was only taxed once, where he was resident or last living if on the move, so the lists form a useful directory of names of people wealthy enough to attract attention for the subsidy at a particular date.

The lay subsidy rolls have been much studied by historians seeking to trace the etymology and evolution of surnames, their distribution and comparative rate of hereditary stabilization over time and in different parts of the country close to or remote from the Royal Court. The lists can be utilized to demonstrate continuity of settlement, migration patterns, and occupational concentrations, using locative, topographical and occupationally derivative or associated names as the key. Often, however, the list from a previous subsidy was purloined without any revision, and because of evasion and undervaluation we are not presented with a true picture of individual or communal riches. A comparison of numbers of payers and sums raised among contemporary local communities and over a longer period, and between different economic regions can help us to evaluate their relative and changing status, and a scrutiny of the totals prised from individuals can illustrate local social stratifications.

The lay subsidy of 1/20th imposed in 1327: the assessment for 'Broughtone and Newentone' and other vills and townships in the hundred of Bloxham, Oxfordshire, reveals what each person was to pay. The names of several women are included. E179/161/9 m10r

A record of the collection of the first of a triple subsidy of a twentieth, voted by the Temporalty in Parliament in 1327 (1 Edward III), taken from the hundred of Bloxham in Oxfordshire, included forty-eight residents at Broughton and Newenton (North Newington), who together gave £3–1s–4d ranging from contributions of sixpence up to four shillings, and which formed part of the hundredal collection of £56–5s–11d.[3] This list, coming twenty-one years before the first outbreak of the Black Death in 1348, perhaps enshrines the community's population at its medieval zenith. It has been reckoned that the plague decimated Oxfordshire's population by up to thirty-seven percent;[4] complete families and whole generations were wiped out in the space of a few weeks, many of the weakened survivors succumbing to later outbreaks. The 1327 list reveals two Palmers (a pilgrim or itinerant monk), a ffaukenere (falconer), a ffabre (smith), and a ffreman; there is an ad Montem (Atthill), atte Chace, and atte Bruggende (Bridgend), a de Bloxham, Pleistowe and de Bedeford, indicating where they lived or came from; there are female as well as male taxpayers, who would have been single or widowed householders, for a married woman's property was vested in her husband, while a dependant unmarried daughter living with her parents would have no goods of her own.

Early Poll Taxes

From 1334 until 1523 only the Commissioners' and collectors' accounts exist, but there are miscellaneous documents relating to their appointments or to enquiries conducted in connection with the subsidies. During this interval of almost 200 years other sporadic taxes of a special nature were levied from time to time, of which the most famous were the Poll Taxes of 1377 (51 Edward III), 1379 (2 Richard II) and 1381 (4 Richard II), and which afford us another glimpse of community populations about thirty years after the depredations of the Black Death. The first, in 1377, was at a flat rate of a groat (fourpence) mulcted from all the laity aged fourteen and over, except regular beggars, and from unbeneficed clergy excluding the mendicant orders, while beneficed clergy paid a shilling apiece. This tax disregarded personal wealth or status and must have caused severe hardship to people struggling to eke out a living. In 1379 the tax was accordingly graded to make the collection more equitable, poor couples and individuals aged sixteen and more paying a groat, artificers between sixpence and two shillings according to status, substantial merchants half a mark (6s 8d), and, at the apex, earls contributing £4. Only regular beggars were exempt. The last, in 1381, aiming to raise 100,000 marks, recommended a rate of three groats per person aged fifteen and above, while any deficiency from the poor was intended to be made up by higher contributions from wealthier inhabitants, to a maximum of sixty groats per person; the minimum permitted was a groat from a married couple. This provoked civil unrest, chiefly in Kent and East Anglia, culminating in the Peasants' Revolt of 1381, and the tax was never again attempted until the reign of Charles I, although it was implemented to exact money from aliens living in the King's realms in England, Ireland, Wales and France in 1440, 1442 and 1449, was granted as an annual imposition on aliens during the lifetime of Henry VI from 1453, and was collected by Edward VI in 1482 and Henry VII in 1487. The revamped lay subsidy from the reign of Henry VIII onwards included a poll tax on aliens who would not otherwise have been liable.

The lists of names are arranged in the same way as for the subsidies, incorporated on rolls filed in the Exchequer. In 1379 and 1381 occupations are frequently recorded, and husbands and wives noted together, though the wives were generally not identified by name. The format of the lists, not compiled by grade or status, suggests that they were drawn up in street order, but because the tax gave rise to so much antagonism we are not given a complete view of population size, spread or prosperity within a community. As everyone over a certain age was liable, regardless of sex, theoretically population totals can be calculated, but as we do not know the age structure of any one community we cannot determine what proportion fell beneath the minimum age threshold, a problem compounded by the high and unevenly spread casualty rates incurred by the plague a generation before. Names present in one list and not the others is indicative of death, mobility or evasion, or for a woman, her marriage, while people newly reaching the minimum age may be detected in 1381, when it was a year lower than the previous levy.

Other medieval taxes were the Ninth imposed in 1341–2 (14–15 Edward III), the two subsidies on real estate (worth 500 marks a year in 1404/5, 6 Henry IV, and £20 a year in 1411–12, 13 Henry IV), the mixed tax on knights' fees and householders imposed in 1427–8 (6 Henry VI), on knights' fees in 1430–1 (9 Henry VI), a grant of wool made in 1338 (12 Edward III) and again in 1347 (21 Edward III) and a voluntary gift voted in 1337 (11 Edward III), and there are some extant lists of contributors, but the very nature of the taxes means that they represent only a tiny segment of the total population.

Henrician Embellishments

In 1523, Henry VIII elaborated on the lay subsidy by adding a tax on personal wealth centred on the capital value of movables or annual income from land, wages or offices of profit. An isolated precedent had been set in 1449/50 (28 Henry VI), but this time it endured until superseded by the Hearth Tax in 1663. Over the next 140 years there were more than thirty lay subsidies voted by Parliament, some a single levy, but others in multiples spread over several years and paid in full or by tiered instalments, the moneys going to maintain the peace, uphold the religion of the realm, to defray the costs of military or naval expeditions abroad, to quash rebellions in Scotland or Ireland, or to quell threatened foreign invasions. Thus the nominal listing of taxpayers was revived, and notes kept of outstanding arrears, which also found their way to the Exchequer. The rolls are organized like the earlier subsidies, but some contain two columns of figures, the first being the valuation, and the second the assessment or receipt at the prevailing tax rate. Many also record the nature of wealth, be it in goods, lands or wages.

The first of the new lay subsidies was voted for four years from 1523 (14 and 15 Henry VIII).[5] Rating was done each year between the Feasts of St Michael (29 September) and St Martin (11 November) by between two to six substantial inhabitants of each county, city and town, depending on population size, under precepts issued to them by Commissioners nominated by the House of Commons or by the King. The Commissioners were only to serve in their own counties, divided among the hundreds. Assessment was effected at the current or last abode if absent, and people with two or more places of residence were given certificates of assessment (known as certificates of residence) discharging them from more than one liability. The penalty for evasion was a double charge. The Commissioners rated each other and their names were recorded alongside other taxpayers, whereas peers were assessed by the Lord Chancellor or others appointed by the King and were to be held responsible for tax on the wages of their servants and other lodgers. The nominal lists were delivered to the Hundredal Constable and from him to the High Collector, for transmission to the Exchequer by the Morrow of St Hilary (14 January) 1523/4, and in the three succeeding years, the money forwarded by the Octave of the Purification (9 February), having been collected in by the parish and petty constables and sent via the Hundredal Constable to the High Collector. Payment was to be in English or certain specified foreign coins, which bore their true weight, or in plate of a particular description and value, thus allowing some versatility for merchants and aliens, for those without ready cash, and ensuring prompt settlement. Exemption was extended to the inhabitants of Wales, Ireland, Calais, Guernsey and Jersey, the English residents of the Cinque Ports, the counties of Northumberland, Cumberland and Westmorland, the Bishopric of Durham, and to Brighton and Westbourne in Sussex 'at such tyme as the same towne was lately destroyed and burnyd with fyer', while scholars and students at named Universities, Colleges and Inns of Court were released from any liability.

The procedure to be followed in 1523 and adopted as the regular method of rating and collection, shows how bureaucratic the system was, and that the original lists therefore changed hands several times, copies of them being made for despatch to Westminster. The Hundredal Constables seem to have neglected to check that the new lists were not merely repetitions of the old, so the reliability of them is suspect, especially from the reign of Elizabeth when the poundage was fixed and remained constant. Moreover, the Commissioners were recruited from the most powerful and influential local landowners with a vested interest in keeping their own valuations low, while the annually elected parish constables may not have been very rigorous in carrying out their duties, which were unpaid.

In theory there should be four consecutive lists of taxpayers running from 1523/4 until 1526/7; in practice perhaps one or two survive per hundred, but from these we may detect the disappearance of certain people or surnames, suggesting death, migration or extinction of the male line, and the emergence of widows or other family representatives, and strangers with new households or whose wealth had newly entered the tax band.

The 1523 subsidy imposed a levy of a shilling in the pound for each of the first two years on natives' lands possessed or held to their use in fee simple, fee tail, term of life or term of years, by execution of ward, by copy of a court roll, or at will in any castles, Honours, manors, lands and tenements, rents, hereditary services, annuities, fees, corrodies, or profits of the clear annual value of £50; a similar charge was made on natives' personalty worth £20, sixpence in the pound on capital values over 40 shillings and below £20. Personalty was defined as coin, plate, stock of merchandise, all manner of corn and blades severed from the ground, household stuff and all other goods and chattels movable within and outside the kingdom, all debts 'which in conscience he trusts will be paid' with deductions for money the taxpayer himself owed and intended to settle, and for wearing apparel of all persons, except gold jewels (later statutes extended this to cover pearls, other stones and to silver jewelry). Natives aged at least sixteen, with goods amounting to 40 shillings, or daily, weekly or yearly wages of 20 shillings a year, were to contribute fourpence in the pound. Aliens were singled out to pay at double rates, those falling outside the three categories but aged sixteen or more at the time of assessment being subjected to an annual Poll Tax of eightpence.

From the Statute we can see that it was the person taking the profits of lands, rather than any feoffee, who was to be taxed; personalty both at home and abroad was to be considered, as well as any debts not deemed bad, though an allowance was to be made for the taxpayers' own liabilities to encourage their payment; clothes were excluded, which was somewhat generous, considering the finely ornamented fabrics and furs of which they were made and how much they were prized as gifts and evidence of status. Wages

of landless labourers also attracted tax, so whilst they may have had insufficient goods to render them liable, a primitive form of income tax was their lot. Aliens were hit most, for none over sixteen escaped some kind of contribution. Certificates of residence rarely survive from Henry's reign, and where they do, they will be found bound up with the assessments and returns, but there is a series of them running between the reigns of his son Edward VI and Charles II,[6] showing where people with dual land ownership were taxed, to which there is a typescript nominal index.

In the third year (1525/6) only landed incomes were liable, on the same basis as before, while in the fourth year personalty worth £50 was to be taxed at one shilling in the pound, in both cases aliens paying double. No person assessed in the third year was to be assessed in the fourth, nor was anyone paying tax on land to be assessed on his goods in the first two years and vice versa, making the maximum number of liable years three per taxpayer.

Two lists of taxpayers survive for the hundred of Bloxham in 15 and 16 Henry VIII (1523/4 and 1524/5).[7] John and Juliana Fardon are shown at North Newington as jointly having to pay 18d on wealth amounting to £3, but the nature of it is not recorded. Recourse to the Statute shows that it was based on their goods, taxed at sixpence in the pound on personalty worth over 40 shillings, and thus we know that they would have paid nothing in the third and fourth years.

Because people were assessed to pay on whatever category formed the bulk of their wealth, we do not know how much they were worth altogether, for while annual income from land might have exceeded the capital value of any goods, it might not have been by much, and thus a substantial portion escaped any levy.

Part of the assessment of Broughton, hundred of Bloxham, Oxfordshire, for the first year of a four-year lay subsidy, 15 Henry VIII (1523/4), featuring the names of John Vardon and Juliana Vardon, who were to pay 18d. From the surviving lists of the second payment in 1524/5, it would appear to be based on wealth of £3. The statute reveals that this was based on their goods. E179/161/198 m30Bd

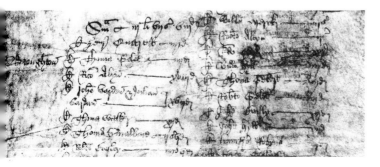

Later Tudor and Stuart Taxes before the Civil War

From 1571 (13 Elizabeth I)[8] the rate was fixed and the subsidy payable in two portions, 1s 8d in the pound on natives' personalty worth £3 in the first year, and one shilling in the pound in the second, or 2s 8d in the pound on their annual income from land worth 20 shillings for the first year, and 1s 4d poundage in the second, with aliens being doubly charged. The Poll Tax was set at fourpence for non-taxpaying aliens and denizens, a lower age limit of fourteen being adjusted down to seven in 1576.

Charles I further refined the lay subsidy in 1625, by making it punitive against known Roman Catholics. Since 1558, fines had been imposed for non-attendance at church and the moneys devoted to the parochial poor. In 1581 the shilling penalty was increased to £20 a month, and absenteeism became an indictable offence. The fines were collected by sheriffs, who were given powers of arrest and imprisonment for refusal or default. In 1586 the Exchequer was granted authority to seize and retain a recusant's goods and two thirds of his lands until he conformed. From 1591 until 1691 the annual Recusant Rolls[9] of the Pipe Office note in Latin under each county in England and Wales the lands taken, from whom and at what date, the rents due from them, any arrears, the name of such person to whom the Crown subsequently had let the property, the total debt and details of its payment; a record was also kept of seized goods and chattels and their value; and finally a note was made of new convictions certified to the Exchequer giving the name and abode of the recusant, the period of dissent, date of conviction, the amount of the accrued fine and whether any further action was taken to secure payment. Whilst not confined to Papists, the Rolls do not indicate the recusants' religious predilections, some of whom were known Protestant Dissenters and Quakers. Sometimes clerical errors crept in, so parochial and other sources should also be checked such as Archdeacons' Visitation records and county Quarter Sessions Rolls, both series held locally.

In 1625 (1 Charles I)[10] the grant of 'the free and cheerfull Gift' of two entire subsidies made Popish recusants convict of seventeen or over and persons aged twenty-one who had failed to take Holy Communion within the previous year liable to double rating or the Poll Tax, like aliens and denizens. Possibly the Recusant Rolls were used as a means of reference to ensure no-one escaped. In 1640[11] indicted Roman Catholics were also attached, though not yet convicted, a practice dropped by his son, Charles II.

So the monarch was entirely dependent on the goodwill of Parliament in granting him subsidies to meet particular emergencies and to settle retrospective debts, rather than in anticipation of future expenditure. Charles I, during his eleven years of personal rule from 1629 until 1640, operated through his Council to raise taxes by issuing Royal Writs. The most notorious of these taxes was Ship Money. Customarily this was provided by seaports to defray the cost of shipbuilding, but in 1635 Charles tried to extend it to inland towns. It was based on rents, annuities and offices, and because it was imposed in each of the three years to 1637, seemed destined to become perpetual. The relatively few extant lists of Ship Money payments are among State Papers, Domestic,[12] the writs and orders directed to sheriffs are included in the Privy Council Registers.[13]

Ship Money and other non-Parliamentary taxes were declared illegal by the Long Parliament of 1640–53. Faced with crises in Scotland and Ireland, and in order to pay off the Army, settle the peace and reduce public indebtedness, five tax statutes were enacted in 1640: to grant four entire subsidies to be paid in two instalments by 27 February 1640/1 and 1 April 1641,[14] two subsidies to be assessed by 20 October 1641,[15] a graded Poll Tax to be forthcoming not more than ten days after its proclamation,[16] a 'speedy contribution and loan' to be paid by 1 June 1642,[17] and finally a grant of £400,000, the fixed county quotas to be realized in two instalments in May and November 1642,[18] and the collection of which was left to the discretion of the county Commissioners, but based on natives' goods worth £3 and upwards, lands, offices of profit or annuities providing a clear annual income of 20 shillings, and aliens and Popish recusants paying double, or if not liable, paying a Poll Tax of 2s 8d a head along with non-communicants aged twenty-one or more. Undoubtedly the lists of names of subsidy payers would have been the main source for this levy and their relative worths being juggled to meet the quota.

Any money not forthcoming for the six subsidies within eight days of being demanded were to be raised by distress or forfeit, with a final expedient of imprisonment. The Poll Tax laid down prescribed sums from everyone over the age of sixteen and not in receipt of alms, according to title or degree, to be mulcted from Londoners and inhabitants of counties within an area of ten miles of the City within four days of the public proclamation of the Act, a longer period being allowed for counties further afield. Payment was not to be in farthings 'to the intent the same may be paid and received with more expedition'. The lowest contribution was sixpence, and the highest £100, required from dukes. The titled, down to the rank of esquire aged twenty-one or more, public office holders in the law, cities and boroughs, in the City Livery Companies and in the Church, had graded scales of payment, Popish recusants convict paying double and widows a third of the appropriate rate. In chapter 12 we shall see that William Dyer, a freeman of the Fishmongers' Company, and listed as

A warrant issued under the Act of Contribution for the Relief of His Majesty's Distressed Subjects of the Kingdom of Ireland, for the Treasurers of the City of London to pay out certain sums from the residue, 28 April 1642. The total amounted to £342, the highest amount going to Silvester Kennedy, one of the members of the House of Commons in Ireland. SP28/193

a milliner in New England, was liable.[19] According to the Statute his contribution would have been a shilling; had he been a liveryman he would have paid £5. Anyone lending £100 by 1 July 1640 was to receive eight percent annual interest on the loan, while anyone able to dispend that sum in a year from lands, leases, stock or otherwise, was expected to subscribe £5, those with disposable incomes of £50 40 shillings, of £20 five shillings, £10 two shillings or £5 a shilling. Merchants were assessed according to their status as freemen, strangers, or involvement in the home or foreign trade, as craftsmen or artisans. The surviving returns made by the London Livery Companies form an extremely useful directory of their officers and freemen in the mid-seventeenth century, some of whom followed other trades or migrated abroad.

The charitable loan to relieve the King's distressed subjects in Ireland was supervised by parochial churchwardens and overseers of the poor in England and Wales, notice of the Act having first been published by the sheriffs, mayors and parsons in churches and chapels. The parochial donations were handed over to the High Constable of the hundred together with nominal listings of the amounts from each contributor, and which were then passed on to the sheriff for transmission to special Receivers and Treasurers before the deadline of 1 July 1642. Some of the parish lists are filed in the Exchequer, but others are kept among State Papers, Domestic.[20]

The Parliamentary Committees

On the outbreak of Civil War in 1642 Parliament financed its activities by operating through Committees sitting in London Livery Company Halls, and whose decisions and orders filtered down to County Committees. In 1643 the lay subsidy was completely overhauled, and substituted by weekly and monthly assessments on land and personalty, and whose amounts varied according to Parliament's needs. Secondly, it put an end to the farming out of customs and widened excise duties. Thirdly, it sought out and punished the King's supporters by the imposition of fines and sequestration (seizure) of their lands. Fourthly, it encouraged subscriptions in return for promises of land in Ireland, the receipts and

claims of these so-called Adventurers for Lands in Ireland, 1642–59, being located among State Papers, Ireland,[21] and giving name, abode, status, amount paid and when and details of any assignments.

The revenue-raising committees were for Advance of Money, for the Sale of Fee-Farm Rents or Crown Rents, for Sequestration, for Compounding for the Estates of Royalists and Delinquents, and for Removing Obstructions in the Sale of Delinquents' Lands. Often proceedings started by one resurfaced in another, making the demarcation boundaries difficult to define and greatly added to the delays and inconvenience caused by their deliberations.

The Committee for Advance of Money was the earliest to be embodied, under an Order in Parliament of 26 November 1642. Its members met in Haberdashers' Hall, and later in a private house in Westminster, before being merged with the Committees for Sequestration and for Compounding in 1650. Its purpose was to receive loans in money or plate for the public use at an annual repayment interest of eight percent. Although intended for inhabitants living within twenty miles of London, counties further afield supporting the Parliamentary party were called to account if they failed to subscribe. The ratio of assessment was a twentieth of real and a fifth of personal estate worth £100 or more, but no allowance was given for any decrease in value owing to the unrest. Some people tried to avoid payment by distributing their goods among friends, or by absenting themselves: the Committee's response was to authorize a distress on their goods and to charge its expenses for an auction 'by the candle', the bidding being completed when the candle burnt out. However, no-one absent overseas was charged, nor was a person with residences in town and country liable to a double rating. In June 1643 a sub-committee was set up to mitigate assessments considered too high, though half the amount had first to be remitted, and then affidavits were taken valuing the estate and deductions made for any debts incurred before June 1642. If any of this proved to be false, the remaining half fell due. By August 1646 the assessments were restricted to Royalists and any earlier non-contributors, further limited in June 1648 to the King's supporters whose lands were in sequestration. From March 1648/9 Royalists who had compounded were to be taxed in accordance with the particulars they themselves had furnished about their landed and personal wealth, but were rendered exempt if their composition had been fully paid. Details of the enquiries made by the Committee between 1642 and

The petition of Humphrey Taylor and his wife Elizabeth to the Commissioners for Advance of Money, December 1651. Her elder sister Mary married Walter Dunch to whom part of Elizabeth's portion was entrusted. He lent £500 to Sir William Walter and others on a penal bond. They sought to recover the money after legal proceedings were suspended on the premise that the money had gone to help the King. SP19/125 p194

1656 are in State Papers, Domestic, and have been calendared and printed.[22]

The Committee for Compounding for the Estates of Royalists and Delinquents was the most important of the Parliamentary Committees, and had its origins in the Committee to raise money for the Scots Army. From September 1643, it sat in Goldsmiths' Hall, as the Committee for Scottish Affairs, and was empowered to draft a list of citizens of London and Westminster thought capable of lending moneys, but in July 1644 it began to deal with 'delinquents' (the King's supporters), Papists and recusants, and this became its speciality. From August 1644, delinquents prepared to sacrifice part of their estates to safeguard the rest and protect themselves were permitted to pay a composition. The resulting documentation came to be known as 'Royalist Composition Papers'. The rules for composition were that the fine was to be based on a fraction of the difference between what the estate was worth over two years before the war, and its current value. The valuation was left to the compounder, but was to be certified by the county committee, and he was to be restored only to the lands for which he had compounded. Any debts owing to him were taken as debts to the State unless compounded for. Prominent named individuals were to compound at a third of the valuation, everyone else at a tenth, and if the fractions proved insufficient, they were to be increased to a half and a sixth respectively. Later, the proportions varied according to the date of surrender and the extent of the delinquency.

The fine was paid in two equal portions, the first promptly and the balance within six weeks. If the fine remained unsettled after six months, the land became forfeit. Rents, in the meantime, were frozen. Sometimes the Committee consented to part of the estate being sold to pay the composition. Those able to prove their surrender by 1 December 1645, compounded at the lowest rate, having first taken the National Covenant in defence of the Protestant faith and the liberties of the subject against the King's forces, and sworn the Negative Oath denouncing the Pope's supremacy over the Church and denying the Catholic tenets, and having lived orderly lives thereafter, otherwise the higher rate was due. Special favour was extended to persons compounding on their own discovery by 1 May 1646, but later compositions were invariably at the higher rate. After 3 October 1646, the whole estate was forfeit if delinquency was proved, although any worth less than £200 were not to be seized.

Sir William Walter, an Oxfordshire baronet, tried to compound in November 1645, and finally made discovery of his delinquency in July 1646, paying a fine of £1,430, being a tenth of his valuation. Any concealment of estates led to a composition based on four years' value of them, and forfeit of personal goods. On 3 December 1650, Sir William paid a further £177 for undervaluations (see chapter 7). Latterly, concealments revealed by anyone other than the owner were redeemed only by payment of half the estate's full value and a shilling in the pound given to the informer. Advowsons and rights of patronage were, however, exempt.

The Committee also handled the estates of Royalists in sequestration. Sequestration, being the seizure of all a delinquent's property, eventually led to his land being sold off at six or eight years' rent and his goods disposed of. It occurred on an information rather than after self-discovery while the matter was being investigated; if delinquency was proven the owner was permanently deprived of it, but allowed back a fifth for the maintenance of his children while another fifth of the proceeds went to the informer. In cases of recusancy the offender was allowed a third of his estate back. In April 1651, seizure and security of delinquents' estates was defined: thereafter the rents remained their property and they could retain their personal estate on security of twice its value as a precaution against any further delinquency. An Act of Pardon and Oblivion, passed in December 1651, exonerated from sequestration any estates of delinquents not already seized.

The records of these two Committees, bound among State Papers, Domestic, have been calendared and printed, 1643–60,[23] but the work of the other Parliamentary Committees has not yet attracted such attention, except for the Sales of the King's Goods and Lands, and Fee-Farm Rents effected by Trustees, which can be traced among the printed calendars of State Papers of the Council of State between 1649 and 1660.[24] For the rest, they will be found in State Papers and Commonwealth Exchequer Papers[25] arranged by subject rather than by date.

These substantial records are invaluable for what they reveal about the King's known or suspected allies and religious recalcitrants of the period, the topographical distribution of Royalist support, and how real property values plummeted during the Civil War. But where Royalists were in the ascendant the county committees were over-indulgent to delinquents, and protected friends and relatives while persecuting their enemies and settling old scores. The example of the Walter family in chapter 7 amply demonstrates the welter of detailed evidence required by the Committees, and may explain the sudden submergence of once wealthy families, for Charles relied on them for loans to cover his war expenses and for billeting his men. An example of how a loan was procured can be seen in chapter 7. Under letters patent of 4 July 1643, Charles offered the New Forest and certain Royal Chases and Parks to several named Oxfordshire gentry including Sir William Walter in return for their acting as sureties for moneys borrowed to offset the Royal debts.

During the Commonwealth, taxation continued to be based on weekly and monthly assessments, while in 1655 the Decimation Tax was imposed on Royalist compounders at a charge of a twentieth of their submitted land valuations and a fifth of their personal property, and the sums were used to pay for the war with Spain and the military policing of England. Reference to these taxpayers may be found among State Papers, in Commonwealth Exchequer Papers, listed by parish, in county bundles.[26]

Tax after the Restoration

Charles II was voted a permanent annual income of £1,200,000 partly drawn from the remaining royal demesne and in compensation for lost revenues after the abolition of feudal tenure in 1660. This was augmented in 1670 and 1671 by money raised on the disposal of fee-farm rents on Crown lands by trustees, copies of the deeds being enrolled on the Close Rolls,[27] but almost all the Crown lands had been surveyed and sold off during the Interregnum and attempts to recover them at the Restoration in many cases proved futile in spite of the sales having been declared void.

In 1661 a free and voluntary present voted by Parliament[28] for the speedy supply of money 'from those who are able and willing to aide your Majesty in this sudden exigencie as a testimony of theire affections to your Majesty and in ease of the poorer sort of yr Subjects' produced another rich crop of county nominal listings. In chapter 9 we shall learn that John Fardon of North Newington gave 2s 6d as one of eleven contributors from the hamlet.[29] In the previous year five tax statutes had been promulgated: a Poll Tax[30] and four fixed levies of £70,000 apiece[31] were followed in 1663 by the final lay subsidy,[32] being four entire subsidies at the standard rate and payable in two instalments before 1 October 1663 and 1 March 1663/4.

Pitfalls and Pleasures of Using the Records

Although the later lay subsidy assessments and returns from 1523 until 1663/4 are far from complete, they are an important source for the genealogist because they predate many parish registers, may mention people who never made wills, and provide clues as to who lived where and when to enable the searcher to turn to manorial material, enrolments of land transfers or title deeds, and where there is a problem of identification, the reader can refer to them in the certain knowledge that a person was taxed only once per levy. Where a name has vanished and is replaced by another of the same surname with property valued at the same amount it may suggest continuity and kinship, and indicate approximately the period to start searching for a burial or will, a probate inventory and change of land tenancy. Sometimes a father and son may be assessed in the same place; when the relationship ceases to be shown the searcher may look for the death or migration of one of them bearing in mind evasion or a loss of prosperity as other factors. A sequence of lists reflects continuity of settlement, the spread of a surname over a particular area. Anyone with immigrant or Roman Catholic ancestors may find evidence of residence and name in the lay subsidies available from no other source, especially as they were subjected to a Poll Tax if not liable on other grounds, but only on having attained a minimum prescribed age.

The Hearth Tax

Soon after the Restoration a wider-reaching tax was introduced. From 25 March 1662[33] the occupiers of every dwelling and other house and edifice, all lodgings and chambers of the Inns of Court, Inns of Chancery, Colleges and other Societies of England, Wales and Berwick-on-Tweed, were to be charged with the annual payment of two shillings for every fire hearth and stove, rendered in two equal instalments starting at the Feast of St Michael 1662 and the Feast of the Annunciation (25 March) 1663. Within six days of being given notice by the constables, headboroughs or tithingmen or other parish officers, the owners or occupiers were to deliver to them in writing a true account of their total number of hearths and stoves. In default of this, or in the absence of any occupiers, a notice was to be pinned to the door requiring an account, and the officers were given a right of daytime entry to collect the information themselves, and to furnish the next county Quarter Sessions after 31 May with a nominal list of people refusing or neglecting to respond. The clerk of the peace enrolled the accounts, made a parchment duplicate and under the signatures and seals of three or more justices of the peace returned it to the Exchequer within a month of the Sessions. Anyone refus-

---

Receipts for the Hearth Tax, 18 October 1662, from householders in the parish of Sarsden, hundred of Chadlington, Oxfordshire. Sir William Walter paid £1 4s. As this was the first of two equal payments of two shillings per hearth, we can conclude that his house contained 24 firehearths. Some of the payers have added their signatures. E179/255/4 Part 2, no 157

ing or neglecting to pay up was to suffer distress and the sale of his goods by the collector, and within twenty days of the collection the money was remitted to the High Constable with a list of payers and defaulters. Further time limits were set for passing these on to the sheriff, who in turn sent them to Westminster. At every stage a small commission was extracted as remuneration, the highest cut of three-pence going to the sheriff, and the lowest, of a penny, to the collector and to the clerk of the peace.

Any subsequent variation in the number of hearths was notified in writing and a duplicate sent to the Exchequer. No-one living in a dwelling worth less than a pound a year full improved rent was to be liable: two from among the churchwardens, overseers of the poor and the minister were to certify in writing to two magistrates that such a person did not occupy lands of his own or others to that value, nor did he have in his possession or on trust for him any lands, goods or chattels worth £10, in consequence of which the constable was to make no return. No blowing house, stamp furnace or kiln or private oven in a house, or hearth or stove in a hospital or almshouse for the relief of the poor and whose endowment and revenue was less than £100 a year was to be charged.

In the resulting confusion accounting mistakes were made, so a clarifying Act was passed the fol-lowing year,[34] enabling justices of the peace to issue warrants to the High Constables to authorize the petty constables to give public notice to occupiers to provide true written accounts of their hearths and stoves within ten days to the appropriate constable, headborough or tithingman, who was then, in company with two other substantial inhabitants, to enter the houses and inspect them in order to endorse or amend the accounts before they were sent to the High Constable. A roll of names and number of chargeable hearths was to run in one column, and those of exempt persons in a second column, the information finally going to the Exchequer in dupli-cate form as before. Even then, not all the defects had been resolved, so a further statute of 1664[35] attempted to curtail false returns, inadequate col-lections and sundry fraudulent practices. After 24 June 1664, from time to time, the King, with the advice of three of his senior officers of State, was to appoint honorary officers, offering sufficient security and taking the corporal oath, to receive and collect the duty, to view and number the chimney hearths and stoves, and to examine the rolls, certificates and returns made into the Court of Exchequer. In company with a constable or any other public official they were to enter any property during the day to

establish whether there were any more hearths than had been notified in the last certificate, and make amendments. Such inspections were to take place every year and be certified to the clerk of the peace, and then to the King's Remembrancer in the Exch-equer. They were also responsible for the house to house collections of dues and arrears. If an occupier refused or defaulted for more than an hour after the demand, the officers might at any time with the assistance of the constable, levy distress on his goods, deducting costs of not more than half the duty before restoring the balance of the sale proceeds to the offender. Any proven violence shown towards the officers was punishable by imprisonment for up to a month. Arrears more than two years old were to be discounted. An occupier vacating a liable house before the half-yearly Feast transferred the charge to his successor; anyone found stopping up, defacing, covering or concealing a chimney hearth or stove and proved by confession before a magistrate was to pay double; anyone letting out lands belonging to a house, dividing the building into several dwellings or letting them out within the past year in order to pretend exemption through poverty was to pay like any other; no-one inhabiting a house with more than two chimneys was exempt unless lodged in an almshouse. Thus the collection of the tax was to be rigorously applied, but any appeal could be placed before a justice of the peace for decision.

From 1666 the Hearth Tax was farmed out, but brought back under Crown control in 1668, before being farmed out a second time in 1674, which means that extant Exchequer duplicates relate only to the years between Michaelmas 1662 and Lady Day 1666, and from Michaelmas 1669 until Lady Day 1674, though some for the intervening years have found their way into county record offices.

The Hearth Tax was abolished in 1688 by William and Mary,[36] the last collection being on 25 March 1689, as it was considered 'Grievous to the People . . . a great Oppression to the Poorer sort but a Badge of Slavery upon the whole People Exposeing every mans House to be Entred into and searched at plea-sure by Persons unknowne to him'.

The extensive lists of names and numbers of chargeable hearths, rather than the amounts due or collected from them, are arranged, like the lay subsid-ies, by county, hundred, and then by parish rather than by vill or township as before. They are prefaced by the date of the statute, and of collection, and give the names of the constables or collectors, written in English. Much has been made of these rosters as a clue to house size and personal status, to the social structure and layout of parishes by giving names in order of perambulation, and as the basis of formulating population totals, the 1688 returns being used by the seventeenth-century demographer Gregory King to estimate England's inhabitants. In 1664 exempted persons were also identified, so, theoretically, every householder occupying property worth more or less than one pound should be recorded. As such it is an excellent source for surname distribution in the mid-seventeenth century immediately prior to the plague and to the Fire of London and the consequent mortalities and migrations.

Where parish registers are defective after the spoliations of the Civil War, the Hearth Tax returns and other taxation lists are perhaps the best evidence we have of continuity of residence or movement, of new generations emerging as adult householders, and although covering a very short time span, must be considered an invaluable genealogical source.

Later Stuart Poll Taxes

Charles II also drew funds from graded Poll Taxes imposed in 1660, 1666/7 and 1677/8, the lowest contribution being a shilling, and everyone aged sixteen and over being liable, with the exception of almspeople, and children remaining with their families who by their poverty did not pay any Church or poor rates. William and Mary followed suit in 1689, 1690, 1694 and 1698, though very few nominal lists survive, including one among the records of the Lord Steward's Department, being an assessment book of 30 July 1689,[37] listing royal servants below stairs, their relations and servants; but for the remainder, a few will be found among the county lists in the Exchequer series, following on from the lay subsidies and Hearth Tax, and others are in county record offices.

Return of Poll Money for the parish of St Martin's in the Fields, Piccadilly Ward, Middlesex, 30 April 1677. Note that wives and children, aliens, lodgers and servants were recorded though not always named. This list relates to non-payers, considered too poor for any distress of goods to be levied against them, or those who were gone away or dead. E179/143/349

Land Tax

William and Mary's usual mode of taxation was by the grant of aids, whether in fixed county quotas, or at so much in the pound on personal wealth in goods (less any debts), offices (excluding military or naval), lands, mines or tithes. In 1696/7 the enabling statute described the aid 'as well by a Land Tax as by several Subsidies and other Duties payable for one year',[38] perhaps reflecting where the bulk of the revenue emanated. Starting on 25 January 1696/7, everyone over sixteen was to pay a total tax of 4s 4d, by monthly instalments of 4d, wives and almspeople only exempted. Additionally, a further levy was imposed on the wages of domestic servants and those under covenant (excluding day labourers), journeymen and hired servants at 13d in the pound when earnings were between £4 and £8 a year, rising steeply to 2s 6d poundage on earnings of £8 up to £16, and 4s 4d on wages above this amount. People with personal estates of £100 or more were to pay £1–5s for every £100, wholesalers and retailers £2–10s for every £100 of stock in trade, farmers and graziers 12s for every £100 of stock, all contributions being payable in twelve monthly instalments, while manors, lands, quarries, annuities and rent charges attracted three shillings in the pound on their full yearly value. The Land Tax soon became a regular annual impost, but the lists of assessments are to be found locally rather than in the Public Record Office, with one notable exception. In 1798 it became possible for landowners to exonerate themselves from future liability, or in cases where the tenant paid the tax to purchase it, the money being collected as usual for the term of the lease or demise but treated as rent in arrears and passed on to the landowner as third party redemptioner.[39] A contract with the Tax Commissioners recorded the lump sum paid sufficient to buy three per cent Bank annuities and yield a tenth more than the tax. The returns for that year for England and Wales are filed with the records of the Inland Revenue,[40] organized under county, hundred and parish, the latter's boundaries not always coincident with the ecclesiastical borders. The names of proprietors, occupiers, sums assessed and date and registered number of any contract by which redemption and exoneration was granted appear under their headings. In chapter 9 we shall see that Thomas Fardon owned land in Adderbury West, Oxfordshire; the registered contract of 17 April 1799 reveals that the freehold property of about five acres attracted 10s

11d a year in tax (based on four shillings in the pound). In consideration of £10–19s–7¾d paid by him, sufficient to purchase £20–0s–3½d three percent Bank annuities, he was granted redemption.[41] The tax continued to be paid, but he received a fifth of the amount as an annuity. From 1798 too, owners of land valued under a pound a year were exempt from the tax, so the lists do not record every proprietor. Roman Catholics were doubly charged and there are a few certificates of returns among the registrations of Papists' Estates in the Exchequer from 1715,[42] as well as appeals against the double liability from 1828 onwards in the Inland Revenue records.[43]

As the 1798 assessments form a comprehensive centralized survey of landownership, occupancy and

Michael Henry Blount of Mapledurham, Oxfordshire, gentleman, seeks leave to appeal against the Tax Commissioners' rejection of his claim against paying double Land Tax on his estates at Mapledurham Chawney and Mapledurham Gurney, in 1873, as a Roman Catholic. IR23/122

values at the end of the eighteenth century, unmatched by any other listing during the era between the Hearth Tax a hundred years before and the post-1836 tithe apportionments, they are a flagpost for locating people and their property, although proprietors might well be resident elsewhere, and not every occupier was listed. Because the returns from 1745 were to be used as evidence of qualification to vote in Parliamentary elections, the 1798 lists reveal whether and where an antecedent was enfranchised, and by consulting printed Poll Books we can discover where he actually lived and how he cast his votes.

The Land Tax accounts are filed in the Exchequer and the office of the Inland Revenue, but are merely the fixed annual parochial quotas without names.

Other Assessed Taxes

The tax on births, marriages and burials, on childless widowers and bachelors over twenty-five from 1695 until 1706 merits no returns in the Public Record Office, but other levies of duties or taxes, on windows (introduced in 1696), hair powder, armorial bearings, inhabited houses, male servants, four-wheeled carriages, wheeled carriages and taxed carts, riding horses and those used in husbandry, and on dogs, while not evidenced by any lists of payers, are traceable among the receipts of surcharges imposed on defaulters, the county bundles of dated scraps of paper giving their names and addresses and the penalties. These are filed with the dated receipts of Income Tax payments effected in six equal instalments, arranged by county, and then by parish, for the period 1799–1802 and from 1803 until 1816, and including lists of defaulters, and salary receipts of local tax commissioners.[44] The Lord Chamberlain's Department has also deposited registers of Income Tax returns of members of the Royal Household between 1854 and 1869, and of other tax levies beginning in 1759.[45] They range from the chimney sweep to Garter King of Arms, from the page of the backstairs to the Master of the Tennis Court, the entries giving the salary and assessed tax after any deductions of each named individual.

The above Exchequer records are as yet untouched by the genealogist, probably reflected in the rather sketchy class list to them, but there waits a treasure trove for the resourceful searcher.

In the Treasury papers, yearly lists of persons paying duty on coaches, Berlins, landaus, chariots, calashes, chaise-marines, chaises, chairs or caravans from 1753 until 1766,[46] on silver plate between 1756 and 1762 (with lists of actual and suspected defaulters, 1757–68, and in 1776),[47] and on male servants in 1780,[48] are also relatively untouched. They are arranged alphabetically by county or county borough, with London and Westminster residents listed last, and then by initial index of surnames, giving abode, the basis of liability and the sum paid. For instance, David Garrick of Southampton Street, Covent Garden, London, paid six pounds in tax for the year ended 5 April 1756 on his four-wheeled chariot and two-wheeled chaise.[49] A transcript of the 1780 tax on male servants is similarly arranged, but gives the number of servants rather than the duty assessed on them for each person.

Returns of persons in confinement for non-payment of taxes between 1848 and 1856 may be found among the records of the Inland Revenue,[50] and there is also a series of Assessed Tax cases running from 1823 until 1858, which has been partially indexed.[51]

Income Tax return of members of the Royal Household for the year ended 5 April 1855. Included is Hon. the Rev. G[erald] Wellesley, another nephew of the first Duke of Wellington, whose salary of £600 a year as Resident Chaplain attracted £35 in tax at 1s 2d in the pound. The Chimney Sweeper, William Andrews, had £6–9s–5–d deducted from his salary of £111. LC3/36 p1

Surname	Forename	Address	Carriage						
Gibbon	Cha.s	Scotland Yard	A Chaise	1	4	1	4	1	4
Germain	Lady Betty	St James's Square	2 coaches 2 chariots, & a chaise	4	1 18	4	1 18	4	1 18
Godolphin	Earl	Stable Yard St James's	A Coach & Chariot	2	8	2	8	2	8
Graham	Dan.l	Pall Mall	A Coach & Chariot	2	8	2	8	2	8
Graham	Tho.s	Pall Mall	A Chariot	1	4	1	4	1	4
Grant	Alex.r	King Street St James's Square	A Chaise		1 2		1 2		1 2
Gwynn	Fra.s	Scotland Yard	A Coach	1	4				
Grubb	Henry	Strand	A Chair		1 2		1 2		
Green	Frances	Greens Yard Castle Lane Westm.r	A Coach			1	4	1	4
Griffiths	Wm.?	Queen Street Westminster	A Chariot & in 1756 a coach &c.	1	4	1	4	2	8
Gibson	Geo.e	Whitehall	A Coach & Chariot	2	8	2	8	2	8
Giles	Jn.o	Russell Street Cov.t Garden	A Chair		1 2		1 2		1 2
Garrick	Dav.d	Southampton Street Cov.t Garden	A Chariot & in 1755 a chaise &c.	1	4	1 1 6		1 1 6	
Goodwin	Henry	Mill Bank Westminster	A Chaise		1 2				

Stamp Duty

The Board of Stamps was established in 1694 to supervise charges on legal proceedings, commercial, financial and other formal documents including conveyances and leases written or engrossed on paper, vellum or parchment. The stamps and stamped sheets were sold locally by distributors receiving their commission by way of poundage, and assisted by sub-distributors on a lesser rate. From 1813, as we shall see, William Wordsworth served as Stamp Distributor for Westmorland and part of Cumberland, appointed his son William as a sub-distributor, and was succeeded by him when he resigned in 1842 (see chapter 10).

During the eighteenth and nineteenth centuries the range of stamp duties widened to encompass newspapers, pamphlets, lottery tickets, apprentices' indentures, advertisements, playing cards, dice, hats, gloves, patent medicines, perfumes, insurance policies, gold and silver plate, hair powder, armorial bearings and legacies. Few of these are represented by any form of nominal list, the Audit Office accounts recording the county collections, but the names of some London newspaper proprietors between 1712 and 1848[52] and printers and publishers from 1816 until 1844[53] may be found here and among Inland Revenue material. The Board also oversaw licensing

The Register of Payments of Duties on Coaches and other Carriages, 1751–6. Under London, David Garrick is portrayed as living in Southampton Street, Covent Garden, paying tax of £4 on a four-wheeled chariot in the year ended 5 April 1751, and also for a two-wheeled chaise in the years ending 5 April 1755 and 1756. T47/2

duties on hawkers and pedlars, hackney carriages, pawnbrokers, horse dealers, attorneys, patent medicine vendors, plate dealers, appraisers, bankers, post-horses, stage-coaches and game. Correspondence from local officials to the Board may well yield references to licensees, and this is bound up among the records of the Inland Revenue.[54] In 1757 the Board took over management of wine licensing on the abolition of the Wine Licence Office, and was itself merged with the Board of Taxes in 1834, and came under the Board of Inland Revenue from 1849.

Usually only the Distributors' accounts survive, but nominal lists exist for the duty on apprentices levied between 1710 and 1811,[55] legacy duty from 1796,[56] licences to hawkers and pedlars from 1697 until 1699,[57] and the stamped indentures of articles of clerkship of attorneys and solicitors, commencing in 1729.[58]

Apprenticeship Books, among the Inland Revenue records,[59] set out the date when duty was paid, the name, address, profession or trade of each master, the name of the apprentice, the date of the indenture and number of years for which he or she was bound out or remaining if the apprenticeship had been assigned to another master, the premium paid for the training, and the amount of duty. Up to 1752 the name, residence, status or occupation of the father or guardian was normally included. The duty was based on sixpence in the pound on premiums up to £50, a shilling in the pound on premiums exceeding this and payable on the total amount; it was due on indentures made within fifty miles of the London Mortality Bills within two months of the date they were signed, the documents being sent to the Receiver General for stamping before three months had elapsed, but within six months outside this area, though the duty was still to be paid to local agents within two months otherwise the indenture was void. The indentures were required to be dated and to record the full premium or its equivalent if not paid in money, so that duty could be calculated. The penalty for non-compliance was a double charge, half going to the Crown and the other half to the informer, whose course of action was however limited to no more than a year after the expiry of the apprenticeship.

The City or Town registers note the numbered daily entries of indentures stamped in London between October 1711 and January 1811, while the Country registers cover the period from May 1710 until September 1808. No details are given of apprentices bound out by the parish or public charity, but there must also have been many indentures which slipped through the net, including the five shilling premium paid by Thomas Gainsborough's nephew, Gainsborough Dupont, for his apprenticeship in January 1772 (see chapter 6). There are typescript indexes of dutiable apprentices running from 1710 until 1774, and of their masters from 1710 to 1762, both on open access,[60] and from which it can be ascertained who else the masters employed, and when and where an apprentice might have become a master himself. The Books are useful in tracing the origins and paternity of apprentices, the trades for which they were trained and by whom. Sometimes the master was from the same neighbourhood and had moved away, or was a kinsman. The premiums are a guide to the cachet attached to particular crafts and trades. As apprentices were usually taken on for seven or eight years, at about the age of twelve or fourteen, a rough surmise can be made of their approximate years of birth, and their abodes are a clue to birthplace. The wills of masters often mentioned apprentices, who may have continued to work for them for wages

once the term was completed. Sometimes the master died during the apprenticeship and the business was taken over by his widow, or the indenture was transferred to someone else. Indentures were assigned if there had been disagreements, closure of business, or to ensure a variety of experience. For instance, George Garrick, articled to a provincial attorney on 16 March 1740/1 for £105, had duty paid of £5–10s in July, the extra £5 being allotted for his washing,[61] while Richard Wordsworth's provincial articles of 1768 were transferred in June 1772 to a London practitioner, attracting duty of a penny-halfpenny on the five shilling premium in 1768,[62] but 3s 9d in 1772 on a premium of £7–10s.[63]

Legacy Duty on personal estates was first imposed in 1780, but because of widespread evasion was overhauled and reintroduced in 1796, and in 1812 brought under the control of the Legacy Duty Office. The Office had access to all wills and grants of letters of administration proved in the English and Welsh ecclesiastical courts, and had a right to call for all settlements, deeds of gift or other documents under which claim for duty might arise, and abstracts were taken from them. The 1796 legislation provided for duty on legacies, annuities and residual estates totalling over £20, but spouses, direct descendants and ancestors of the deceased were freed from any duty on their gifts. Another Legacy Duty Act in 1805 stipulated that any real estate directed to be sold to pay legacies or residues was to be included and from hereon gifts to spouses and parents only were exempt. After the Stamp Act of 1815 exemption was afforded strictly to the spouse. The rates of duty from 5 April 1805 were one percent in the pound on gifts to children and other descendants (and from 1815 the parents), and lineal ancestors of the deceased, the residuary legatee or next of kin, three percent on legacies to siblings and their descendants, five percent on gifts to uncles and aunts and their descendants, six percent in relation to great-uncles and aunts and their descendants, and ten percent on kinsmen of any other degree, or to strangers in blood. The books were kept open for fifty years to allow for any contingent gifts to vest which might attract duty. Any person receiving two or more distinct legacies which together totalled £20 though individually less was brought within the ambit of duty. In 1853 the Succession Duty Act made duty payable on the gratuitous acquisition of real estate worth more than £100, and the Probate Act of 1881 on personal property of similar value, on the death of the former owner, spouses only being protected against the levy. When repealed in 1949 the only duty then in force was

Estate Duty, imposed in 1894 and payable on all property passing on death, and this in turn was replaced by Capital Transfer Tax in 1975.

The yearly nominal indexes up to 1903[64] give reference to the abode, probate court, and register in which details of the deceased's estate will be particularized. The registers[65] supply information thought relevant for duty purposes, arranged under double-page headings, setting out the date of the will and when and where it was proved (or where there was no will when and in which court a grant of letters of administration was made), the name, address and occupation of the deceased, and the names and addresses of the executors or administrators, with a total valuation of the estate. Details of all legacies, to whom given and on what terms, and the relationship of the beneficiaries to their benefactor are recorded in abbreviated form, with annotations of their subsequent deaths or marriages. Finally, details of the amount of duty paid and at what rate are entered, with the date it was received. Reference is given to Residuary Account numbers, but unfortunately most of these records have been destroyed, though the Death Duty Accounts of selected famous people have been preserved,[66] including that of William Wordsworth, on whose estate duty was paid in 1859, nine years after his death, because of the later death of his spouse (see chapter 10). Selected correspondence and papers in connection with disputed cases are also filed among the records of the Inland Revenue,[67] together with all other material relating to the duties.

Table 2 *List of State Tontines and Annuities. (The above information has been extracted from F. Leeson's* A Guide to the Records of the British State Tontines and Life Annuities of the Seventeenth and Eighteenth Centuries, *1968.)*

Year	Tontine	Nos of nominees	Year	Life Annuity	Nos of Nominees
1693		1,002			
			1745		522
			1746		941
			1757		772
1766		138			
Irish Tontines		Total Irish			
1773		1,019 (170)			
1775		982 (167)			
1777		1,560 (383)			
			1778		53
			1779		133
1789		8,326			

The Death Duty Registers are helpful because they may record relationships which were not given in the will itself, and provide information on deaths of beneficiaries; the indexes help locate the appropriate court where probate was effected, and in the case of some West Country wills and administrations destroyed during the Second World War are the only surviving evidence we have of their contents. However not all estates were large enough to be scrutinized, and even some which were were considered too small to be worth the effort involved in quantifying duty.

Tontines, Annuities and Lotteries

Records relating to lotteries may be found in a variety of public records: they were held to provide public finance for specific projects, or were organized with royal protection by individuals. The Million Lottery, set up on 13 March 1694/5, led to the formation of the Million Bank on 19 July 1695 and which was intended to run for 199 years. The Bank was dissolved by a resolution of the Committee of Directors on 29 November 1796, when the remaining stock was converted to reduced Bank annuities at three percent, Bank annuities at one percent more, and three percent Consolidated Bank annuities (consols) apportioned out among the surviving proprietors while any unclaimed funds were transferred to the Accountant General of the Court of Chancery. Among Chancery Masters' exhibits[68] is a formidable array of ledgers recording notifications of deaths of nominees and by whom notified, 1696–1798, cashbooks containing the same information between 1725 and 1798, receipt books from 1695 until 1798, Minute Books of the meetings of Directors and sub-committees between 1700 and 1798, dividend books from 1701 until 1796 in which the signatures of the recipients, the dates, dividend numbers and amounts are recorded against the total invested, accounts and stock transfers, 1734–96, arranged chronologically giving the date, name and address of the proprietor and to whom the specified stock was to be assigned, and finally a book containing the signatures of the original subscribers, their addresses and capital ventured between 1695 and 1700.[69] There are also printed lists of names of proprietors as at 25 June 1793 and 25 June 1795, arranged by initial index.[70] From these

A LIST of the NAMES
OF THE
PROPRIETORS of the MILLION-BANK,
JUNE the 25th, 1793.

Note, Those marked ** are qualified, by their Stock, to be chosen DIRECTORS at the ensuing Election, on *Wednesday* the 3d of *July* next, at their House in *Nag's-head-Court, Gracechurch-street, LONDON:* And those marked * have a Vote, and no Person more than One.

A.

FRANCIS Motley Austen, *Esq;* *Lamberhurst, Kent*
    Abraham Atkins, *Esq; dec.*
Mrs. Agatha Alewyn, *Amsterdam*
Gillis Alewyn, *Esq; Amsterdam*
Mr. Samuel Avila *Mile End Old Town*
Mrs. Esther Agace *Clapton, Middlesex*
The Rev. Mr. Edward Arrowsmith, *dec.*
Mrs. Martha Avery, *dec.*
Mrs. Elizabeth Adams *Kingston upon Thames*
Dr. Swithin Adee, *dec.*

B.

SIR James Burrow, *dec.*
    Robert Burrow, *Esq; Temple*
    Herman Berens, *Esq; Throgmorton street*

C.

DAME Elizabeth Collet, *dec.*
    Richard Crop, *Esq; Lincoln's inn-fields*
Jona Cholmley, *Esq; dec.*
Mr. Abraham Calkoen, *Amsterdam*
Robert Child, *Esq; dec.*
Samuel Castell, *Esq; Lombard-street*
Messrs. John Coape, Will. Hood, John Danvers & Francis Gregg *No Description*
Thomas Curteis, *Esq; dec.*
Sir Thomas Clavering, Bart. *Axwell Park, Durham*
Charles John Clavering *Bathfield, Northumberland*
Augustus Pechell, *Esqrs. Bloomsbury square*
The Right Hon. Charles Sloane Lord Cadogan, Robert Thompson, John Offley, and George James Williams, *Esqrs. No Description*
Thomas Coventry, *Esq; Serjeant's inn, Fleet street*
Joseph Cotton, *Esq; Charter-house square*
Mrs. Hana Capadose Machado, Aron Van Isaac Capadose, *dec.* and David Capadose Pereira *Amsterdam*
Mrs. Mary Clarke *Epsom, Surry*
George Children *Tunbridge*

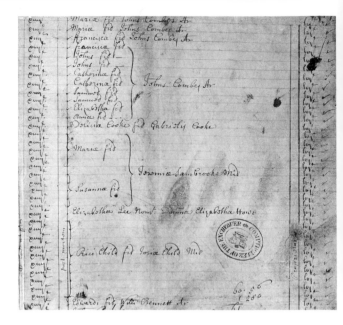

ABOVE *Certificates of sums received for the purchase of annuities. Under a statute of 9 William III c5 (1698) the first State Tontine, set up in 1693, was varied to permit existing holders of life annuities to invest a further £56 per £100 so far subscribed in return for an annual yield at 14% for 96 years. The names of many of the children of the proprietors are included as nominated lives. The two columns of figures represent the annual interest and the money paid. E403/2379*

The Premiums or Benefits in ỹ Fourth Class is continued ———— 86

Number Entitl. Premium | Names Surnames and Places of Abode of the Persons to whom they belong | Premiums or Benefits to which Numbred Ticketts are Entituled

5963 | Thomas Madockes of the Bank of England Gent. | 200 Prin. 12 Ann. Int. Two Hundred pounds prin. The Ann. Int. whereof is Twelve pounds.

7451 | Jonathan Willoughby of St Martins in ỹ Fields Perukemaker | 200 Prin. 12 Ann. Int. Two Hundred pounds prin. The Ann. Int. whereof is Twelve pounds.

1873 | Isaac Helbut of St Catherine Creed Church Lond. Merch. | 200 Prin. 12 Ann. Int. Two Hundred pounds prin. The Ann. Int. whereof is Twelve pounds.

1477 | Samuel Rodes of St Bridgetts Lond. Distiller | 60 Int. Sixty pounds for ỹ first Years Int. as drawn next before a premium of One Thous. pounds.

1898 | William Winchurst of St Giles's Cripplegate Lond. Gent. | 1000 Prin. 60 Ann. Int. One Thousands pounds prin. The Ann. Int. whereof is Sixty pounds.

3320 | Samuel Clarke of Coleman Street | 60 Int. Sixty pounds for ỹ second Years Int. as drawn

TOP LEFT *Names of proprietors of the Million Bank on 25 June 1793, listed in initial alphabetical order, and under a variety of addresses at home and abroad. The Bank was wound up in 1796 and the remaining stock partly distributed among the survivors. Many of the books and ledgers of the Directors since 1694/5 have found their way into Chancery Master's Exhibits. C114/23*

ABOVE *Register of beneficiaries in the Classis Lottery of 1712, showing the capital paid for an annuity and the lottery ticket numbers allotted. Many of the proprietors lived in London, so the lists form a directory of names, addresses and qualities of wealthy residents, and provide clues to City Livery Company and apprenticeship records and to parish registers. E401/2599*

records we learn that Anna Maria Van Praet of Antwerp, a spinster, held £375 of stock and this was divided into £225 in reduced Bank annuities, £191–5s at the level rate and £197–16s–3d in consols.[71] On 3 August 1787 a stock transfer was effected to her under the will of Alida Catharina Geelhand, widow of Joannes Baptista Van Praet, Esquire, late of Antwerp, for whom a London merchant acted as

Among Exchequer[73] and Audit Office[74] records are names of subscribers, dates and amounts invested for other late seventeenth-century and subsequent loan schemes in return for annuities and entry into a lottery prize draw. Two registers of beneficiaries in the Adventure of £2,000,000 on 20 December 1711 and the Classis Lottery for £200,000 less in 1712,[75] list under each of the five classes, depending on when the purchases were made, the number of the ticket, the name and residence of the proprietor entitled under the premiums, the principal sum and attendant benefits, and at the end of the volumes the names of owners of unclaimed premiums which were then put into the lottery to be used as prizes.

Altogether there were eleven other Government schemes between 1693 and 1789 (see Table 2), made up of six tontines of which three were Irish, and five life annuities. Whereas an annuity offered a series of payments at equal intervals throughout a given term in return for a capital investment, the life annuity was paid out only during the duration of a nominated life. Once the nominee died the proprietor's interest also ceased. Often they were the same person, sometimes a public figure was nominated. A tontine annuity was bought by more than one person and as each nominee died the annuities based on their lives correspondingly increased for the surviving proprietors until the last one died and the money became vested in the Government.

Of the original tontine in 1693 there are several printed lists of nominees in the British Library and elsewhere, which can be linked to certificates of sums received for the purchase of ninety-six-year annuities in 1698.[76] They list (in Latin) the names of proprietors, the ventured sums, and the nominees. It was not unusual for there to be five or six of the proprietor's children cited as nominees, so while no addresses are given, family networks are established, and this source is largely unknown. The printed lists give ages and addresses of surviving nominees at varying dates.

The second English tontine, in 1766, had only 180 shares subscribed, and the names of the 138 nominees were formed into classes according to precedence of application. Any half-yearly payment not demanded within twenty days of the year's end was forfeited for the benefit of the other annuitants. The ledgers, among the records of the National Debt Office,[77] give the number, name and address of each proprietor, the consideration money paid, the annuity, and the names, addresses and ages of nominees, their respective dates of death and the name of any proprietor's assignee. A record was kept of who was still alive at certain dates, the entries revealing that the last beneficiary in the tontine died in 1859. A Posting Book of 1766[78] contains an index of nominees together with annotated notes of later half-yearly payments, defaults and dates of death.

The third English tontine, in 1789,[79] divided the nominees into six classes by age bands, the annuity varying according to class, increasing to a maximum of £1,000 a year for the last survivor, but again it was under-subscribed. The next year a further statute allowed tontine holders to exchange their shares by 20 September for annuities having $69\frac{1}{4}$ years to run at £4–5s for every £100–5s share, payable in half-yearly instalments starting on 5 April 1791. The Treasury took the remaining shares and found Government nominees to fill the classes, who were drawn from resident British subjects among the peerage, baronets, justices of the peace, lords of manors and their issue, church dignitaries, College fellows, governors of the Charterhouse, Foundling or Christ's Hospitals, and those registered in the books of the Amicable Society for Insurance of Lives in Serjeants' Inn. The other nominees were distinguished as 'Contributors' Nominees' in the registers. The age of Government nominees was proved on submission of the baptism register or an affidavit recording details of age, residence and parentage; a similar rule applied to the contributors' nominees. Those overseas produced certificates from the Governor or his Deputy of any Settlement, from a British minister if living in Europe, or from the Chief Magistrate if elsewhere, and penalties were high for falsified documents. Payment of the capital sum was made in six monthly instalments of £15 after the initial deposit of £10–5s per share, the last falling due on 29 January 1790, and failure to pay on the due dates meant that what had already been submitted was forfeit to the use of the public. The Master Ledgers are supplemented by printed lists issued in 1792[80] and setting out the debenture number, nominee's name and age in October 1790 when the tontine commenced, his rank or other description, and often his parentage and residence. They are arranged alphabetically within each class, and dates and ages at death were later interpolated. Similar updated lists were published annually and distributed among the surviving annuitants, and an announcement made in *The London Gazette*.[81] Within a month of the death of any nominee, the proprietor was to notify the Auditor; if they were one and the same person, if no payment was demanded for two years the nominee was considered dead and the annuity shared out among the survivors of the class. Any payment received after the known death of a nominee was to be forfeit at treble its value and attracted a fine of £500. Every half year, on 5 April and 10 October, each nominee either reported in person to the Auditor at the National Debt Office to prove his survival, or the annuitant produced a life certificate signed by the minister and parish churchwardens, a sworn affidavit made before a judge at Westminster or a local magistrate, or commanding officer if in the Services, or a British consul if resident abroad. Government nominees had proof of existence certified by the incumbents of the parishes where they lived. Some of the life certificates survive for 1831 for contributors' nominees,[82] and between 1832 and 1840 for those of the Government.[83] Other supporting documents of birth, marriage and death were also filed, the names of nominees entered in the margin and being indexed at the back of each volume.[84] Bundles of 'Tontine Annuities Dead Orders'[85] record on the dorse of the original printed debentures details of assignments arranged in order of decease; and there are other evidences such as will extracts, abstracts of administration grants and assignments during the period 1802 until 1878.[86]

The printed list in 1792 shows 2,435 contributors' nominees in the first class, all aged under twenty on each of whom an annuity of £4–3s was paid to the proprietor, while the lowest number of nominees was in the sixth class covering those aged sixty and over and on these fifty people £5–12s was the annuity. The payments were free of tax, deemed as personal estate, and any transfer was exempt from Stamp Duty. The transfers were recorded in books kept at the Bank of England and signed by the concerned parties or their attorneys. Any assignment by will did not come into effect until that part of it was entered at the Bank; in default of a bequest, the benefit went to the executors. The Bank held the original books of the names of the first proprietors and of the principal sums paid for the certificates granting the annuities, duplicates of which were then sent to the Exchequer.

There are similar registers covering the Irish tontines of 1773, 1775 and 1777,[87] but for these all the lives were those of contributors' nominees.

The first three annuities, of 1745, 1746 and 1757, offered lottery tickets on the purchase of life annuities of a certain value. The Ledgers[88] are arranged by number and give the date of purchase, the name and address of all 387 proprietors, details of consideration money and the names of contributors, the number of lottery tickets allocated, and the annual return on the investment, the name and address of the nominee or nominees, plus age at the time of purchase, and when death occurred or the last annuity was paid. An index of nominees in 1745 has been published.[89] For the 1746 annuity no names of contributors are recorded,[90] while the Ledgers for the 1757 annuity[91] include the names of parents of the nominees, though sometimes it is not clear where the name of the proprietor and the nominee was the same whether it was actually one person or two.

An analysis of the annuities has revealed that most of the proprietors and nominees came from London and Middlesex, though in 1746 over a third were Dutch;[92] where status can be established, it appears to range from tradesman to nobleman, and a sizeable proportion were widows or spinsters.

The last two annuities were more modest in scale, the one in 1778 being for a life annuity or for term of thirty years, with the opportunity of buying lottery tickets. The Ledgers[93] record details of assignments as well as the names of the fifty-three nominees, their ages, and dates of death, and the dates of purchase, the names of the proprietors, how much was invested and the annuity. The final annuity and lottery, offered in 1779,[94] was for a life annuity or term of twenty-nine years.

An Assignment Ledger[95] for the first three annuities records transfers and the authorizing wills, administration grants, marriage settlements and other deeds, arranged in chronological order and giving the original debenture number and amount involved, but not the year. Transfers of the 1745 annuity are included in the published index.[96] There are also bundles of Tontine and Annuity Dead Orders[97] which mainly duplicate what is in the Ledger, Posting Book and Assignment records, but sometimes contain death certificates of nominees. For the 1778 and 1779 annuities, a book of endorsements[98] repeats

List of Government Nominees of the Great English Tontine of 1789, arranged in classes according to age. The First Class comprised children aged under 20. Government Nominees were resident British subjects chosen from a pre-determined social or professional background to make up the numbers as the Tontine was undersubscribed, though they derived no financial benefit. Notice the schools many of the children were attending in 1790 when the list was printed. NDO2/15

N° of the Order.	Names of Nominees.		Age in Oct. 1790	Rank or other Description.	Residence of Nominees.	
			Yrs.			
1481	Guise	Berkeley William	15		Neesdon school	Middlesex
1482	Guise	John Wright	13		Elmore school	Gloucestershire
1483	Guise	Powell Colchester	11	Children of Sir John Guise, Bart. (and Dame Elizabeth his wife)	Westminster school	
1484	Guise	Martin George	10		Westbury upon Severn school	Gloucestershire
1485	Guise	Jane Mary Catherine	9		Churcham	Ditto
1486	Guise	Christopher William	7		Withington	Ditto
1487	Gurdon	Anna Maria	11		Assington	Suffolk
1488	Gurdon	Brampton Philip	10	Children of the Rev. Philip Gurdon (and Sarah his wife) lord of the manor of Assington, Suffolk	Dedham grammar school, Essex	
1489	Gurdon	Laetitia	6		Assington	Suffolk
1490	Gurdon	Jemima	4		Ditto	Ditto
1491	Gurdon	Elizabeth	2		Ditto	Ditto
1492	Hackett	Andrew	18		Witham	Warwick
1493	Hackett	Mary	15	Children of Andrew Hackett, Esq. (and Elizabeth Ann his wife) lord of the manor of Moxhall, in the county of Warwick	Witham	Warwick
1494	Ditto	Ditto			At school at Litchfield	Staffordshire
1495	Hackett	Charlotte	13		At school at Litchfield	Staffordshire
1496	Hackett	Francis Beynon	6		Sutton Coldfield school	Warwick
1497	Haden	Mary Anne	10		Wednesbury	Staffordshire
1498	Haden	Elizabeth	8	Children of the Rev. Alexander Bunn Haden (and Mary his wife) in the commission of the peace for the county of Stafford	At school at Bilston	Staffordshire
1499	Haden	Alexander Bunn	7		At school at Aldridge	Staffordshire
1500	Haden	Francis Waltie	6		Wednesbury	Staffordshire
1501	Haden	Sarah Waltie	4			
1502	Hadley	Sarah	11	Daughters of Jeremiah Rayment Hadley, Esq.		

information on nominees' deaths, and of assignments found in the Ledgers.

Privately compiled nominal indexes to all the above tontines and annuities are currently being transferred to the Society of Genealogists.

Other registers of annuity purchases are among Exchequer records, principally the collection between 1558 and 1650:[99] the names and offices of contributors are listed together with the sums they invested, but no addresses; registers of assurances and wills for the years between 1681 and 1718 are indexed at the back and record appointments of administrators of residuary estates in a variety of probate courts, and annuity assignments, in a mixture of English and Latin.[100]

Licences

The licensing activities of the Stamp Office are represented by two nominal registers of hawkers and pedlars between 24 June 1697 and 24 June 1699,[101] among the records of the Audit Office. The 4,469 entries are listed numerically, giving the date, abode and number of horses traded with, as well as the date and amount of security offered under bond. Evidence of licences to wine retailers survives among Chancery material,[102] and concerns those issued by the patent holders during the reign of Elizabeth. The licence allowed the sale and purchase of wine in taverns, limited by statute[103] to a fixed number in certain named cities, boroughs, ports and market towns, and extended in 1576 to include every thoroughfare, clothing town, haven and fishing town. A restriction was placed on the price of Bordeaux wines, sack and malmsey. The bundles of dated counterpart indentures, signed by the patentee and licensee, are arranged alphabetically by county, then chronologically by regnal year. Compositions for offences against statutory prices and measures of wine were also recorded in the Exchequer during the same reign;[104] Lenten Certificates, 1593–1641,[105] relate to taverns inspected in the City of London and found to be selling unlicensed drink and killing, dressing or eating meat without licence between Shrove Tuesday and the Tuesday after Palm Sunday, contrary to a proclamation in 1561, while a series of Victuallers' Recognizances[106] undertaking to uphold the proclamation during this and the subsequent two reigns are filed chronologically under appropriate counties.

The Wine Licence Office was set up in 1679. Among the records of the Audit Office are the annual accounts of local agents from 1682 until 1757,[107] which include also the names of retailers in arrears, arranged alphabetically by county, then by place of business, and giving details of the overdue amounts. In 1738 John Gainsborough of Sudbury in Suffolk was reportedly two years behind and owed the Office three pounds and a further ten shillings for trading without a current licence.[108]

The Valuation Office

The Valuation Office originated in 1909 as a branch of the Estate Duty Office, hiving off in 1910 to undertake a general valuation of land in Great Britain for the purpose of assessment and collection of land value duties. Valuation districts were accordingly established, further sub-divided into civil parishes, but whose boundaries did not always coincide with the ecclesiastical borders; for instance, a person seeking Lavenham in Suffolk in the class list will be singularly unsuccessful for it was incorporated into the civil parish of Cockfield, in the valuation district of Bury St Edmunds. Each property was allocated an assessment number, which can be identified on the specially printed Ordnance Survey maps.[109] The resulting Field Books[110] run chronologically by property number for each parish and the entries give corresponding map references. Valuation Books were also prepared (commonly called 'Domesday Books'), but these, with the exception of the City of London and Paddington,[111] are in county record offices. The Field Books contain all of what appears in the Valuation Books but add a detailed description of the property. The Turner family of Lavenham once ran the Black Lion Hotel in the High Street (see chapter 5). When surveyed and valued on 30 October 1914, as property number 431, it was described as belonging to William Bantock and occupied by Maulden and Son who had let it out to G. Springett, Junior, on a yearly rental of £60. The freeholder was responsible for the annual Land Tax of £2–17s and for the tithe of 2s 10d, for insurance and repairs, but the rates and other taxes were payable by the occupier. By then it was seen as an old property of lath and plaster and tiled construction, having a veritable rabbit-warren of rooms, including one used as a bank, six bedrooms and private quarters as well as several bars. Outside there was a stable, barn, a coach-house, piggery, wash-house and other amenities, the whole property's estimated gross market value being £1,100, of which a tenth was calculated for the site value less any buildings. The gross rateable value of the buildings was however much lower. These Books are a fascinating source of information on housing at the start of this century, which can be supported by photographic evidence of the period.

Tithes

Tithes were payable to the incumbent of the parish, or lay impropriator, from the annual produce of the land a person occupied by way of crops (predial), grazing animals (mixed) and labour (fishing or milling for example). Some parishes converted their payment in kind to money especially at the time of enclosure, but in 1836, the remaining English and Welsh parishes still following the old system of contributing a tenth of their produce were placed under the Tithe Redemption Commission. A complete perambulation was made to ascertain how much commutation had already taken place, and to gain a consensus among parochial landowners and tithe-owners for commutation, or where this was not possible, to make an award. Commutation was based on a septennial average of the price of corn in Great Britain, apportioned out according to the annual value of each affected property. A map[112] was drafted for each parish or township marking out and numbering the land subject to tithe, and an accompanying schedule of apportionments[113] recorded alphabetically in columns the names of landowners, and against these the occupiers, plot numbers, name and description of the land, its state of cultivation, extent in acres, roods and perches, and the amount of apportioned rent charge payable to the tithe-owner. The maps and apportionments were almost all completed by 1842, but often altered apportionments were added to them later, as in the case of Abigail Turner's property in Lavenham which was reduced in order to allow for the building of a new road and a railway line in 1869, and so the rent charge was accordingly adjusted.[114] The Tithe Act 1936 converted existing rent charges into sixty-year annuities payable to the State, with compensation offered to the tithe-owners. New maps were compiled,[115] updating ownership and confirming the annuities in District Apportionments.[116]

This task was interrupted by the War, and not all have survived, but the maps are almost working copies of the earlier nineteenth-century survey.

These maps, like the Valuation Office maps between 1910 and 1914, show exactly where a particular property lay, its extent, ownership and occupancy. The tithe maps have the attraction of being drawn close to the census year of 1841, and whereas precise addresses were rare for this count, they can be located on the map together with neighbouring properties, and their proximity to road and water networks determined. They also give a glimpse of parishes forty years apart, and forty years after the 1798 Land Tax assessments, and so chart any change in ownership or occupancy. However, not every owner or tenant was included; some property was free of the tithe; the owner listed might have been a long leaseholder rather than the freeholder, while the named tenant might have been one of a group whose names do not feature in the schedule. Nonetheless these sources in the records of the Inland Revenue can be used to add to the family's more recent history.

The other ecclesiastical imposition was on incomes from benefices worth more than £50 a year, drawn from first fruits and tenths to form a perpetual fund administered by the Governors of Queen Anne's Bounty for the augmentation of incomes of poor clergy after 1704. The Office of First Fruits and Tenths, set up by Henry VIII in 1540, was abolished in 1827, and its records[117] transferred to the Governors. Conveyances of lands to provide income for the benefices are enrolled on the Close Rolls to 1903[118] and thereafter in the Enrolment Books of the Supreme Court.[119] Certificates of institutions to livings above and below the threshold date from 1544 until 1912,[120] though not complete for every diocese, and there are records of payments of first fruits running from 1535 until 1822 among the Exchequer archives.[121] An index to livings, arranged by diocese, and ranging from 1556 until 1838, is on open access, and sets out the name of each new incumbent, his patron and the date of presentation. These Institution Books are a relatively straightforward means of finding beneficed clergy as long as one knows the parishes. In chapter 1 we met John Rushworth, the Vicar of Fillongley in Warwickshire, brought to the attention of the Court of King's Bench in 1733.[122] When he resigned and his successor was instituted to the parish on 20 December 1758, his income was given as under £50, and so he would have been in receipt of the Bounty.[123]

4

STRANGERS AND SETTLERS

In the last chapter we saw how lists of taxpayers and defaulters fix our ancestors in place and time; but what of those we expected to have been there and were not, and what of the people we suspect may have been immigrants or strangers, or gone overseas: what are the sources for finding out more about them?

Migrants and Immigrants

– The Census –

Any of the centralized archives may contain evidence of migration, by alluding to a place of origin, work-place or abode other than where a person's activities were recorded. The most fruitful nineteenth-century archive is the census, for here we have a sequence of nominal household listings, taken at ten-year intervals from 1841, and which formed the basis of a total population count of the United Kingdom, the Channel Islands and the Isle of Man. Taken on the Sunday nights of 6 June 1841, 30 March 1851, 7 April 1861, 2 April 1871 and 3 April 1881, the available returns[1] provide personal details of age, birthplace and occupation of all people sleeping in inhabited houses and elsewhere, and when the census of 5 April 1891 becomes open in January 1992,[2] we shall have a span of sixty years to scrutinize. The Irish and Scottish Returns are held in their respective countries, the others are in the Public Record Office.

Access to the microfilms of the census returns is by place-name index, for enumeration was done by city and borough, parish and township, village and hamlet, divided up into enumeration districts of about two hundred households each, or as many as the enumerator could be expected to reach in a day to hand out the household schedules. The completed forms were collected up the day after the census count, the information transferred to an Enumer-ator's Book which was then signed by him, inspected and signed by the District Registrar, and finally by the Superintendent Registrar before being sent to the Registrar General in London. There is a series of Ordnance Survey maps available,[3] plotting out the boundaries of the various Registration Districts, a complete set extant for England and Wales and London in 1891, and incomplete sets for 1870 and 1921.

Some of the larger towns have street indexes to them as an aid to locating specific addresses, and these are indicated in the Registration District volumes to which the place-name indexes are the key. The 1851 census of a number of places has been extensively trawled to compile personal name indexes, and copies of them can be inspected. At present a massive project is in hand to collate a countrywide nominal index of the 1881 census, which will be an invaluable con-tribution to the location of individuals and others of the same surname.

The 1841 census is the least informative because no signification of birthplace is given beyond whether it was or was not in the same county where the person was recorded, or in Scotland, Ireland or foreign parts; ages over fifteen were rounded down to the nearest five. The later returns contain ages and birthplaces supplied by the heads of household and are not always accurate, indeed ages may alter by more or less than ten years by the time of the next enumeration. Often a string of different birthplaces is delineated for family offspring, offering a clue at least to when the family was in a particular place, but not why, although the nature of parental occupation may well be the reason. Sometimes, where neighbours practising similar trades or skills have identical or contiguous birth-places, this may suggest group migration. Marking out family birthplaces on a map may indicate a direc-tional flow of migration, so that pre-census sources can be consulted along the line of movement. Frequently the family did not come from far afield, but was attracted by better work opportunities and regular wages; the death or disability of an elderly relative might create the need for someone to take over a business or farm, prosperous relatives might employ or apprentice other kinsfolk, rural workers join the drift into industrial towns and cities to take up jobs in factories, on the railways, or in burgeoning municipal departments, or be enticed by stories of travellers of life in the city, and added to these was the huge influx of Irish itinerant labour leaving rural poverty to collect in the northern ports before going off to find work on the roads and railways. The most mobile group was probably aged between fifteen and thirty, but even when a wife and children were to be supported many people still moved about, unfettered by landownership.

Special returns of staff and inmates of prisons, penitentiaries, houses of correction, prison hulks, workhouses and almshouses, hospitals, infirmaries and asylums, public and endowed schools, colleges, barracks and other public or charitable institutions were filed at the end of the census of the places they served, or alternatively at the end of the Registration District. Some of these were not local people, although most were, and workhouses, for example, were the final resorts of destitute people from a number of parishes within the local Poor Law Union, as well as temporary refuges for impoverished strangers. Unfortunately, the returns of 1861 merely give their initials, and the entries for each census state their position in the institution rather than in family groupings. From 1851 it was the size of such communities which determined whether they were to be separately treated, or included in the body of the household listings, between one and two hundred occupants being the criterion.

Soldiers and officers in barracks merited special returns if considered large enough; otherwise they will be found with other households. Royal Naval personnel ashore were enumerated wherever they spent census night, while crews and passengers on board vessels in British ports appear to have been separately recorded in 1851, although no returns survive. From 1861, commanders of vessels in home waters were given naval schedules to complete, giving rank or quality, marital status, age and birthplace of all on board, with similar personal details about any passengers. The returns for ships in port or at sea can be found at the end of the census class for 1861; thereafter the returns for ships in port were filed at the end of the Registration District of the appropriate port.

Merchant seamen and passengers staying on shore overnight were recorded where they slept; in 1851 those aboard British ships in port or at sea engaged in the home trade (defined as the United Kingdom coastline, the Channel Islands, Isle of Man or Europe from the Elbe to Brest) were enumerated by port customs officers, who distributed ships' schedules to the masters of all vessels arriving between 15 March and 30 March, for collection on 31 March from ships still in dock. Vessels absent on home trade were given schedules in advance or on putting into port during the month ending on 30 April. The returns give the ship's position at midnight on 30 March, but few of them are extant. In 1861 a similar arrangement was applied, schedules being handed out between 25 March and 7 April, and 8 April to 7 May to masters of ships in the home or coastal trade; in 1871 the period was from 25 March until 2 May, and in 1881 from 26 March until 3 May. Ships away from port in the home trade were omitted from the 1891 census and schedules passed to vessels arriving between 30 March and 30 June. Thus enumeration of merchant shipping was over a course of time rather than on one night, to allow for ships out of port. The 1861 returns are to be found with those of Royal Naval vessels, and from 1871 they are filed at the end of the returns for the port or place where they were on census night or where the schedules were eventually handed in. Fishing vessel crews were probably enumerated in 1851, but no returns survive; a shorter period, from 4 April until 20 April 1861, was followed by one commensurate with other merchant shipping before census night but with a shorter interval afterwards (to 14 April 1871 and 15 April 1881). In 1891 the timescale was made universal for all merchant shipping. The returns are filed with those of the merchant vessels.

Inland craft arriving at ports or areas served by customs officers were treated as merchant ships, but nominal lists exist only from 1861; people on boats on canals and inland waterways were enumerated at their moorings on census night, by 'trustworthy persons' selected by the District Registrars, who previously had compiled a list of vessels with the help of wharf owners and managers of canal companies. The standard ships' schedules were used and the returns are located at the end of the appropriate Enumeration District or Registrar's Sub-District. From 1871 the task was taken over by the enumerators, so the returns are found at the end of their districts. In 1881 barges and other boats arriving during the course of census day were also recorded. Particulars about age and birthplace of those on board show where they came from, which unlike the returns for sea-going ships, may be fairly local.

A more difficult group to trace are the numerous unemployed who 'tramped' the country in search of work. Sometimes a publican would give them space in an outbuilding, or at other times they slept rough. Since these places did not constitute inhabited houses they were not enumerated; many must have been missed out of the June census of 1841, as they roamed about seeking casual farm labour or were sleeping close to temporary jobs. All we have are the numbered summaries of males and females sleeping in barns, sheds, tents and in the open air, and similarly for 1851. In 1861 nominal lists appear in a 'List of persons not in houses' which were filed at the end of the household schedules, and from 1871 their names were entered in whatever road, lane or outhouse they found themselves spending the night. In 1871 the occupants of two tents set up in River Street, Attercliffe, Sheffield, in Yorkshire, revealed themselves as a family of gipsies, tinkers and clothes peg makers, going under a curious set of names and aliases (Black Bird, Cox, Granney, Black Sandy and Frightful to name just a few), and of uncertain marital condition.[4] The 1881 census of Lavenham in Suffolk includes a group of tramps lodged at the Crown and Anchor in Prentice Street, and emanating from places as diverse as Ipswich in Suffolk, Burnley in Lancashire, Royston in Hertfordshire, and Sleaford in Lincolnshire.[5]

Railway and coach passengers were enumerated at the house or hotel where they stopped or took up residence the following morning, though at Southampton in 1841 both railway staff and the occupants of a train on the platform appear to have been listed.[6] Travellers arriving late and leaving early were to be noted as over or under twenty and 'N.K.' where age and name were not known to the host. People on nightshift duty were probably recorded at home with the rest of the household, and from 1851 provision was expressly given for this if they returned there the day after the census. One interesting case of shift (or shifty) work can be found in the 1861 census of the City of Bristol, where a man was listed as head of household with his wife and young family, while at another address in the City the head was absent and the 'wife' enumerated with a similar brood, whose paternity according to their birth certificates was quite clearly his.

– Non-Parochial Records –

A birthplace might not necessarily be where a person was baptized and his or the informant's memory or

knowledge might prove defective. The census does not reveal a person's religious affinity: his parents may have carried him a considerable distance, perhaps as much as twenty miles, so that he could be baptized in accordance with their beliefs. The non-parochial registers of meeting houses in England and Wales form an important source for tracing where adherents actually resided.[7] Information about births and baptisms in deposited registers has been fed onto the county microfiche of the International Genealogical Index (the I.G.I.), but place of residence, father's occupation and mother's maiden name were not incorporated, so where the I.G.I. is consulted the microfilms of the original registers should always be examined for additional information. Most of the registers were collected up in 1840, others in 1857, while some were deposited much later than the original Commissions set up to scrutinize and authenticate these records so that they could be produced as legal evidence. Because marriage in places other than an Anglican church was forbidden after 25 March 1754, few of the registers contain wedding entries, except for the deposited Minutes of the Quarterly Meetings of the Society of Friends[8] who, with the Jews, were granted exemption by the Statute.[9] A number of non-parochial registers (principally the bulk of Roman Catholic volumes) are known to exist either in churches, chapels, county record offices or in other places. Few of the deposited registers commence before 1689 when the Act of Toleration permitted Protestant congregations to erect meeting places for worship under a licence, so while the class index may show the date of a chapel's foundation as being at the end of the seventeenth century, the registers themselves may start only in the late eighteenth; many meeting houses changed denomination; some ministers regarded the registers as their personal property and carried them to a new congregation for use, perplexing the searcher attempting to scan them. A good number of registers were not authenticated because they did not meet the statutory requirements: singled out for exclusion were the baptisms and marriages celebrated before 1754 at the Fleet and King's Bench Prisons, the Mayfair Chapel, the Mint in Southwark and other places whose registers were deposited in the Registry of the Bishop of London in 1821, and transferred to the Registrar General in 1840. They are to be found in a distinct class.[10] One of the marriages contracted at the Mayfair Chapel, near Hyde Park Corner in London, was between Thomas Gainsborough, the artist, and Margaret Burr, on 15 July 1746 (see chapter 6). Like many others who were not Londoners, they gave convenience addresses in order to marry in secrecy, to avoid a scandal, parental wrath, to speed matters up, or to take advantage of the other party's weakness for the bottle or some other vulnerability, without any hindrance or awkward questions. Another unauthenticated series are the births and baptisms at the British Lying-In Hospital in Endell Street, Holborn, in London, between 1749 and 1830, of children born to distressed poor married women, especially those of service personnel, and whose admission was by recommendation.[11] From 1814 the baptism entries include details of parents' abode. The admission entries, running from 1749 until 1868,[12] note the father's occupation and place of settlement (or marriage after 1849); a number came from places outside London and the mainland, so it is worth considering this source, whose contents like the authenticated non-parochial registers have been fed onto the I.G.I.

The registers and certificates of birth of Presbyterians, Independents and Baptists, issued and kept in Dr Williams' Library in London between 1742 and 1837,[13] relate to people overseas as well as British residents, whose births perhaps appear in no surviving or deposited non-parochial register. As parents registered their own births with those of their children, the earliest entries predate 1742. There are photocopied indexes[14] on open access, which are broken down into period and by initial letter of surname, and setting out the registration numbers. Two certificates were produced by the parents, signed by their minister, the midwife and other witnesses at the confinement, and providing the name and sex of the child, his parents' names, those of the maternal grandparents, and the date and place of birth. The details were copied into the register and one of the certificates retained, while the other was returned endorsed with the registration number. From 1828, the certificates resemble formal signed declarations by the parents, and the entries are filed alphabetically. A similar system was established at the Wesleyan Methodist Metropolitan Registry, Paternoster Row, London, in 1818, and there is also an index to births and baptisms registered there until its closure in 1838.[15] The registers indicate the Wesleyan Circuit to which the parents belonged and include some births overseas. Both these records contain complete families whose births were brought together for registration and who may well have been born in a variety of places, and thus they afford a useful directory of migration.

The birth certificate of John Landells, born on 17 January 1806, and registered at Dr Williams' Library, Red Cross Street, London, on 8 July 1812, along with those of his brother and two sisters. His maternal grandparents' names are given. The signatures of the two witnesses would have been secured before the journey to London, and the parents were Dissenters. RG5/49 no 241

– Wills and Family Disputes –

Another major genealogical source, wills, can also be tapped to trace migrants. Wills proved in the superior ecclesiastical court of the Prerogative of Canterbury (P.C.C.), and extending from 1383 until its abolition in January 1858, contain the detailed wishes and instructions of testators which they trusted would be carried out on their death by their executors.[16] A wish for interment in a particular church or churchyard, or in a family vault or plot, gives important clues to parishes of origin, while legacies or devises of land left to benefit the poor of a birthplace, to childhood friends and relations are evidence of strong and persisting connections, and where residences were held in town and country, servants, employees and apprentices stood to gain as well as kinsmen. Where land was mentioned one may surmise migration at some earlier time.

Sometimes the validity of a will was challenged. The pleadings[17] are full of autobiographical and biographical detail about the contestants and their movements and activities up to the time of the alleged facts, and are supported by the sworn depositions[18] made by witnesses, and relevant exhibits[19] produced to the court. The signed depositions record the age, birthplace, present occupation and address of each witness as well as any other personal information deemed appropriate to the suit in answer to the various Interrogatories put to him. It is well worth the effort of tracking down these statements in cases concerning places where forebears lived or held property. The yearly will calendars indicate if there was litigation by the insertion of marginal notes 'by decree' or 'by sentence' against the testator's name. There is also an index of the allegations, 1661–1858, arranged both under the name of the deceased and the prosecutor; early depositions between 1657 and 1809[20] are not indexed, though the later ones between 1826 and 1858[21] are. Appeals up to 1834 went to the High Court of Delegates, whose proceedings[22] and muniment books[23] may add more to the overall picture, and both are indexed.

Disputes concerning real estate and its inheritance were heard in the Equity Court of Chancery. The bills, answers and further pleadings[24] are a goldmine of genealogical information about social and geographic mobility, and the reasons or circumstances behind them. Unfortunately, the haphazard organization of the records up to 1714 makes searching them time-consuming. The deponents were drawn from people well-known to the suitors, but whereas the ecclesiastical depositions invariably give birthplaces, these do not.[25] The Bernau Index of names of deponents has already been mentioned in chapter 1.[26] The exhibits produced to the Masters in Chancery in an eighteenth-century case about the Walter estates in Oxfordshire,[27] include ledgers of payments of wages and salaries to local tradesmen and family retainers who may have been recruited from the households of friends and kinsmen elsewhere, or transported from one country house to another, from a town residence to a country mansion, rather than hired locally, or were passed on by personal recommendation as grooms and gardeners, footmen and butlers, cooks and governesses. Thus a knowledge of local landowners, their marital, friendship and patronage ties may suggest possible lines to pursue when a person suddenly appears in an area, or a clergyman is newly instituted to a living over which the family had the right of presentation. The dated correspondence, diaries and journals of these people can be used to trace their movements and acquisition of staff, and to discover their frank opinions about them.

The other Equity Courts, of Exchequer and of Requests, also contain helpful genealogical information among the pleadings and depositions.[28] There is a typescript list of Exchequer deponents between 1559 and 1695, arranged by county, and a series of place-name and personal name indexes for the Court of Requests up to the reign of James I, making a search of suits concerning places where forebears were known to be a viable proposition. The Statham disputes from 1558 until 1562 in the Court of Requests and Chancery show how much information can be given by witnesses about migration (see chapter 8).

– Taxation Lists –

Another group of records used to trace migrants are the taxation lists. In the same way as the county microfiche of the International Genealogical Index demonstrate the distribution of a surname in period and place, so the parish rosters form a directory of names of liable people. Certificates of residence from the 1550s until the 1660s[29] testify to dual residency and where the liable person was actually living at the time of assessment. Perhaps the most helpful taxation lists are the entries of payments made on apprenticeship indentures between 1710 and 1811,[30] for residences of both the parties are recorded, including up to 1752 that of the parent or guardian, which is indicative of birthplace. The registered contracts for redemption of the Land Tax, commencing in 1798,[31] also give the address of concerned landowners, which may be different to where the land actually lay, hinting at earlier migration.

Inquisitions post mortem on the lands of tenants-in-chief of the Crown, from the mid-thirteenth century until about 1660,[32] record marriage alliances, land grants and purchases in places other than where the holder lived at the time of his death, while proofs of age of heirs attaining twenty-one, and the supporting statements of witnesses to the birth, baptism or their celebration frequently refer to their own places of origin and employment.

Correspondence between the Boards of Guardians of Poor Law Unions and the Poor Law Commissioners in London from 1834 until 1909[33] is full of reports on poverty-stricken people seeking help and shelter; the harrowing accounts of how they came to be there and their physical and mental state on arrival in the Union, impart details of age, birthplace, marriage and employment as well as on the route they had travelled. Some were ordered to be returned to a former parish of abode, and the decision was reported in the correspondence. Details of temporary residents hired to work on public building enterprises, outbreaks of smallpox and other epidemics leading to removal of the afflicted to isolation hospitals, also find their way into the correspondence, to which there is a subject index up to 1920.[34]

(3)

Reputed Fathers of Bastards in Arrear with their Accounts.

Atkinson John, late of Kendal, weaver
Bains Robert, of Kendal, butcher
Baron Thomas, of Kendal, weaver
Barton Charles, of Kendal, waiter
Beetham William, of Holmecales, bobbin-turner
Beck Robert, of Kirkland. woollen-spinner
Chapman Thomas, of Garstang, ostler
Earl James, late of Kendal, tobacconist
Goulden James, of Kendal, cloth-dealer
Gudgeon Robert, of Kirkby Lonsdale, shoemaker

Holme Thomas, of Kendal, shoemaker
Heap James, of Kendal, weaver
Hodgson George, of Holme, labourer
Hogg Andrew, of Cockermouth, hatter
Hudson George, of Kendal, labourer
Jackson John, of Salford, painter and plasterer
Jackson Hind. late of Kendal, joiner
Knowles Matthew, late of Kendal, currier
Kirkbride Thomas, late of Kendal, shoemaker
Mason William, of Kendal, weaver

Pennington Joseph, of Strickland Ketel, husbandman
Riding William, late of Blackburn, weaver
Robinson George, late of Bowness, bobbin-turner
Robinson William, of Kendal, stone-mason
Rowand Francis, late of Kendal, cropper
Settle Benjamin, late of Kendal, carpet weaver
Shaw George, of Kendal, assistant in timber-yard
Stringer Joseph, of Kendal, weaver
Tatham Thomas, of Kirkland, weaver
Thornton Henry, of Preston, ostler

List of Persons receiving Weekly Relief from the Churchwardens and Overseers of the Township of Kendal.

NOTE.—In submitting to the Rate-Payers of Kendal the following List of Persons now receiving Parochial Relief, it is particularly requested that whoever may see any of the Individuals named herein living idly, when work may be had, or drinking in public houses, will give information to the Churchwardens or Overseers.

Pauper's Name.	Age.	Earn-ings.	Pen-sion.	Pauper's Name.	Age.	Earn-ings.	Pen-sion.
		s. D.	s. D.			s. D.	s. D.
Appleby, widow, Mr Geldard's Yard	74	2 0	1 6	Murray Alexander, Stramongate	71	2 0	1 0
Airey, widow, North Fell-side	77		2 0	Newby Betty, Beast Banks	55		2 0
Atkinson Sarah, Sandy's Close	81		2 0	Oddy Jane, Longpool	81		2 0
Airey Jane, Far Cross Bank	67	1 0	1 6	Parker Simpson, Stricklandgate—lame	60	1 0	2 0
Anderson Agnes, Stricklandgate	70	1 6	1 6	Pepper Alice, Stramongate—lame	87		2 0
Anderson, widow, North Fell-side	79	0 6	2 0	Pepper Agnes, Stramongate—very poor health	65		2 0
Bowman, widow, Captain French Lane—infirm	76		2 0	Petrie Mary, Peat Lane—infirm	78		2 0
Brown, widow, Black Hall Yard—infirm	80		2 0	Pearson Margaret, Slip Inn Yard—infirm	72		1 6
Birkett Thomas, Sandy's Close	19		1 6	Poole James, Stricklandgate—very bad health	16		2 0
Barber Mary, Stricklandgate	63		1 0	Rowand, widow, George Braithwaite's Yard	71	0 6	1 6
Braithwaite, widow, and 3 children	32	2 0	2 6	Rooking Jane, All-hallows Lane	71	1 6	1 6
Bains, widow, and 2 children	53	3 6	2 0	Rook Elizabeth, Old Shambles—bad health	68		2 0
Bateman John, & wife, and 3 children, Bonning Yeat	48-39		2 0	Rook Grace, North Fell-side	88		2 0
Clement Betty, All-hallows Lane	68	1 6	1 6	Rigg Ann, North Fell-side—confined to bed	48		2 0
Cherry Margaret, All-hallows Lane	89	0 5	1 6	Radcliffe Cicely, Wildman Street	73	0 8	1 6
Cooper, widow, North Fell-side	76		2 0	Ridley, widow, and 3 children, Gibson's Place	46	5 0	2 0
Carter Richard, North Fell-side	76	2 6	2 0	Robinson Elizabeth, and 4 children, Old Shambles	34	4 0	3 0
Carlisle Ann, Wildman-street	84		2 0	Rigg George's children, Kirkland	10-5		2 0
Clarke Betty, Far-cross-bank	67	1 0	1 6	Rigg Harriet, and 4 children, Highgate	40	8 0	5 0
Crayston Mary, Nag's Head Yard	64	1 0	1 0	Rennison Christopher, and wife, Far-cross-bank	74-76	3 6	1 6
Chambers Anthony, Highgate	18		1 6	Rigg Maria, Highgate	40		1 0
Carradus Thomas, and wife, and 6 children	39-38	10 0	2 0	Sharpe Joseph, Captain French Lane	74		2 6
Carradus, widow, and 6 children, Highgate	36	2 0	5 0	Shaw Nancy, Miss Carter's Yard	72	0 4	2 0
Dixon Margaret, Captain French Lane	71		2 0	Saul, widow, Natland	60	0 6	1 6
Dixon, widow, Slip Inn Yard—bad health	81		2 0	Simpson Hannah, Old Shambles	75	0 6	1 6
Dent Francis, North Fell-side	84		2 0	Sinkinson James, Fold	75		2 0
Dobson Dorothy, Hospital	75		2 0	Sanderson, widow, Stricklandgate	78		2 0
Dodd Alice, Longpool—bad health	78		2 6	Stockdale John, Far-cross-bank	81		2 0
Dixon, widow, and 2 children, one of which is very ill	41		2 0	Swaine, widow, Knipe's Yard—bad health	71		2 6
Dover Isabella, Captain French Lane	11		1 6	Simpson James, and wife, Old Shambles	52-51	5 0	1 0
Dent John, & wife, & 5 childn., Stricklandgate—lame	44		6 0	Thompson Ann, Miss Postlethwaite's Yard	56	0 6	2 0
Gardener's children, Kirkland	10,8,3		2 6	Thompson Mary, and 2 children, All-hallows Lane	56		2 0
Goulden John, Pawnbrokers' Yard	50		4 6	Tanner William, Far-cross-bank—bad health	45		2 0
Gilkinson, widow, 1 child, Kirkland	21		2 0	Troughton Ellen, North Fell-side	10		1 3
Glover Jane, Market-place	73		1 6	Troughton, widow, do.	65		2 0
Goad Hannah, Badenoch's Yard	77	0 9	2 0	Troughton Thomas, do.	6		0 0
Garnett Harrison, Bentham	80		1 6	Troughton John, and wife (ill), South Fell-side	70-71		2 0
Hall Sarah, Mr Benson's Yard	8		1 6	Taylor Sarah, North Fell-side—ill	29		2 0
Hallhead, widow, All-hallows Lane	74	1 0	1 6	Thompson Mary Ann, Low Wood	12		1 6
Harker Jane, Stramongate	67	1 0	2 0	Wilson Jane, Wind-mill Yard—bad health	74		2 0
Hallhead William, Capper Lane—infirm	66		2 0	Winn John, and wife, Highgate	74-66		1 6
Hallhead William, All-hallows Lane	8		1 0	Wilson Mary, North Fell-side	86		2 0
Harrison Jane, Entry Lane	69		2 0	Willan Agnes, Pack Horse Yard	65	2 0	1 6
Hodgson James, Wildman-street	65	1 0	1 0	Wilson Dorothy, Black Hall Yard—infirm	80		2 0
Jackson Marian, Entry Lane	58	1 0	1 6	Wilson Thomas, and wife, Caroline Street	74-70	2 0	1 0
Johnson, widow, and 2 children, Stricklandgate	58	1 3	3 0	Wilson, widow, Wildman Street—nearly blind	67		1 0
Johnson, widow, Castle-street	60	1 0	2 0	Walmsley Anthony, Kentmere	75		1 0
Jerkinson Betty	61		2 0	Wilson Isaac, Brewery Yard	82		2 0
Knowles Margaret, Stricklandgate—infirm	78		2 0	Wilson Isabella, Stramongate	70		2 0
Langhorne Sarah, Stricklandgate—bad health	50	1 0	1 6	Wilson James, & wife, & 4 children, Moffett's Yard	50-40	2 0	5 0
Levens Christian, North Fell-side	48		2 0	Welsh, widow, Highgate	67	1 6	1 0
Masterson Betty, Stricklandgate	68	1 6	1 0	Wearing Thomas, & wife, & 4 children, Castle Street	41-40	3 0	6 0
Mattinson Dorothy, Stricklandgate	70	1 6	1 0	Wade, widow, and 4 children, Stricklandgate	41	1 0	5 0
Musgrove Joseph, and wife	73-72	3 0	2 0	Whittan, widow, & 5 children, Captain French Lane	49	3 0	6 0
Musgrove Margaret—bad health	43		2 0	Wharton, Edward and Agnes, Stramongate	74-77	4 0	3 0
Musgrove John, and wife, and 2 chld. (he being lame)	35-33	5 0	2 6	Young, widow's children, All-hallows Lane	14-15	3 0	2 0

Mothers of Illegitimate Children.

NOTE.—p signifies that the Children are entirely paid for by the reputed Fathers; pp that part payment is received; and n that nothing is obtained.

		s. D.				s. D.				s. D.
Armstrong Mary		n 1 9	Heap Ann		p 2 0	Scott Agnes		p 1 6
Bell Jane		pp 1 6	Johnson Sarah		p 2 0	Speight Mary		n 1 6
Barns Jane		n 1 6	Lonsdale Emma		p 1 6	Swindlehurst Jane		p 2 0
Carradus Elizabeth		n 1 6	Nicholson Mary		p 1 0	Troughton Margaret		n 1 6
Dent Elizabeth		n 1 6	Prickett Isabella		pp 2 0	Wilson Margaret		pp 1 6
Fleming Elizabeth		n 1 6	Rowlandson Susan		p 2 0	Workman Elizabeth		p 1 6
Franklin Ann		p 1 0	Rooke Agnes		p 1 6			

KENDAL: PRINTED AT THE MERCURY OFFICE, BY GEORGE IRWIN.

List of Kendal, Westmorland, Poor Law Union Outdoor Relief recipients, being a 'Statement of the Accounts of the Overseers of the Poor for the township of Kendal 25 March 1835 – 25 March 1836.' The various headings speak for themselves. MH 12/13581

Aliens

– Change of Name –

But what of non-native migrants? Surname is the most obvious indicator of immigrant ancestry, perhaps augmented by family knowledge and documentation, but this may not be immediately apparent. A good number of immigrants had their surnames involuntarily changed by local officials struggling to write down unfamiliar names; others anglicized them as a deliberate act, either by translation or by spelling them phonetically. More formal methods of change of name were by deed poll, royal licence, Act of

Parliament, statutory declaration or advertisement in the press. By the late nineteenth century the first was the most common device, and permanent enrolment was effected on the Close Rolls (from 1903 in the Enrolment Books of the Supreme Court), though this was not mandatory. The annual initial indexes to the Close Rolls generally record the former name, but from 1905 both are invariably included. Often name changes were published in *The London Gazette*,[35] and after 1914, if central enrolment was required, its publication here was obligatory.

Applications for change of name by royal licence stem from the seventeenth century and were usually combined with the assumption of a coat of arms associated with the family name to be taken. Petitions up to 1781 may be found among State Papers, Domestic,[36] thereafter in the Warrant Books of the Home Office.[37] From 1783 too, petitions were referred to officers of the College of Arms for advice, the applications and their reports up to 1837 being filed in the Home Office.[38] Warrants for the name change were entered among State Papers, Domestic, and after 1782 in the Home Office Warrant Books, followed in 1868 by a special series devoted to changes of name, which runs up to 1969.[39] Both the Home Office series are indexed.

Private Acts of Parliament were an expensive method and not much used from the mid-nineteenth century. Some of them have been published up to 1713 in *Statutes of the Realm*, and appear on the Parliament Rolls,[40] perhaps merely under the Statute's title.

From 1916, however, enemy aliens resident in Britain were forbidden to change their names, a restriction extended in 1919 to all foreigners, the only exceptions being where a royal licence was applied for, where special consent was granted by the Home Secretary, or when a woman assumed her husband's surname on marriage. The first two were announced in *The London Gazette*. The ban was finally lifted in 1971, though the limitations placed on non-enemy aliens had already long lapsed.

– Denization and Naturalization –

The most readily accessible source on immigrants is the series of volumes of printed and typescript indexes of Acts and Certificates of Naturalization and of Patents of Denization, covering the period of 1509–1935.[41] The essential difference between naturalization and denization is that the former grants rights as a British subject in accordance with prevailing legislation, whereas the latter, under letters patent

from the Crown, can be as wide or as narrow as the monarch chooses. Generally denization restricted any right to inherit land, and did not give full mercantile privileges in order to preserve Customs and tax receipts at the higher alien rate. Since 1844 naturalization has come within the department of the Home Secretary.

The first traced example of a foreigner being recognized as English appears in 1295.[42] During the Middle Ages, as many of the King's subjects travelled abroad to do trade, settle on Continental estates, or to fight, and produced offspring a problem was caused over rights to land inheritance in England. The solution was found in a statute of 1351,[43] and reinforced a decade later,[44] under which such children were recognized as the rightful heirs to their fathers' English estates.

From 1529 aliens in England were required to swear an oath of allegiance to the King;[45] in 1609, with anti-Catholic feeling running high, James I extended it to all naturalized persons.[46] The oaths of allegiance and supremacy were to be administered at eighteen, on submission of a Sacrament certificate signed by the minister and two churchwardens of the church where the Anglican Communion had been taken. Echoing the fourteenth-century legislation, in 1677 Charles II granted naturalization to all persons born abroad to his subjects during the Civil War and Commonwealth (14 June 1641–24 March 1660/1), on condition that within the next seven years they took the Anglican Sacraments and swore the oaths;[47] similar rights were conferred on the children of English subjects in war service in France and Flanders in the years 1689 and 1690, and again between 13 February 1689/90 and 25 February 1698/9, provided that within five years of reaching fourteen they took the Anglican Sacraments.[48] An act of 1708[49] granted automatic naturalization to all foreign Protestants taking the two oaths and making a declaration of allegiance to Queen Anne, the Protestant Succession, and against the Pretender and the Bishop of Rome in one of the central courts of record, or at Quarter Sessions. The central enrolments, with the certified proofs of having taken the Sacraments within the previous three months, have been partially published,[50] but the originals are bundled or sacked under each court.[51] In 1711 this part of the Statute was repealed, but a further section, granting naturalization to all children born abroad to British subjects, was maintained, amended in 1730 to include those of only native paternity, and from 1773 it was accorded to their grandchildren.

The preamble to the 1708 Act stated that 'The

increase of people is a means of advancing the wealth and strength of a nation'; it was thought that once allowed the advantages and privileges of natural born subjects, many strangers of the Protestant and reformed religion would come, particularly the Huguenots, who after the Revocation of the Edict of Nantes on 22 October 1685 had flocked out of France by sea or overland routes to escape further persecution. Later statutes were directed at relaxing restrictions on naturalization in times of war, need or difficult trading conditions, for instance all foreigners serving the British Crown during the war from 1 January 1739[52] for two years, and for a similar period from 25 March 1777,[53] were to be regarded as British subjects, as an inducement to recruitment of mariners and seamen, and to encourage commerce. Aliens seeking naturalization in the English Plantations between 1740 and 1775 could do so once they had been resident seven years, had sworn the oath of allegiance and taken the Anglican Sacraments, or in the case of Quakers had made an affirmation of fidelity and of abjuration.[54] Returns do not survive for all the American and West Indian colonies, but there is a printed index of them on open access.[55]

In 1844 the system was completely overhauled.[56] Any alien wishing to be naturalized was to present a written memorial to the Secretary of State at the Home Office, recording his age, trade, and duration of residence in this country. A certificate of naturalization was issued at the Home Secretary's discretion, and the oaths of allegiance and succession administered. The recipient was however barred from serving in Parliament or on the Privy Council. Under this Act, a woman married to a native or naturalized person automatically became a British subject, while anyone born out of the British dominions of a native-born mother was permitted to take real or personal estate, although aliens from a friendly country were restricted to holding only personal property, and land for up to twenty-one years and intended as a place of residence. The 1870 Naturalization Act[57] dispensed with this last restriction, but the electoral franchise and public office remained closed to unnaturalized aliens. After five years' residence, and with an inten-

The enrolment on 20 March 1685/6 of letters patent of 5 March granting denization to David Garric and other immigrants. Their names betray a strong French element, a reflection no doubt of the great influx of Huguenots escaping persecution, especially after the Revocation of the Edict of Nantes in 1685 which removed all their privileges. C66/3286 no 4

tion of settling in this country, an alien could henceforward apply for naturalization, but its refusal did not permit any appeal. In chapter 11 we shall see that Karl Marx's application was rejected in 1874, and a request for an explanation turned down, though from surviving internal memoranda in Home Office papers we now know why. From this Act up until 1915 also stem the Declarations of Nationality, renouncing citizenship of another country, and the Declarations of Alienage renouncing British Nationality, organized under headings according to category of Declaration.[58] Certificates issued under the British Nationality and Status of Aliens Act 1914 and running up to 1949 are filed in the same series of Home Office material, along with Declarations of British Nationality between 1948 and 1950 made under the Burma Independence Act 1947.

The petitions, memorials, letters and ancillary papers relating to naturalization and denization may be found in State Papers, Domestic up to 1782[59] and then in the records of the Home Office.[60] Authorizations for denizations are located in the Signet Office Docquet Books,[61] as well as King's Bills,[62] both arranged chronologically by month, and finally the grants were enrolled on the Patent Rolls.[63] Between July 1681 and August 1688 some denizations were effected by Order in Council and are contained in State Papers, Domestic.[64] A number of denizations were granted in batches, in response to group applications submitted by agents. For example, those of David Garric and his wife and son Peter in 1685/6[65] and 1688[66] were listed alphabetically among a host of other Huguenots.

The Private Acts of Naturalization are kept among the records of Parliament, but the Huguenot Society has published those between 1509 and 1800.[67] The Acts refer to place of origin or birthplace and the parentage of each alien, and thus are an immensely important source. Naturalization certificates from 1844 until 1873 are enrolled on the Close Rolls,[68] and subsequently among Home Office records,[69] along with earlier naturalizations from 1789.[70] The indexes [71] to them set out the applicants' names, country of origin, place of abode, and the date and reference number of the certificate, though the records themselves remain closed for one hundred years. The certificates add details of trade or occupation, and of any spouse and issue, while the signed memorials and petitions inform us about the applicants' date and place of birth, religious persuasion, father's name and occupation, the date of arrival in England and where subsequently resident and for how long, why denization or naturalization

was requested, and contain supporting testimonials as to good character.

From the naturalization papers it is thus possible to reconstruct the movements of aliens since arrival and which can be tested against the census if close to the relevant years when they were taken. From the census it will be seen that the pattern was for certain areas to attract clusters of immigrants, so for example the Marx family in Dean Street, Westminster, in 1851,[72] was one of many alien households in the street, though sadly, only countries rather than places of birth are indicated. Incoming passengers on board British and foreign merchant vessels arriving in port between 25 March and 2 April 1871 were also enumerated, giving details of marital status, age, occupation and birthplace, a prototype for the later returns, all of which are filed with the other shipping returns under the respective ports of arrival.[73]

– Ships' Passenger Lists –

Passenger lists of incoming travellers run in a continuous series from 1890 until 1960,[74] although a few others survive between 1878 and 1888. They relate only to people docked at British ports from or bound for places outside Europe and the Mediterranean Sea, unless the ships came from elsewhere and had put in to European ports to pick up passengers. Filed among the records of the Board of Trade, they are organized by port, chronologically by date of entry, and then by vessel. From 1906 until 1951, Registers of Passenger Lists[75] may be culled on open access to discover the months of arrival of ships at every British port. After 1920, the exact date is noted.

The ships' passenger lists reveal the name, age and occupation, address in the United Kingdom and the date of entry to the country of every alien on board. Slightly earlier than this and a reasonable substitute for the passenger lists are the certificates of arrival of aliens at English and Scottish ports between 1836 and 1852, stored in Home Office records, and to which there are nominal indexes for 1826–49,[76] although the certificates between 1826 and 1835 are no longer extant. They range chronologically by number, and bear the port, date of arrival, the ship's name and its port of departure as well as the name, country and profession of each alien, his signature and any other remarks, such as whether he had been issued with a passport. Many of them were merchants, presumably travelling regularly from Continental bases. Another Home Office series of returns, once known as Lists of Immigrants, covers the years 1836–69,[77] but they are not indexed. Running according

ABOVE *The certificate of arrival on 22 August 1849 of Michael Rosenthal, a rabbi, from Prussia, at the Port of London, which he duly signed. Sources such as this, though incomplete, are often the only means of tracking down incoming passengers in the first half of the nineteenth century. HO2/185*

RIGHT *A request from the Portsmouth Magistrates to the Secretary of State at the Home Office for advice on whether they were empowered to issue a pass to Louis Stephen Lucas, a teacher of the French language, for him to go regularly from his home at Fareham to attend Sunday church in Portsmouth, 11 October 1793. HO1/1*

to date of arrival, they are listings provided by ships' masters coming from foreign ports and delivered to customs officers. From one of these, we know that on 27 August 1849, the *City of Boulogne*, bound from Boulogne to the Port of London, carried among its passengers one Charles Marx, a Doctor by profession and a native of Prussia (see chapter 11).

– Passes and Passports –

Passport issues by mayors of ports to aliens are located in Home Office records, and date from 1793.[78] The name and occupation of the holder, and his residence during the previous six months are given together with references to any wife or family. They appear mainly to have been granted to merchants allowing them to pass to a specific place. Reports on movements of aliens, and persons under suspicion of spying are also incorporated in this series.

Refugees

There is much information about refugees fleeing from the French Revolution, chiefly among the Bouillon Papers, 1789–1814,[79] and which concentrate on the Channel Islands, especially émigrés in Jersey, those of the Foreign Office from 1793 until 1815,[80] and among the unbound papers of the Privy Council, 1777–1814,[81] and in the War Office, 1794–1816,[82] for which there are comprehensive descriptive lists or nominal indexes. Pension applications and payments may be found in Treasury records,[83] concerning remittances made by the French Refugees Relief Committee between 1792 and 1828, and to Breton and Norman refugees from 1793 until 1831.[84] Treasury papers are a useful source for tracing fiscal claims and awards of allowances to refugees of other nationalities in the late eighteenth and nineteenth centuries, for example the sums paid out to distressed American refugees in 1781 and 1782, and to Poles from 1841 until 1856;[85] allowances to refugees of Polish and Spanish origin paid out from 1855 to 1909 may be inspected in the records of the Paymaster General's Office.[86]

The most prominent group of immigrants in the late seventeenth and early eighteenth century were the families of Huguenots arriving from all parts of France during the events leading up to and after the removal of royal protection in 1685. They have been extensively documented in Huguenot Society publications. The registers of births, baptisms, marriages and burials of foreign Protestant churches in England[87] have been printed by the Society, drawing on the deposited originals of the Walloon, French, Dutch and Swiss congregations in London and other towns and cities, the earliest of which begins in 1567 and the latest of which ends in 1857. There is a partial manuscript nominal index to a few of the registers on open access. The registers were written in the vernacular, the very full baptism entries including the mother's maiden name and sponsors, the marriages the names of witnesses. In chapter 11 we shall see what the registers of the church in Threadneedle Street in the City of London yielded about the first generation of Garrics. As it was common for the families of immigrants to intermarry, the names of sponsors and witnesses may be a guide to later alliances, the Garrics for instance married twice into the ffermignac family, members of which acted as sponsors at Garric baptisms. Where perhaps the origin of one and not the other is known, this may be a clue to where the unattributed person came from. Registers of other foreign churches, such as the Greek and Russian congregations of the Orthodox Church in London, may be found among the series of unauthenticated material deposited with the Registrar General.[88] There is also a series of baptism, marriage and burial certificates among the records of the Court of King's Bench between 1693 and 1831 and which includes Jewish names.[89]

Tracing Aliens in Other Sources

Aliens always attracted special attention for taxation, paying double, or an extra Poll Tax; nominal listings and what they reveal for the genealogist have been outlined in the previous chapter, but suffice it to say that the Huguenot Society has published a Return of Aliens in London between 1523 and 1625,[90] based on the lay subsidies and drawing on other sources where they were mentioned, such as State Papers, Domestic, and not restricted to the metropolis as the title suggests, but recording names of people in provincial centres like Norwich and Colchester, and ports such as Sandwich and Rye.

Because denizens were generally forbidden to inherit land, and from 1701 they and naturalized aliens were banned from public office, the wealthy and influential group of Dutch courtiers and merchants who had followed William III to England, and the Hanoverians who later attended George I from 1714, had few outlets for their money. Consequently they invested in the various Government fund-raising schemes and their names can be seen dotted around the lists of contributors and proprietors of annuities and lotteries set up in return for loans. The names and addresses show a strong Continental element, and many of the nominees lived well into the eighteenth century. By patiently working through the ledgers of dividend payments, the assignments and dates of death of nominees, it is possible to trace changes of address, marital status and when the annuity ceased altogether.

Wills of aliens leaving property in England mention legacies and gifts to relatives abroad, for example the Austrian widow of David Garrick left monies to her niece in Vienna, in her will drafted in 1819 (see chapter 11), while the actor's uncle, another David Garric, was a wine merchant resident in Lisbon, Portugal, and hurriedly made a holograph will in December 1736, while temporarily lodged in Surrey, leaving bequests to the benefit of poor French refugees in the care of Threadneedle Street church, and to several friends and relations whose names are obviously French. Foreign merchants like Garric may be referred to in State Papers, Domestic[91] and Foreign,[92] and in Exchequer Accounts[93] in their pursuit of privileges and deals, or compensation for loss because of hostilities to which Britain was a party.

Emigrants

There is a cornucopia of material concerning British subjects travelling abroad to settle, exploit and defend new territories, to fight or to do trade, to escape religious or political persecution, or poverty, or going involuntarily as convicts. Overseas descendants will hopefully have scoured all available sources in their own countries before starting investigations here, will have reached a point where no earlier reference to a forebear can be found, or even better, have positive information on when and where he came from. This is rare.

The first American colony to be settled was Virginia, permanent colonization beginning with the establishment of Jamestown in 1607, after an earlier failed attempt at Roanoke in 1585. Not far behind came the West Indian Islands of Bermuda in 1612, St Christopher in 1624, Barbados in 1625 and Nevis in 1628; New England and Maryland were the homes of largely Puritan, and a mixture of Protestant and Roman Catholic migrants respectively, the first colonized from 1620, and the latter from 1634.

The early emigrants were a disparate group of gentlemen and yeomen, adventurers, merchants, paupers, orphans, debtors, indentured servants and criminals, whose geographic origins were just as diverse. After 1620 their numbers were increased by negroes brought from Africa, a trade which mushroomed from the 1650s, and which greatly enriched the merchant shippers and the planters who hired them to secure slave labour.

– Ships' Passenger Lists –

Passenger lists of early settlers are few. Scattered among the Exchequer Port Books,[94] the Privy Council[95] and Colonial Office records,[96] they have been extensively explored and printed.[97] The information varies from being a scant list of names to a roster of individuals denoting ages, occupations, family relationships and parish of origin arranged by ship and recording when and which port it sailed from and its destination. The prefatory information may refer to the obligatory oaths of allegiance administered to passengers over eighteen. Where origin is not stated for an individual those of other passengers in the party may afford a clue, especially helpful in cases where the surname was unusual, as a search can be made of the county microfiche of the International Genealogical Index to see whether it is there. Where ministers took members of their congregations with them sometimes their place of origin can be tracked via his, which may be reasonably well documented. The names of emigrant ministers going to America and the West Indies in return for the Royal Bounty may be found among the records of the Treasury and Exchequer, commencing in the reign of Charles II, and these have been published.[98] Evidence of passage may also be found in licences to pass beyond the seas, 1634–9 and 1677,[99] for the most part from Gravesend to Barbados, Virginia, Maryland, and New England. Other listings are of the rogues, vagabonds, idle and disorderly persons and sturdy beggars transported by Quarter Sessions from 1662, and whose names were notified to the Privy Council, among whose records are also the names of convicted felons similarly transported from 1615.[100] Merchant ships were chartered using Treasury funds: the Money Books of the Treasury contain nominal lists of convicts for the period

Part of a roll setting out a probate inventory of the goods, chattels and credits of John Crow, junior, a merchant of London, appraised on 22 June 1692. His total assets amounted to £10,489–7s–7d. The items illustrated here reflect his business interests in England, Ireland, New England and the West Indies, and show the extent of credit he was able to extend to others. PROB4/8572

1716–44[101] who were sent to the colonies mainly from London and the Home Counties, and these name the ships and destinations up to 1742. The lists have now all been published.[102] Other transportation lists appear in Treasury Board Papers from 1747,[103] while appeals from convicted prisoners for a reprieve or pardon are to be found in Privy Council Papers[104] and State Papers, Domestic.[105] Pardons granted on condition of transportation are entered on the Patent Rolls[106] from 1654, giving the name, occupation, abode and intended colony of each person. Having located the county of origin a search of surviving Assize Court Indictments and the Crown Minute Books will elaborate on the charge and sentence.[107]

Planters and Servants

Another important group of settlers were the numerous indentured servants whose passages were paid in return for their labour. Treasury papers include the weekly returns of English and Welsh emigrants between 1773 and 1776, and of Scots sailing to America in 1774 and 1776.[108] There is a card index to the English and Welsh entries on open access, the entire list having also now been published.[109] The names of the servants are arranged by port and particulars given about age, employment, former residence and destination and for what purpose. For instance, Thomas Sewell, twenty-two, a bookkeeper from Westmorland, bound for Virginia as an indentured servant for four years, was one of fifty-six such people to sail on the Elizabeth from the Port of London in December 1773.[110]

The indentured servants were needed to help on the plantations. Any territories captured or settled were taken in the name of the Crown, which in turn conferred grants of land to companies and proprietors for organization into settlements or for resale. The colonists eventually became autonomous, so many of the land grants will be found in the former colonies rather than this country, but petitions for grants, for offices, privileges and favours, for judicial decisions, and letters and charters directed to London by the colonial governors will be found amongst the Privy Council Registers and Papers, and the Plantation Books, which have been calendared and printed for the period 1613–1783.[111] The chief sources of information on land grants, which especially in Virginia and Maryland were tied to the headright system under which a settler paying the passage of other emigrants

'An Account of all Persons who have taken their passage on board any Ship or Vessel to go out of this kingdom from any part of England with a description of their Age, Quality, Occupation or Employment, former residence, to what Port or Place they propose to go and on what Account and for what purposes they leave this Country, from 31 May–7 June 1774, distinguishing each Port.' Most of these passengers sailing on board the crick Princess Carolina from Shoreham in Sussex were bound for Dieppe and Paris on business or for pleasure. T47/9 f160

was entitled to a minimum acreage, are Original Correspondence, America and West Indies, 1606–1807, which is calendared as far as 1738,[112] and Correspondence and Entry Books, Colonies, General, 1662–1782,[113] the Patent Rolls and Chancery Masters' Exhibits.[114] Treasury Solicitor's records also feature details of land in West and East New Jersey, Pennsylvania and New England, which was divided up into 1,600 shares of the West New Jersey Society in 1691, and which was wound up only in 1923.[115] The wills and probate inventories of first and second generation planters and their families give precise locations and extents of their estates, down to the names of creeks which formed their boundaries. The will of William Dyre of Sussex County in Pennsylvania, proved in the Prerogative Court of Canterbury in 1690,[116] refers to 2,000 acres of grazing land there, 196 more in different parts of the county granted to him on the survey for settlement, a further 200 acres in Newcastle County, land in Narraganset County in New England, in Providence Plantation, Rhode Island, Dyer's Island, and the Clabbord Islands in Cascoe Bay, New England. Thus he was not confined merely to landownership in one colony. The place names given to such estates may be reminders of their home parish, and references may be made in wills to relatives still in England, in the same way as kinsmen overseas were named in their wills. Indexes to the wills of American colonists proved in the above Court up to 1858 have been published.[117] The probate inventories of goods and merchandise left in England by merchants and traders dying overseas show the strong nexus between the two bases, and reveal the extent of borrowing and lending, a practice often not resolved without protracted litigation in the Court of Chancery or of the Exchequer as joint ventures foundered. Disputes about property left in England by colonists are fairly common and provide information about trading practices, wide kinship networks, and migration to do business, especially when backed up by letters, deeds and business records lodged as exhibits.

American Loyalists

During the American War of Independence, 1775–83, subjects remaining loyal to the British Crown were faced with a choice of crossing into Canada, especially to Nova Scotia, of making their way to the West Indies, or of returning to England, though some elected to stay under the new republican government. In the records of the Audit Office, the two series of memorials and petitions of claimants seeking compensation and an annual pension for their support and resultant loss of land and property contain a feast of genealogical detail as well as telling how they reached their present plight.[118] The formal initial approach was the prelude for a deluge of marriage certificates, abstracts from wills, affidavits, inventories of personal goods, animals and rents, letters about children and servants, about the nature of help given to the beleaguered British troops, and the financial and physical suffering sustained during rebel incursions, and all designed to reinforce the claim for a decent award. In chapter 12 we shall see how the resourceful Captain Jahleel Brenton spirited away his young sons on board one of his ships after he had been forced to flee his Rhode Island estates. The claims cover the years 1776–1831 and 1780–1835, the latter having been calendared and printed and the former series indexed. Another index to claimants is in Treasury records,[119] being the temporary allowances and pensions paid out to them between 1781 and 1831 and 1788 and 1839 respectively, giving the name, abode and profession of each recipient and the allowance and quarterly payments. In the same series are also the Minute Books of the American Loyalists' Claims Commission, 1784–1804, set up to investigate applications.[120] An index of claimants' pensions and allowances over the years 1786–1827 is to be found in the Audit Office.[121] Claims also arose after the cession of East Florida to Spain, and there is an index of claimants, 1740–89, giving access to the title deeds and other evidences produced to the East Florida Claims Commission and now filed among the Treasury papers.[122]

Among the Foreign Office records of claims arising out of the war between 1782 and 1795 is a graphic list of items to be donated to 'Loyalists going to Nova Scotia and who are really poor', compiled on 14 June 1783:[123] a spade and an axe were to be given to each family, with four yards of woollen cloth, seven yards of linen, two pairs of shoes and stockings and a pair of mitts for the men, three yards of woollen cloth, six yards of linen, two pairs of stockings but only one of shoes, and a pair of mitts for the women, and for the children over ten years old two yards of woollen cloth, six yards of linen, a pair each of stockings and mitts, with one-and-a-half yards of woollen cloth and three yards of linen for younger progeny. So loaded and attired, we can imagine the refugees trudging to safety and to their allocation of six months' provisions each once they reached their destination.

Later Emigrants

From 1783 material relating to British migrants to the United States will therefore be found amongst the records of the Foreign Office, in the letters and papers sent by British consuls from various cities and ports, and there are subject indexes to these.[124] Included among General Correspondence is a collection of relief and protections from impressment offered to American seamen from 1797 and which certify their American citizenship. They give the name, and any assumed name, age, birthplace and place of baptism, physical description, and details about living parents, their place of residence and the father's occupation of each sailor. There were questions about any wife and siblings and where they lived, where the seaman had been educated, at what age and to what trade he had been apprenticed and when the term was completed, and how protection had been acquired. For example, in Baltimore on 13 January 1806 John Smith was examined by the Collector of Customs.[125] He was then twenty-two, a man five feet tall and of a ruddy complexion, with bluish-grey eyes and curly hair. He admitted being born in Newcastle in Northumberland, and was baptized at Stockdale under the name of John Marloe. His parents continued to live there, where his father was a tailor. He himself was unmarried and had four sisters living in England. He was educated in Newcastle and was bound apprentice at the age of twelve, went to sea for seven years, and the apprenticeship was completed in 1803 when he was nineteen. He paid a dollar for his protection to the Collector at Baltimore, having obtained it through a shipmate, a native of Germany with a wife and children in Philadelphia, and with whom he had sailed out of that city. His friend had sworn before the Notary Public that 'Smith' was born in Boston, whereupon he was given a certificate to deliver to the Collector, who granted him a protection.

– Ships' Passenger Lists –

Passenger lists of ships departing from ports in the United Kingdom and bound for places out of Europe and not within the Mediterranean Sea survive between 1890 and 1960[126] when they were discontinued. They are among the records of the Board of Trade, filed by year, by port. As with incoming vessels, the Registers of Passenger Lists, on open access,[127] are an easier way of tracing which ships left port after 1906. The

Part of the examination of 22-year-old John Smith, born John Marloe, an American seaman, by the Collector of the District of Baltimore, Maryland, 13 January 1806, as to his family background and career. He was born at Newcastle in Northumberland, and was certified as an American citizen giving him protection from impressment. FO5/49 f155d no 68

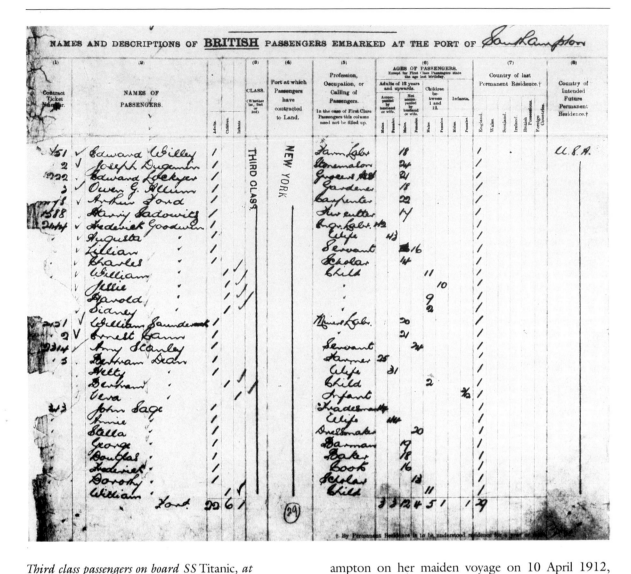

Third class passengers on board SS Titanic, *at Southampton, 10 April 1912, including the families of Frederick Goodwin and John Sage, bound on the 17-day voyage to New York as emigrants. None of them made it; they were all drowned when the ship struck an iceberg on 15 April. Only a quarter of the third class passengers were rescued. BT27/780B*

lists themselves contain details of age (except for first class passengers), occupation and abode, country of citizenship, permanent residence or intended residence of all passengers, according to class of ticket. A number of intending voyagers may also be found lodged in hotels and other places in the port of departure on census nights, and these will provide information on others in their party who perhaps came to see them off. The SS *Titanic* left South-

ampton on her maiden voyage on 10 April 1912, with 922 passengers on board. She called at Cherbourg and at Queenstown in Ireland before embarking on the journey to New York. Of the 2,201 known people on board, only 711 were rescued when the ship hit an iceberg on 14/15 April. Leslie Williams, a pugilist, aged twenty-eight, travelled third class on his way to settle in America;[128] John Sage, a tradesman of forty-four, was another passenger going third class with his wife and nine children, the youngest of whom was eleven.[129] Also on board were foreign nationals, listed separately, and providing information on name, age, country of which they were subject, and at which port and on what steamship line they had arrived in the United Kingdom. Many of these came from Eastern Europe. The list of casualties produced to the enquiry by the Ministry of Transport recites the name, nationality, birthplace, age, class, date and place of embarkation and of death, the cause of demise (invariably drowning), and the last residence of all passengers and crew who were lost.[130] All of the Sages were drowned. Their last address was given in Peterborough, in Northamptonshire, and the father's birthplace was London. The boxer, Leslie Williams, also perished. His home had been in Tonypandy, Glamorganshire, where Mrs E. Williams was described as his next of kin. His birthplace was given as Cardiff.[131] There is a nominal index of passengers on open access.

On the back of each passenger listing were recorded details of all births, marriages, injuries and deaths on board, with an account of any apprentices employed and their dates and ports of indenture and the date and reason for leaving the ship. The registrations of vital events are identical to those civil registrations of England and Wales from 1 July 1837, except that the birth entries give the parents' nationality and last abode, and the deaths, the nationality, birthplace and last address of the deceased.

Records of births, marriages and deaths at sea between 1854 and 1890 and 1902 and 1919 are kept among the Board of Trade records,[132] based on the above lists.[133] There are also miscellaneous returns of marriages and deaths from British and foreign ships, 1836–89, in the deposited records of the Registrar General,[134] with indexes on open access. The latter registers also contain significant numbers of births, baptisms, marriages and deaths of British subjects throughout the world, from 1627 until 1958,[135] and Foreign Office records also contain short runs of similar registrations, of title deeds, and probate records of Britons living and working abroad.

Using the passenger lists as the base the searcher may well be able to locate the birth certificates and marriages of many nineteenth-century passengers, though these records lie outside the scope of this book.

– Passes and Passports –

Seventeenth-century licences to go beyond the seas to places other than the American and West Indian colonies are filed in the Exchequer, ostensibly pertaining to travel to the Continent, especially Holland, 1621 and 1637, and a few to passengers going to Ireland between 1632 and 1633, to France in 1634/5, and to soldiers off to serve in the Low Countries in 1631/2, Utrecht, Vienna and elsewhere in 1631, and those taking the oath of allegiance before embarking for the Low Countries at various dates from 1613 until 1633, and there are also earlier licences from 1573 until 1578.[136] Before the First World War, passports were rare, but Entry Books containing abstracts of Passes issued between 1697 and 1784 may be found among State Papers,[137] and

List of third class passengers who drowned when the SS Titanic *struck an iceberg on 15 April 1912, showing the family of John Sage, their ages and last address. Note the passengers of foreign provenance, coming from as far afield as Syria and Bulgaria, all presumably hoping to emigrate to America. MT9/920/201 no 17*

others in the Foreign Office from 1748 until 1794.[138] Later registers, from 1795, are also filed in the latter Office,[139] but have been heavily weeded, though the indexes remain.[140] Passports were granted for a single journey; any further use required the counter-signature of the appropriate minister or consul of the country to be visited. The registers, running as far as 1948, are arranged chronologically and give date, number and destination as well as the name of the holder. Indexes for the years 1851–61, and 1874–1916, give the name and passport number and the date of issue, so are the key to the surviving registers. Correspondence in connection with passport applications may be inspected for the period 1815–1905.[141] After this, only a selection of it has been preserved, reference to it being by card index on open access. Passport applications may also be examined for 1796 until 1811 in General Correspondence of the Colonial Office,[142] and includes colonists.

– Compensation Claims, and the Slave Trade –

Compensation claimed and awarded to British subjects abroad for war losses or as a result of local disturbances involving British intervention, may be found among Treasury, Foreign Office and War Office records.[143] For instance, American and British claims concerning the North-East Frontier after Treaties in 1794 and 1814,[144] and after cessation of hostilities in 1871[145] are found in the records of the Foreign Office; indexes and selected civilian claims for compensation for loss or property requisitioned in South Africa during the Boer War in the years 1902 and 1903 are located in the War Office.[146]

The Slave Compensation Commission was set up in 1833 to relieve slave proprietors in the dominions. The indexed proceedings and registers of claims in the Treasury records contain valuations, original claims and counter-claims, contested cases, certificates for compensation and awards made between 1834 and 1846.[147] Other proceedings, relating to the joint British and Portuguese Slave Trade Commission from 1819 until 1824, are among the records of the Foreign Office,[148] Minute Books of the Court in Jamaica survive between 1843 and 1851,[149] and there are records of slaves and slavers in Cape Town, Havana and Sierra Leone, in Treasury and Foreign Office material.[150] Cases brought before the High Court of Admiralty cover the years 1805 until 1877.[151] Details of the awards are recorded in the Audit Office, 1835–46,[152] while the National Debt

Office[153] has a run of material, including marriage and death certificates of claimants, with the date of any Treasury warrant authorizing compensation, and its amount relating to the West Indies between 1835 and 1842.

Records of the Royal African Company, in the Treasury archives,[154] include the sales of hundreds of shiploads of slaves between 1673 and 1816, mainly in the West Indies, but also in Virginia and South Carolina. Names of purchasers, the numbers of slaves and their cost, are recorded with the date and place

Notification to the Slave Compensation Commissioners of the death on 7 August 1835 of a claimant, Marie Therese Laurent, proprietor of a slave on the island of Dominica, by her sister and joint claimant, Marie Claire Laurent, and sworn on 9 September 1835. NDO4/28

of the sale. There are indexed Treasury registers of names of plantation owners from 1813 until 1834 in which details are given of negroes held in slavery. Slave registers, arranged by parish, for Jamaica and other West Indian islands, the Cape of Good Hope and Ceylon, 1817–32, provide details about personal and plantation slaves. There are various parochial returns of slaves in the West Indies in 1832, and an incomplete index of those in Ceylon in 1819.[155] Among the Foreign Office records too are the registers of slavers at Havana from 1819 until 1869,[156] and of suspected slavers at Cape Town between 1843 and 1870;[157] Colonial Office material includes a census of liberated slaves taken in Sierra Leone in 1831,[158] and registers of those emancipated from 1819 until 1868,[159] and an alphabetical list of slaves in Surinam compiled in 1811.[160]

Convicts

British convicts transported to Australia from May 1787 until 1868 may be traced in a variety of sources. The colonies used were New South Wales, 1787–1849, to which about 84,000 men and women were sent, Van Diemen's Land, 1803–53, Norfolk Island, 1843–55, both of these taking a total of over 67,000 convicts, and Western Australia, 1843–68, which received under 10,000 male transportees. A census of New South Wales, taken in 1828,[161] including people who went as free settlers and those born in the colony, has been published,[162] listing alphabetically the names, ages, occupations, employers, residences, religious denominations, and nature of settlement of each inhabitant, and if appropriate, the court of trial, the sentence, period of transportation, and the ship and year of arrival. Other listings, like this in the Home Office, relate to the years 1788–1821 (organized by males and females), with general musters in 1806, 1811, 1822, 1825 and 1837.[163] There is a list of convicts embarked in 1787, and of those arriving from 1828 until 1834. Pardons granted in New South Wales and Tasmania between 1834 and 1859, and incomplete lists of convicts in Tasmania between 1808 and 1849, also contain personal details. The information garnered from these is normally sufficient to enable an examination of the Assize Indictments, the records of Old Bailey Sessions (from 1834 the Central Criminal Court),[164] and of the Annual Criminal Registers of England and Wales,[165] all of which give details of the charge. For instance,

Nature of employment of emigrant settlers and convicts in New South Wales, 1822, showing the type of heavy work they endured. The numbers relate to the workers under the oversight of the named individuals. CO201/119 f268d

George Robert Woodrow, labourer living in York Street, Sydney, and aged forty-nine in 1828, was transported for seven years and arrived in 1815 on board the *Baring Island*.[166] The Annual Criminal Register showed that he was tried for bigamy at the Lent Assizes for the City of Worcester in 1814;[167] the Assize Indictment for 12 March[168] gave him as a labourer living in the city (not always found to be true), and that he was charged with marrying at St Mary's Kingston-on-Hull, Yorkshire, Ann Jenden on 25 September 1806, and while she was still living marrying Jane Stinton at Hallow in Worcestershire on 14 June 1813, before being apprehended at Worcester on 14 August 1813. When the information was laid against him his occupation was given as a guard of the Mail from London to Worcester, and his first wife as a resident of Oxford.

Convict transportation registers, 1787–1867,[169]

similarly mention the place and date of trial and length of servitude. Death sentences were often commuted to terms of transportation, and petitions between 1819 and 1854[170] may be consulted after looking at the alphabetical registers of petitions and their outcomes, 1797–1853.[171] Convicts awaiting transportation were held in prisons or prison hulks, quarterly returns of which run between 1802 and 1876.[172] They list the name, age, offence, the date and place of conviction, the sentence, surgeon's report and one on the behaviour of every inmate. Medical journals from 1817–53 and 1858–67[173] give details on the health of passengers during the voyage, and there is a card index of ships on the open shelves. These, like the log books,[174] are among the records of the Admiralty, the logs being listed under 'transports', while mercantile ships brought into use between 1786 and 1859 are located under the Board of Trade.[175]

Free Settlers

Names of wives petitioning to join their husbands may be found in Privy Council records for the years 1819–44,[176] between 1848 and 1873 among Colonial

Office records,[177] and from 1849 among those of the Home Office.[178] They give, chronologically by number, the name and address of each applicant, the names or number of children and their ages, the relationship to a named convict, his sentence, the date and destination of the convict ship, and the name and address of a referee and when his reply was received.

Details about free settlers appear also in the Home Office returns and lists cited for New South Wales. It is also worth consulting the Entry Books and Correspondence in relation to specific colonies, and similar series under Emigration, the last of which relates to the period 1817–96.[179] For example, New South Wales Original Correspondence from 1784 includes names of convicts and settlers from 1801 until 1821,[180] while there is a typescript index on open access to later correspondence between 1823 and 1833. The papers of the Colonial Land and Emigration Commission also have information on Australasian settlement from 1833 until 1894,[181] and these usually have integral subject or nominal indexes.

Collections of colonial newspapers invariably contain a lot on strongly local matters, birth, marriage and death announcements and advertisements placed by settlers. *The New Zealand Journal* of 18 March 1843[182] records that the first body of settlers did not arrive until early in 1840, and was composed mainly of missionaries, traders, whalers and runaway sailors and convicts. By October 1842, there were between 11,000 and 12,000 Britons on both Islands, the greatest concentrations being in Wellington and the Northern shore of Cook's Strait (6,000), at Nelson (2,100) and Auckland (1,900).

Applications made by convicts' families for a free passage to join them in Australia, 10 March 1849. The names, ages and addresses of applicants are given with the wife's maiden name, as well as details of the convict and his date and ship of transportation. CO386/154

Registry Number Col. Off. Letter	No. of Application	Convict's Name	Ship in which Transported	Names of Persons included in Permission	Residence	Married		Single		Children			
						Male	Female	Male	Female	Boys 1-14	Boys Under 1	Girls 1-14	Girls Under 1
120	320	Donelly. James Free passage	"Augusta Jessie" 1838	Ann (Donelly) McGill . John . Elizabeth	Lockport Cheshire 3. Mottram Street Oakwood. Cheshire	✓ ✓ ✓	38 18			✓		12	
120	321	Reardon. Jas..	"Neva" 1833	Eliz.th Reardon White . William . James . Maryann . Elizabeth . Martha	Stratton Cornwall	✓ ✓ ✓ ✓ ✓ ✓	40	20 18	16 16 15	✓		✓	

Public Service lists, 1895–1916[183] give the names of people sent to the colony of New South Wales on government business, and other similar lists relate to colonies elsewhere.

Applications for purchases of land in the colonies may be located among Original Correspondence; for example, the New Zealand applications give the name, abode, date of registration, deposit paid, and choice of town, suburban or rural property of each aspirant, whose name went into a ballot held by the New Zealand Company at intervals between 1839 and 1850.[184] The deposit allowed the contributor to nominate within six months up to four adults for a free passage for every £100 paid, and who were to be selected in accordance with the Land and Emigration Board Regulations from mechanics, handicraftmen, agricultural labourers, or domestic servants intending to go and work for wages. The names of nominees, their trades, ages, and children, and the name of the ship in which they sailed are also recorded, together with the details of when the balance was received. There are extant lists of landowners in New Zealand, arranged by settlement, for the period 1839–53,[185] stating whether the owner was resident, and giving the acreage of town, suburban and rural land, and purchase or exchange details, and the numbers of the land orders. Under the Regulations, the cost of land was fixed at not less than a pound an acre and was to have been put to auction at least once, with not less than a ten percent deposit being paid out at the time of the sale, and the balance within one calendar month. No lot was to exceed one square mile in extent. Other registers relate to shareholders of the Company between 1840 and 1853, to dividend payments from 1840 until 1843, deeds of transfer and registers of share certificates from 1840 until 1853,[186] many of whose holders owned land in the colony.

Assisted Emigration

The Colonial Land and Emigration Office was established in 1833 to receive applications for land grants and free passages to Australia and New Zealand, acting through its local agents, who by way of remuneration and refund of expenses, extracted a commission of two-and-a-half percent on land sales, and a pound for each married couple, seven shillings for every single adult passenger enlisted. The Emigration Office Regulations were devised in February 1842[187] to control assisted and free passages to the colonies in Australia and New Zealand. The people most in demand were shepherds and farm servants, those involved in the building trade, carpenters, sawyers, joiners, plasterers, brickmakers, bricklayers, stonemasons, quarrymen and limeburners, country blacksmiths able to shoe horses, wheelwrights, harness-makers and 'a moderate number of tailors and shoemakers': in other words, anyone able to build himself a country from scratch was welcome, and traders and shopkeepers were to make their own way in order to serve the manual workers. Anyone hoping to buy land was ineligible for a free passage, and likewise inmates of workhouses or people in habitual receipt of outdoor relief. The most desirable emigrants were young, childless and married, and a supporting marriage certificate had to be produced at the time of application. No family could be accepted where there were more than two children under the age of seven, nor were families to be broken up. Single women were not admitted unless accompanying their parents or near relatives, or as domestic servants of lady cabin passengers, preference being accorded to those used to farm and dairy work, sempstresses, strawplaiters and domestics, while single men were only allowed in numbers matching those of the single women. The age band of accepted adults was normally to be from fourteen up to thirty-five, and all must have been vaccinated or have had the smallpox. Anyone found ineligible might be allowed to pay the bare contract price of the passage (£17–£20 for adults over fourteen) at the discretion of the Commissioners. References as to character, health and employment performance were sought before any decision was reached about applicants. Once an application was accepted, notice was given of the ship and date of sailing, a deposit of a pound being required to secure a ticket and which was refunded on arrival in the colony, but the expense of reaching the port of embarkation was up to the emigrant. In chapter 12 we learn that the young Walker family, bound for New Zealand in May 1842, had its travel expenses to London paid for by the parish of Grasmere in Westmorland.

Food, mattresses and bolsters and cooking utensils were supplied on board, but the emigrant had to produce his own blankets and sheets, towels, cutlery and tin or pewter plates, and drinking mugs. The mattresses and bolsters they were allowed to keep if 'they conduct themselves well during the voyage'. Passengers were to bring their own clothing, which was inspected at the port to ensure it was sufficient for a healthy trip, the lowest acceptable quantity being stipulated as six shirts, six pairs of stockings, two pairs of shoes and two complete suits of exterior clothing for the men, six shifts, two flannel petticoats, six pairs of stockings, two pairs of shoes and two gowns for the females. The usual voyage was estimated to take four months depending on the season, and emigrants were advised of the extremes of climate through which they would pass. Two canvas bags per family were recommended, as access to any heavy boxes or chests kept in the hold would only be granted once every three or four weeks. Trade tools were also allowed, but no bulky agricultural implements or furniture.

The applications for free passages to New Zealand survive for the period 1839–50[188] among the New Zealand Company's Original Correspondence. The two volumes are arranged alphabetically by surname and there is an index volume[189] giving the number of each application and resulting Embarkation Order (ticket number). Affixed to them are the returned testimonials from employers, parish priests and physicians, about the candidates' sobriety, integrity, industry and occupation and expressing an opinion about suitability as settlers. The form indicated the intended colony of settlement, the applicant's name and address, marital status, trade or calling, and whether he was receiving parish relief and for how long; details of employment were to be included with the name and address of an employer and parish priest so that the references could be commissioned about him; the names of all parties to the application were given with their ages at last birthday and its date, and information

Register of Seamen's tickets, 1845–54, showing the variety of birthplaces of merchant mariners. The figures on the Out columns represent the ship's registration, and the port registration numbers, followed underneath by the registration number of the port the seamen sailed from and the day and month in that year. Under 'Home' the bottom sequence indicates the registration number of the port and the day and month of disembarkation. BT113/10

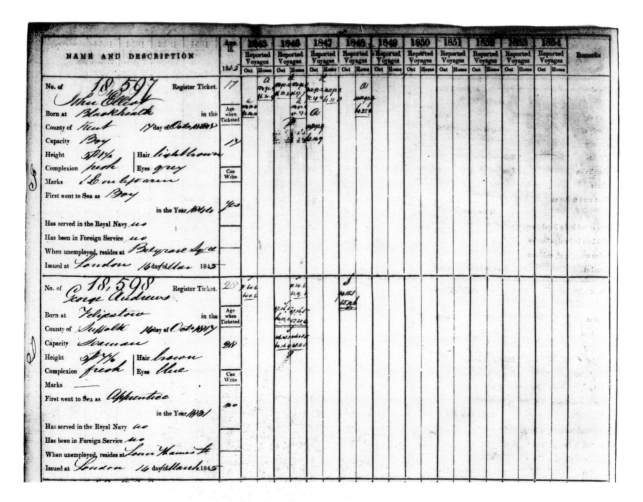

given on vaccination and the smallpox, literacy and reading ability, and ending with an assurance that once accepted the candidate would be willing to work for wages. His signature and those of two respectable witnesses were attached, publicans or beer and spirit retailers being specifically excluded. The physician produced an examination certificate testifying that none of the family was seriously mutilated, deformed or otherwise afflicted by a life-shortening, physical or mental energy sapping ailment, and that they were all entirely clear of any infectious or contagious disease. The Medical Journals of emigrant ships from 1815 to 1853[190] would have us think otherwise. These and the surgeons' returns of death on voyage,[191] filed among the Colonial Office and Admiralty records, show how hazardous the journey was. For example, the *Euxine*, sailing on 14 October 1859, arrived at Madras on 23 January 1860, with 391 passengers under the care of Dr Clarence Chapman.[192] Seventy-three soldiers' wives and children had died en route, the first on 20 October of diarrhoea. The same day there was an outbreak of the measles which carried off another forty-five people up to 6 January, and scarlet fever was responsible for six of the deaths between 20 December and 22 January. Most of the victims were under twelve years old. Conversely, there were two births on board. The names of all of them are preserved, and the volumes indexed by ship's name. Appointments of ships' surgeons are also found in the Colonial Office.[193] Payment was by result, depending on how many live passengers were landed, the rate increasing with the number of voyages undertaken, and preference being given to those who had already served satisfactorily at sea. Some went on from the Australian colonies with other emigrants bound for India or China, and then to the West Indies before returning home. In such cases the return passage allowance of £60 from Australia was reduced by half and was claimed retrospectively on arrival back in Britain.

There are also lists of cabin passengers bound for New Zealand between 1839 and 1850,[194] giving name, occupation, age and destination, the number of adults, age bands and sex of any children in the party, lists of candidates for employment in the colony for the same period,[195] some memoranda and agreements to work, and the signed, dated and witnessed receipts of remittance money of 18s a week paid out by the directors of the New Zealand Company to the wives of employees between 1841 and 1844, arranged by settlement.[196]

What has been said of the Australasian colonies is equally true of free settlers going to Cape Colony from 1820, to British North America from the 1830s and to other places.

The Poor Law Union papers from 1834 to 1909[197] also include information about assistance given to pauper emigrants. The subject index[198] to the papers is the best means of reference. Correspondence between the Poor Law authorities and the Emigration Commissioners from 1836 to 1876,[199] and from the General Board of Health to the Commissioners in 1853 and 1854[200] contains details about individual parish-assisted emigrants, filed among the records of the Ministry of Health.

The Armed Services

Movements of guards and garrisons of British Army personnel, of Royal Marines and the Royal Navy,[201] can be tracked down through the service records of officers, the attestation and discharge papers and

The Quarterly Return of 1 April–30 June 1856 of out-pensioners of the Chelsea and Greenwich Hospitals from the District of Toronto, Canada. From this we can trace their movements after retirement, and it enables us to discover more of their careers from the Muster Books and the Attestation and Discharge Papers. WO22/204

ABOVE LEFT *Continuous Service Engagement Book of Royal Naval Seamen. Although they date only from 1853, retrospective details of service can take the searcher back to the earliest part of the nineteenth century. ADM139/8*

ABOVE RIGHT *Lieutenant-Colonel Ralph Gore, on half-pay in HM's Service and Ordnance Storekeeper at Quebec, presents a petition to the Lieutenant Governor of the Province of Lower Canada for a land grant in the townships of Ireland and Halifax, 29 August 1825. The family details record that he fought at the Battle of Waterloo. He requested an extra 6000 acres so that he could establish Irish settlers. CO384/51 p113*

OPPOSITE PAGE *Edwin Colwell's claim for an increase to his Army disablement pension for the year ended 30 June 1924; all the papers relevant to the pensioner are filed together, from 1889 when he made his claim for an arm injury through to his death in 1932. PIN71/2009*

P.W.P 1069 F W M

For Year ended 30. 6. 24

E. Colwell

M.P.A. 110.

DECLARATION BY A PENSIONER CLAIMING AN INCREASE OF PENSION UNDER THE PENSIONS (INCREASE) ACTS, 1920 AND 1924.

Any Person who knowingly makes a False Statement or False Representation for the purpose of obtaining or continuing an Increase of Pension, or for the purpose of obtaining or continuing such Increase at a Higher Rate than that appropriate to the Case, either for Himself or Herself or for any other Person, is liable on Summary Conviction to Imprisonment for a Term not exceeding Six Months, and, in the Case of a Pensioner, to Forfeit any Pension or Increase of Pension Payable to Him or Her.

NOTE.—The instructions on pages 3 and 4 should be carefully read and complied with.

1. (a) State whether you are married or unmarried, or a widower or ~~widow~~ ..   *Married.*

† Child includes stepchild, but not grandchild or adopted child.

  (b) If a widower or ~~widow~~, state whether you have a child† or children under sixteen years of age at the present time, dependent on you ; and if so, give date of birth of youngest child ..   ————

  (c) If married, state whether you are living with your wife (or ~~husband~~) ..   *Yes.*

2. State your age at the present date, giving date of birth..   *16/Nov ⁴/1869*

3. State your total means, for the twelve months ending this date, received from all sources, as set out in full and *30 . 6 . 1924* in detail on this Form, including the amount of your original pension (*exclusive* of any increase given under the Pensions (Increase) Acts) ..   *My wife and I work together £156.13.11*

4. If you are a married man, state the means of your wife, received from all sources as set out on this Form ; if ~~you are a married woman, the means of your husband~~ ..   *included in above. Earned jointly*

I declare that, to the best of my knowledge, information and belief, the above statements are true.

§Signature of claimant   *Edwin Colwell.*

Pension or Establishment No. *FWP, PWP 1069, FWM.*

Retiring Rank of { Pensioner ~~Pensioner's husband~~ } *Private.*

Residence   *86 Hanover Street Brighton Sx*

Occupation   *Dress Shirt Maker.*

Employer's name and address *J. Osborne and Co, 51,52 East St Brighton*

§Declared and subscribed before me this   day of   192 .

Not to be signed by the claimant.

*(by *Edwin Colwell* who made his mark thereto in my presence)

For persons qualified to attest see instruction 11 on page 4.

Alfred Vitler -   Name.

   Residence.

Station Sergeant 26 Qualification.

(Attestors are requested to state their qualifications in accordance with the instructions.)

* Strike out unnecessary words.
§ A Claimant unable to write must make his mark and have it duly witnessed by the attestor. Where a Claimant signs by means of a mark, the Declaration should be read over to him or her by the person who attests the Declaration, who should satisfy himself that the Claimant understands the purport of the statements signed by him or her.

The warrant of 28 November 1803 for a grant of letters of administration to be made to Joseph Canavan, by his attorney Benjamin Hitchins, after the death of his son John Canavan, a private in the 30th Regiment of Foot in Egypt on 20 June 1801. The estate was less than £5, but because he was a soldier dying overseas the bona notabilia rule did not apply and it was dealt with by the Prerogative Court of Canterbury. PROB14/429 no 74

muster rolls of soldiers up to about 1913, in the attestation forms, description books and service records until about 1900 for the Royal Marines, and in the occasional returns and records of service of commissioned and warrant officers, the Continuous Engagement Books and service records of Royal Naval ratings recruited before 1891, and for the last two Services, in the ships' musters[202] transporting them all over the world. Their pension registers give addresses to which any gratuity or weekly allowance was paid, wherever the retired servicemen settled, be it in Britain or overseas. The dates of death are generally noted in all the pension records, for officers in the Paymaster General's Office, for the rest in the War Office, Admiralty and Ministry of Pensions.[203]

We shall see in chapter 13 how William Godfrey Dunham Massy's career as an Army officer and those of other soldiers in the 19th Regiment of Foot can be traced from commission or enlistment to the time when they went to pension.

Many soldier pensioners were encouraged to emigrate to the colonies with their families, especially between 1846 and 1851. There are lists of ex-military men going to Australia and New Zealand between 1830 and 1848 in War Office records,[204] while material in the Colonial Office includes the names of North American settlers, 1837–8,[205] among whom may be found many former Army officers already stationed there and who were applying for land grants, offering as they did so personal details about themselves and their families.

Wills or administration grants relating to English and Welsh estates of armed personnel dying overseas may be traced among the records of the Prerogative Court of Canterbury up to January 1858, when the Court was abolished. The yearly calendars of names list their residences as 'Parts' rather than the actual country or seaboard. Warrants for the issue of a grant or commission to swear the executor of a will give the date and place of death, the rank or quality of the deceased, his regiment or ship, and his marital status, before recording the name, address and relationship of the next of kin or the applicant, and the total value of the estate.[206] An indexed series of naval wills for the years 1800–60 (ratings)[207] and 1830–60 (officers)[208] is contained in Admiralty records, attached to applications made by relatives for back-pay. Another indexed collection of similar wills, covering the years 1786–1882 relates to ratings and Marines.[209]

Once an ancestor's career is known the information about him may be amplified by gleaning the reports sent back from the Front by the General Officers Commanding, and the published Despatches highlighting acts of outstanding bravery. The latter appear in *The London Gazette* along with nominal lists of casualties, both dead, reported missing or captured.

Prisoners of War

Names of British prisoners released by the American rebels in 1783 can be found in Treasury papers,[210] those released by Spain from 1798 until 1807 in those of the Admiralty.[211] Admiralty registers record the names of primarily naval prisoners and internees held in France, Tangier, Spain and America at periods between 1779 and 1815, with a list of prisoners exchanged from 1780 until 1797,[212] almost all of which material is unfortunately unindexed. They provide details of the place of confinement, the date and circumstances of capture and their eventual disposal.

British prisoners of war taken in the Crimea, 1854–6 and by the Boers, 1899–1902, may be found listed in *The London Gazette*, but are incomplete and generally name only the officers arranged under regiment. British and Dominion prisoners held in Germany, Turkey and Switzerland in 1916 are among Air archives, though chiefly relate to Army personnel;[213] a further list of prisoners in German camps in July 1915 is preserved in Admiralty records[214] and includes crews from two vessels captured in May that year. The Foreign Office material documents prisoners held in Austro Hungary from 1915 until 1916, in the Balkans in the former year, in Belgium, France, Germany, Egypt and Turkey, and embracing British civilians interned in Germany, for the period 1916–19.[215] Notifications of death while in confinement may be found in the Registrar General's registers, along with military casualties in France and Belgium from 1914 until 1921, and these are indexed.[216]

Prisoners of war in enemy hands during the Second World War include, among Air records, nominal rolls of Royal Air Force and Allied prisoners detained in individual camps between January 1943 and September 1951, and of those held by the Japanese from November 1942 until September 1945,[217] and there is an alphabetical list of British and Dominion Air Force prisoners in German hands for the period 1944–5.[218] Reports on escapes, lists of Air Force prisoners and those reported captured in Occupied Europe, and the reports on individual Royal Air Force personnel supply background information on them up to the moment of being taken.

Royal Marines known to be in German hands between 1939 and 1945 merit their own roster in Admiralty records,[219] while lists of naval men in German-run camps also survive.[220] The Foreign Office records contain details of prisoners of war and internees in Germany in 1942, the names of missing servicemen circulated to camps in 1941, British subjects in Italy in the same year, and taken prisoner there and in Greece, and the names of British subjects in enemy territory on whose behalf remittance payments were made, also in 1941.[221] The deaths of civilians, internees and servicemen and of crews of aircraft lost in flight, may be found among the registers of the Registrar General, to which there is an index.[222]

Lists of British and Commonwealth prisoners seized or suspected captured by the enemy during the Korean War, 1951–3, may be traced among the records of the War Office,[223] along with a list of Commonwealth prisoners in January 1954.[224]

Conversely, lists of French army prisoners, 1698–1703, are located in the Audit Office:[225] their petitions and complaints up to 1816 are filed in the Admiralty.[226] Names of French prisoners taken in the Low Countries from 1793 until 1796 are also in the former Office.[227] The ships' musters of Royal Naval vessels invariably include names of foreign prisoners taken during naval engagements, which were recorded in the daily entries of the ships' logs.

Admiralty registers of foreign prisoners from 1755 until 1815[228] are listed by depot or prison ship, then by nationality and provide detailed descriptions of them, their places of birth, capture and ultimate disposal, by exchange, parole or release. Some of the volumes are indexed by prison or prison ship, rather than by location. The nationalities covered are French, American, Spanish, Dutch, Danish, Russian and Prussian men, held in Britain and other places. Russian prisoners taken during the Crimean War are listed in the War Office,[229] and some of those treated in hospitals are mentioned in the Admiralty hospital musters.[230] They may also be traced in the deposited material of the Russian Orthodox Church in London, filed in the unauthenticated series of registers of the Registrar General.[231]

Two lists of German subjects interned in 1915 and 1916 are also contained in the records of the War Office, organized as army, naval and civilian categories, and giving regiment or ship, or the home address of each.[232] There are also filed among the papers of the Ministry of Health, representative medical records of admission and discharge of German and Belgian sick and wounded prisoners, arranged by Field Ambulance, casualty clearing station, or wherever treated, for the duration of the First World War.[233]

For the Second World War, nominal lists of prisoners temporarily interned in the Tower of London are contained in War Office records,[234] while lists of those detained in the colonies are found in the appropriate Office. Selected Home Office personal files on internees, 1940–9, are mainly concerned with enemy or neutral aliens, though some British subjects held under Defence Regulations feature amongst them.[235] Some of these records are however closed for fifty years.

General Correspondence of the Admiralty, War Office and Air Departments should also yield more information about the conditions under which prisoners were held and what action was taken to help release them.

Refugees

Information about European refugees of the First and Second World Wars may be found among the ships' passenger lists of the Board of Trade, as they made their way to find a new life. Among the records of the Ministry of Health are alphabetical history cards on Belgian families, 1914–18, giving name, age, relationship, wife's maiden name, the allowance granted and to what address it was to be paid.[236] Provision was similarly made for ex-Polish servicemen who fought with the Allies, under the Polish Resettlement of 1947.[237] Details of cash allowances or maintenance in camps or hostels afforded to certain groups of Poles and their dependants who arrived in Britain from September 1939 may be tracked down in a series of the National Assistance Board records[238], but some of this material is closed for seventy-five years.

II

The Sources at Work

*The remaining chapters contain examples of the
information to be derived from records in the
Public Record Office.*

5

THE TURNER AND
PLENDERLEATH FAMILIES

The Turners of Lavenham, in Suffolk, have been traced through a sequence of census returns to illustrate the changing composition of a rural Victorian household, and then linked into local archives, the parish registers of baptism, marriage and burial. The house where they made their home can be plotted among the records of the Tithe Redemption Commission and the Valuation Office, and lastly the Death Duty Registers show what became of the family's property.

The account of the Plenderleath murder in 1851 shows what a rich resource are the Assize documents, which include copies of the report on the coroner's inquest and the sworn depositions of witnesses. Again, resort has been made to the census returns, for the victim was the District Registrar of the Longtown area of Cumberland and his assailant one of the enumerators.

The Black Lion Inn, High Street, Lavenham, Suffolk, c.1870

In the Guildhall at Lavenham in Suffolk hang two small paintings. One is of a man with a clutch of children of assorted sizes stringing along behind him, and the other is of a black lion. The man is Westrop Thomas Turner, landlord of the Black Lion Inn, at 19 High Street, Lavenham, until his death in 1856: the children are his offspring. The 1851 census of Lavenham, taken on the night of 30 March, showed the innkeeper living in the High Street with his wife Abigail, who at thirty-two was a year older than her spouse.[1] By then they had six sons and a daughter, one born every year from 1841 until 1846, and thereafter in alternate years, and, like their parents, they were natives of Lavenham. With two female

RIGHT *The census taken on 6 June 1841 of the parish of Lavenham, Suffolk, showing at the bottom of the page the household of Thomas Turner, a yarnmaker, resident in the High Street. There are six houses, comprising eleven households (demarcated by single diagnonal lines drawn through the column immediately to the left of the names where a building is shared by more than one household, and double diagonal lines when the house complement ends). Note, however, that servants are shown as occupying separate households from their employers so this may be misleading. HO107/1011 Book 17 f5 p2*

BELOW *The Turner Family in 1849; from left to right: Harry, 14 months; Charles, 2 years 5 months; Frederick, 4 years 2 months; Westrop, 5 years 5 months; Mattham, 6 years 8 months; Thomas, 7 years 10 months.*

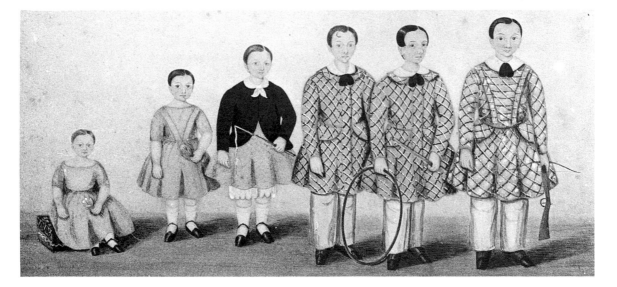

103

ABOVE *Westrop Thomas Turner (1819–56), farmer, maltster and brewer.*

servants, an hostler, a boy and a lodger, the household had fourteen occupants in all.

On 6 June 1841, the night of the previous census, Westrop and Abigail were part of Thomas Turner's household in the same street.[2] He was a yarnmaker aged fifty-six, and Westrop was employed as a wool-stapler. Yarnmaking had long been one of the major occupations of Lavenham, but by the late eighteenth century was in decline, the domestic spinning of fine worsted yarn superseded by mechanization. Thomas Turner's business was one of the last representatives of a once flourishing industry. In 1851 Thomas, also born at Lavenham, had become a woolstapler too, buying in raw material for manufacture rather than spinning it himself it seems. His home was shared with a ten-year-old granddaughter, Maria Mary Smith, and he had taken on a female servant to look after them.[3] Ten years later, on 7 April 1861, his address was

BELOW *The 1851 census return of the town and parish of Lavenham, Suffolk, showing under schedule no 60, the household of the innkeeper, Westrop Thomas Turner, in the High Street. A son, Mattham Turner, was lodged in 1861 in the Lavenham household of Mary Ann Day's older brother, William, and was described then as a farming pupil. HO107/1790 f175 p15*

given in the census as The Woolstapler's Shop, in the High Street;[4] his house contained the servant and three Smith grandchildren besides himself: one, William Thomas, a young man of twenty-two, was also a woolstapler, and his birthplace was given as London. Mary Maria Smith had found work as a dressmaker, but the youngest grandchild, Alice Jane, aged sixteen, was not working. At the Black Lion Inn, in the High Street, Abigail Turner, by now a widow aged forty-four, was the publican.[5] Of her children only a four-year-old daughter Elizabeth remained, together with one of the servants, now a nurse. On the night of 2 April 1871 the Black Lion was given its number in the street and Abigail's household had expanded to include her unmarried brother William Mattham, aged sixty-five, and of no occupation, while her two children, Harry, twenty-three, and Abigail H., nineteen, both assisted in the business with the help of two servants.[6] On 3 April 1881 Abigail was describing herself as an hotelkeeper and farmer, employing four men and two boys.[7] Her brother William was still lodged with her, together with her two children as before. Harry's age was given as twenty-seven and Abigail's as twenty-five, conflicting with the ages predicted from the census ten years before, yet Abigail was presumably the person completing the schedules on both occasions as the head of household.

From the sequence of five census returns we can see that the Turners were in continuous residence in the High Street for more than forty years, and in the same house for thirty of those years. The household of Abigail was at its greatest in 1851, when it was full of her burgeoning family, and as the children left home so it shrank back, but later took in an elderly unmarried brother and a granddaughter. She continued to run her husband's hostelry for at least twenty years after his death, calling on the services of her descendants, but never remarrying in spite of being left with three children under ten years of age and heavily pregnant when he died. She gave birth to at least nine children, the eldest of whom was born when she was twenty-four, and the youngest when she was forty, and she may well have had more who were born and died between census years; as a relatively young woman in 1857 she could have expected a longer childbearing period.

The forenames used by the parents for their children reflect the father's names in reverse order for the first-born son, his mother's maiden name for the second, and the father's first name for the third (possibly this was the maiden name of his paternal grandmother), and among the rest there appear to have been two Abigails, one born in 1850 and the other in 1852, suggesting an infant death.

If we look at all the Turner households in Lavenham during the forty-year period from 1841, we can count twelve of them (composed of fifty-seven people) in 1841, living in the High Street, Potland Place, the Market Place, Prentice Street, Shilling Street and the Common, in a total population of 1,871. By 1881 there were seventeen Turner households containing fifty-three people, in a population of 1,838, and they lived mainly in the High Street, but also in the Market Place, and Bolton, Church, Shilling and Water Streets, and the Common. No household was ever larger than Abigail's at the Black Lion Inn in 1851. No Turner lived alone in 1841 or 1851. One of the households in 1841 was headed by a seventy-seven-year-old matriarch, Elizabeth Turner, living in Shilling Street.[8] From subsequent searches of a transcript of the parish registers of Lavenham baptisms[9] it transpired that she was mother to the fifty-five-year-old and thirty-year-old men with her in the house that night, as well as to twelve other children, all baptized between 1783 and 1809. Of the eleven other Turner households in 1841 three were headed by her sons and two by grandsons, and all except one Turner household can be traced back to a marriage in nearby Hadleigh in 1750,[10] between Elizabeth's parents-in-law, Ardley Turner and Susan Deeks, who themselves spawned ten offspring. Westrop Thomas Turner was her husband William's great nephew, being the son of Thomas Turner by his second marriage, to Susan Westrop, and grandson of Ardley Turner baptized in 1750, the eldest child of Ardley and Susan.[11]

The parish registers of Lavenham[12] show that Abigail Turner was pregnant at the time of the 1841 census; her first child was baptized there on 9 August, two months later. Her eldest daughter, Abigail, was buried on 21 April 1851, less than a month after the 1851 census, and a further two daughters, Abigail Harriet and Emily Ann, were baptized together on 13 November 1853, although we do not know if they were twins. Emily Ann and another infant daughter, Mary, were buried within a few days of each other, in June 1856, and in October their father followed them to the grave. The couple's last child was baptized Elizabeth on 15 February 1857, a posthumous daughter. Abigail therefore was mother to eleven children, two of whom were born and died between 1851 and 1861.

The Turners pursued a variety of occupations ranging from those which were wool-linked, to bricklaying, agricultural labour, shovelmaking, hempweav-

No. of Schedule	Road, Street, &c., and No. or Name of House	Houses (Inhabited)	Name and Surname of each Person	Relation to Head of Family	Condition	Age Males	Age Females	Rank, Profession, or Occupation	Where Born	Whether Blind or Deaf-and-Dumb
30	High Street	1	Charles Cury	Head	Mar.	34		Ag. Labourer	Suffolk, Lavenham	
			Ellen do	Wife	Mar.		32		do Preston	
			Elizabeth do	daur.	Un.		12	Sunday Scholar	do Lavenham	
			William do	son		9		Ag. Boy Labourer	do do	
			George do	son		7		scholar	do do	
			Sarah do	daur.			3		do do	
			Harry do	son		1			do do	
31	High Street Glaziers Shop	1	John Abbott	Head	Mar.	40		Plumber & Glazier	do do	
			Mary Ann do	Wife	Mar.		40		do Preston	
32	High Street	1	Harriet Death	Head	W.		63	Farmer of 80 acres, employing 3 men and 1 boy	do Lavenham	
			Sarah Hickman	Sister	Mar.		45		Middlesex, London	
			Susan Matthews	serv.	Un.		18		Suffolk, Cockfield	
33	High Street Glaziers Shop	1	Charles Clemence	Head	Mar.	47		Plumber and Glazier	do Pakenham	
			Sarah do	Wife	Mar.		51		do Lavenham	
34	High Street Black Lion Inn	1	Abigail Turner	Head	W.		44	Innkeeper	do do	
			Elizabeth do	daur.			4	scholar	do do	
			Theodosia Smith	nurse			69	servant (nurse)	do do	
			Sarah Bulmer	serv.	Un.		20	House Servant	do do	
35	House with Shop High Street	1	John Tiffen	Head	Mar.	72		Ag. Steam Machine Owner	do Acton	
			Mary Anne do	Wife	Mar.		60		do Lavenham	
			Ruth Teverson	sister in law	W.		70	Lady, late Farmer's Wife	do Alpheton	
6	Total of Houses... 6					7	14	Total of Males and Females...		

ABOVE *Part of the 1861 census of Lavenham, Suffolk, showing at schedule 34 Abigail Turner as the widowed innkeeper at the Black Lion Inn, in the High Street. By now only the youngest of her children remained at home. RG9/1134 f12 p6*

BELOW *Part of the 1881 census of Lavenham, Suffolk. Schedule 63 records the household of Abigail Turner, a widow aged 64, which included her unmarried brother, William Mattham, and a granddaughter. Three of her family assisted her in running her hotel and farm, which employed four men and two boys. RG11/1833 ED12 f36 p10*

No. of Schedule	Road, Street, &c., and No. or Name of House	Houses (Inhabited)	Name and Surname of each Person	Relation to Head of Family	Condition as to Marriage	Age Males	Age Females	Rank, Profession, or OCCUPATION	WHERE BORN	(1) Deaf-and-Dumb (2) Blind (3) Imbecile or Idiot (4) Lunatic
	High Street		Emily Pain	Daur			1		Lavenham, Suffolk	
60	do	1	James F Ellerton	Head	Mar	30		Gardener	do	
			Emily do	Wife	Mar		29		do	
			Esther do	Dau	Unm		8	Scholar	do	
			Thomas do	Son		6			do	
			James do	Son		3			do	
			Frederick do	Son		1			do	
61	do	1	Charles Mills	Head	Mar	72		Boot Maker	Suffolk	
			Charlotte do	Wife	Mar		72		Seydon	
62	do	1	William Ward	Head	Mar	72		Retired Merchant Clerk	Ipswich	
			Elizabeth do	Wife	Mar		64		Colchester, Essex	
			Betsy Woods				80	Family Farms Wife	Bradfield, Suffolk	
63	do	1	Abigail Turner	Head	W		64	Hotel Keeper & Farmer	Lavenham do	
			William Mattham	Brother	Unm	75		Lodger	do	
			Abigail H Turner	Dau				Assistant	do	
			Harry do	Son		37			do	
			Mary R Amos	Grandau			12		do	
			Mary A Amos	Servant				General Servant	do	
			William Day	Visitor	Mar	49		Farm Labourer	Waldingfield, Suffolk	
64	do	1	Charles Fisk	Head	Mar	43		Plumber	Denton, Norfolk	
			Mary A Fisk	Wife	Mar		39		Rimsford	
			Kate do	Dau	Unm			Apprentice to Dressmaker	Lavenham	
			Abigail do	Dau				Servant	do	
			Elizabeth do	Dau				Scholar	do	
			George do	Son		10			do	
5	Total of Houses... 5					12	13	Total of Males and Females...		

NOTE.—Draw the pen through such of the words of the headings as are inappropriate.

Part of the Estate Duty Register entry relating to Westrop Thomas Turner, of Lavenham, Suffolk, whose will was proved in the Archdeaconry Court of Sudbury on 24 April 1857. The estate was valued at £1,500 on 13 July 1857, but Duty was not paid till after his widow Abigail's death on 21 September 1884, as she had been left his estate for life. As his spouse the gift was exempt, but provision had been made for the estate then to he equally divided amongst the surviving children, who were liable. Details of the deaths of some of them are included and the estate revalued at £2,458–10s–6d attracting 19s Duty. Abswp means the legacy was absolute with a proviso (a conditional legacy). IR26/2112 f592

ing and carrying in 1841, to running bakeries, grocer's shops, a victualling business, marine stores, and a butchery, to pig dealing, milling and wood sawing, to Army service, in later years. The women became dressmakers, silk throwsters, hempspinners, horse-hair weavers, strawplait and straw bonnet makers, reflecting the new industries introduced to Lavenham, and by 1871 one was a schoolteacher.

Abigail Turner was interred at Lavenham on 25 September 1884, having outlasted four of her sons (Harry, her assistant, had been buried in December 1881, aged thirty-three), and four of her five daughters. Her father-in-law, Thomas Turner, died in 1864. His will was proved in the District Probate Registry, at Bury St Edmunds, on 4 March 1864.[13] The Death Duty Register for that year[14] contains a list of the thirteen properties which he held in the High Street at Lavenham, the barn, stable, yard and buildings in Bears Lane, devised to seven of his Turner and Smith grandchildren, plus three legacies to other Turner grandchildren and two to servants. The residue of his estate was valued at £1,012–19s–10d and on 16 May

1864 duty of £10–2s–7d was paid. The Register records that he was a woolstapler and yarnmaker of Lavenham, and that he died on 15 February that year.

Although he had died on 20 October 1856, duty of £24–11s–9d on his son Westrop Thomas Turner's estate of £2,458–10s–6d was not paid until 25 February 1885,[15] because he had devised his copyhold messuage in Lavenham and all other copyholds, together with his personal estate to his wife Abigail for life or until her remarriage, and gifts to spouses fell outside the ambit of the duty. This would also explain why she never remarried, as she would then have lost the inn. On her death (on 21 September

Part of the Ordnance Survey map of Lavenham, Suffolk, 1904, used by the Valuation Office. Lavenham formed part of the civil parish of Cockfield, in the Sudbury Division of the Valuation District of Bury St Edmunds. The Black Lion Hotel was given reference no 431 when the Valuers' Field Book was compiled in 1914. By then the Hotel had passed out of the Turner family. IR 127/9f 329

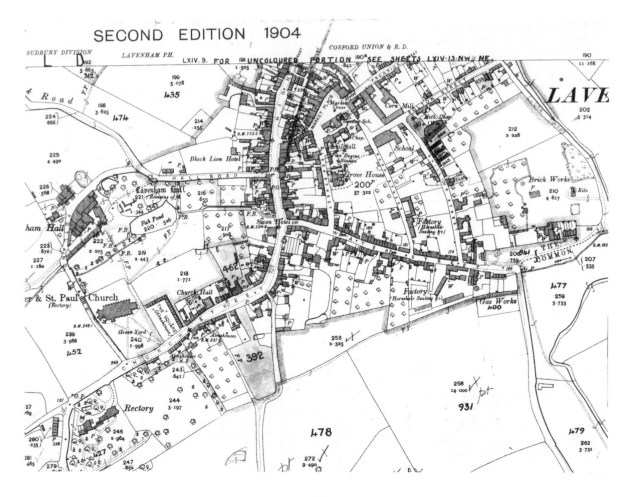

1884) her husband's estate was to be sold and the proceeds equally divided among his surviving children in accordance with the instructions given in his will. The Death Duty Register names the seven children alive at the time the will was drafted, plus his posthumous daughter for whom provision had been made in a codicil. The entries are annotated with details of some (but not all) of their deaths prior to that of their mother, so from these we know that Thomas W. Turner died on 23 February 1860, Westrop on 4 July 1873, and Charles on 8 October 1874.

An Ordnance Survey map of Lavenham, based on a 1904 revision of an 1883 Survey,[16] was used by the Land Valuation Department of the Inland Revenue for tax purposes between 1912 and 1915. On a scale of 1:2500, the map indicates where the Black Lion Hotel stood. A smaller scale map, 1:1250, marks out the boundaries of Lavenham properties, and the Hotel was given assessment number 431.[17] The valuation district covering Lavenham was that of Bury St Edmunds, and it was incorporated in the Field Book of the civil parish of Cockfield.[18] The Lion Inn's gross value, with a garden, was £1,104, the inn itself occupying thirty poles, and the garden two roods and fourteen poles. The property's gross annual value was calculated at £45, with a rateable value of £29 for the inn and £8 for its garden, and attracting the tithe rent charge of £4. The Field Book also tells us how many

rooms the inn contained and to what uses they were put. By the time of the Valuation the inn had passed into the ownership of William Bantock of Preston in Suffolk, and was occupied by G. Springett, Junior. Eight Turners were listed in the Field Books as occupiers of property in Lavenham, but only one of them was also the owner, although Mattham Turner of Acton owned a cottage in Church Street, occupied by Miss Turner. Altogether Mattham owned twenty-three cottages in Church Street, Bears Lane, High Street, Market Street, Lady Street, the Common, and in Water Street; he owned a house and a shop in the last. There was also a barn, stable and pasture in the High Street, left to him by his grandfather Thomas Turner in 1864, given assessment number 435.

An earlier map of the parish, drawn up in 1841 by the Tithe Redemption Commissioners,[19] marks out the plot numbers of properties owned or occupied by Thomas Turner. He and Samuel Turner owned and occupied adjacent sites on one side of the High Street, while a Thomas Turner also owned three properties on the opposite side of the road which were exonerated from the tithe, and four other plots in the neighbourhood were either owned or occupied by Thomas Turner.[20] Seven of the properties were cottages and gardens, but there was over an acre of brick meadow used for pasture (plot 400), and half an acre of orchard (plot 601). From the transcript of

The Valuers' Field Book of the civil parish of Cockfield, Suffolk, showing the gross valuation of property no 431 in Lavenham. It was intended to levy a tax on the site less the value of buildings, timber, fruit trees and other things growing on the land, but was never implemented. A detailed description of the layout, use and state of repair of the Black Lion Inn when inspected, in July 1913, shows how it was less than 30 years after Abigail Turner's death. IR58/15839

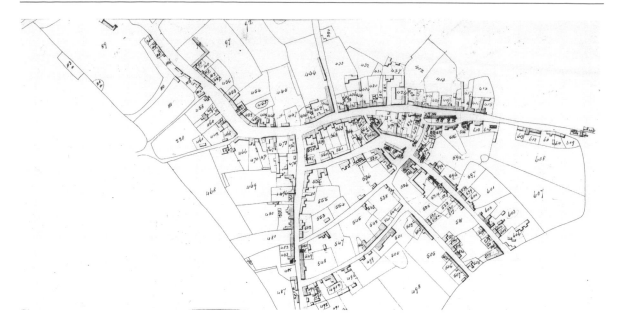

LANDOWNERS.	OCCUPIERS.	Numbers referring to the Plan.	NAME AND DESCRIPTION OF LANDS AND PREMISES.	STATE OF CULTIVATION.	QUANTITIES IN STATUTE MEASURE.			Amount of Rent-Charge apportioned upon the several Lands, and Payable to the Rector		REMARKS.
					a.	r.	p.	£ s. d.		
Turner Thomas	Himself & others	419	House Orchard &c			3	12			No 411
		420	do & Garden				12			N B M 1239/198
	Himself	400	Brick Meadow	Pasture	1		17			
					2	.	1	19 .		
Warner Thomas	Hurrell William	564	The Greyhound Inn			1	13			
Winthrop Charles	Teal Ferdinand Frederick & others	481	House Garden & Orchard			3	2	6		M. 25323.
West Mary	Good Timothy Jr									

C.C.—London: Printed and Published (by Authority) by Shaw and Sons, 137 & 138, Fetter-lane.

TOP *A section of the tithe map of the parish of Lavenham, Suffolk, surveyed by A. Russell in 1841, marking out properties affected by the commutation of the tithe. Nos 419, 420 and 400 (not shown), belonged to Thomas Turner, and were situated in the High Street. Samuel Turner owned and occupied plot 421. Lower down the street plot no 436 was the Black Lion Inn, later the home of Westrop Thomas Turner. A Thomas Turner also owned plots 582, 583 and 576. IR30/33/266*

ABOVE *Part of a schedule of the tithe apportionment of the parish of Lavenham, Suffolk, made on 9 February 1843. From this we can see that Thomas Turner owned and occupied four plots, totalling over two acres, on which the new annual rent charge of 19s was fixed. The accompanying map identifies the plot only by number. IR29/33/266 p15*

the parish registers of Lavenham I discovered that Thomas Turner's next door neighbour, Samuel, was the third child of William and Elizabeth (aged seventy-seven in 1841 and living in Shilling Street). The 1841 census[21] shows that he was a bricklayer, and entered on the same page is his younger brother, Thomas Turner, another bricklayer in the High Street. To add to the confusion there were another four adult Thomas Turners heading households in Lavenham of whom only the above two were in the High Street. It is thus impossible to be certain on the tithe apportionments alone whether the yarnmaker was owner of all or any of the properties; surviving title deeds and manorial Court Baron records might elucidate this.

The local tithe agent visited Lavenham on 24 February 1842. He reported that a notice of the proposed commutation of the tithes was posted on the principal outer door of the church on 9 February 1841, and the first meeting of landowners was advertised in the

Pedigree of the Turners of Lavenham, Suffolk

AUDLEY TURNER = SUSAN DEEKS
of Hadleigh, Suffolk | marr 7 Feb 1749/50,
1749/50 | at Hadleigh

AUDLEY TURNER = ANNE GRISS
bp 1 Apr 1750, | marr 5 July 1778, at
at Hadleigh | Lavenham, Suffolk

THOMAS WESTROP = MARY GIBLING
of Lavenham, 1781 | of Little Waldingfield,
| Suffolk, marr 19 Nov 1781,
| at Lavenham, by Licence

WILLIAM TURNER = ELIZABETH LAMBERT
bp 15 June 1758, | bn c.1764, of Shilling Street, Lavenham,
of Lavenham | 1841, marr 8 Oct 1782, at Lavenham,
| there bur 10 May 1842, aged 79

other issue
3 sons
5 daughters

ANNE =
bp 5 Dec 1782
at Lavenham,
there marr
28 Feb 1811,
and died
4 Apr 1814,
aged 31, M.I.
at Lavenham

THOMAS TURNER
of High Street, Lavenham, 1841–64 wool-
comber, 1813, yarn mker, 1819, woolstapler, 1840, bp 16 Oct 1783 at Lavenham,
held land, shops and a wool hall in High
Street, and Bears Lane, Lavenham, died
15 Feb 1864, M.I. at Lavenham, will dd
21 Dec 1863, pr 4 Mch 1864, Death Duty
paid 16 May 1864

= SUSAN
bp 27 Mch
1797, at
Lavenham
bur 3 Sept
1821, at
Lavenham,
aged 24,
M.I. there

other issue
2 sons
4 daughters

ARDLEY TURNER
of Shilling Street,
Lavenham, 1841,
shovel maker, bp 9 Oct
1785 at Lavenham,
aged c.55 in 1841, bur
29 Apr 1845, at
Lavenham, aged 59

LAMBERT TURNER
of Shilling Street,
Lavenham, 1841–81,
baker, bp 11 June
1809, at Lavenham,
there bur 28 Dec
1881, aged 72

= JANE BOGGIS
bn c.1809, of
Thorpe, Suffolk,
marr 4 Feb 1830,
at Lavenham,
aged 42 in 1851,
52 in 1861, dead
by 1871

other issue
6 sons
6 daughters

WILLIAM = ANNE
SMITH | bp 18 Aug 1811,
| at Lavenham,
| there marr 9 Mch
| 1837, by Licence,
| died 11 Jan 1847,
| aged 36, M.I.
| at Lavenham

MARY
bp 25 Jan 1813,
at Lavenham,
there bur
30 May 1831,
M.I.

WESTROP THOMAS TURNER
of High Street, Lavenham, 1841–56, woolstapler 1840, farmer 1842, Innkeeper
1844–56, bp 15 Aug 1819, at Lavenham,
held copyhold land in Lavenham, d ed
20 Oct 1855, M.I. at Lavenham, will dd
19 May 1855, pr 24 Apr 1857, Succession
Duty paid 25 Feb 1885

= ABIGAIL
of the Black Lion Inn, High Street,
Lavenham, 1861–84, Innkeeper, 1861–71,
hotelkeeper and farmer, 1881–84, bn c.1817,
at Lavenham, there marr 6 Oct 1840, named in
husband's will, 1855, to have his land for life,
died 21 Sept 1884, M.I. at Lavenham, will dd
16 Feb 1876, pr 9 Jan 1885

WILLIAM MATTHAM
of Black Lion Inn,
High Street,
Lavenham, 1871–81,
bn c.1806, at
Lavenham, aged 65
in 1871

HENRY WESTROP
TURNER, bp 30 July
1821, at Lavenham,
there bur 3 Aug 1821

other issue
7 sons
2 daughters

WILLIAM THOMAS SMITH
of High Street, Lavenham,
1861, woolstapler, bn
c.1839, at London, Middx,
aged 22 in 1861, named
in grandfather's will, 1863,
to have a shop and wool hall in
High Street, Lavenham

MAFIA MARY
dressmaker, 1861,
bn c.1841, at
Lavenham, aged
20 in 1861, named
in grandfather's
will, 1863, to have
moiety of a shop
in High Street,
Lavenham, then
marr

ALICE JANE
bn c.1845, at
Lavenham, aged
16 in 1861,
named in grand-
father's will,
1863, to have
moiety of a shop
in High Street,
Lavenham and
4 cottages

THOMAS WESTROP
TURNER, bp 9 Aug
1841, at Lavenham,
aged 9 in 1851,
named in father's will,
1855, died 23 Feb
1860, aged 18, M.I.
at Lavenham

MATTHAM TURNER
of Monks Eleigh, Suffolk,
1876, farmer, bp 23 Sept
1842, at Lavenham, aged
8 in 1851, named in
father's will, 1855, and
grandfather's will, 1863,
to have moiety of
property in Bears Lane,
Lavenham, executor of
mother's will, 1885

WESTROP TURNER
bp 4 Feb 1844, at
Lavenham, aged 7 in
1851, named in
father's will, 1855,
and grandfather's
will, 1863, to have
moiety of 3 cottages
in High Street,
Lavenham, died
4 July 1873

FREDERICK TURNER
bp 3 Apr 1845, at
Lavenham, aged 6 in
1851, named in
father's will, 1855, and
grandfather's will,
1863, executor of
mother's will, 1885

CHARLES TURNER
of London, 1874, bp 26 Dec
1846, at Lavenham, aged 5
in 1851, named in father's
will, 1855, grandfather's
will, 1863, to have moiety of
property in Bears Lane,
Lavenham, died 8 Oct
1874, M.I. at Lavenham

HARRY TURNER
of the Black Lion Inn, High Street,
Lavenham, 1871, bp 7 Apr 1848,
at Lavenham, aged 3 in 1851,
named in father's will, 1855,
grandfather's will, 1863, to have
moiety of 3 cottages in High
Street, Lavenham, bur 13 Dec
1881 at Lavenham, M.I.

ABIGAIL
bp 31 Mch 1850,
at Lavenham,
aged 1 in 1851,
there bur 21 Apr
1851, M.I.

ABIGAIL HARRIET
bp 13 Nov 1853, at
Lavenham, named
in father's will,
1855, grand-
father's will, 1863,
mother's will, 1876

EMILY ANN
bp 13 Nov
1853, at
Lavenham,
there bur
9 June 1856,
M.I.

MARY
bp 24 May
1856, at
Lavenham,
there bur
13 June 1856,
M.I.

ELIZABETH
bp 15 Feb 1857, at
Lavenham, aged 4 in
1861, named in grand-
father's will, 1863,
mother's will, 1876,
bur 16 Apr 1875, at
Lavenham, M.I.

The details in italics refer to sources held outside the Public Record Office

Bury and Norwich Post on 17 and 24 February.[22] The meeting itself took place at the Greyhound Inn at Lavenham on 4 March, and there were six adjournments. The final agreement was provisionally executed on 3 July 1841, and was signed by fifteen of the forty-six landowners. The Great Tithe was payable to a lay impropriator, a rope manufacturer living in London, and amounted to £26–9s for 98 acres of land; the Small Tithe, due to the rector, was worth £436 a year. After detailed calculations and deductions the rent charge was fixed at £931, £894 of which was to go to the rector and £44 of which was apportioned on his glebe. Thomas Turner's High Street holdings were liable to 19s a year, on 2 acres and one pole.

A copy of the notice of apportionment was attached to the church door and another left at the Swan Inn together with a draft of the apportionments and a map for the inspection of any interested party.

The report described the parish in 1842: the soil was considered to be a strong loam on a clay subsoil, and the land wet and in want of drainage, being very flat. The arable was cultivated 'in the usual Suffolk mode' of the four course shift, of fallow, barley at four quarters an acre, clover or beans in tares, and wheat in three quarters an acre. The pasture near the town was deemed to be good and full of herbage, but the remainder was cold and wet and not very productive. The greater proportion was mown. The underwood was held to be good and at ten years' growth would make £10 an acre. The arable and grasslands were thought capable of much improvement, having a good staple of loam, but were perceived as miserably wet. So much for Lavenham one hundred and fifty years ago.

There were seven later amendments to the original apportionment.[23] Abigail Turner, as an owner-occupier, was affected by an adjustment made on 18 August 1869 and brought about by two acres, two roods and twenty-six poles being taken from her holding of seven plots of arable and pasture amounting to fifty-seven acres and twenty-two poles, for use by the Great Eastern Railway Company and for the new road. Her rent charge was reduced to £20–3s. A further adjustment was made on 20 June 1878 when two-and-a-half acres of pasture in Swans Meadow, owned by her son Mattham and occupied by her, had the rent charge changed to 13s 6d a year.

The Lavenham Land Tax assessment for 1798[24] is partially divided into streets: in Bolton Street George Turner was the occupier of property owned by John Mattham and assessed at $10\frac{1}{2}d$ in tax. Thomas Westrop owned land occupied by Ardley Turner, on

which $11\frac{1}{4}d$ was due, but we do not know in which street this lay. They were future brothers-in-law, for Ardley's son Thomas married Thomas Westrop's daughter Anne in 1811, and, later, another daughter Susan sometime between her death in 1814 and Westrop Thomas Turner's baptism in 1819.

In contrast with the domestic harmony of the Turners' establishment at the Black Lion Inn, a North Country pub was the setting for an exciting series of events arising from the 1851 census.

On Tuesday, 10 June 1851, three friends, John Ward, John Graham and William Kirkpatrick, went for an evening drink at the Bush Inn, at Longtown in Cumberland. Soon afterwards, they were joined by Thomas Plenderleath, the local District Registrar of Births and Deaths, but Kirkpatrick, objecting to his company, shoved Plenderleath out into the passage. After a short interval Plenderleath returned with a crony and sat down on a sofa nearby, called for some whisky and commented that 'the pether' (meaning Kirkpatrick) would not strike at him. Kirkpatrick had been a pedlar or hawker by trade and was generally known by that name. Provoked by this remark, Kirkpatrick jumped up, seized a poker and threatened to split open Plenderleath's skull, but was restrained by his friends. Downing a glass of rum, he brandished the poker again and made another threatening gesture. Plenderleath offered to buy him a drink, at which Kirkpatrick tried to strike him and was pulled away.

Kirkpatrick was aggrieved by events earlier in the day when the three men had gone to Plenderleath's house to receive their fees for acting as his nominated census enumerators at the end of March. The Superintendent Registrar had also been present at the payout. Kirkpatrick had complained that he was underpaid by five shillings. Plenderleath had replied that he had received all that was owing to him and if he would not take it then the Superintendent would. He had ordered Kirkpatrick out of the house, calling him a swindler and accusing him of withholding two volumes of books on the life of Napoleon which Kirkpatrick had borrowed from him. Kirkpatrick had taken the money, signed the receipt and left, highly agitated.

In the bar Kirkpatrick now raised the matter again and Plenderleath acknowledged that two shillings were still outstanding as his fees. At this Kirkpatrick angrily tossed a glass of spirits at him before sitting down, pouring out another glass and despatching it too in Plenderleath's direction. This time Plenderleath said nothing, but wiped himself down with a handkerchief before inviting Kirkpatrick to come and sit beside him and have a drink, and if not, then he would sit next to Kirkpatrick. He went over and perched on Kirkpatrick's chair. Kirkpatrick sprang up and grabbed him by the throat with both hands, pressing hard. John Ward and the publican, Jonathan Foster, quickly pulled him off. Plenderleath's head fell forward on his chest, the fingers of his left hand began to twitch, and the two men momentarily supported him before he collapsed against the oven. He was lifted onto the sofa, the doctor was summoned, and he was carried home on a chair, stupefied. He lingered on unconscious for a fortnight before succumbing on 24 June. A coroner's inquest was held at the inn the next day and adjourned to 27 June.[25] John Ward signed his written statement, describing himself as a shoemaker, and setting out the above

Part of a book containing the depositions taken on oath from witnesses at the coroner's inquest on the death of Thomas Plenderleath, at the Bush Inn, Longtown, in Cumberland on 25 and 27 June 1851. The two Plenderleaths were his sons and signed their statements. ASS145/69

story. There were twelve witnesses in all, and fourteen jurymen (each of whom had been bound on a recognizance of £10 to appear).

Ward told the inquest that after the attack he went home to find Kirkpatrick waiting for him. Thereafter he was frequently visited by him, always enquiring about Plenderleath's condition, until his arrest on 16 June. He said that Kirkpatrick was a single man whereas his victim was married with a grown-up family. A Carlisle doctor, Henry Lonsdale, then testified that he had examined Plenderleath on 11 June and found him paralysed and unconscious. He had tried unsuccessfully to rouse him by pain. He had helped Dr Rome conduct the post mortem, six hours after demise. No external bruising had been evident on the body but the left side of the brain had suffered much softening, and he concluded that death was due entirely 'to the violence and force used by Kirkpatrick as described by Ward ... a blood vessel was ruptured both on the brain and within the Structure'.

Two of the other witnesses were sons of the deceased, Robert Plenderleath and Joseph Plenderleath, Junior. The latter merely testified to his father's age being sixty, while Robert reported that he had been standing opposite the inn, his mother having gone inside to fetch her husband, when he saw figures outside in the passage. He crossed the road, thinking them to be his parents. One of the figures said, 'I've done the bloody Buggers goose this time', while his companion laughed and turned to urinate against the wall. History does not relate whether Kirkpatrick had paid for the drinks he so freely dispensed.

The verdict found by the jurors was one of wilful murder against William Kirkpatrick.

Kirkpatrick stood trial at the Summer Assize and Gaol Delivery for Cumberland, part of the North Eastern Assize Circuit, held at Carlisle between 4 and 6 August 1851. He was one of twenty-six defendants. The Court Minute Books[26] record that it was presided over by one of the Barons in the Exchequer and one of the Justices in the Court of Common Pleas, and the Justices assigned to deliver prisoners from gaol and to hear and determine 'all Treasons Felonies Trespasses Contempts Offences Nuisances and Misdemeanours committed within the said county'. Firstly their Commissions were read out to the Court, and on the second day the Grand Jury of twenty-three were sworn in, comprising an Honourable, a Knight, four members of Parliament and seventeen esquires, all of whose names and addresses were noted down, while the names of the petty jury of twelve were set down.

William Kirkpatrick's was the ninth case to be heard. He pleaded not guilty, was found guilty of manslaughter and sentenced to six months with hard labour in the House of Correction. From the other entries in the Minutes it emerged that five of the defendants, convicted of burglary, armed robbery with violence, and carnal knowledge of a girl under ten, were ordered to be transported for periods varying between ten and fifteen years. Of those found guilty Kirkpatrick's was the third lightest sentence. The Court also dealt with charges of rioting, kidnapping, forgery and embezzlement, assault, larceny, libel and one case where a parson was accused of shooting with intent to do bodily harm.

The bundle of indictments for the Summer Assize[27] sets out full details of Kirkpatrick's alleged offence, as well as the plea, verdict and sentence. He was described as living in the parish of Arthuret and a labourer. On the dorse of each indictment is a list of the witnesses sworn in Court. At Kirkpatrick's trial there were eighteen of them, including Sarah and Robert Plenderleath. Because he was tried for murder the report of the coroner's inquest was attached to the indictment, signed by him and his jury. The depositions taken at the inquest were also produced in evidence, but filed in a separate series together with depositions from other inquests.[28] However, witness

statements seldom survive from trials other than where death was involved, and the evidence given in Court can generally only be gleaned from the pages of contemporary local newspapers or printed proceedings such as those of the Old Bailey Sessions (after November 1834, the Central Criminal Court) sitting in London.

Unfortunately no Gaol Calendar has been deposited for this Assize so we do not know Kirkpatrick's age nor the name of the committing magistrate when he was arrested on 16 June.

The 1851 census of Longtown, in the parish of Arthuret, shows that Thomas Plenderleath lived in Esk Street.[29] He was Registerer (*sic*) and Proprietor of houses. He gave his age as fifty-eight and his

---

The census of the town of Longtown, parish of Arthuret, Cumberland, taken on the night of 30 March 1851. Schedule no 56 embraces the household of Thomas Plenderleath, 'Registerer (Proprietor of Houses)' and his family in Esk Street. He supervised the census of the town and other places within his Registration District, but survived less than three months, being killed by one of the census enumerators. HO107/2428 f242 p8

birthplace as Longtown, like his two sons Robert, an apprentice stonemason of twenty, and Thomas, aged fourteen, and infirm. His wife Sarah, fifty-two, came from Carlisle. Of the other son, Joseph, called at the inquest, there was no trace, so he may have been temporarily absent or living away. Other Plenderleaths were found, and notably a household in Bridge Street, headed by Andrew Plenderleath, a tea dealer aged thirty.[30] In the same street lived John Ward, the shoemaker, aged thirty, with his wife and four young children,[31] and William Kirkpatrick, living alone, describing himself as a retired draper of fifty-one, and a Scot.[32] The Bush Inn was also in the street, though not named in the census. The publican, Jonathan Foster, mentioned in John Ward's statement at the inquest, can be identified from the census as a married man of twenty-nine.[33]

Ten years earlier, Thomas Plenderleath[34] was living in Eskbank Street, Longtown, with Sarah, Joseph Plenderleath, an ironmonger aged about twenty, Elizabeth and Sarah, both about fifteen years old, Robert, eleven, and Thomas, five. He was already Registrar and signed the two Enumeration Books for Longtown in the third week of June.[35]

District Registrars were appointed by the local Boards of Guardians of the new 1834 civil Poor Law Unions, whose boundaries were adopted for the purposes of establishing Superintendent Registration Districts of Births, Marriages and Deaths in England and Wales commencing on 1 July 1837. The Clerk to the Board of Guardians generally became the Superintendent Registrar, while his district was subdivided into smaller districts of about seven parishes each for registration of births and deaths, under the supervision of District Registrars. The District Registrars were responsible for their own accommodation and were paid 2s 6d for the first twenty entries of births and deaths in a calendar year, and then 1s for every entry registered thereafter. The onus lay with the Registrars to travel to the houses in their area where these events occurred in order that they might be recorded. They were given a strong lock-up iron box to hold the registers, which were supplied by the Registrar General in London for distribution by the Superintendent Registrars. Once every three months the local registrars had to furnish their superintendents with copies of the entries of births and deaths during the preceding quarter for verification, before they were forwarded to London and fed into the national registration system, and where a quarterly alphabetical index of names was compiled.

The District Registrars were often recruited from the ranks of Poor Law Union officers. Thomas Plenderleath was the vestry clerk of the parish of Arthuret by 28 March 1834,[36] and he helped prepare a list of all those people receiving parochial outdoor relief, who were in the workhouse, or who had given birth to bastard children during the year ended 26 March 1835. In all £1,157–5s–6½d had been paid out during that time, and the Overseers of the Poor Accounts were, like the list, produced for inspection by the Board of Guardians of the Longtown Poor Law Union. Robert Little, the future Superintendent Registrar, was one of the four overseers.

Starting in 1841, it was also the duty of the District Registrar to fix the size of the enumeration districts in his area for the decennial census. None was to contain more than two hundred inhabited houses nor less than twenty-five, the distances between the houses being the determining factor, as no district was to include 'a larger extent of country than an able-bodied and active man, visiting every house therein, can go between sunrise and sunset in a summer's day'.[37] These boundaries were subject to revision in the light of local administrative changes and the alterations notified to the Registrar General's Office in London, which also held a copy of the registrars' original plans of the enumeration districts.

The District Registrars were sent an instruction and memorandum book for each enumerator, plus a set of household schedules for delivery by the enumerators a few days before the designated night of the census and for collection the day after. The memorandum book was used to make notes about unoccupied buildings and people temporarily absent, or sleeping under cover in places not deemed as houses for census purposes, as well as detailing the order in which the schedules were delivered and recovered. The enumerators used this as a guide when the information was transferred from the schedules to the Enumeration Book. The nominal entries were written in black lead pencil specially provided for the 1841 census, though ink was to be used for the population summaries and for all the later censuses. Each Book contained a set of Directions and a specimen page for guidance and was prefaced by a brief geographical description of the district, written by the enumerator, with its number, county, Parliamentary division, hundred, parish and township to which it belonged, and the titles of the Superintendent and local Registrars' districts. From 1851 this was greatly modified to record the county and Parliamentary division, the registration districts, and the number of the enumeration district, with a short description of the district setting out the names of streets, house numbers and administrative areas contained in the

Book. The enumerators totalled up the number of male and female entries on each page and summarized them in tables at the front of the Book, adding the numbers of males and females temporarily absent or present with the reasons, and those sleeping elsewhere than in houses. The Book was then signed and produced to the District Registrar with the household schedules for his inspection and signature. The Superintendent Registrar was then supposed to examine the Book and countersign it before transmission to the Registrar General's Office.

The enumerators were required to be aged between eighteen and sixty-five, intelligent and fit, with an ability to read and write well and have a knowledge of arithmetic. They were to 'be temperate, orderly and respectable, and be such a person as is likely to conduct himself with strict propriety, and to deserve the goodwill of the inhabitants of his district'.[38] For their efforts they were usually recompensed with a fixed sum and then paid for every hundred persons over four hundred enumerated, with excess travelling expenses for ground covered to deliver and collect up the schedules. This low rate of payment caused much consternation among enumerators. One was moved to complain in his Book in 1851, 'The enumeration of this district [All Hallows, Barking, London] was undertaken by me in the belief that I should be fairly paid for my services. I was not aware that all the particulars were to be entered by the enumerator in a book, the work without that, being ample for the sum paid, nor had I any idea of the unreasonable amount of labour imposed. the distribution collection &c of the schedules together with the copying of the same, occupied from two to three hours for every 60 persons enumerated, and for this – the *equivalent* is – ONE SHILLING!!! What man possessing the intelligence & business habits necessary for the undertaking, would be found to accept it, if aware of the labour involved? How then can a correct return of the population be expected? He who proposed the scale of remuneration, should, in justice be compelled to enumerate a large district, such as this, upon the terms he has himself fixed.'[39]

William Kilpatric (*sic*) signed his name on the returns made of the 295 inhabitants of Kirklinton Middle township, in the parish of Arthuret.[40] There were fifty-eight houses for him to call at, and perhaps help illiterate heads of household complete the schedules, or give advice to those who did not understand what was being asked of them. Part of his task also included asking at each house whether any schooling was being provided there, and if so another form was left for completion. The book was signed on 7 April,

Plenderleath attached his signature on 12 April and Robert Little, the Superintendent Registrar, on 19 April 1851, but it was not until 10 June that he was to receive any money. Among the other enumerators appointed by Thomas Plenderleath were Robert and Andrew Plenderleath, presumably his relatives. At the end of one district he was complaining about the way in which the enumerator had noted the four males and three females in tents, and the three females in a barn at Breconhill,[41] so he obviously did spend time looking at the work of his nominees.

The February 1988 edition of the International Genealogical Index, a series of microfiche produced by the Society of Jesus Christ of Latter Day Saints (the Mormons), can be conveniently consulted for entries of Plenderleath baptisms and marriages in Cumberland. The *Vital and Parish Listings* reveal that the I.G.I. has a complete coverage of marriages at Arthuret between 1686 and 1855, and a high percentage of the baptisms there from 1666 until 1870. As the census gave approximate birth years, and birthplaces, a look for the baptism of Thomas Plenderleath around 1793 or 1791 quickly produced an entry on 1 August 1790, the child of Robert Plenderleith (*sic*) and Mary Mitchelhill. Because the I.G.I. groups all surname variants together, and then alphabetically by Christian name in chronological order, it was possible to find the marriage of Thomas Plenderleath and Sarah Thompson on 22 January 1820, at Carlisle St Mary, and the baptism of their son Thomas on 4 September 1836 at Arthuret. Plenderleath is a common surname in Cumberland making the work of extracting entries of other issue more daunting. To ease this problem I looked under the column recording parents' names and wrote down the details of the other six children they were listed as having had baptized between 1820 and 1833, as well as finding Andrew Plenderleath's baptism entry in 1821. He was son of John Plenderleath and Jane Latimer, married at Arthuret on 4 January 1820, and again I scanned the microfiche for more of their children, and for those of Andrew himself. From the entries on the I.G.I. it would seem that Robert and Andrew Plenderleath, the two census enumerators in 1851, may have been the District Registrar's son and nephew respectively, but Thomas also had a brother Robert, baptized in 1795, so the former enumerator may have been him.

From the I.G.I. it was also possible to discover that Thomas Plenderleath's wife Sarah was baptized as the daughter of Joseph Thompson and Mary Nicolson on 18 November 1798, at St Mary Carlisle, the church where she subsequently married.

Pedigree of the Plenderleaths of Longtown in Cumberland

ROBERT PLENDERLEITH = **MARY MITCHELHILL**
of Main Street, Longtown, Cumberland, 1841, farmer, bn c.1761 in Scotland, aged c.80 in 1841 | bn c.1761, in Cumberland, aged c.80 in 1841

THOMAS PLENDERLEATH = **SARAH**
of Eskbank Street, Longtown, 1841—51, Vestry Clerk and Assistant Overseer of the Poor of the parish of Arthuret, Cumberland, c.1829—37, Registrar of Births and Deaths, 1841—51, and proprietor of houses, 1851, bp 1 Aug 1790, at Arthuret, died 24 June 1851, at Longtown, aged 60, Coroner's Inquest, 27 June 1851

daughter of JOSEPH and MARY THOMPSON, bp 18 Nov 1798, at St Mary Carlisle, Cumberland, there marr 22 Jan 1820, aged 52 in 1851

ROBERT PLENDERLEITH
bp 25 Apr 1795, at Arthuret

JOHN PLENDERLEITH = **JANE LATIMER**
of Main Street, Longtown, 1841, farmer, bp 26 June 1797, at Arthuret, aged c.40 in 1841 | bn c.1806, in Cumberland, marr 4 Jan 1820, at Arthuret, aged c.35 in 1841

JAMES PLENDERLEITH
bp 5 July 1805, at Arthuret

JOSEPH THOMPSON PLENDERLEATH, of Eskbank Street, Longtown, 1841, iron-monger, bp 10 Sept 1820, at Arthuret, aged c.20 in 1841, witness at Coroner's Inquest on his father, 27 June 1851

MARY
bp 13 Nov 1821, at Arthuret

ELIZABETH
bp 16 Oct 1823, at Arthuret, aged c.15 in 1841

SARAH
bp 17 Sept 1826, at Arthuret, aged c.15 in 1841

ROBERT PLENDERLEATH
of Esk Street, Longtown, 1851, stone mason (apprentice), bp 16 May 1830, at Arthuret, aged 20 in 1851, witness at Coroner's Inquest on his father, 27 June 1851

FANNY
bp 7 Apr 1833, at Arthuret

THOMAS PLENDERLEATH
bp 4 Sept 1836, at Arthuret, aged 14 in 1851

ANDREW PLENDERLEATH = **ISABELLA JOHNSTON**, bn
of Bridge Street, Longtown, 1851, tea dealer, bp 10 Jan 1821, at Arthuret, Census enumerator, 1851, then aged 30

c.1820, at Longtown, marr 11 Oct 1844, at Arthuret, aged 31 in 1851

ROBERT PLENDERLEATH
bp 5 Aug 1824, at Arthuret, aged c.15 in 1841

THOMAS PLENDERLEATH
bp 17 Apr 1827, at Arthuret, aged 12 in 1841

JOHN PLENDERLEATH
bn c.1832 in Cumberland, aged 9 in 1841

JAMES PLENDERLEATH
bp 25 June 1837, at Arthuret, aged 4 in 1841

ANN
bn c.1840, in Cumberland, aged 1 in 1841

JOHN PLENDERLEATH
bp 10 May 1845, at Arthuret

ROBERT HILL PLENDERLEATH
bp 23 Aug 1846, at Arthuret

ELIZABETH
bp 28 July 1848, at Arthuret, aged 2 in 1851

JANE
bp 11 May 1851, at Arthuret, aged 1 mth in 1851 Census

The details in italics refer to sources held outside the Public Record Office

It must be stressed that the I.G.I. rarely includes deaths or burials, so it gives a distorted picture of family events, as some of the recorded infants died before reaching maturity; secondly, not all parishes are included, nor comprehensively, nor for a consistently defined period; third, the entries are fed into the Index to comply with a fixed layout, ignoring any extra information contained in the original register; fourth, the data are only as good and accurate as the person feeding them onto the computer, so are open to error, omission, duplication, mistranscription, transposition, misalliance and wrong parish or date attribution; and fifth, it is not clear exactly what calendar is being observed in the vital period before 1 January 1752, when the year began on 25 March – entries in the hiatus months are therefore ambiguous. For all these reasons, however tempting it may be to ignore them, it is essential that the original parish registers be checked, using the I.G.I. only as a rough guide to the sought-after entry, or to the distribution of a surname in time and county, and should never be used without consulting the appropriate *Vital and Parish Listings*.

6

THE GAINSBOROUGH FAMILY

In this chapter we shall look at the family of Thomas Gainsborough, the eighteenth-century artist, also a Suffolk man, born in 1727 not far from Lavenham, in the market town of Sudbury. Material used includes the baptism registers of the Old Meeting House of the Independent Congregation in Sudbury, bankruptcy records concerning his father's failed business, an application for a patent of invention made by his brother, and his own life history.

Thomas Gainsborough, the artist, was baptized on 14 May 1727 at the Great Meeting in Friars Street, Sudbury, Suffolk.[1] He was the son of John and Mary Gainsborough, six of whose other children were taken there for baptism between 1711 and 1725, from their house in nearby Sepulchre Street. Five cousins, children of Thomas and Elisabeth Gainsborough, were also baptized in the Meeting House from 1709 until 1717: three were baptized privately because of

sickness. Subsequent Gainsborough entries relate to their descendants; the last, a great-granddaughter of Thomas and Elisabeth, was born in 1786.

The Great Meeting was founded about 1662, and originally it was Presbyterian. After the Declaration of Indulgence, issued on 15 March 1671/2, John Parish was granted a licence on 1 May 1672 to hold meetings at his house in Sudbury.[2] Between April and June that year forty-nine Suffolk folk obtained similar licences. The baptism registers survive from 25 April 1707, and when they were sent to the Commissioners in London in September 1837 for examination and authentication so that they could be produced in a court of law as evidence of birth and parentage, the denomination was given as Independent. The burial

118

registers, starting in 1739, were retained by the minister, and are now in the Suffolk Record Office in Bury St Edmunds.[3]

When Thomas was six years old his father's business as a clothier foundered. *The London Gazette*, issued for Tuesday 26 June to Saturday 30 June 1733, announced that a Commission of Bankruptcy had been awarded against him.[4] Being declared a bankrupt, John Gainsborough was 'required to surrender himself to the Commissioners on the 9th and 30th July next, and on the 10th of August following, at Ten in the Forenoon, at the Bell Inn in Siblehedingham, in the County of Essex, and make a full Discovery of his Estate and Effects; when and where the Creditors are to come prepared to prove their Debts ...'. In the meantime no debtors or people holding any of his property were allowed to pay or give delivery to him but only to those whom the Commissioners should appoint.

The Docket Books of the Court of Bankruptcy tell us that the award was made on 22 June 1733 at the instigation of three creditors, all clothiers living at Glemsford in Suffolk.[5] On 4 July John petitioned the Lord Chancellor, insisting that he had in no instance whatever committed any act of bankruptcy.[6] He asked that the Commission be superseded, or that there should be an issue at law to determine whether he was a bankrupt before or at the time of the issue of the Commission and that the Commission be stayed. The Lord Chancellor ordered all the parties or their agents to attend him on the matter of Gainsborough's petition. At the meeting, on 25 July 1733, the Solicitor General represented the petitioner and the Attorney General the creditors; the petition was read, affidavits were produced including those of John and Mary Gainsborough, and a hearing of the allegations on both sides ensued. The Lord Chancellor ordered that the Commission be stayed pending an issue at law, to be tried in the next Term or as soon as possible thereafter in the Court of King's Bench, sitting in London, with the creditors as plaintiffs and John Gainsborough as the defendant. If the parties differed about the issue they were to refer to one of the Masters of the Court of Bankruptcy, and after the

FAR LEFT *Portrait of John Gainsborough (1683–1748), by his son Thomas, c.1750–1. Courtesy of Gainsborough's House, Sudbury, Suffolk.*

LEFT *Part of the register of the Greater Meeting of the Independents, Friars Street, Sudbury, Suffolk, showing the baptism entry of Thomas, son of John Gainsborough, on 14 May 1727. The family later assigned some of their land to the Meeting for use as a burying ground. RG4/1861 p15*

RIGHT *Bankruptcy Order made by the Lord Chancellor on 25 July 1733 on the petition of John Gainsborough of Sudbury, Suffolk, clothier, 4 July 1733, challenging the recent Commission of Bankruptcy awarded against him. The Order calls for a trial of issue at law to be heard in the Court of King's Bench to determine whether the petitioner was actually bankrupt at the time of the Commission. B1/12*

trial either side could apply to the Lord Chancellor for further directions.

The London Gazette for Tuesday 16 October until Saturday 20 October 1733, reported that the Commission had been suspended under the Great Seal, 'Therefore all Persons that are indebted to the said John Gainsborough, or that have any of his Effects in their Hands, are forthwith to pay and deliver the same to the said John Gainsborough, or they will be sued by Mr Henry Stanyford, Attorney at Law, in Friday-Street, London.'[7] No further legal action seems to have been taken and no later applications were made to the Lord Chancellor, suggesting that the parties reached an agreement.

A clue as to what happened is contained in the will of John's brother Thomas, also a clothier based in Sudbury, drawn up on 23 February 1738/9 and proved in the Prerogative Court of Canterbury on 5 April 1739.[8] From the amount of personal and real estate he held there and elsewhere in Suffolk it is apparent that his business had prospered. He himself lived in the Calendar House, and he mentioned 'the house my Bror John Gainsborough lives in with three Tenements All which were purchased by my . . . son John of my said Bror John and at that time conveyed to my said son', presumably to provide him with the necessary cash to settle his debts. But Thomas remained anxious about his brother's ability to stay solvent, for the will continued '. . . as I am fearful that should my Brother John Gainsborough live many years he may come into such Circumstances as may stand in need of some assistance towards the procuring the necessarys of Life and if that should be the Case with him My will is that my Executors do make provision out of the Overplus of my Estate that he may be paid five shillings a week during his life.' John's surviving seven children were left £10 apiece and he also seems to have taken an active interest in advancing the careers of two of the sons, as the will stated, 'I have for some years past taken upon my Self the care of Humphery Gainsborough one of the sons of my Brother John Gainsborough who is now in London a pupill at the academy where Mr Emes is Master In order to be trained for the Ministry' and accordingly £20 a year was now to be set aside towards the cost of this training, for three years. Thomas, Humphery's youngest brother, was to be cared for by his uncle's executors (his wife Elizabeth, and their sons John and Samuell), 'that he may be brought up to some Light handy Craft trade likely to get a comfortable maintenance by And that they do give him any sum not Exceeding £20 to bind him out to such trade . . .', with a further legacy of £10 if

he proved to be sober and likely to make good use of it 'the better to Enable him to set out into the world'.

John and Humphry Gainsborough, the older sons, were both inventors. John remained in Sudbury but Humphry became a dissenting minister, ending his life at Henley-upon-Thames in Oxfordshire. He invented 'a Steam Engine upon a New Construction, which will, as your Petitioner apprehens, be much more useful to the Publick than the common Steam Engine, by its having a much greater Power and Velocity', and petitioned the King for a patent to have the sole use and benefit of it within England, Wales and the Town of Berwick-upon-Tweed and in all the King's Colonies and Plantations abroad for fourteen years.[9] It was referred to the Attorney or Solicitor General on 6 February 1775, but James

Humphry Gainsborough's petition for a patent for invention to have a 14-year monopoly on the use of his Steam Engine. On 6 February 1775 it was referred to the Attorney General, was challenged by James Watt, and before arbitration could take place Gainsborough died. SP44/265, p355

Watt, who had taken out the first of a series of patents on his own Steam Engine on 5 January 1769, apparently challenged the petition and a meeting was arranged with the Solicitor General to settle a possible breach of patent law.[10] Humphry died little more than a year after his petition, leaving the matter unresolved, and his working model was kept in the garden of his brother's house in Pall Mall, Westminster, until 1785, by which time it was in a sorry state.[11] Humphry's will, made on 26 September 1761, had bequeathed everything to his wife and sole executrix, Mary Gainsborough.[12] She predeceased him, so on 29 August 1776, Thomas, as his brother and one of the next of kin, was granted letters of administration with will annexed, to settle his affairs.

Thomas Gainsborough was married on 15 July 1746, aged nineteen, to Margaret Burr, at St George's Chapel, Hyde Park Corner, London.[13] The register described him as a resident of the parish of St Andrew's Holborn, and his bride as living in St George's Hanover Square (in whose bounds the chapel stood). These premises, also called the Mayfair Chapel, were established by Rev. Alexander Keith about 1730.[14] He performed marriages at a guinea each, including the cost of a certificate, but without the necessity of a prior licence, the reading of banns, or parental consent being obtained for minors. Although irregular, the marriages were nonetheless binding until Hardwicke's Act for the better preventing of Clandestine Marriages was implemented on 25 March 1754. On the last day of its existence sixty-one marriages took place in the private house which had served as the chapel since 1743 or 1744. Custom was summoned up via advertisements in the press, giving precise instructions on how to reach the chapel, and how to recognize it. The house apparently had a porch resembling that of a country church. Such was its success that in 1742, while forty marriages were celebrated in the church in Hanover Square, more than seven hundred were performed at the chapel. This had a notably adverse effect on the church's income, so the rector brought a suit against Keith in Doctors' Commons, alleging that he had officiated and performed divine service in his church without prior licence or leave from the Bishop of London, and for which he was duly excommunicated at the end of 1742. In Hilary Term 1742/3 a writ of trespass and contempt against the form of the Statute made to prevent clandestine marriages was filed on an information by Richard Dovey.[15] Keith had been in Holy Orders since 24 June 1712, and on 23 November 1742 'with force and arms' had married Robert Hume and Mary fford in the Church of St

Richard Dovey appears before the Court of King's Bench (Crown Side) to claim his half of the £100 forfeited by Rev. Alexander Keith about whose activities in marrying a couple without Banns or proper licence Dovey had laid an information to the King in the Court in Hilary Term 16 George II (1742/3). KB28/165, m7

George Hanover Square, without banns or licence, in contempt of the King and his Laws 'To the evil and pernicious Example of all others in the like Case offending and against the peace of our said present Sovereign'. Keith had forfeited £100 for the offence, divided between the King and the informant. In Easter Term Dovey appeared before the King in person, sitting in the Court of King's Bench, where he requested his share of the fine and for due process of the law to be awarded against Keith.[16] The Sheriff of Middlesex was commanded to arrest him and compel him to answer the charges. He was taken into custody on 25 April on a writ of *capias excommunicatum* from the Court of Chancery, and committed to the Fleet Prison on 14 May, for want of bail.[17] He entered a plea of not guilty.[18] A trial by jury was ordered and took place in Trinity Term 1743, at which he was convicted.[19] He died in the

A page from the Fleet Prison Commitment Book containing details of the Rev. Alexander Keith's committal on 14 May 1743. To a writ of habeas corpus the Sheriff of Middlesex replied that Keith had been detained on a writ of capias excommunicatum for performing an illegal wedding in the church of St George's Hanover Square; the writ was returned to the Court of King's Bench (Crown Side) on 18 November 1743. PRIS1/9 p262 no 861

Fleet Prison on 13 December 1758, and one of his clerks, James Frith, went to collect his effects, including three of his marriage registers in one of which Gainsborough's wedding is contained.[20] The registers were deposited in the Church of St George Hanover Square, while others from the chapel, lodged in the Bishop of London's Registry, now rest among the unauthenticated volumes in the Public Record Office.[21]

After his marriage Gainsborough returned to live in Sudbury. The I.G.I. of Suffolk reveals that his two daughters were baptized there. The family moved to Bath in 1760,[22] where he took on as his apprentice his nephew Gainsborough Dupont. According to the I.G.I. his mother Sarah was married to Philip Dupont on 6 May 1745, at St Gregory's Church in Sudbury. The original apprenticeship indenture survives, dated 14 January 1772.[23] It gives five shillings as the premium paid for the apprenticeship, but avoids duty payable at 6d in the pound. In 1780 Thomas did however pay duty on the two male servants in his employ at his house in Pall Mall,[24] where he had set up home in 1774.[25]

Gainsborough Dupont was given a legacy of £100 under his uncle's will, made on 5 May 1788, and proved in the Prerogative Court of Canterbury on the oath of his widow and sole executrix, Margaret Gainsborough, on 22 August 1788.[26] The sum was intended to be in full satisfaction of all claims and demands he might have on the artist, and in return Gainsborough forgave him all debts owed to him up to the time of his death. Another clause in the will made it clear that if the nephew were to make any claim for work done or on any other account then

the legacy was revoked, and the executrix was instructed to charge him for board, washing and lodging and only the balance paid out to him. Dupont was also given such of his models, implements and utensils in the painting business, oils, colours, varnishes and such like as the executrix deemed useful to him, while she herself was to have the rest of his artist's equipment, his drawings, paintings, pictures and prints of all kinds.

From the will of the painter's cousin, John Gainsborough, of Sudbury, crapemaker (*sic*), dated 16 February 1771, it is obvious that he flourished.[27] He possessed houses in Sudbury (including the one in which his uncle had lived) and elsewhere, had investments in Government stock, and securities, held Old South Sea and Bank annuities, and shares in lead mines and the London Bridge Waterworks. Some of these had been inherited from female relations as he readily acknowledged. Like his father and his son John after him, he left money for the Meeting in Sudbury, and detailed instructions for his funeral. He asked that his remains be carried by ten of his workforce to the vault where his parents, his wife, and some of his own children were buried, and that they each be paid ten shillings and receive hatbands and gloves. The minister reading the funeral service at the interment was to be similarly kitted out, while the minister preaching the sermon additionally received a scarf, a ring and two guineas. There were to be six pallbearers who were each to have a hatband, gloves, scarf and rings. Rings were to be purchased for the two executors, his daughter and thirty-one other named relatives and friends, at a cost of one guinea apiece.

Pedigree of Gainsborough of Sudbury, Suffolk, and Pall Mall, Middlesex

JOHN FENN =
named in son-in-law's will, 1738/9

THOMAS GAINSBOROUGH = ELISABETH
of the Calendar House, | named in
Sudbury, Suffolk, clothier, | husband's will,
1738/9, he'd houses in | 1738/9,
Sudbury, farms at Glemsford, | executrix 1739
Falkenham, Trimley and
Alpheton, all in Suffolk,
will dd 23 Feb 1738/9, pr
5 Apr 1739

MARGARET
named in 'brother' THOMAS
GAINSBOROUGH's will,
1738/9, as owning shares
in River Stour, and in
London Bridge Waterworks

JOHN GAINSBOROUGH = MARY
of Sudbury, clothier, 1733,
Commission of Bankruptcy
awarded against him 22 June
1733, suspended Oct 1733,
licensed to retail wine at
Sudbury, 1738, named in
brother's will, 1738/9

MATHIAS GAINSBOROUGH
named in brother's will,
1738/9, as deceased ◆

other issue
2 daughters

MARY = JOHN GAINSBOROUGH = MARGARET
of Sudbury, crapemaker,
1771, bp 23 Sept 1711, at
Indep. Great Meeting,
Friars Street, Sudbury,
named in father's will
1738/9 (executor 1739)
to have land in Sudbury
and farms at Glemsford,
Falkenham and Trimley,
paid tax on a chariot at
Sudbury 1757–61,
1764–5, and on silver
plate, 1756–62, 1764–6,
will dd 16 Feb 1771, pr
7 Apr 1773 and
10 Apr 1773

MARGARET
named in
father's will,
1738/9,
brother's
will, 1771,
marr by
1738/9 to
WILLIAM
SHEPHERD
= ◆

other issue
2 sons
2 daughters

PHILLIP =
DUPONT

SARAH
bp 28 Aug
1715, at
Indep. Great
Meeting,
Friars Street,
Sudbury,
marr 6 May
1745, at
St Gregory
Sudbury,
named in
uncle's will,
1738/9

HUMPHREY
GAINSBOROUGH, of
Henley-upon-Thames,
Oxon, Minister, 1761, bp
13 Apr 1718, at Indep.
Great Meeting, Friars
Street, Sudbury, named
in uncle's will, 1738/9,
as apprenticed for the
Ministry, in London,
petitioned for a Patent
for Invention of a Steam
Engine 6 Feb 1775, will
dd 26 Sept 1761, pr
29 Aug 1776, marr
MARY, who dsp before
her husband

THOMAS GAINSBOROUGH = MARGARET
sometime of St Andrew's | BURR, of
Holborn, Middx, 1746, City of | St George's
Bath, Somerset, 1772, Pall | Hanover
Mall, St James's Westminster, | Square, Middx,
1780–88, painter, bp 14 May | 1746, marr
1727, at Indep. Great Meeting, | 15 July 1746,
Friars Street, Sudbury, | at the Mayfair
named in uncle's will, 1738/9, | Chapel, Hyde
to be apprenticed, executor | Park Corner,
of brother's will, 1776, paid | Middx, named
tax on male servants, 1780, | in husband's
will dd 5 May 1788, pr | will, executrix
22 Aug 1788 | 1788

other issue
2 sons
3 daughters

MARGARET
bp 22 Aug 1751, at
St Gregory,
Sudbury, named in
father's will, 1788

MARY
bp 3 Feb 1748/9, at
All Saints, Sudbury,
named in father's
will, 1788, then
marr to — FISCHER

JOHN GAINSBOROUGH = SUSANNAH
of Sudbury, clothier, 1789, | named in
bn 16 Oct, bp 1 Dec 1752, | husband's will,
at Indep. Great Meeting, | 1789,
Friars Street, Sudbury, | executrix 1791
named in father's will,
1771 (executor 1773) to
have land in Sudbury,
farms at Falkenham and
Trimley, cwn will dd
10 Aug 1789, codicil dd
1 Jan 1790, pr
17 Nov 1791

MARY
bn 10 Oct
1755

ELIZABETH
bn 22 Aug, bp
29 Sept 1758,
at Indep. Great
Meeting,
Friars Street,
Sudbury,
named in
father's will,
1771, to have
an estate at
Panfield, Essex

ANNE
bn 26 Feb 1766,
bp 12 Nov 1786,
at Indep. Great
Meeting, Friars
Street, Sudbury,
aged 3 (sic)

GAINSBOROUGH DUPONT
apprenticed to his uncle
14 Jan 1772, named in
uncle's will, 1788

THOMAS GAINSBOROUGH
bn 7 May 1784, named in father's
will, 1789, to have a house in
Sudbury at 21

JOHN GAINSBOROUGH
named in father's will, 1789,
as under 21, to have his
father's house in Sudbury

MARIA
bn 14 Nov 1782, bp — 1783, at Indep.
Great Meeting, Friars Street,
Sudbury, named in father's will, 1789

EMILY
bn 26 July 1786,
named in father's
will, 1789

The details in italics refer to sources held outside the Public Record Office

heretofore made I do publish and declare this alone to be and contain my last Will and Testament In Witness whereof I the said Thomas Gainsborough have to this my will contained in four Sheets of Paper set my Hand to each of the first three Sheets and my hand and Seal to this last Sheet this fifth day of May in the year of our Lord one Thousand Seven Hundred and Eighty Eight and in the Twenty Eighth year of the Reign of our Sovereign Lord George the Third by the Grace of God of Great Britain France and Ireland King Defender of the faith and so forth –

Signed Sealed Published and Declared by the said Thomas Gainsborough the Testator as and for his last Will and Testament in the Presence of us who in his Presence and at his Request and in the Presence of each other have hereunto subscribed our names as witnesses thereto

Tho Gainsborough

Jo. Allen Junr

Richd. Holden

22 Aug: 1788.

Margaret Gainsborough Widow the Relict of the deceased and the Sole Executrix named in the within written Will was duly Sworn as such.

G & N. Gotling.

Before me Geo. Harris. Surrogate.

The Testator Thomas Gainsborough Esqre was late of the Parish of Saint James Westminster in the County of Middlesex deceased and died this Month./-

Among the personal goods at his house left to his son John was a chariot. Between the years ending 5 July 1757 and 5 July 1761, he was paying £4 a year in duty on this, and £1 a year for the years ending 5 April 1764 until 5 April 1766.[28] Previously he had owned a four-wheeled chaise, attracting £4 in annual duty for the three years up to 5 April 1756.[29] John Gainsborough was also paying duty of £1 a year for silver plate weighing 400 oz in each of the years ending 5 July 1756 until 1762, and again from 1764 until 1766.[30]

John Gainsborough made his will eighteen years after his father, on 10 August 1789.[31] He was also a clothier living in Sudbury. One of the four executors appointed in the will was Rev. John Mead Ray, minister of the Old Meeting, and who was still there at the time of his death in January 1837, according to the preface of the baptism registers.[32] John

The signed latter part of the original will of Thomas Gainsborough, of Pall Mall, parish of St James's, in the Liberty of Westminster, Middlesex, dated 5 May 1788. It was proved in the Prerogative Court of Canterbury on 22 August the same year, and the month of his death. PROB1/20

Gainsborough had set aside a piece of ground for burials at the Old Meeting and he made provision for the annual interest of £4–6s–2d on a principal sum of £143–14s left by his uncle Thomas Gainsborough of London to be regularly paid to the Treasurer of the Old Meeting as he himself had done every year on 1 February, but the capital was to remain in his family. So the family's strong connection with the Meeting was maintained for at least eighty years and over a period of three generations.

What follows is the cautionary tale of the decline and fall of an Oxfordshire baronet's family, starting with its misplaced support of Charles I against Parliament during the Civil War for which it paid a heavy financial price, and ending in the Court of Chancery as a century's squabbling and bad estate management came to litigation. The records chiefly belong to the State Paper Office in relation to the Stuart and Commonwealth period, and the Court of Chancery for the Hanoverian.

Sir John Walter, of Sarsden, Knight, Lord Chief Baron of the Exchequer, made his will on 11 December 1626.[1] He was seised (possessed) in fee simple of the Oxfordshire manors of Sarsden and Lyneham, which during the lifetime of his first wife he had conveyed to feoffees to hold to the use of himself and his heirs, to enable him to dispose of them. The Statute of Wills 1540 allowed him to devise up to two thirds of his land to whomsoever he wished; the other third was destined under feudal law for his eldest son, William Walter, as heir, so that the Crown could exact a relief on the death of Sir John as a tenant in chief. Sir John chose to leave the two thirds to William and the heirs male of his body, thus creating a fee tail. If William were to die without male issue provision was made for the land to devolve to his son David and his heirs in remainder, in default of which, jointly to Sir John's daughters Mary, Elizabeth and Margaret and their heirs forever in fee simple.

Elizabeth and Margaret were each given £2,500 as marriage portions (increased by £500 in a codicil of 25 November 1629), payable on the day of marriage or at eighteen, whichever came sooner. In the meantime £80 apiece was to be applied annually for their maintenance, paid out at Christmas, Lady Day (25 March), Midsummer and Michaelmas (29 September) by his wife Anne as his executrix. He had previously assured certain unnamed lands to the use of his son David, from which his wife was to extract the profits until he reached twenty-one and use them

for his schooling and learning in the best and most profitable manner. He went on '. . . And I would have my sonne to undertake the profession of the lawe or some other honest profession to the glory of god and good of his Countrie and not live idlely or vainely'. Any balance was to be paid out when he was twenty-one or used to purchase land for him. To help him in his studies, David was given his father's books, notebooks and papers in the Temple and elsewhere, except at Sarsden. The furniture there, household implements, white plate and books were reserved for the eldest son.

Sir John confirmed gifts already made by him for the perpetual support of a preacher at Churchill, the income of the parson of Sarsden and for the maintenance of five Fellows and scholars in Jesus College, Oxford. He left moneys to relieve the poor of seven specific parishes, including one in London, bequests of £3 each to his male servants and 40s each to the females, payable on the day after his funeral, and he hoped that there might be 'a convenient monument over my buriall place expressing the person of myself and my two wives and children' though the burial itself was left to the discretion of his executrix. The legacies were to be raised from his personal estate and if this proved insufficient, then from the leases he held on lands in Churchill, Cutslow and Bruern, except those which formed part of his wife's jointure (widow's pension). The leases themselves were to go to whomever held the manors of the same name by his gift or as his heir. Three years later, on 25 November 1629, he modified his will, by adding the first of three codicils: the Principal and Fellows of Jesus College, Oxford, were left £2,000 payable within a year of his demise, but this was reduced to £1,000 on 16 November 1630, as 'on better perusal of my estate I find it will not bear so great a legacy'. He had lent his 'cousin' Bell £2,000 using copyhold lands in Wimbleton as security. If the debt remained unpaid at Sir John's death the bond was to pass to his executrix. By 17 November 1630,

Pedigree of the Walter Family of Sarsden, Oxfordshire

EDMUND WALTER = **MARY**

of Ludlow, Shropshire, sometime Chief Justice of South Wales, and Member of the Council in the Welsh Marches, died and bur 1592, at Ludlow

daughter of THOMAS HACKLUIT, of Eyton, Herefordshire

MARGARET = *daughter of WILLIAM OFFLEY, of London, Middx*

Sir JOHN WALTER Kt = **ANNE** *daughter of WILLIAM WYTHAM, of Ledstone, Yorks, named in husband's will, 1626, executrix 1630, dsp by him*

2nd son, of Sarsden, Oxon, *bn 1590, at Ludlow*, held the manors of Sarsden, Lyneham Merriscourt, Lyneham Finescourt, Churchill, and Kingham, the reversion of Bruern Mill, the dissolved monastery of Godstow, Isle of Godstow, the manors of Wolvercote and Cutslow, advowsons of Sarsden and Churchill, Oxon, lands at Ludlow, Stanton Lacy, Moor Overton and Batchcote, all in Shropshire, and Heyop, Llangynllo, Beguildy, in Radnor, Lucton, Ludford, Richards Castle and Elton, Herefordshire, *knighted at Greenwich, 18 May 1619, Chief Baron of the Exchequer 10 May 1625*, by deed dd 29 Sept 1626, set up salaries for priest at Sarsden and lectureship at Churchill, died 18 Nov 1630, will dd 11 Dec 1626, codicils dd 25 Nov 1629, 16 Nov 1630, pr 19 Nov 1630, I.P.M. 13 Aug 1633

MARY named in father's will, 1626

ELIZABETH named in father's will, 1626, under 18

MARGARET named in father's will, 1626, under 18

Sir WILLIAM WALTER Bt = **ELIZABETH** *daughter of THOMAS LUCAS, of St John's, near Colchester, Essex*, granted Admon of husband's goods, 1675

of Sarsden, bn c. 1605, aged 25 and more, Nov 1630, named in father's will, 1626, held entailed estate in manors of Sarsden, Churchill, Lyneham Merriscourt, Kingham, Bruern and Chilson, Oxon, cr Baronet by Letters Patent dd 16 Aug 1641, compounded for his estates, 28 Nov 1645, fined 9 July 1646 and 3 Dec 1650 for supporting King Charles I, Admon granted 24 Nov 1675

DAVID WALTER of Godstow, 1646, bn 6 Oct 1611, aged 21 on 6 Oct 1632, assured of lands in Shropshire, Radnor and Herefordshire by his father, 20 Sept 1626, named in father's will, 1626, petitioned Committee for Compounding, 6 Aug 1646, fined 19 Dec 1646, and 11 Dec 1650, for supporting King Charles I

ANNE 2nd daughter, named in settlement 30 and 31 Aug 1670

(Lady) MARY = daughter of Rt Hon. JOHN (TUFTON), Earl of Thanet by MARGARET, marr settlement dd 30 and 31 Aug 1670

Sir WILLIAM WALTER Bt of Sarsden, succeeded his father to the title, 1675, barred the entail on the Lyneham manors by Fine dd 10 Nov 1680, will dd 5 May 1692, pr 14 Feb 1697/8

(Lady) MARY = *daughter of ROBERT (BRUCE), Earl of Elgin and Earl of Ailesbury*, marr settlement dd 22 Mch 1677/8

THOMAS WALTER youngest son, named in settlement, 30 and 31 Aug 1670

MARY named in father's will, 1692, marr by 23 June 1698, co-defendant in Chancery suit, 19 July 1722, and another by 22 June 1748

= **Sir ROBERT RICH Bt** of Sonning, Berks, co-defendant in Chancery suit, 19 July 1722

WILLIAM WALTER died aged c. 12 months

Sir JOHN WALTER Bt of Sarsden, succeeded his father to the title, 1693/4, suffered a common recovery of the manors of Lyneham, Trinity Term 1695, seised in fee simple of the manors of Sarsden, Churchill, and Kingham, and other lands there and at Bruern, 1718, named in father's will, executor 1697/8, died 11 June 1722, sp, will dd 30 Oct 1718, pr 9 Mch 1722/3

ELIZABETH named in husband's will, 1718, to have his lands for life or her widowhood, joint plaintiff in Chancery suit, 9 July 1722, party to deed of lease and release, 10 and 11 Sept 1722, settlement 18 Jan 1723/4, marr 2nd c. Sept 1724, *died 12 July 1748*

= **SIMON (HARCOURT)** *Viscount Harcourt*, named in will of Sir JOHN WALTER, 1718

Sir ROBERT WALTER Bt of Sarsden, succeeded his half-brother to the title, 1722, named in brother's will, 1718, to have lands after the widow's death or remarriage, joint plaintiff in Chancery suit, 9 July 1722, grantee of lands in Lyneham by deeds 10 and 11 Sept 1722, party to settlement 18 Jan 1723/4, died sp 16 Nov 1731, will dd 7 Oct 1731, codicil dd 16 Nov 1731, pr 16 Dec 1731 and 22 June 1748

(Hon.) ELIZABETH LOUISA = daughter of Hon. HENRY BRYDGES, D.D., marr settlement dd 19 and 20 Dec 1729, named in husband's will, executrix, 1731, to have his manors for life, marr 2nd c. June 1740, and died c. 18 Aug 1740

= **BARNEVAL**

JOHN ROLLE of Stephenson, Glos, named in brother-in-law's will, 1731, deceased

= **ISABELLA CHARLOTTE** named in father's will, 1692, under 18, named in brother's will, 1731

at least 2 sons alive 1731

other issue 1 son 4 daughters

The details in italics refer to sources held outside the Public Record Office

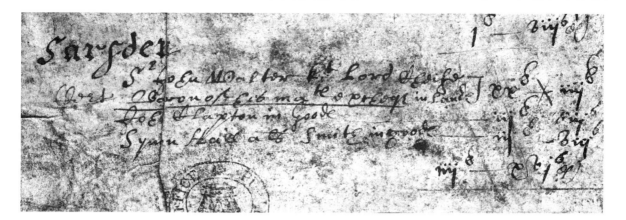

The Lay Subsidy assessment of Sarsden, hundred of Chadlington, Oxfordshire, 3 Charles I (1627). Sir John Walter, Knight, Lord Chief Baron of the Exchequer is liable to pay four shillings on land there worth 20s a year. In the margin is a note that a certificate of residence had been issued to him to avoid any double liability in other places. E179/164/467

the date of the final codicil, he was in possession of the lands and his wife was assigned them 'to the intent that she should deale lovingly and courteously with my cosen Bell'. Shortly afterwards he died, for on 19 November 1630 his will was proved in the Prerogative Court of Canterbury on the oath of his widow, Dame Anne Walter.

The King's Escheator for the county held an inquisition post mortem in the City of Oxford on 13 August 1633, on a brief of mandamus issued from the Court of Chancery.[2] Aided by information supplied by the fifteen sworn local jurors he was to determine what lands Sir John had held in Oxfordshire directly from the Crown on the day of his death, who was his next heir, the relationship between them, and whether the heir was twenty-one. The jurors deposed that Sir John was seised in his demesne of the manors of Sarsden, Churchill and Lyneham, and held the site of the dissolved monastery of Godstow and the Island of the same name. He had a reversionary interest in lands once belonging to the dissolved monastery of Bruern on the death of Lady Anne Cope, a widow; he was seised of divers lands in Shropshire, Radnor and Herefordshire, assured to his second son, David, by a deed of feoffment of 20 September and a deed of bargain and sale of 20 October 1626. The Godstow estate and the manors of Wolvercote and Cutslow had come to him under

a marriage settlement of 30 October 1622 with his present wife Anne. He died on 18 November 1630 without any living issue by her, and his son and next heir was William Walter, Armiger, then aged twenty-five and upwards. The second son attained twenty-one on 6 October 1632.

Thus the inquisition post mortem amplifies the will's allusions to Anne's jointure and the assurance allotted to David.

We can learn more about Sir John from published work. *The Knights of England*, ed. W.A. Shaw, 1906, records that he was knighted at Greenwich on 18 May 1619. Soon after his accession in 1603, King James I had issued orders requiring sheriffs and borough officers to summon all those possessed of £40 a year to receive the dignity of knighthood (and its attendant obligations). After 1616 and up to 1827 it was extended to include male heirs born to baronets, who were required to become knights at twenty-one, and a register of the new Knights Bachelor was instituted at the College of Arms in 1622. *The Dictionary of National Biography* ascribed his birthplace as Ludlow in Shropshire and his mother as a native of Herefordshire; presumably his parents were the source of his landholdings in those counties. His father, Edmund Walter, was Treasurer of the Inner Temple from 1581 until 1583, and was later a member of the Council of the Welsh Marches. Sir John was his second son, and followed his father to the Inner Temple to study law. He established a large practice in the Courts of Exchequer and Chancery, and in 1613 was made Attorney General to the Prince of Wales and Trustee of his revenues. On 10 May 1625 he was created Chief Baron of the Exchequer.

By 1609 he was installed at Sarsden, for the Lay Subsidy of that year assessed him as liable to pay *32s* on land there worth £12, at *2s 8d* in the pound.[3] In 1623 he was given a certificate of residence as proof

The certificate of residence of Sir John Walter, Knight, at Sarsden, hundred of Chadlington, Oxfordshire, recording his payment of £4 on £20 worth of annual landed income, as part of the third subsidy, 21 James I (1623). It was issued by the two Commissioners for the county and gives the name of the High Collector of the hundred. E115/409/62

that £4 had been exacted from him on land at Sarsden worth £20 (at the rate of 4s in the pound), to avoid any further tax elsewhere.[4]

Two later enrolments on the Close Rolls, in Trinity[5] and Michaelmas Terms 1649,[6] show that Sir John set up a trust on 29 September 1626 for the appointment of a lecturer at Churchill 'for the preaching of the word of God' and for the advowson, right of patronage and power of presentment to the Church of Sarsden to be vested in three trustees. The trustees were to be replaced when one survivor remained, so that the trust continued forever. The money to pay the two annual salaries of £50 was to come out of the profits on his land at Shipton-under-Wychwood and at Lyneham Merriscourt, in Oxfordshire. When a vacancy arose for the lecturer, through death, removal or other departure, the successor was to be freely chosen from among the best scholars of the University of Oxford, without any outside pressure or interference. Any vacancy at Sarsden was to be filled by the lecturer at Churchill. The enrolments were of the Indenture of 6 July 1649 conveying the rights and powers to the new trustees, including Sir William Walter, eldest son of Sir John, and of the

deed of bargain and sale effected on 18 December 1649, whereby the land was transferred to them to the use of themselves and their heirs subject to the Trust. Subsequent enrolments record similar indentures, each reciting the previous changes of trustees and the descent of the current Walter trustee from the grantor of 1626.[7] The succession of incumbents and the names of the patrons can be traced for the diocese of Oxford in the indexes known as the Institution Books, running from 1558 to 1838.[8]

The gift to Jesus College, Oxford, is referred to in *Founders' Kin, Privilege and Pedigree*, by G.D. Squibb, 1972. Apparently the Principal and Fellows declared that preference should be given to Sir John's kindred in the hope 'that posterity will be as well dispos'd and as mindfull to do the like'.[9]

David Walter, the second son of Sir John, was destined for the law. Unlike his father, he did not become a student at the Inner Temple, but was admitted to Lincolns Inn on 28 October 1630, when he was nineteen, a month before his father's death.[10] Of his later life it is known that he had four judgments of outlawry brought against him in 1641 and 1648, when lands were seized to pay debts.[11] He was involved with his elder brother in raising money for the King's cause against Parliament;[12] by 1663 he was one of the Grooms of His Majesty's Bedchamber and with his brother served as one of 57 Commissioners for Oxfordshire nominated in the 'Act for granting four intire Subsidies to His Majestie by the Temporaltie'.[13]

William, the eldest son, was created a baronet by letters patent dated 16 August 1641, for himself and the heirs male of his body.[14] Sir William Walter's support for his monarch had grave financial repercussions. Taking advantage of Parliament's offer in August 1644 to take only a portion of the estates of those 'delinquents' willing to confess and voluntarily compound, and so preserve the rest of their property, in a petition of 28 November 1645[15] he admitted helping the King, but claimed it was because of his obligation as his sworn servant. As the whole of his estate in Oxfordshire lay in the King's quarters, he was forced to help him in 'this unnatural war' with Parliament. For two years he had refused all other employments on the King's behalf, and was utterly against his actions. He deeply regretted what he had done and submitted himself to the justice of the Committee (for Compounding with Delinquents). His estate, he reckoned, was worth £800 a year, £100 of which went in payments to the Church (to the lecturer of Churchill and the parson of Sarsden); he had also incurred debts before the troubles, and had

Part of the enrolled indenture of 18 December 1649, by which John Lloyd bargained and sold land in the parish of Shipton-under-Wychwood, Oxfordshire, and elsewhere to Thomas Gate, Sir William Walter, Baronet, and William Littleton, subject to the trusts and uses set up by Sir John Walter, Knight, by an indenture on 29 September 1626. Lloyd had been granted the lands himself by Gate on 6 July 1649 on condition that he immediately sold them to the above parties. Gate was the only surviving trustee of the original grant and this was a device to ensure the trust's continuation. The trust provided a salary for the parson of Sarsden and lecturer at Churchill in Oxfordshire. C54/3485 m38, no 2

charge of six small children. His income from his estate was now less than a quarter of what it once was, and he hoped that this would be taken into consideration. The five local Commissioners at Woodstock were not impressed, for on 8 June 1646 they reported to the Committee at Goldsmiths' Hall in London that £800 was an undervaluation, as Sir William was generally reputed to be worth £1,200 a year at least;[16] investigations revealed that he had recently sold lands in Leicestershire, Wales and elsewhere to reduce his annual income, and 'his delinquency is for opposing the petition for reformaçon and promoting one to the Contrary, for takeinge upp armes for the King, one of the first in this County of Oxon, and puttinge in execution the Commission of Array, and continuing with him most part of these Warrs, theis are the delinquencys for wch the said Sr Wm Walter stands sequestrerd'. So by then his land and its rents had passed into the custody of the Committee.

On 7 July 1646 Sir William gave his reply.[17] As the King's man he went and remained in the City of Oxford for some time and was there obliged to obey the commands of the King and his Party. By June 1645 he wished to make his peace with Parliament. To this end he had obtained a pass for his servant to go to London and present a petition that he might compound. The Committee declined to proceed, suspecting that because he was in the King's quarter he might refuse to perform any order. In July another attempt was made, this time by his solicitor in an appeal to the Committee of the Lords and Commons for Irish Affairs. A contract was drawn up granting him a pardon, but before it could be signed the House of Commons issued an order that no compositions for delinquency could be made by any other Committee than the one based at Goldsmiths' Hall. In November Sir William finally had his petition accepted and he appeared in person before the Committee on 4 April 1646. As required, he took the Negative Oath on 9 May, and the National Covenant on 29 June. He supplied detailed particulars of his lands, held by him as tenant in tail in possession (they were entailed in his father's will). The manor of Sarsden, with various customary rents belonging to it, was valued at £286 a year before the troubles; there were also twelve guineas' worth of customary rents for which his tenants paid a fine of three years' current rent at each change of tenancy; the manor of Churchill and its customary rents were valued at £216 a year, and Lyneham at £141–6s–8d. His goods and chattels, household stuff and implements he estimated as worth £150, but the Committee at Banbury had appraised them at £173 and sold them, contravening an order made by the Committee at Goldsmiths' Hall. An inventory of these was furnished on 2 May 1646.[18] There were twenty-five rooms in all in the mansion house at Sarsden, and the layout, nomenclature and list of their contents offer a fascinating

An inventory of the goods and chattels of Sir William Walter in and about his house at Sarsden in Oxfordshire, made on 2 May 1646 and produced to the Commissioners for Compounding with Delinquents, so that the 10% fine could be assessed for his support of Charles I. The sale value was given as £150. Altogether the contents of 25 rooms were listed, affording a marvellous glimpse of how a seventeenth-century mansion was furnished. SP23/183 p49

glimpse of life in a country house in Stuart England. There was the bigger parlour, the lesser parlour, the dining room above the hall, the bedchamber adjacent to it, two balcony chambers, a nursery, a kitchen, washhouse and brewhouse, three chambers for the maids, a turret chamber and a gatehouse. To heat them all were at least eight fireplaces with their accoutrements, and a goodly number of various types of sleeping amenity, ranging from the feather bed and old velvet tester in the bedchamber next to the dining room, to the four flock beds for the meaner servants in the three low rooms, and the truckle bed in the turret chamber. Outside there were seven milch beasts, two young heifers, six rearing pigs and a breeding sow, plus a goodly number of horses including '5 colts running in ye grounds' and two mares for the saddle. Later he submitted a catalogue of goods left unclaimed at Oxford, then under siege.[19] These included 'three peeces of hangings of fflorist imagery' and six wall pictures, of total value £30. A further particular outlined his debts. He himself was owed £2,220, but unfortunately he had run up fifteen debts of his own to the tune of £4,160: there was an annuity of £80 already four years in arrears; there was a mortgage of £1,000 for 40 years, set up on 1 June 1631, on lands in Churchill, redeemable on payment of £1,000 on 1 June 1632, and of the yearly value of £120. The mortgagee had taken on a double-edged sword, for he feared to collect the rents because of the troubles and the King's Garrisons; there was a loan of £1,500 with interest added, with a penalty of £3,000 for non-payment set out in a bond; there was an outlawry against him in the sum of £200: a writ of error had been brought, but not certified in the Court of King's Bench, so the judgment still stood, and interest on this bond for four years amounted to £64, or 8 percent a year. No wonder he wrote plaintively 'I am worse at this present in my estate by reason of this Warr; since these troubles began; at ye least five thousand pounds'. He was shortly even worse off, for on 7 July 1646 the Committee fined him £1,430 as his composition, based on a tenth of the value of his estate. This was paid on 11 August.[20] On 20 November 1650, a further fine of £177 was served on him for adjusted valuations,[21] besides which a tenth of his rents were paid to the Commonwealth for the year ended Michaelmas 1648.[22]

As if this was not a big enough blow, there soon came another. This time it was in connection with loans made to the King for which Sir William and his brother David had offered security. On 25 November 1651, the Commissioners for Advance of Money, sitting in Haberdashers' Hall, London, recorded that Sir William and Mathias Valentine had disclosed certain letters patent granted to them by the King on 4 July 1643, in which the New Forest and other Royal Chases and Parks were assured to them in return for acting as sureties in sums totalling £10,045–14s–5d they had secured to enable him to conduct the war.[23] With interest added, Sir William's share came to £2,574–2s–8d. He alleged that £705 had already been satisfied by the payment of £400 to those persons to whom he stood bound. Having now supplied a list of all the lenders' names so that the money could be claimed for the Treasury, he was respited from paying the balance and protected from any legal action by the other lenders until the rest of his share was got into the use of the State. The two men were to have a fifth of the money brought in, as a reward. But then Elizabeth, wife of Humfrey Taylor, gentleman, swore an affidavit before the Commissioners on 31 December 1651.[24] She alleged that £500 lent by her brother-in-law, Walter Dunch, about February 1642, at Sir William's behest, on a bond of £1,000 conditioned for payment of £540, was actually held by Dunch on trust for her. Dunch was now dead and Elizabeth wished to recover the debt. She said that he had been coerced into the loan, having at first refused. He lived at Newington, between the King's Garrisons at Oxford and Wallingford and had been seized by a party of dragoons and imprisoned in Wallingford Castle, and his goods and cattle impounded, and the latter starved. The grief had partly contributed to his death.[25]

On 28 January 1651/2 the Commissioners ordered Sir William to appear before them with the petitioner to answer the charges.[26] An affidavit was produced from James Hall, of New Inn, Middlesex, gentleman.[27] He affirmed that about Easter Term 1648, he was retained by Elizabeth Taylor's husband and instructed to sue Sir William and David Walter to the outlawry. He caused a writ of extent to be issued to the Sheriff of Oxfordshire for a valuation to be made of their lands, which amounted to £900 a year or more. The Sheriff had several writs of *levari facias* (execution) to seize the rents and profits from the land to satisfy the debt, but he had failed to make returns. In due course the Sheriff was committed for contempt, whereupon he produced a return that £200 had been collected. Sir William promised Hall that he would pay c. £250 to Elizabeth 'for that he the said Sr Willm and his brother David might be discharged of this bond'.

Sir William made answer on 20 February.[28] He averred that he had never at any time borrowed any money from Dunch, or acted as a surety for its repayment. When the King's Garrison was at Oxford he was summoned to attend the King as his sworn servant and as one of the Committee of Oxford. He was received in the King's Privy Chamber at Christ Church College and told that some people in the county intended to lend money, but expected a bond in return. Sir William, his brother David, and Sir Thomas Chamberlain were asked to be sureties. Sir William went to the lodgings of Sir Edward Hyde at All Souls, Oxford, where the bond was sealed. It was for repayment of £500 to Dunch, on penalty of £1,000. Sir William never received any money himself from Dunch. About five years later, Dunch took the bond in his own name for his own use, and died childless and apparently intestate, leaving a personal estate of £6,000 and real estate worth £600 a year. The Commissioners ruled that because there was some difficulty in the case it should be referred, with the consent of both parties, to Mr Brereton for the case to be stated and a report placed before Parliament for its judgment.[29] Either party could place an objection to the report. In the meantime no further proceedings were to be instituted. Parliament issued an Act of Pardon, whereby the £540 was discharged from sequestration.[30] On 14 April 1652 Elizabeth

The Hearth Tax return for Sarsden, hundred of Chadlington, Oxfordshire, 17 Charles II (1665), including the name of Sir William Walter, Baronet, who was to be charged on 24 hearths. Three of the householders were discharged from payment by reason of poverty, and they were probably his tenants, as he was also lord of the manor of Sarsden. E179/164/513 m51r

and her husband claimed their expenses of £80, over the four years spent in pursuit of the matter. They alleged that the just debt formed the greatest part of their estate, which they relied on for their livelihood; they now hoped to receive the benefit of the law for its recovery.

G.E.C.'s *Complete Baronetage, 1611–1800*, 1902, tells us Sir William Walter later served as Sheriff for Oxfordshire for the year 1656–7. At Michaelmas 1662 he was paying tax of £1–4s, being the first of two instalments of the 2s levy on every firehearth and stove in his house at Sarsden.[31] Three years later he was again assessed on his twenty-four hearths, so he seems to have recovered from his earlier vicissitude.[32] In 1675 he died and was succeeded by his son William.

By an indenture of 10 November 1680, Sir William Walter, as tenant in tail in possession, covenanted with John Crispe and William Crispe to levy a fine before the end of the following Hilary Term, in order to bar (destroy) the entail on the manors of Lyneham and Finescourt.[33] The Crispes were the querients (purchasers) in the fine, and Sir William the deforciant (vendor). The fine was enrolled by the chirographer in the Court of Common Pleas in Michaelmas Term 1680, and in return for consideration of £70 paid to him by the Crispes they were given possession of the land for life and for the heirs of John Crispe forever.[34] The indenture recorded that this fine and any others entered by Sir William should be for the use of him and his heirs forever and for no other purpose, but this is not stated in the fine itself. In effect the Crispes were created temporary trustees and the estate was enlarged to a base fee. Under this, his own male line was ruled out of the remainder, and once his male descendants all died his uncle David Walter's heirs became entitled following the will of their grandfather, Sir John Walter. In the meantime he could convey the land to whomsoever he pleased but only for the duration of his own male line. The fine was proclaimed in four consecutive Legal Terms.

In Trinity Term 1695, his son and heir, Sir John Walter, levied a similar fine with two other gentlemen.[35] On 29 June 1695 he was party to an indenture with these two whereby he bargained and sold them the Lyneham and Finescourt estate, so that he could bring a writ of entry against them as tenants,[36] and suffer a common recovery of the land thus converting the base fee into a fee simple and putting an end to the entail.[37]

By the time Sir John made his will on 30 October 1718, all his estates were held in fee simple.[38] They were devised to his wife Elizabeth for life or widowhood, if they had no issue, and then to his half-brother, Robert Walter and his heirs forever. In this way he provided for his next of kin at the expense of his heir at law. Elizabeth was given the power of granting leases for up to twenty years at the best rent, but without fine, with a power of re-entry for non-payment. Thus she held a life estate (as tenant for life) determinable on remarriage or death, and Robert Walter was the remainderman, as he had a right to future enjoyment of the land. Robert was allocated all the silver plate and household furniture at Sarsden after her remarriage or death, but the furniture in her bedchamber, the jewels, and pictures including a portrait of Sir John and herself by Sir Godfrey Kneller, were reserved for her personally. All his debts, and legacies of £1,100, were to come out of the residue of his personal estate, and if this proved insufficient, then from his lands. Robert was entrusted with the silver fountain inscribed to Queen Anne, to leave it to whoever was given the dwelling house at Sarsden so that it 'may be therein perpetually preserved in remembrance of my Duty and gratitude to her sd late Majestye'. G.E.C. informs us that he was a Clerk of the Green Cloth, the counting house of the Royal Household.[39]

Sir John died on or about 11 June 1722, without any issue. Not long afterwards, the validity of the will was challenged.[40] On 9 July Dame Elizabeth Walter, the widow of Sir John, the only son and heir of Sir William Walter by his first wife, Lady Mary Tufton, combined with Sir Robert Walter, eldest son of Sir William by his second wife, Lady Mary Bruce, in bringing an action in the Court of Chancery against Sir Robert Rich, of Sonning in Berkshire, Baronet, and his wife Dame Mary, the only daughter of Sir William's first marriage, full sister and heir at law of Sir John, and not named in his will.

As his heir she would have inherited his fee simple lands if he had died without making a will, or the will proved invalid; she and her husband had apparently spread rumours that they doubted there had been a will, that it was not properly executed (signed by him and attested by three credible witnesses), that he was not of sound and disposing mind and memory, to the detriment of the complainants. The complainants asked that a writ of subpoena be issued to the Richs to appear and prove their allegations and to abide by any order that the Court might make. The defendants' answer was to refer themselves to such proofs that the complainants might produce that the will was valid. Dame Mary Rich doubted that Sir John was actually able to dispose of the lands as they were his under settlement only, and as such she was next entitled to them as his heir at law. They ended by requesting that the suit be dismissed and their costs and charges 'most wrongfully sustained' be awarded them. The three witnesses of the will's signature supplied written depositions at Dame Elizabeth Walter's mansion house at Sarsden on 11 January 1722/3, in answer to the Interrogatories put to them on the complainants' behalf by four Commissioners appointed by the Court. Their names, abodes, status, ages and length of acquaintanceship with Sir John were noted, together with their accounts of how the will was executed. The dénouement was not long in coming, for the will was proved in the Court of Chancery, and in the Prerogative Court of Canterbury on 9 March 1722/3, on the oaths of the two executors.

One of the Commissioners, Nathaniel Sturges, a clerk in Holy Orders, was instituted to the living of

The institution of Nathaniel Sturges, MA, to the Rectory and parish church of Sarsden, in the deanery of Chipping Norton, diocese of Oxford, on 24 December 1720, on the death of the previous incumbent, George Vernon, and on the presentation of the two patrons, Sir John Walter, Baronet, and Robert Walter, Armiger. 'Comp' indicates that the salary was over £50 a year so would not attract Queen Anne's Bounty. E331/OXFORD/19 no 6

Sarsden on 24 December 1720 on the presentation of Sir John Walter and his half-brother Robert, as joint patrons, and thus claimed the annual income of £50 established by their great-grandfather in 1626.[41] There he remained until his death created a vacancy, filled on 25 November 1762 on the presentation of John Walter and Dennis Rolle, Esquires.[42]

Sir John died leaving considerable debts. The probate account lists what he still owed after his personal estate had been swallowed up in attempting to pay them, the funeral expenses and cost of proving his will (and presumably the legal costs for the suit brought against the Richs).[43] The debts amounted to £2,766–13s–7d, and with the funeral charges of £249–16s–8d, his liability was £3,016–10s–3d before payment of the three legacies totalling £1,100. His personal assets (less his books) were put at £1,057–11s–1d. Out of this the funeral bill was settled, but a balance of £1,958–19s–2d was outstanding. He

had, in March 1712/13, entered a bond in the penal sum of £2,000 conditioned for payment of £1,000 to his half-brother, Robert, only part of which had been reimbursed, and so £1,500[44] was added to the list. Altogether, Sir John was indebted in £4,558–19s–2d, which became chargeable on his manors and other lands.

In order to pay off these debts a tripartite agreement was made on 20 June 1722 between his widow as the tenant for life in possession, his half-brother as the remainderman, and Sir John's two executors as trustees of his estate, to vary the arrangement outlined in the will.[45] Under the agreement Sir Robert Walter offered to waive the bond of £1,500 and to make an allowance of £100 for books bequeathed to him by Sir John. He agreed to raise £3,088–19s–2d within four months to meet the debts and legacies and so save the estate intact and free from any encumbrance or mortgage. This having been achieved, an indenture of lease and release was drawn up on 10 and 11 September, with the same parties: Sir Robert was to have for life certain lands in Lyneham, currently out on six leases for lives and bringing in £204–6s–6d in annual rents, to offset the money he had raised. Another indenture, of 18 January 1723/4,[46] granted him the right to fell timber on these premises to make up any deficit and in satisfaction of any more of Sir John's debts which might be uncovered. He was now conveyed the rest of the Lyneham estate, of a total annual rental of £295–13s–6d, to enable him to live in a style more suited to his quality, subject to payment of the two salaries of £50 at Churchill and Sarsden established by his great-grandfather. He was advanced £1,000 by Sir John's widow to pay his own debts and the executor of one of Sir John's creditors. This advance was to be recovered, with 5 percent interest added, by means of Dame Elizabeth exercising her power during widowhood of granting leases for terms up to 99 years determinable on three lives, commencing in possession or at the end of existing former leases, at the best rents. Once the loan was recouped, the power ceased, but she could continue to create leases of not more than 21 years, without fine, at the best improved rent, and reserving a right of re-entry for non-payment, on any lands of which she was possessed. On her remarriage or death the power to grant both types of lease was to pass to her successor, Sir Robert Walter, or whoever else was entitled to the premises. If any of the £1,000 remained unpaid the trustees were to find it from the rents or by mortgaging the estate.

Provision was made for Dame Elizabeth in the event of her remarriage. An annual rent charge of

Diagram 4: The 1723/4 Settlement of the Walter Oxfordshire manors under two co-existing Trusts

Lady (ELIZABETH) WALTER Widow of Sir JOHN WALTER Bt, settlement dd 18 Jan 1723/4 creating two Trusts, reserving powers of leasing for 21 years, (and for 99 years determinable on 3 lives to recover the £1,000 advance and interest) for widowhood. → ABRAHAM BULLEY SAMUEL ROCK Trustees:–

Trust ends on death of grantor ← grantor if Sir ROBERT dies in her lifetime, and any wife sp.

a) 100-year Trust on land leased out at Sarsden and Lyneham to raise an annual income of £500 for Sir ROBERT WALTER and his heirs forever: advanced £1,000 to be repaid at 5% interest under 99 year leases by grantor, with power reserved to Trustees to settle any outstanding balance by rents or mortgage at her death or remarriage.

b) 200-year Trust of Oxfordshire manors for grantor's widowhood.
↓
Sir ROBERT WALTER and his heirs, paying £800 pa rentcharge for life to the grantor, with right of re-entry reserved to her for any arrears.

Trust ends on death of grantor ← grantor if Sir ROBERT dies in her lifetime, and any wife sp. £800 pa rentcharge then ends, and she takes all rents for as much of 200 years as she lives.

At the death of Sir ROBERT's childless widow in 1740 £110 of the annual rentcharge was in arrears, plus £1,500 in rent arrears from tenants on the estate charged with this £800 annuity. Sir ROBERT had also mortgaged part of these premises, leaving uncertainty about who was responsible for paying out the interest, while his widow had granted leases of 99 years on trust for herself and her executors, leaving little room for manoeuvre by the hapless grantor.

£800 for life was payable from the estate passing then to Sir Robert. Sir John's executors were appointed trustees of all the manors and lands subject to the above charges. After Sir Robert's demise the lands at Lyneham, already his for life, were to be held by them for a hundred years for the benefit of his heirs. If he were to die before Dame Elizabeth, and any wife and issue likewise, then the rents and profits from these estates were to be enjoyed by Dame Elizabeth and her assigns for her natural life, and at her death the hundred-year-term come to an end. The rest of the premises were to be held by the trustees for two hundred years for the benefit of Sir Robert's heirs. If she remarried and Sir Robert, his wife and issue predeceased her, the £800 annuity was to end and she was to have the premises in the 200-year-term for life, subject to any leases or mortgages, and any arrears of the rent charge and £1,000 advance were to come out of the rents in this term. The 200-year-term ceased at her death.

During his lifetime, if the rent charge was in arrears for twenty-one days, Dame Elizabeth had the right to distrain Sir Robert's goods until the debt was made good. If after thirty-one days it was still not fully satisfied she had the power of re-entry to the capital messuage at Sarsden and other lands, to exact the rents and profits until the debt was redeemed. Sir Robert covenanted to repay her or her assigns within six months of her remarriage or death any of the advance and rent charge unsatisfied.

To prevent any disputes between them, Sir Robert indemnified Dame Elizabeth against payment of the two salaries of £50. If she became re entitled to have possession of the estates on the death of Sir Robert's widow and any issue, then she was to have for her lifetime the use of the silver plate, household goods and furniture at Sarsden left her for her widowhood by her husband, except what Sir Robert should bequeath by will. He agreed to levy a fine in the Court of Common Pleas barring the entail on the Lyneham rents of £204–6s–6d before next Hilary Term, by conveying them to the trustees.

This strict settlement was prepared to meet almost every eventuality. So what actually happened? In September 1724 Dame Elizabeth Walter remarried,[47] to Simon, Lord Viscount Harcourt (left £1,000 in her previous husband's will). The premises passed to Sir Robert, and the rent charge of £800 payable out of their rents, came into operation. Sir Robert himself took a wife, soon after executing a marriage settlement on 19 and 20 December 1729, under which his bride, the Honourable Elizabeth Louisa Brydges, was to have a marriage portion of £6,000, and his lands

were conveyed to trustees.[48] He died without issue on 16 November 1731, seised in fee simple of all his lands, subject to the rent charge and the salaries. His will was made on 7 October 1731, by which time he was 'infirm in health'.[49] After requesting burial in Churchill church among his ancestors, he left a series of complicated instructions for the devolution of his estate, setting up another strict settlement. For the want of issue, Sir Robert's own wife, Elizabeth Louisa, was to have a life estate in his manors and other lands and tenements, with full power to grant leases for 99 years or lesser term, determinable on a maximum of three lives, on lands already let out by lease within the last twenty years, or by copy of the Court Roll during a similar period. All other lands could be leased by her for not more than twenty-one years, to commence in possession or within one year of the date of the lease, at the best improved rent, without fine, and with a right of re-entry for non-payment. The capital messuage at Sarsden and its outhouses, gardens and curtilage (courtyard) were not to be leased.

After her death the manors were to pass under a succession of life estates and entails. Firstly, such second son of his sister Isabella Charlotte and the late John Rolle, of Stephenson in Gloucestershire, as was alive at Sir Robert's death was to have the life estate (this was a contingent remainder). At the same time two trustees were to be appointed to preserve the contingent remainders under the fee tail which was to take effect on his death: the first, second, third and all other sons (as yet unborn) of the said second son of John Rolle and Isabella Charlotte and the heirs male of their bodies were to have the manors in succession, and in order of seniority and priority of birth. In default of any such issue, remainder over was to the third son of Sir Robert's sister and his male issue, then the fourth son and so on until all the male issue was extinct. When this happened further life estates and entails were to come into force, the last of which was for the lawful heirs of the body of Sir Robert's sister, and reversion to his own right heirs forever. A condition was that on taking possession of the manors, each person had to assume the surname of Walter in lieu of his own, and to adopt and use the arms of Walter for himself and his descendants, otherwise the estate was to pass to the next person in the line on similar conditions.

In theory, therefore, the will effectively tied up the descent of Sir Robert Walter's land for many generations and ensured the survival of his surname and coat of arms.

The tenants for life, in addition to receiving the

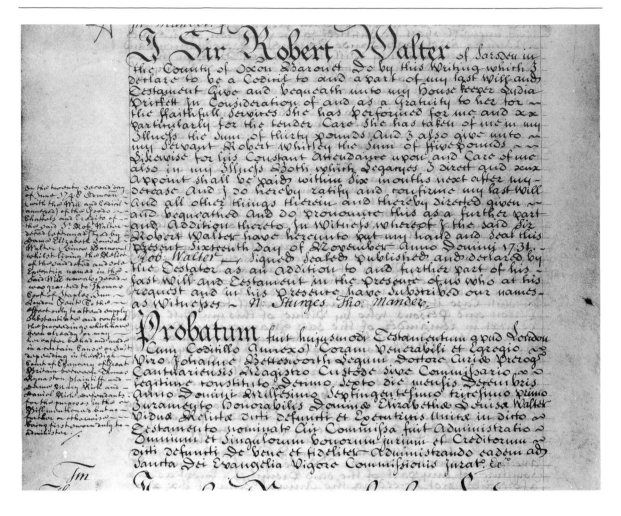

ABOVE *The codicil of 16 November 1731, attached to the will of Sir Robert Walter, Baronet, of Sarsden, Oxfordshire, and proved with it in the Prerogative Court of Canterbury on 16 December 1731, on the oath of his sole executrix, his widow Dame Elizabeth Louisa Walter. The Rector of Sarsden, N. Sturges, and his attorney, Thomas Mander, were the witnesses. A later grant of administration with will annexed was made on 22 June 1748 for the purposes of a case in the Court of Chancery in which Sir Robert's half-sister was involved as a defendant. PROB11/648 q318, f296d*

RIGHT *A page from the sale catalogue prepared in 1732 itemising the contents of the house and outbuildings at Sarsden, Oxfordshire, once the home of the Walter family. It shows what was in the greenhouse and lists the Berline Chariot and its trappings. The other examples of Chancery Master's exhibits, lodged about 1748, are a bill of £2–0s–9d for making a scarlet rug coat and velvet breeches for Sir Robert Walter in 1725, the amazing collection of shoes ordered by his wife between 1734 and 1737 accompanied by a plaintive request from H. Mountague for payment, and finally a letter sent by Lady Walter from London in 1735 to her Steward, John Peisley, asking for more money and a dozen pigeons a week to be sent to her. C110/136*

rents and profits, had power to lease any of the premises except the capital messuage for up to twenty-one years at the best improved rent, without fine, and to create a jointure not exceeding £600 a year for such woman or women as they should marry, by a written deed attested by two or more credible witnesses.

To his wife Sir Robert bequeathed his jewels and the furniture from their bedchamber, her closet and dressing room, plus his silver plate and household goods, except the silver fountain which was to go as an heirloom with the books there and elsewhere to whoever was entitled to the manor or mansion house of Sarsden.

[10]

The GREEN-HOUSE, Numb. LI.

Twenty bay Trees in Tubs; 30 Orange Trees in Tubs, 10 Orange Trees in Pots, 8 *Mecnemplanny*'s or Winter cherries, 29 Myrtles in Pots, 23 Orange Trees in Pots, 3 *Adam*'s Needles, 4 Ragworths in Pots, 2 Honey Trees, 1 currant Tree, 1 Hollander in a Tub, 1 Strawbery Tree, 6 Watering Pots, 25 blue and white Earthen Pots, 17 brown Earthen Pots, a Brass Pump, Water-Tub, 2 Casting Nets, Drag Net, 8 Forest Chairs, 2 Sieves, 8 Forms, Spanish Table, Earthen Pots, 34 Iron Hoops, 4 Tubs iron-hoop'd, Iron Dogg, 4 Scythes, 2 Pair of Sheers, Turfing Iron or Reel, 4 Hoes, Iron Bar, a Gun, 3 Wheel-barrows, Hand-barrow, 2 Rakes, 20 Lead Pots, 10 large Earthen Pots, 4 Stone Rolls and Frames, large Iron-cast Roll, Wood Roll, 2 Stone Jarrs, 3 blue and white Earthen Pots, Hair-brush, 2 large Settles.

Numb. LII.

Matted Bedstead, Feather-bed, Bolster and Pillow, brown Rug, 3 Blankets, 2 Chairs, Close-stool, Chest, Pewter Pot, Skillet, 2 Prongs, Chariot box.

Numb. LIII.

Corded Bedstead, Flock-bed and Bolster, 3 Blankets, Table and Lanthorn.

Numb. LIV.

Seven Collars, Corn Bins, 2 Buckets, a Sconce, Wheelbarrow, Shovel and 3 Prongs, a Berline Chariot lin'd with blue Cloth, Tar-barrel, and Tub-cloth to cover the Chariot, 2 Water-brushes.

Numb. LV.

Bedstead, Serge Furniture, Feather-bed, 2 Bolsters, 3 Blankets, Coverlid, Elbow Chair, Cane Chair, Wood Chair, Stool, Table, Pair of Doggs, Cupboard, 2 gilt Sconces, 13 Pair of Bowls, and 3 Jacks.

In the WARDROBE, Numb. LVI.

A large Quantity of Table-Linnen, Bed-Linnen, and all other Sorts of Linnen, with several large Boxes to keep Linnen in.

The

The will was proved in the Prerogative Court of Canterbury on 16 December 1731, on the oath of his widow, as sole executrix. A marginal note in the probate register records that on 22 June 1748 letters of administration with will annexed of the estate left unadministered by her at her death, were granted for the purposes of legal proceedings already begun in the Court of Chancery between Thomas Kynaston as plaintiff and Dame Mary Rich and Daniel Rich as defendants.[50]

Lady Walter died in August 1740, having taken a second husband a couple of months earlier, but administration of her goods was not granted until May 1746. Under the prevailing 1723/4 agreement, Lady Harcourt re-entered the premises. There were arrears of £1,500 in rents from the lands subject to her annuity, which itself had a shortfall of £110. At Lady Harcourt's direction, the surviving trustee mortgaged the premises to recover the rent charge arrears for her executors. Sir Robert had also mortgaged part of the estate, but Lady Harcourt paid none of the interest on this. In June 1733, his widow granted a series of leases for 99 years determinable on the lives of three of her Brydge siblings to a friend, Henry Perrot, to hold on trust for her, her executors, administrators and assigns until she should direct otherwise by deed, writing or will.[51] Henry Perrott was also one of the trustees under the settlement set up by her husband's will. She had already sold all the house contents at Sarsden, plus plants, shrubs and garden statuary, at an auction in June 1732.[52]

Lady Harcourt died in July 1748, whereupon John Rolle, now Walter, became tenant for life. He was left to sort out the financial exigencies of the estate. He initiated proceedings in the Court of Chancery against Thomas Mander, the family's attorney and estate steward, who had been responsible for drafting the leases and the collection of rents by the bailiff.[53] In May 1749 Counsel's opinion was sought on several matters:[54] although Lady Harcourt had been in possession of the mortgaged lands long enough to settle the rent charge arrears it was considered that the profits she received were for her own use by right under the 1723/4 agreement, and should not be used to pay any arrears owed to her by the failure of her predecessor, Lady Walter. Lady Walter's personal estate was responsible, unless the rents from the land had been insufficient to pay the annuity, in which case the plaintiff was to consult with her administrator. The mortgage entered by Sir Robert was deemed to be a debt on his own personal assets, and failing that, on his real estate. One of the leases granted by Lady Walter in 1733 actually exceeded the

powers given her under her husband's will, for the former lease, which it replaced, had been created in 1680, more than twenty years ago, but the rest of them were held to be binding on Mr Walter, even those on trust to Henry Perrot, which now presumably passed to her heirs at law, the Brydges, until the leases fell in.

The three boxes of exhibits,[55] lodged with the Masters in the Court of Chancery, contain a wealth of estate books of rents, leases and accounts, counterparts of indentures, and neatly tied and referenced bundles of correspondence, itemized bills, signed receipts for wages, services, goods and accommodation, and for collections of Land and Window Tax, poor and Church rates from the Walters and their tenants, plus the sale catalogue of the 56 lots from the house and its outbuildings for the 1732 auction. The material covers a period of more than thirty years from the 1720s. Thanks to these folded slivers of paper we can reconstruct a picture of the estate and how it was run 100 years after the Civil War. There were tradesmen's accounts, bills from local and metropolitan purveyors of groceries, spices, wines, shoes, dress fabrics, lace and house furnishings mixed up with fuel bills and charges for estate repairs and maintenance. The overriding impression is of a household in a muddle, living beyond its means and sliding inexorably towards financial catastrophe. It seems as if Sir Robert's widow aimed to deprive her successors of any enjoyment of the land by stripping the house of its contents and tying up the land in long leases for the benefit of her own kin, while the rest was allowed to deteriorate to grave need of repair. In this she seems to have had an ally (unwittingly or otherwise) in the attorney, who failed to collect or hand over rents, to the great detriment of the tenants, who were confronted with huge bills for arrears or the threat of eviction or legal action. For instance, the invalid lease, of land at Lyneham, was granted to Henry Perry in 1680 for 99 years determinable on three lives.[56] The last life ended in 1730, so Lady Walter granted a twelve-year lease of the same land to William Hasted at £75 annual rent for the first six years and £80 a year for the remainder.[57] In June 1733 she granted a 99-year lease determinable on three lives to Henry Perrot.[58] In August 1746 steps were taken to recover the rent arrears from William Hasted. The bailiff wrote to the attorney that Hasted was forced to sell off his animals and crops to pay them, after a valuation had been made of his goods.[59] The rent was apparently paid to the undersheriff on the direction of Thomas Mander, so legal action must have been taken to enforce the debt.[60] In November and December there was a string of urgent correspondence from Nathaniel Sturges to Mander, unsuccessfully trying to recover the money, so that he could pay some bills.[61] John Walter wrote to Mander asking whether he knew anything of the affair. He had learnt that the money had been handed over to Mander and deposited with his banker in London.[62] In March Walter ordered that £40 of the money be delivered to his aunt, Mrs Walter, in the Strand, and the balance forwarded to Rev. Sturges at Sarsden.[63] In August 1751 one of the estate trustees wrote to Mander ordering him to quit possession of the premises or face a writ of ejectment or other necessary legal proceedings.[64]

One box yielded an abstract of Sir Robert's title to the various manors, drawn up on 4 November 1729:[65] it began with a lease and release of 30 and 31 August 1670, by which his grandfather, Sir William Walter, granted them to trustees for the use of himself until the marriage of his eldest son and heir apparent, William Walter, with Lady Mary Tufton, daughter of the Right Honourable Margaret, Dowager Countess of Thanet. The bride was to have a portion of £5,000. After the marriage was consummated, his demesne at Churchill was to be retained by Sir William for life, out of which he was to pay £200 a year in rent to the couple for maintenance, with the power of distress for non-payment. Sarsden manor was to be his son's for life, thereafter his widow's as her jointure and then their first and other sons were to hold it in tail male, in default of which any heirs male by any other marriage contracted by William, and then the right heirs of Sir William. Similar provisions were made regarding the other manors. A trust was set up for 500 years with power to grant 21- or 99-year leases determinable on three lives at the ancient usual rents, out of which was to come £500 a year for life to Dame Elizabeth, Sir William's wife; £20 a year was to be raised for his youngest son Thomas Walter; a sale or mortgage was to achieve a portion of £2,500 for his second daughter Ann if so directed by him in a deed or will, with £60 a year for her maintenance.

Should William die without male issue, then £5,000 was to be raised for the portions of any daughters, with maintenance until eighteen or marriage. If William or his male heirs offered security to the trustees for the performance of the above charges after the death of Sir William, then the 500-year term was to be surrendered to him. William was finally given power to create new 'uses' after his father's demise.

The abstract records that William and Mary had a son, William, who died at about twelve-months-old, John (later Sir John Walter), and a daughter Mary (married to Robert Rich). On 10 November 1680 William barred the entail of the estate in a fine levied to John and William Crispe. His will, made on 5 May 1692, gave his daughter Mary £5,000 and a further £1,000, payable out of the yearly rents and profits of the land passing to her brother John if their father's personal estate proved insufficient. On his marriage with his second wife, Lady Mary Bruce, various lands in Churchill had been placed under a Trust to raise £800 a year for her life in lieu of dower. At her death (in 1711) they passed to their eldest son Robert, with remainder to any other issue, under their marriage settlement. If John paid £2,750 within ten years of his father's death to his half-brother, then the mansion house at Churchill was to be his for his use and for his heirs in fee simple. Under the will William and his second wife's second son William was bequeathed £1,000 at twenty-one, for which the son gave a receipt on 6 November 1702. One daughter was given a marriage portion of £2,000 and the other four portions of £1,500 each, payable at eighteen or on marriage from the fines and profits of his estates. But if John were to pay or secure any of these, then the estate was to be discharged of the liability.

There were further transactions made by Sir John Walter up to the time of his death in 1722, all recorded in the abstract, which thus is an immensely useful summary of the landowners' activities stretching over almost sixty years, explaining how Sir William Walter's descendants came to possess their estate, on what terms and limitations, how that estate was tied by payments of portions and annuities, and what was done with it by means of lease and mortgage, marriage settlement or will, fine and common recovery.

It is not surprising that by the early eighteenth century the estate was exhausted. Once the rents ceased to come in, valuable leases had been given under trust and the personal estate disposed of, financial crisis was not far away. But then, there were no male heirs of the body of Sir Robert in 1731; his nephew was left to pick up the pieces, the silver fountain and the heirloom books. It must have been a pattern repeated in many other families.

8

THE STATHAM FAMILY

I stumbled on this pedigree purely by chance. Having just seen the film *A Man for All Seasons*, in which a woman of Leicester tried to bribe Sir Thomas More, the Lord Chancellor, it occurred to me that the records of this Court might usefully be explored for the sixteenth-century Derbyshire family of Statham I was currently researching. The personal name index revealed the surname, and the requisitioned case papers produced a wonderful array of genealogical detail taking the family back to the fifteenth century. Here is the story.

On 22 October 3 and 4 Philip and Mary (1556) John Statham addressed a bill of complaint to the joint sovereigns in their Court of Requests at Whitehall, seeking a remedy against Sir Henry Sacheverell, Knight.[1] His grievance concerned lands in the Derbyshire parishes of Snelston, Alsop and Rossington (Roston), which he claimed were granted by certain feoffees to his antecedent, John Statham of Morley,

in the same county, by a deed of entail dated the Feast of St Michael the Archangel 32 Henry VI (29 September 1453). John was given the land for life, after which a fee tail male was set in train, starting with his son Nicholas and the male heirs of his body, in default of which there were similar successive remainders to his other sons Thomas and Henry with remainder over to John Statham of Horsley, Derbyshire, and the male heirs of his body.

After the grantee's death the lands duly passed to Nicholas, Thomas and Henry, who all died without male issue, so that they eventually came by right to the complainant, as son and heir of William Statham, a mercer of London, the son and heir of John Statham of Goverton in Nottinghamshire, the son and heir male of John Statham of Horsley, the complainant's great-grandfather. But 'Dyvers dedes, Evydences charters wryttyngs & mynyments concernyng the premysses only Appertaynyng to yor said Subiect were casually come into the hands & possession of one

The undated replication of John Statham to the answer of Sir Henry Sacheverell, Knight, taken on 12 January 1556/7 and returned to the Court of Requests. Statham denied that Sir Henry's mother was seised in fee tail general of the disputed premises in Derbyshire or that after her death they descended by any right to Sir Henry as her son and heir, and now wished the Court to hear the case and make an award.
REQ2/26/48 no 8

The pedigree drafted on 24 October 1544 by Thomas Merydale of London, on the instructions of Sir Henry Sacheverell, Knight, of Morley, Derbyshire, the defendant in a suit brought by John Statham, son of William Statham, late of London, mercer, in the Court of Requests in 1556. The family tree sketches their common ancestry and shows how Tudor genealogies were set out. Sacheverell's aim was to establish that he was John's next heir. REQ2/26/48 no 5

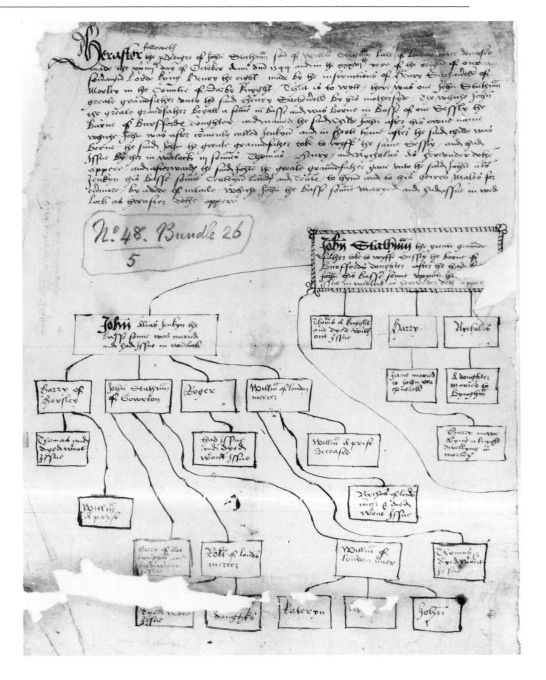

Sr Henry Sacheverell Knyght Thomas Alsoppe of Alsoppe in the Countie of Derby & Agnes Parker wydowe of Snelston in the said Countie who by meanes therof have contryvyd & devysid dyvers & sondry secret estates to be made of & in the premysses of them selffs & to dyvers other to theyr uses unto yor said Subiect unknowyng And to the dysherytyng of yor said Subiect for ever'.[2] Without the deeds Statham was impotent at common law, and was denied his rents and profits, so his only recourse was to find a remedy through one of the Courts of Equity. His bill ended with the entreaty that the defendants be summoned to appear before the Court and abide by its judgment.

On 18 November 1556, under their Privy Seal, the monarchs sought instructions from the Court on how to proceed. A fiat (decree) was issued requiring an answer from the defendants by the Octave of St Hilary next (20 January 1556/7). The answer was taken at Morley on 12 January by one of the Court's

Commissioners. The defendants alleged that the bill was uncertain, insufficient in the law, and outside the jurisdiction of the Court, for the complainant was a wealthy man, and was not a member of the Royal Household. They asked for the case to be transferred to a common law court, but if compelled to give an answer, then they would say that Sir Henry's mother, Jane, wife of John Sacheverell, and later called Jane Zouche, was seised of the land as the rightful heir in fee tail general under a lawful conveyance made to her ancestors long before the 1453 deed. After John Sacheverell's death, Jane continued to enjoy the estate until her demise about forty-six years ago (*c.* 1510/11), when it devolved on her son and heir, Sir Henry Sacheverell. He entered the premises, took the rents and profits and granted leases to Thomas Alsop and Agnes Parker. Sir Henry denied that he had custody of any other evidences than those affecting his own right and interest, and cast doubt on whether there ever had been any such deed and whether the grantors had been entitled to the estate as it was already entailed to his own forebears. The defendants called for the case to be dismissed and an award made of their reasonable costs. To this John Statham responded with a replication, to which the defendants retaliated with a rejoinder.

Two lists of interrogatories were then drawn up by the suitors. The depositions were taken at Westminster on 7 May 1557 for the defendants and five days later for the complainant. The signed depositions, made by the sworn witnesses, refer to the interrogatories by number, so without these lists of questions the reader would be disadvantaged. John Statham's witness was Thomas Merydale, of Coleman Street in the City of London, aged about forty-eight. He was asked if he knew Sir Henry Sacheverell to pay rent to Richard Jervys of London on John's behalf, and if so how much and how often. He deposed that he was a servant of Jervys for about thirty years. Jervys had married Statham's mother. After the death of Harry Statham, son of Robert Statham, a mercer of London, Jervys had delivered Merydale a little red paper book for him to draw up a rental of the annual sums due to the complainant from the disputed lands and elsewhere in Derbyshire. Jervys gave the rental to a carrier from Derby to enable him to collect the rents and hand the money over to Jervys for Statham. Sacheverell's rent was forty shillings a year; sometimes this was paid to the courier, but sometimes it was brought to London by others for him, to whom Jervys gave receipts. He continued to pay rent after Harry Statham's death 'until suche tyme as the sd John Statham cam frome beyonde the seea'. The

deponent was asked whether he had written the annexed pedigree, when, where, and by whose instruction and on what occasion. To this he answered that on 24 October 1544, while Statham was still abroad, he had drafted the chart at his master's house in Bow Lane, London, after Sacheverell and Jervys had talked together about the complainant. Sir Henry had said in Merydale's hearing that if Statham were to die without male issue he would be his next heir. The pedigree was constructed at his suggestion to demonstrate his claim. Further questions related to a visit paid by John Statham to Sir Henry Sacheverell in August 1556, when the defendant was asked to surrender the land. The deponent was asked to substantiate Sir Henry's response. Merydale averred that he had ridden with Statham into Derbyshire to Sacheverell's house, where a lengthy discussion took place. Statham had queried the defendant's title to the land. Sacheverell had replied that he held it as his ancestors had done and that an award made by the Abbot of Darley or Dale set out his rights, but Statham said that this award in no way affected his own title, and asked for the land to be restored to him otherwise he would seek a legal remedy. Sacheverell then appealed to his goodwill, asking to be treated no worse than his forebears had been.

The final interrogatory sought and received confirmation that Statham had immediately afterwards peaceably entered his lands without any resistance. Merydale added that he and Statham had then returned to London the same day.

The pedigree chart shows that the complainant's great-grandfather John was the base born child of John Statham and his future wife Sessly (Cecily), the Baron of Burford's daughter, and was commonly called Jenkyn. His parents subsequently married and produced three more sons. John alias Jenkyn was granted certain lands for himself and his male heirs by a deed of entail. He moved to Horsley, married and had progeny of his own, as recorded on the family tree.

After issue was joined, Sir Henry Sacheverell died, about November 1558, and was succeeded by his 'cosen and heyre', John Sacheverell, who entered the land and took its profits, and also came by the deeds and evidences. John Statham issued a reviver, citing him as the new defendant, and this was filed in the Court on 14 February 1 Elizabeth (1558/9). A writ of subpoena directed Sacheverell to appear before the Court in the Quindene of Easter next (9 April 1559). No further documentation survives there, but from the later Chancery Proceedings we know that the case was dismissed because the Court of Requests had no warrant or authority to make a decree without the consent of both parties, and this was lacking from the defendant.

The suit soon resurfaced in the Court of Chancery with the presentation of a similar bill to the Lord Chancellor.[3] John Sacheverell's answer was the same as Sir Henry's in the Court of Requests. A replication from John Statham, filed in Easter Term 3 Elizabeth (1561) was rather more expansive. Apparently, the premises had been let by Henry Statham of Nottingham to the defendant's grandfather, Sir Henry Sacheverell, for as long as both parties could agree, at an annual rent of forty shillings, which Statham received for twelve years until his death, when the estate descended to his 'cousin' and heir male, Henry Statham (son of Robert Statham, another London mercer, the brother of the deceased Henry, making the younger Henry his nephew. Robert and Henry were sons of John Statham of Goverton, and grandsons of John Statham of Horsley). Sacheverell remained as a tenant at will and paid the rent until the younger Henry's death, at which point the complainant became entitled as his cousin and male heir, being the son of Robert and Henry's brother William, mercer of London. Sacheverell occupied the land a further twenty-four years at the same rent, although by now it was worth considerably more. Statham had tried to elicit a higher sum from him, or persuade him to vacate the land so that it might be let out to others for his better gain or advantage. Sacheverell begged to be allowed to stay, at the existing customary rent, for, he argued, he was an old man and not likely to live many more years and so the land would soon be freed for reletting. Statham had concurred with this. Altogether Sir Henry Sacheverell had occupied the land for forty-five years until his death in 1558, when he was followed by his grandson and heir, John Sacheverell, as son and heir of John Sacheverell, his eldest son.

From this time-scale we can perceive that John Statham became entitled to the land in about 1534. Sir Henry first rented the premises around 1513, and paid rent to Henry Statham for twelve years until his demise *c.* 1525, and thereafter to Henry Statham to 1534. It would seem that John Statham was overseas by 1544, but had returned to England by 1556. Possibly he too was a mercer like his father and two uncles, and he certainly lived in London. His time abroad might have been to trade.

The replication asserted that the complainant inherited lands in Derby, Aston and Wilne under the same deed of 1453, and that he had rentals, evidences and books of good authority as proof, plus letters from Sir Henry Sacheverell acknowledging his status as a tenant at will. Statham denied that Jane Sacheverell had ever possessed the premises in tail general, and urged the Court to compel the defendant to deliver the appropriate deeds and evidences to him and to allow him peaceful enjoyment of the land under his right and title.

On 22 October 1561 an Order was issued by the Court to the defendant to rejoin or lose the benefit.[4] In other words, judgment would otherwise be given on the basis of what had already been submitted. The

Entry Book of Chancery Decrees and Orders, including the decree made by Sir Nicholas Bacon, Knight, Lord Chancellor, on 4 May 4 Elizabeth (1562), after a hearing of the plaintiff, John Statham's case, and in the absence of the defendant, John Sacheverell. The latter had failed to produce any good title to the contested lands, whereas Statham presented an ancient deed of feoffment and deed of entail, in support of his bill of complaint. The decree gave Statham the right of entry to the premises, pending any better evidence to the contrary which the defendant might offer. C33/26 f351r

rejoinder was received soon after, amounting to a straightforward denial of the allegations, a challenge to the existence of the 1453 deed, and an insistence that the reason for the suit's dismissal out of the Court of Requests was because the complainant had failed to prove his title.[5]

A further Order of 11 November gave the parties two dates on which to produce their witnesses, a week and a fortnight hence;[6] on 21 November a Commission was awarded to examine those for the plaintiff;[7] on 4 February 1561/2 publication of documents between the parties was sanctioned.[8]

A hearing of the matter took place on 4 May 1562, resulting in a Decree on 11 May in favour of the plaintiff.[9] The defendant had defaulted, had not been represented by Counsel, and the pleadings and depositions on his behalf had not sufficiently proved his right to the lands, whereas the plaintiff had showed the Court 'not onely one fayre auncient dede of feoffament wherby the sayd John Statham of Morley did enfeoff the sayd Willm Dethick Esquier Willm Morton John ffletcher Willm Sheffeld Henry Sankye and others of and in the premisses To have to them and to their heyres And also one dede wherby the same Willm Dethyck and others his sayd cofeoffees did demyse the premisses unto the sayd John Statham for tearme of his lief wth the remayndor thereof over in manner and forme as in the sayd bill and replicacon of the sayd complt is alledged', and the depositions of his several credible witnesses had contained enough to convince the Court that he and his antecedents had continuously and quietly received the rent from the premises for forty years. The plaintiff and his assigns were authorized to enter and enjoy the land and its rents at forty shillings a year from the Feast of St Michael the Archangel next, without any let or hindrance from the defendant, his assigns or agents, until such time as he could furnish the Court with good evidence to the contrary.

An appeal must have been lodged, for on 12 June 1562 another hearing was fixed, for the second week in Michaelmas Term.[10] Four days later an order was made for a writ of subpoena to be sent to the defendant to summon him to Court.[11] A second decree was issued on 5 December, after the hearing on 25 November.[12] Under this, the plaintiff was henceforward to hold, occupy and enjoy the lands for himself and his heirs forever, on the same conditions

Part of the enrolled decree of the Equity Court of Chancery, 4 May 4 Elizabeth (1562) by which John Statham, the complainant, was given judgment in default of the defendant, John Sacheverell's, appearance and lack of evidence of good title to the disputed lands in Snelston, Alsop and Roston in Derbyshire. Statham was given authority to enter them and enjoy the rents from Michaelmas (29 September) until Sacheverell should show good proof to the contrary. This section sets out at length the background history to the case and the descent of the lands, before putting the defendant's argument. C78/21 no 30 as before. The lands at Snelston, Roston and Norbury were valued at forty-nine shillings annual rent, while the defendant was ordered to immediately satisfy the plaintiff all accrued average rent arrears of forty shillings a year. The rest of the land under dispute, in Alsop, was referred for determination at common law, by commencement of an action for its recovery by the plaintiff against the defendant, provided that none of the tenants or occupiers was ousted without reasonable warning. A copy of the decree was enrolled among the Court records, summarizing the arguments put by both sides, and setting out the extent and nature of the affected premises, comprising, as it did, two messuages, 300 acres of land, 40 acres of meadow, 100 acres of pasture and 100 acres of wood. The decree also expressed the Court's view that the defendant's earlier default was due to a desire to delay rather than put an end to the matter.

From the above case we can follow the progress of litigation from receipt of the initiating bill of complaint to the final outcome, punctuated with the various orders and decrees issued to the parties giving the Court's instructions and decisions; we can see the time lapses between one stage and the next. A suit could be commenced in more than one Court, being thrown out of one and dealt with by another with wider powers. From the content of these documents we can learn how and when the original entail was created, how the land descended and how crucial it was that the owner retained possession of the deeds of title, for without any 'office copies' to refer to, the common law could not help him once they were lost or in another's custody. We can observe how the various remainders were extinguished as male heirs became extinct, so that little more than a hundred years after the original grant the land ought to have come to the great-grandson of the fourth remainderman. This was another important reason why the deed should survive: to enable the remaindermen to be identified, and eventually the reversioner in fee simple, should all the male lines be exhausted. Although fees were required for centralized enrolment of land grants and transfers, it did at least ensure a permanent record which could not be tampered with or destroyed.

Because legal proceedings often relate to people and events many years before, whose actions and behaviour were relevant or gave rise to the disputes, the detailed accounts about them can be of immense value to the genealogist, with the caveat that this information was used to argue a case and may not always be utterly reliable. What emerges from them is a studied awareness by the parties of their ancestry

inasmuch as it affected their rights and titles. When possession of land was the basis of power and privilege this knowledge was important. We are given family relationships, sometimes tenuous and remote, details of residence, movements, careers and occupations from which we can approximate the dates of certain events. Where these relate to a period before parish registers, when perhaps wills were not made or do not survive, or are insufficient in themselves, legal records can prove invaluable in sorting out ambiguities and explaining certain actions and situations. They also lead the searcher in other directions, to inquisitions post mortem, taxation lists, Heraldic Visitation pedigrees, private family and estate papers of the contestants, monastic cartularies and muniments, manorial, City Livery Company records, and centralized enrolments and collections like Ancient Deeds, Feet of Fines, and other incidental matter such as Patent and Close Rolls, Letters and Papers of King Henry VIII and State Papers, which might yield references to mercers trading at home and abroad, and of course to other litigation before and after the case in point, in the common law courts and those of Equity.

The genealogist is also reminded how loosely a generic term such as 'cousin' was applied. In one Chancery document alone it was used to connote a grandson, a nephew and a first cousin. Interpretation of the word is thus often entirely dependent on the internal evidence of the document in which it occurs.

In Hilary Term 7 Elizabeth (1564/5) John Statham made a final concord or agreement with Lawrence Wright as querient, in connection with lands at Snelston and elsewhere. The chirograph is missing, but from the entry in the manuscript indexes to Feet of Fines we can conclude that Wright was the purchaser.[13] It may have been a device used by Statham to bar the entail and create a base fee before its enlargement to a fee simple by a common recovery, using Wright as his collaborator. We would thus expect to find another deed by which this was done. Of the original fifteenth-century entail no trace has been found among Ancient Deeds and Feet of Fines.

The will of Nicholas Stathum, the first remainderman, was proved in the Prerogative Court of Canterbury on 5 August 1472, having been written in his own hand on 15 July.[14] He wanted interment in the Church of St James Garlickhithe if he died in London, and for a month of prayers to be recited for him there and for the souls of his parents, John and Cecill, and for those of nine other named individuals, whose exact relationship to him is unknown. Money was left for painting the image of Our Lady in Morley Church and he bequeathed £9 to be distributed among his brother Jankyn's children and servants 'for divers causes þat move my conscience and þat it be done by thavice of my sustre Dame Elizaberth and of my brother Herry and if part therof be distribut among his servantes and to the priory of Bridsalpark [Breadsall Park, in Derbyshire] I wol þat it well done'. He seems to have died leaving a daughter Anne, and his capital wealth appears to have been considerable.

From the proceedings in the Court of Requests we know that Jankyn was his eldest brother, alias John, born out of wedlock to their parents. The will nowhere mentions the entail and at this date land could not be willed directly, so we do not know what other land he owned and what would have passed to his daughter Anne as his heiress. In the absence of an inquisition post mortem, the only evidence we have of the pattern of descent of freehold lands lies in legal proceedings and deeds of sale or gift of the estate to others.

The allusion to Morley church is clarified by the litigation, for this parish is where his parents resided and presumably where he was born. Provision for his burial in church may suggest that a tomb or some other memorial was erected to him, whose inscription and decoration would further increase our knowledge about him and his immediate family.

Sir Thomas Statham, Knight, predeceased his brother Nicholas, for his will and testament were proved in the same Court on 19 January 1470/1.[15] The testament was drafted on Monday after the feast of St John the Baptist 9 Edward IV (26 June 1469) and the will on Thursday after the Feast of St James the Apostle (26 July 1470), in which he left lands to various people for terms of their lives. This means that he cannot have followed his brother into the fee tail estate, and it is clear that he left no son, though he was twice married. He asked for burial in Morley church, on the south side of the chancel at St Nicholas' altar end, under the low wall, which was to be taken down to accommodate a marble stone (costing six marks). It was to be laid over his body and was to portray the three kneeling figures of himself and his two wives, each holding a roll to the Blessed Virgin Mary and to St Christopher, and displaying over their heads three shields containing his arms quartered with those of his spouses. Elaborate funeral instructions were given, affording a glimpse of late medieval ritual: there were to be six torches burning about his body on the day of burial, to be carried in procession by six poor men clad in white gowns and hoods. Afterwards the torches were to go to the chapel at Smalley and for use at Morley church. The Abbots of Darley and of Dale, and the Priors from Nottingham, Derby and Breadsall Park were entreated to attend with their canons and clerks, friars and priests, and were to be given donations in return. At the interment four oxen, six calves and fourteen wethers were to be slaughtered and eaten with bread and ale, so the funeral must have been one of some size and splendour. Then six hundred masses were to be sung for himself and nineteen named relations

The Charter of 18 May 2 Henry VII (1487) by which William Zouche and his wife Joan, daughter and heiress of Henry Stathum, late lord of Morley in Derbyshire, are confirmed as life tenants of a messuage in Smalley under a feoffment made by Joan. After their deaths the six named feoffees (including William Sacheverell and Henry Stathum) were to grant the remainder to her right heirs forever. Joan was previously wife of John Sacheverell and mother of Sir Henry, the defendant in the Court of Requests in 1556. E326/B3360

(connections not stated, the Christian names were sufficient) in several priories, in a similar form as was entered in the Tables of Record for his father. A priest was to chant daily mass for him at Morley for a year after his death, and another at Smalley, for which each was to have a salary, food, drink, and a black gown. His wife Elizabeth, daughter Cecily, brothers Henry and Nichol, sister Godith (and her daughter Luce), Margaret Stathum and her brothers Henry, little Thomas, and William and her sister Luce were named as beneficiaries. John, Thomas and William Stathum were bequeathed his gowns of different hues and fabrics. Unfortunately the relationship of these last eight people to the testator is not apparent.

The remaining brother, Henry Stathum, died on 29 April 1481. An inquisition port mortem, taken at Derby on 19 November that year, established that his daughter Johanna, wife of John Sacheverell, and aged twenty-one and more, was sole heiress to his manors of Morley and Smalley.[16] According to an Ancient Deed of 18 May 1487 she was then widowed

Pedigree of the Stathams of Derbyshire

JOHN STATHAM = CECILY
of Morley, Derbyshire, held lands in fee at Snelston, Alsop and Rosington, Derbyshire, enfeoffed them by deed dd 29 Sept 1453, named in will of son NICHOLAS, 1472
CECILY — daughter of Baron of Burford, named in will of son NICHOLAS, 1472

GODITH
named in brother's testament, 1469, marr ◆

NICHOLAS STATHUM =
3rd son, named in brother's testament, 1469, executor 1470/1, sometime MP, c.1472, will dd 15 July 1472, to be bur at St James Garlickhithe, London, pr 5 Aug 1472

ANNE
named in father's will, 1472

HENRY STATHUM =
Armiger, 1481, 2nd son, lord of manors of Morley, and Caldelow, held land at Kiddesbey, Smalley, Chaddesden, Spondon, and Winster, Derbyshire, granted land at Derby by Fine dd 9 Feb 1453/4, named in brother's testament, 1469, and will of brother NICHOLAS, 1472, died 29 Apr 1481, I.P.M. 19 Nov 1481

ELIZABETH
named in husband's testament, executrix 1470/1, through RICHARD STATHUM

JOHN als JENKYN STATHAM, of Horsley, Derbyshire, named in will of brother NICHOLAS, 1472, named in deed of 10 July 1476

ELIZABETH
named in deed of 10 July 1476

Sir THOMAS STATHUM Kt
of Morley, eldest son, granted manor of Caldelow, Derbyshire, by Fine dd Easter 1443, held land at Wessington, Derbyshire, Lymm, Cheshire, testament dd 26 June 1469, to be bur at Morley, will dd 26 July 1470, pr 19 Jan 1470/1

CECILY
named in father's testament, 1469, to have land at Wessington

JOHN SAUCHEVERELL =
dead by 18 May 1487

JANE
aged 21 and more, 19 Nov 1481, her father's heir, marr 1st by 19 Nov 1481, granted lands at Smalley for life, by deed dd 18 May 1487, then remarr, died c.1510/11

= WILLIAM ZOUCHE
of Morley, 1487, party to deed with his wife, 18 May

Sir HENRY SACHEVERELL Kt =
of Morley, held land at Snelston, Alsop, and Rosington as tenant at will c.1510/11–1555/6, defendant in suit in the Court of Requests, Nov 1556, dead by Feb 1558/9

other issue
2 daughters

WENYFRIDE
named in husband's will, 1524

= RICHARD JERVYS
of Bow Lane, City of London, Alderman, and mercer, 1524, dead by 12 May 1557

JOHN SACHEVERELL =
eldest son and heir

ALICE
named in father's will, 1524

KATERYN
named in father's will, 1524

JOHN SACHEVERELL
defendant in Chancery suit, Easter 1561, in default of an appearance June 1562

JOHN STATHAM = JOHANE
of Horsley, 1476, when granted his lands at Burnaston, and Berwardcote, Derbyshire, to ROBERT LEEK, 10 July, and of Goverton, Nottinghamshire, dead by 1522, bur in Thurgarton Abbey, Nottinghamshire, named in son ROBERT's will, 1522
JOHANE — named in son ROBERT's will, 1522

ROBERT STATHOM = ANNE
Citizen of London, and mercer, 1522, will dd 29 June 1522, to be bur at St Lawrence Old Jewry, London, pr 17 July 1522
ANNE — named in husband's will, executrix 1522

WILLIAM STATHOM
of London, mercer, 1524, bn at Bleasby, Nottinghamshire, named in brother ROBERT's will, 1522, will dd 21 Aug 1524, to be bur at St Martin's Iremonger Lane, London, pr 31 Mch 1525

JOHN STATHAM
gentleman, 1556, heir to HENRY, referred to in father's will, unborn but expected, 21 Aug 1524, beyond the sea 24 Oct 1544, in England by Aug 1556, plaintiff in the Court of Requests, Nov 1556, and the Court of Chancery 1561, Chancery decree 4 May 1562 ordered his re-entry to land at Snelston, Rosington and Norbury, Derbyshire, deforciant in Fine Hilary Term 1564/5 relating to land at Snelston and elsewhere

HENRY STATHOM
eldest son, of Nottingham, Nottinghamshire, 1530, when granted his lands at Burnaston and Berwardcote to THOMAS MELLOURS and others, 10 July, named in brother ROBERT's will, 1522, and WILLIAM's will, 1524, died c.1531/2

other issue
6 children

HARRY STATHOM
heir to uncle HENRY, dead by Aug 1556

The details in italics refer to sources held outside the Public Record Office

and had remarried William Zouche of Morley.[17] It would seem that Johanna, the forebear of Sir Henry Sacheverell who died in 1558, was a member of the Statham family herself.

Thirty-five years later, Robert Statham, citizen and mercer of London, made his will on 29 June 14 Henry VIII (1522) and it was proved on 17 July.[18] He hoped to be buried before the altar of St Mary Magdalen in the Church of St Lawrence Jewry, in London. The torches at his funeral were to be distributed to the church at Bleasby, and to the abbey and parish church at Thurgarton, in Nottinghamshire, and for use at funerals of the poor in the London parish. Black gowns were to be worn at his funeral by his wife Anne, William and Nicholas Stathom and their wives, and his servants and apprentices. The relationship of these two men to him is not stated. Immediately after his death his mother, Johane Stathom, was to be given £10 to find a priest to sing for his and his father's souls, and to do good deeds amongst the poor for a year. His brothers, Henry and William Stathom, were left fabrics, and his own six children plus the one which his wife was currently carrying were to have a hundred marks apiece, by the custom of the City of London.

Lastly, the will of the plaintiff's father, William Statham, mercer of London, and brother of Robert, was drawn up on 21 August 1524, and proved in the Prerogative Court of Canterbury on 31 March 1525.[19] His burial was to be in the Church of St Martin in Iremonger Lane, London, before Our Lady of Mercy, in the middle of the church, or in a place thought convenient by his executors, John Barnard and Nicolas Stathum. He donated money for a glass window to be installed in the chancel over the high altar of the church at Bleasby, the parish of his birth. The glass was to show his parents with all their children, at the discretion of his brother, Henry Stathum, though his father was actually buried in the abbey of Thurgarton. William left ready money to his wife Wenyfride, and for his three children, Kateryn, Alice, and the one as yet unborn. His father-in-law, John Barnard, sister Margaret Stathum (now living with his mother), the seven children of his brother Robert Stathum, and his sister Elizabeth's children by her first husband, William Jonson, of Horsley, were all bestowed gifts. Among those provided with black gowns to wear at his funeral was Richard Jervys, mercer, the future husband of William's widow. From the will we know that William Statham ran a shop and had at least two apprentices, one of whom was bequeathed £10. If he failed to reach full age, the money was to be used to repair the highway between Gorton (Goverton) and Bleasby, at the discretion of his brother Henry.

The wills tell us the dates between which members of the Statham family died. We know that Sir Thomas Statham was dead sometime after 26 July 1470 and before 19 January 1470/1, and his brother Nicholas between 15 July and 5 August 1472, both without sons, but leaving the third remainderman, their brother Henry, still alive. It is clear that the instructions in the testaments were to be carried out immediately on demise, for they contain a fine attention to the detail of the ceremonial and attire at their funerals. They reveal also a depth of religious devotion, respect for forebears and a social responsibility for almsgiving, manifested especially by Robert, who benefited four London prisons and four guilds, in addition to religious houses. The family maintained close links with its Nottinghamshire and Derbyshire roots, and it would seem that while Robert and William made their way to London, their brother Henry stayed in Nottinghamshire, as he was to supervise various local works. As he had possession of the disputed lands about 1513, he must have been the eldest brother and their father was buried at Thurgarton Abbey some time before this. William was born at Bleasby which explains the oblique reference to the parish in his brother's will, and Gorton is presumably Goverton, where their father lived. As Robert died in 1522, his son Henry was the next heir for want of male issue of the older Henry, and he must have inherited the land after August 1524. William's son John was not born in that month, when his father's will was made, but he must have been alive at the time of probate, eight months later. Of Robert's seven children no son can have produced a male heir, for we know that John was entitled to the remainder in about 1534 on his cousin Henry's death, when he would have been aged nine or ten. Richard Jervys, his mother's new husband, was responsible for collecting his rents, and we know that by 1544 John was overseas, perhaps apprenticed to a mercer, for he would have been aged about twenty, or perhaps was being educated.

The wills indicate a strong likelihood that the churches at Morley, Bleasby and in London will contain memorials to the family. Monastic cartularies, especially from the Abbey of Thurgarton, wills proved in the diocese of Lichfield, the archdeaconry of Nottingham and the Prerogative Court of York, Mercers' Company and City of London records, Heraldic Visitations, taxation lists and inquisitions post mortem would all add to what we know already about the family in the fifteenth and sixteenth centuries.

9

THE FARDON FAMILY

The Quaker family of Fardon, living in Oxfordshire, has been used for a survey of taxation records. The very full Minutes of the Meetings of the Society of Friends, dating between the mid-seventeenth and nineteenth centuries, provide the skeleton onto which the listings can be pinned, and for information on likely earlier generations the taxation assessments can prove invaluable as a name and surname distribution indicator.

A few months before central registration began of births, marriages and deaths in England and Wales, on 1 July 1837, Eliza Fardon died and was buried in the Friends' Burying Ground at Sibford Gower, in Oxfordshire, aged thirty-six. In the Minutes of the Monthly Meeting of Banbury she was described as the daughter of the late Thomas and Susanna Fardon.[1] She was born to them on 14 January 1801 at Sibford Ferris, where her father was a baker,[2] and her parents were married on 6 February 1799 'in a Publick Assembly of the people called Quakers, in their Meeting House at Sibford'. The Minutes recorded that Thomas was the son of Jonathan Fardon, late of Sibford, baker, and Ann his wife, and Susanna the daughter of Jeremiah Lamb of Sibford, a blacksmith, by Ann.[3] Six years later, on 8 October 1805, Richard Fardon, a younger brother of Jonathan, took Susanna's sister Ann as his bride, in a similar ceremony.[4] By then Richard had moved to the City of Worcester and was employed as a glover. Looking through the pages of the Banbury Minutes of births, marriages and burials, it was possible to extend the family tree another three generations back beyond the two brothers to John and Alice ffardon of Northnewton (North Newington, in the parish of Broughton, Oxfordshire), alive in 1656.[5]

In 1654 two pioneer Quakers from Westmorland travelled through Banbury on their way from London to Bristol. During their stay they made their religious beliefs known to the locals in a series of meetings, and a year later their wives paid a visit to the area. As a result, a number of the inhabitants were converted and Banbury quickly became the main centre for Oxfordshire Quakers. They were subjected to ridicule and brutality by their neighbours; some had their goods distrained and were imprisoned by local magistrates for non-payment of church rates and tithes, for refusing to cease meeting or to take the oath of allegiance. North Newington villagers attended the monthly meetings at Banbury, but until 1698 also gathered at Nathaniel Ball's house in the hamlet.[6]

North Newington was largely independent of the influence of the major local landowner, who possessed much of the mother parish of Broughton and lived in the castle there. Unlike his copyhold tenants at will in Broughton, they were leaseholders or freeholders thanks to an earlier lord of the manor who in exchange for his tenants' co-operation at enclosure at the turn of the century had given them a more secure tenancy of their land.[7] William Fiennes, Viscount Saye and Sele at the time of the conversions, was hostile to the Quakers and wrote two violently anti-Quaker pamphlets.[8]

The registers of births for the Banbury Monthly Meeting survive from 1632, marriages from 1662, and burials from 1665.[9] The earliest births must have been recorded retrospectively for some of the first members of the Society. The registered entries express the days and months in figures, as was the Friends' custom, eschewing the names of the months as being pagan. It is important to realize that before the Calendar change in 1752, the first month in the year was March. The births note the names of both parents and where they lived; the burials often give dates of death, ages and parentage of children and adults; the marriages bear the names, abodes and occupations of the parents as well as of the parties directly concerned, and the names of all those relatives and Friends who subscribed their signatures to the marriage certificate as witnesses at the exchange of vows. Many of these lists are extensive, and the task of reconstructing the kinship networks into a wider collateral family is a

Part of the register of the Banbury Monthly Meeting of the Society of Friends, Oxfordshire, recording the death, and burial of Jonathan Fardon of North Newington on the 11th day of the 11th month (November) 1763; note the diverse places of interment. RG6/1332 p224

formidable one. For instance, at Jonathan ffardon's wedding with Elizabeth Lamb on 2 October 1733[10] there were twenty-five relatives present: Benjamin and Elizabeth Lamb were probably the bride's parents, and Richard, Thomas and John ffardon the groom's two brothers and a cousin. Five other Lamb relations signed; Elizabeth Smith was the groom's sister, having married John Smith in 1713;[11] Henry Smith was probably a relative of her husband, or possibly her son; Hannah Archer was probably related through Jonathan's brother Richard's marriage to Mary Archer in 1725;[12] Hannah Fowler, Rachel and William Stevens were connected by the second marriage of Jonathan and Richard's father, Thomas ffardon, with Mary ffowler in 1708,[13] a Rachel Fowler having married William Stevens in September 1733;[14] Alexander Tredwell presumably signed as a relative by virtue of his alliance with Anne Fowler in 1732.[15] This leaves a Gilkes, a brace of Groves, a Harris, a Grisham and a trio of Paxfords. A scrutiny of the earlier marriage registers revealed a female Lamb mar-

rying a Gilkes in 1685:[16] Richard Gilkes may have been a descendant, and similarly the Gilkes marrying a female Harris in 1720.[17] Of the twenty-five names, therefore, ten came from the Fardons' side and nine from the Lambs'. As none of the unattributable surnames feature among those of witnesses at six other Fardon ceremonies between 1708 and 1731,[18] the conclusion must be that they belonged to the bride's family, possibly on her maternal line. Time spent gleaning wills of people of these surnames and of the other witnesses might well produce affirmative evidence of the suggested links, by mentions of Fardons as beneficiaries. Conversely, we can also discover which 'non-Fardon' weddings the family witnessed, which may give clues to other connections. Elizabeth ffardon was present on 6 April (the second month) 1674 when Thomas Gilkes married Hannah Alcock, and Alice ffardon witnessed the marriage of John Warron and Elizabeth Hiorne, a widow, on 3 August (the sixth month) 1674.[19] When Elizabeth ffardon's father John ffardon, alias Vardon, a yeoman

Part of the last will and testament of John ffardon alias Vardon of North Newton [Newington], made on 17 March 1676/7 and proved in the Prerogative Court of Canterbury on 24 November 1677. He mentions lands held for terms of years in both Oxfordshire and Warwickshire. PROB11/355, q115, f153r

of North Newton 'aged of body but of sound and perfect mind and memory', made his will on 17 March 1676/7, proved in the Prerogative Court of Canterbury on 24 November 1677, he left her £200 and his household goods to the value of £10, and gave another daughter, Sarah Alcock, ten shillings.[20] Alice, his wife, was not mentioned, so we must assume that she was already dead, sometime after August 1674 perhaps. Thus the witnesses' names in the marriage registers can be used to find out who was alive at a given date.

Besides his two daughters, John's will mentioned his sons John and Richard, neither of whose births were recorded in the Friends' registers. John ffardon alias Vardon was bequeathed two shillings and sixpence and Richard all the lands in Wootton Wawen, lying close to the Warwickshire border with Worcestershire, held by lease for term of years, for his natural life and thereafter for the use of his children, until the lease fell in. Thomas ffardon alias Vardon, his executor, was devised for himself and the heirs of his body his father's paper mill at Bodicote, on the other side of Banbury, which was also held for term of years, together with the dwelling house where the testator lived and its houses, outhouses, orchards, gardens, yards, backsides and appurtenances, his two

yardlands of arable meadow and pasture ground in the fields of North Newton, and his closes or closing in North Newton at a place called Deepeslad. If Thomas (who was then unmarried) left no such heirs then the lands were to pass after his death to the testator's two grandchildren, John and Richard ffardon alias Vardon, to share equally.

The birth of Thomas, son of John and Alice ffardon, was the only one registered. It took place on 2 September (the seventh month) 1656.[21] On 16 December 1687 he married Hannah, daughter of Nathaniel Ball, a butcher of North Newton,[22] the man in whose house the early Quaker meetings were held. By then Thomas was a yeoman. Their five children's births were registered between 1688 and 1701, and it is their descendants who continued to feature in the registers until Eliza Fardon's burial in February 1837. According to the burial entries, John ffardon of Northnewton died on 12 July 1677,[23] his daughter Elizabeth ffardon being buried on 30 August 1681,[24] and Hannah the wife of Thomas was interred at Banbury on 12 January 1705/6.[25]

On the face of it, it would seem that John and Alice were early recruits to the Society of Friends, especially as Nathaniel Ball witnessed his will, but it may well be that it was their son Thomas, and that he was instrumental in recording his own birth and the death of his father. John ffardon did not witness any of the marriages recorded before his demise, although his wife Alice did so, yet her death is not reported. The parish registers of Broughton unfortunately only survive from 1683, so we cannot see who of the Fardons, if any, remained constant to the Established Church before this.

Joseph Besse's *Sufferings of the Quakers*, published

in 1753, drawing on Quarter Sessions records, covers Oxfordshire for the years 1654–89/90. In 1678 Thomas Fardon was committed to prison at the suit of the Rector of Broughton for a demand of £5 in tithes. While he was in gaol the priest's tithe-gatherer took corn off his ground worth £7.[26] In 1689/90 corn, hay and 'other things' were taken for predial tithes at North Newton from Nathaniel Ball and Thomas Pardon (sic), to the value of £12.[27] This latter entry more than likely is a mistranscription or misprint of Fardon or Vardon.

The registers tell us that branches of the Fardons had installed themselves at nearby Deddington by 1720,[28] were in Sibford Ferris before 1771,[29] and in the cities of Worcester and London in 1805[30] and 1823[31] respectively. From North Newington their bodies were carried to Banbury for burial in the graveyard next to the meeting house, to Adderbury

Part of the register of the Banbury Monthly Meeting of the Society of Friends, Oxfordshire, recording the birth of Thomas, son of John and Alice ffardon of North Newington on the 2nd day of the 7th month 1656. The 7th month was September until 1752, when the Gregorian Calendar was adopted and the New Year commenced on 1 January rather than 25 March as before. RG6/1332 p5

Part of the register of the Banbury Monthly Meeting of the Society of Friends, Oxfordshire, recording the names of relatives and Friends present at the wedding of Thomas Fardon of North Newington and Hannah Ball, on 16 December 1687. Hannah's father Nathaniel Ball and other ffardon and Ball kinsmen can be detected amongst the names. RG6/1220 p106

from nearby Deddington, and some of the family were taken to Sibford Gower and Shutford.

By an examination of the entries we can count the number of Quaker families in North Newington, how long they remained adherents, and conjecture whether they drifted away from the Society, or simply moved to a different district. It has been estimated that about twelve Quaker families lived in the hamlet in the seventeenth century; by the nineteenth there were only two,[32] the decline no doubt exacerbated by the fact that there was no meeting house there, which meant a journey to Banbury for worship. The Fardons were gone soon after 1771. From the registers, too, we can see what occupations the Fardons pursued. They were yeomen, maltsters, clockmakers and bakers, and three found work as a currier, a glover and a schoolmaster.

Beyond the period of the Quaker registers we have to rely principally on extant parish registers, the Bishop's Transcripts of them, wills, manorial records, and title deeds for evidence of earlier filiations. There are, however, fairly regular county listings of taxpayers, dating from the late thirteenth century which are arranged under hundreds, wapentakes or sokes, and then by the towns, villages and hamlets of which they were made up. These lists form a directory of names of local people. In most only those inhabitants liable to pay are named, but occasionally there are lists of people who were exempted by reason of poverty, and of those who were in arrears.

Besides fixing an individual in place and time, the assessments and returns inform us about his current economic status, on what that wealth was chiefly based, and how much of it he was expected to contribute in tax. A sequence of these can trace how that wealth and its nature altered, taking into consideration such factors as fluctuating land values, and shortage of labour pushing up wages. A person's name will appear but once for each levy, and was at the place of his last abode. If his wealth was scattered over several places a certificate of residence was furnished by the Tax Commissioners as proof of payment where he actually lived when the sum was collected. For this reason also, the nominal lists can distinguish whether there were one or two individuals of the same name in the same place at the same time, when other sources may be ambiguous (provided that both fell within the tax band). Suggestions as to continuity of residence, and the succession of tax payers in a family, including their widows, can be derived from a sequence of the lists. For example, a widow's name *in lieu* of that of an individual recorded in the previous assessment with similar wealth or more (allowing for

that disposed of under his will or other arrangement), may indicate the interval during which death occurred, the period to be scanned for a burial, and for a will, grant of letters of administration, and probate inventory. When a person's name disappears it may not always be caused by death, for he could be living and be assessed elsewhere, or have fallen beneath the tax threshold for that particular levy.

Similarly, where a family's origins are unknown, an inspection of taxation assessments and returns over a wider area than where it was last known to be can reveal the surname's distribution and give a clue as to where to look next. The tax lists predate parish registers, and can fill gaps left where they may be defective, and because they date from the late thirteenth century, are an invaluable means by which the origins and development of personal and hereditary names can be studied (be it patronymic, locative topographical, occupational or nickname), together with longevity of settlement, population movement patterns, wealth and size of the community, surname spelling styles and adoption of aliases.

To understand the amounts assessed we really need to read the relevant statutes, for the basis of assessment was not constant. We do not always know, either, if there was any allowance made for subsistence before the wealth of a person was calculated, so the figures given may not be a true reflection of his total financial position. The Lay Subsidies were imposed on movables (goods and chattels or personalty), land or wages, whichever was of the greatest value, so that although a person was taxed on his goods he may also have possessed land and earned wages of lesser, excluded, amounts.

The Lay Subsidy levied by Act of Parliament in 1523, and spread over four years, as we have seen in chapter 3, set the basis of assessment as possession of lands worth £50 annual clear value, at 12*d* in the pound, payable in each of those four years; 12*d* in the pound was payable each year on personalty of £20 and upwards, 6*d* in the pound on personalty worth 40*s* and under £20, and 4*d* in the pound for people of sixteen and over earning daily, weekly or yearly wages amounting to 20*s* or with goods worth 40*s*. Aliens paid double.

At Broughton, in the hundred of Bloxham, John and Juliana Vardon paid 18*d* on £3,[33] category not stated, but we can deduce from the Statute that it was on personalty, rated at 6*d* in the pound because it was worth over 40*s*. By 1542 the goods of John Vardon were valued at £5 and he was paying 20*d* in tax.[34] The rate of the imposition would seem to have been 4*d* in the pound, but the Statute shows that the

Table 3 *The Fardon taxpayers at North Newington and Broughton, Bloxham hundred, Oxfordshire*

Note the various ways of spelling the surname, possibly a clue as to how it was pronounced locally.

Date	Name	Nature	Value	Assessment	Remarks
15 Henry VIII 1523/4	JOHN and JULIANA VARDON	[goods]	[£3]	xviij*d*	Lay Subsidy. Years 1 and 2: based on 6*d* in the £ for
16 Henry VIII 1524/5	As above	[goods]	iij^{li}	xviij*d*	goods worth 40*s* and under £20
34 + 35 Henry VIII 1542–44	JOHN VARDON	goods	v^{li}	xx*d*	Lay Subsidy. Year 1: 4*d* in the £ on goods worth £3 or more
8 + 9 Eliz 1565–67	THOMAS VERDON	goods	iij^{li}	ij*s* vj*d*	Lay Subsidy. 2nd payment: 10*d* in the £ on goods worth £3 +
18 + 19 Eliz 1575–77	THOMAS VERDON	goods	iij^{li}	iij*s*	Lay Subsidy. 2nd payment: 1*s* 2*d* in the £ on goods worth £3 +
23 Eliz 1580/1	THOMAS FFARDON	goods	iij^{li}	v*s*	Lay Subsidy. Year 1: 1*s* 8*d* in the £ on goods worth £3 +
22 James I 1 Mch 1624/5	RICHARD VARDEN	lands	xx*s*	iiij*s*	Lay Subsidy. 4*s* in the £ on lands worth 20*s* pa +
3 Charles I 1627	RICHARD VARDEIN	lands	xx*s*	viij*s*	5 Lay Subsidies. 1st and 2nd payments at 4*s* in the £ on lands worth 20*s* pa +
4 Charles I 23 Dec 1628	RICHARD VARDEN	lands	xx*s*	iiij*s*	4th out of 5 payments at the same rate
18 Charles I 31 May 1642	RICHARD VARNAN and his son JOHN	[county quota]	—	x*s*	Lay Subsidy. 1st of 2 payments
15 Nov 1661	JOHN FFARDING, yeoman	[contribution]	—	2*s* 6*d*	Free and Voluntary present
15 Charles II 29 Oct 1663	JOHN FFARDON	land	[20*s*]	8*s* 0*d*	4 Lay Subsidies. 1st and 2nd payments of 4*s* in the £ on land worth 20*s* pa +
16 Charles II 17 Mch 1663/4	JOHN FFARDON	land	[20*s*]	8*s* 0*d*	3rd and 4th payments at same rate
11 Oct 1662	JOHN FFARDON	hearths	3 hearths	[3*s* 0*d*]	Hearth Tax 1st half of 2*s* tax per hearth
17 Charles II 1665/6	JOHN FFARDIN	hearths	iij hearths	[3*s* 0*d*]	Hearth Tax half-yearly payment at above rate

The Lay Subsidy assessment of Broughton and North Newington, hundred of Bloxham, Oxfordshire, 23 Elizabeth (1581), in which Thomas ffardon is listed as owing 5s in tax on goods worth £3. By far the biggest contribution was to come from Richard ffenys, who was assessed at £5–6s–8d on annual income of £40 from his lands. He was the inhabitant of Broughton Castle. E179/162/345 m6

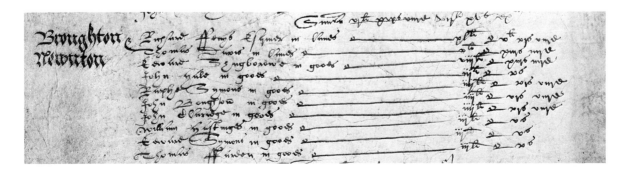

tax was paid in three instalments, and the basis was 8*d* in the pound for goods worth £5 and under £10, 4*d* in the pound to be collected in the first year, and 2*d* in the pound in each of the second and third years. In 1566/7 John's name was absent, replaced by that of Thomas Verdon, whose goods, assessed at £3, attracted 2*s* 6*d* in tax.[35] He was possibly the Thomas ffardon paying 5*s* on goods worth an identical amount in 1580/1.[36] Richard Varden, some 40 years later, in March 1624/5, was assessed at 4*s* in the pound on land worth 20*s* a year clear.[37] As this was after the

enclosure made by Richard Fiennes, presumably his land was now worth more than his goods. In May 1642 Richard Varnon and his son John paid 10*s* in tax as the first instalment towards the £6,418–4*s*– 9*d* contribution from Oxfordshire to make up the requisite subsidy of £400,000.[38] Between 1661 and 1665/6 it is John ffardon's name which appears under Broughton and North Newington (spelt ffarding in 1661, when he was described as a yeoman). Over a period of six years he paid out at least £1–10*s*–6*d* in national taxes: in 1661 he gave 2*s* 6*d* as a 'free and voluntary present' to the King to help with reparations of the royal fishponds and other commodities after the Restoration, and was one of eleven subscribers from his hamlet who raised £1–19*s*–0*d* amongst them;[39] next year he was contributing 6*s* for his three hearths,[40] a year later, on 29 October, 8*s* for his land (at 4*s* in the pound), being the first two of four Subsidies,[41] and the balance of an equal amount on

ABOVE *The first of two payments of a Subsidy taxed and assessed at Banbury, Oxfordshire, on 31 May 18 Charles I (1642). Among the taxpayers contributing to the fixed quota were Richard Varnan and his son John, who paid ten shillings, at Broughton and North Newington, in the hundred of Bloxham. E179/164/493*

RIGHT *The Hearth Tax return of North Newington, hundred of Bloxham, Oxfordshire, made by the constable, John Browne, on 11 October 1662. John ffardon's house had 3 chargeable hearths, and also listed are three women heads of household. E179/255/4, pt 2, p179*

17 March 1663/4;[42] and finally a further 6s for his hearths in 1665/6.[43] Presumably he is the man dying in 1675/6, having left his dwelling house and other land in North Newington to his son Thomas. One feature of these sixteenth- and seventeenth-century lists is that only one Fardon appears in each list for the hamlet with the exceptions of 1523 and 1642, suggesting descent of property almost intact. John's grandson, Jonathan Fardon, who married Elizabeth Lamb in 1733, is recorded in the Treasury Books as having paid an annual duty of £2 to the Officer of Excise for a two-wheeled chaise at his residence in Adderbury in 1754 and 1755.[44] To this was added a two-wheeled chair in 1756, attracting a further £2 in duty, but in 1758 he was contributing merely for the chaise.[45]

The Land Tax assessment for 1798 gave Thomas Fardon as both the proprietor and occupier of land in Sibford Ferris, in the hundred of Bloxham, on which he had to pay 9s 4d.[46] At Adderbury West, 'Mr Fardon' owned land occupied by Josiah Cox, assessed at 10s 11d.[47] A marginal note referred to a contract of 17 April 1799, whereby any future liability for the tax was redeemed and exonerated by a lump sum payment. Looking at the Register of Redemption Certificates, under the reference number cited in the assessment, the contractor's name was given as Thomas Fardon.[48] His landholding was a freehold close of about five acres, on which he paid consideration of £10–19s–7¾d in cash for redemption and received a receipt for it on 21 May 1799. Unfortunately the contract does not identify where he lived.

A glance at the Quaker registers showed that Thomas Fardon of Sibford Ferris died on 3 March 1803, aged thirty-one.[49] Whether he was the Adderbury West landowner is uncertain, but no Fardon was listed as occupying land there in 1798. The only other apparent candidate is his uncle, born in 1732/3,[50] and the last Fardon to register his children's births at Banbury Meeting, and we do not

know what happened to him after 1771. However, there was a Thomas Fardon occupying land at Deddington,[51] the adjacent parish to Adderbury, and other possibilities are that the Adderbury land proprietor was not a Quaker at all, or came from an entirely different branch of the family. Earlier Land Tax assessments, manorial Court Baron minutes, any surviving title deeds or wills may well yield the answer and explain who he was and how he came to own the land and when.

Another useful directory of names is contained in the Association Oath Rolls of 1696. These were signed by the High Sheriff, Deputy Lieutenants and justices of the peace, most of the gentlemen free-

The 1798 Land Tax assessment of Adderbury West, hundred of Bloxham, Oxfordshire; Mr Fardon was the proprietor of the land occupied by Josiah Cox, and the contract date refers to the agreement whereby any future liability was redeemed. There are a number of owner-occupiers on the list. IR23/69 f120d

Certificate of contract no 36,573, dated 17 April 1799, made between the Oxfordshire Land Tax Commissioners and Thomas Fardon for the redemption of the annual liability on a freehold close at Adderbury West, occupied by Josiah Cox. The contract was registered on 15 July 1799, and the consideration money paid over on 18 May. IR24/48

Pedigree of the Fardon Family, of North Newington, Oxfordshire

RICHARD VARNAN = of Broughton and North Newington, Oxon, taxed with his son, 1642

NATHANIEL BALL = of North Newington, 1687, butcher, paid tax on his hearths, 1662 **= HANNAH HASTINGS** marr 20 Apr 1662 at the Friends' Meeting, Banbury, Oxon

JOHN FARDON als VARDON = of North Newington, 1656–76/7, yeoman, held a paper mill at Bodicote, Oxon, and land at Wootton Wawen, Warwickshire, for term of years, 1676/7, contributed a 'free and voluntary present' to King Charles II, 1661, assessed to pay tax on land 1663 and 1663/4, and on hearths 1662 and 1665, died 12 July 1677, will dd 17 Mch 1676/7, pr 24 Nov 1677 **= ALICE**

other issue 2 daughters

JOHN FARDON als VARDON named in father's will, 1676/7

RICHARD FARDON als VARDON, named in father's will, 1676/7, to have land at Wootton Wawen

HANNAH marr 16 Dec 1687 at the Friends' Meeting, Banbury, bur 12 Jan 1705/6, at Banbury **= THOMAS FARDON als VARDON** of North Newington, 1687, maltster 1708, yeoman 1713, bn 2 Sept 1656, registered at the Friends' Meeting, Banbury, named in father's will, 1676/7, to have his house at North Newington, and a paper mill at Bodicote, executor 1677, bur 8 May 1731, at Banbury **= MARY** daughter of CHRISTOPHER FOWLER, of Shipton-upon-Stour, Warwickshire, mercer (dead by 1708), marr 10 May 1708 at the Friends' Meeting, Banbury, bur 10 Feb 1724/5, at Shutford, Oxon

JOHN FARDON of Deddington, clock-maker, 1731, marr 1st 2 Oct 1731, ELIZABETH POTTINGER (who was bur 5 Apr 1734, at Adderbury) and 2nd 8 Nov 1735, MARY COX, of Milton, Oxon, both at the Friends' Meeting, Banbury

ELIZABETH daughter of BENJAMIN LAMB, of Rollright Mill, Oxon, miller, by ELIZABETH, marr 2 Oct 1733, at the Friends' Meeting, Chipping Norton, Oxon **= JONATHAN FARDON** of North Newington, maltster, 1733, bn yeoman, 1763, bn c.20 Mch 1701/2, registered at the Friends' Meeting, Banbury, paid tax on a chaise at Adderbury 1754–5, and also on a chair 1757–8, died 7, bur 11 Nov 1763, at Banbury, aged 61

HANNAH bn 28 May 1694, registered at the Friends' Meeting, Banbury, there marr 20 May 1720, JOHN TUTTY of Hook Norton, Oxon, yeoman

THOMAS FARDON = of North Newington, 1761–71, bn 4 Aug 1737, registered at the Friends' Meeting, Banbury **= ESTHER**

other issue 2 sons 4 daughters

ELIZABETH bn 15 Nov 1771, registered at the Friends' Meeting, Banbury

THOMAS FARDON bn 12 Jan 1769, registered at the Friends' Meeting, Banbury

ELIZABETH bn 24 June 1767, registered at the Friends' Meeting, Banbury, bur 8 Jan 1768, at Banbury

JONATHAN FARDON, bn 9 Mch 1765, registered at the Friends' Meeting, Banbury

HANNAH bn 16 May 1761, registered at the Friends' Meeting, Banbury

MARY, bn 8 June 1763, registered at the Friends' Meeting, Banbury

ELIZABETH bn 22 Feb 1688/9, registered at the Friends' Meeting, Banbury, there marr 16 Nov 1713, JOHN SMITH, of Temple Mill, Swalcliffe, Oxon, miller

RICHARD FARDON = of North Newington, maltster, 1725, bn 6 Oct 1690, registered at the Friends' Meeting, Banbury, died 2, bur 7 Mch 1762, at Banbury, aged 71 **= MARY** daughter of RICHARD ARCHER, of Ascott, Warwickshire (deceased 1725), marr 29 May 1725, at the Friends' Meeting, Banbury

THOMAS FARDON = of Deddington, Oxon, currier, 1720, bn 25 or 26 Apr 1692, registered at the Friends' Meeting, Banbury, bur 19 Sept 1740, at Adderbury, Oxon, aged 48 **= MARY PRESTAGE** of Sibford Gower, Oxon, marr 20 May 1720, at the Friends' Meeting, Banbury, dead by 1781

ANN = bur 4 Nov 1774, at Sibford **= JONATHAN FARDON =** of Sibford Ferris, Oxon, baker, 1771, bn 6 Aug 1740, registered at the Friends' Meeting, Banbury, died 28 Jan, bur 1 Feb 1789, at Sibford Gower, aged c.46 **= HANNAH** daughter of THOMAS HARRIS, of Bloxham, Oxon, yeoman, by HANNAH (both dead by 1781), marr 8 June 1781, at the Friends' Meeting, Adderbury, died 13, bur 16 Oct 1814, at Sibford Gower, aged 70

HANNAH died 10, bur 13 Dec 1778, at Sibford Gower

2 daughters

RICHARD FARDON = of the City of Worcester, Worcestershire, glover, 1805, bn — 1772, registered at the Friends' Meeting, Banbury **= ANN** marr 8 Oct 1805, at the Friends' Meeting, Sibford Gower

EDWIN FARDON bn 15 June 1802, at Sibford Ferris

ELIZA bn 14 Jan 1801, at Sibford Ferris, died 10, bur 19 Feb 1837, at Sibford Gower, aged 36

JEREMIAH LAMB = of Sibford, blacksmith **= ANN**

other issue 2 sons 7 daughters

◆ *3 sons 5 daughters*

THOMAS FARDON = of Sibford Ferris, baker, 1799, bn 30 May 1771, registered at the Friends' Meeting, Banbury, proprietor and occupier of land at Sibford Ferris on which he paid Land Tax, 1798, died 3, bur 9 Mch 1803, at Sibford Gower, aged 31 **= SUSANNA** marr 6 Feb 1799, at the Friends' Meeting, Sibford

JONATHAN FARDON of Islington Road, London, schoolmaster, 1823, bn 1 Nov 1799, at Sibford Ferris, died 14, bur 21 Sept 1823, at Sibford Gower, aged 24

The details in italics refer to sources held outside the Public Record Office

*Part of the extensive roll of names and signatures of
people sworn to defend the King and Government
against the late King James and his adherents and to
avenge any violent or untimely death of their monarch,
and to defend the Protestant Succession. 'The Association
of the high Sheriff of the Deputy Lieutenants and Justices
of the peace most of the Gentlemen ffreeholders and other
princip[ll] inhabitants of ye county of Oxon' and in other
counties was formed after an assassination attempt on
the King. The names include the Grand Jury at the
Quarter Sessions at Oxford on 21 April 1696, though
some signed later or used proxies. John ffardon's name
is in the second column from the left. C213/206*

by proxy, and the General Quarter Sessions, held at
Oxford on Tuesday 21 April, provided the occasion
for a mass signing. Some entries were dated later than
this. The handwriting of the signatures affords an
excellent example of the wide range of styles and
spellings employed by the upper echelons of local
society in setting their names to a formal document
in the late seventeenth century, and it is clear that not
all were able to write their names. A drawback of
the Oxfordshire rolls is that place names were not
invariably listed under each hundred, so we cannot
be precise about where the people came from. A
John ffardon signed on the membrane containing
Glympton residents as well as those of Wroxton,[52]
but these parishes are some miles distant from each
other. Positive identification of Fardon is thus difficult, but if he had signed with his neighbours and
friends, reference back to contemporary Poll Books
of freeholders qualified to vote in the Parliamentary
election of the previous year, parish registers, parish
rate books, and Quaker records of the area where
Fardons were known to be, would probably supply
at least circumstantial evidence as to where he came
from.

holders and principal inhabitants of the English and
Welsh counties, in response to an assassination
attempt made on King William III's life by 'papists
and other wicked and traiterous persons' in order to
instigate a French invasion. The signatories pledged
to support and defend the King's person and Government against the late King James and his adherents,
and to unite together to avenge him should he meet
a violent or untimely death, and to defend the succession to the Crown.

In Oxfordshire, most of the signatures appear to
have been of the people themselves, but others were

[10]

THE WORDSWORTH FAMILY

The activities of William Wordsworth as Stamp Distributor for Westmorland from 1813, and as Poet Laureate from 1843, those of his Uncle Richard, a Customs Officer in Whitehaven, and other Wordsworths involved in the legal profession are chronicled among the archives of the Audit Office, Lord Chamberlain's Department, the Board of Customs and the records of the courts of law.

William Wordsworth, resident of the Lake District and sometime Poet Laureate, was appointed Stamp Distributor for Westmorland and the Penrith District of Cumberland on 6 April 1813, with an annual income of more than £400.[1] The post was conditional on security of £10,000 which he found in two of his benefactors, the Earl of Lonsdale and Sir George Beaumont, Baronet.[2] The bond described him as 'Head Distributor of Stamped Vellum, Parchment and Paper for the County of Westmorland and Part of the County of Cumberland'.[3] Lord Lonsdale had interceded with the Government on his behalf to obtain a post with a pension which would allow him time to pursue his literary work.[4] Dorothy Wordsworth, his sister, wrote to a friend that her brother's predecessor had resigned on account of his inability to conduct the business, which he had delegated to a drunkard with disastrous results. By then the Distributor himself was a septuagenarian, paralysed by a stroke; forty years before the post had been delegated to a servant who waited at table at the Distributor's home at Rydal Mount.[5] In theory the job was a sinecure.

Unfortunately this employment brought no regular salary, nor a pension. Wordsworth was entirely dependent on his fixed commission from the collection of Stamp Duties on newspapers, conveyances and other documents. There was brisk competition among the Distribution Districts and with Head Office in London to collect the various fees from inhabitants and business people operating in several areas. Wordsworth was not accustomed to keeping accounts, so part of his income went to employ a clerk, John Carter, who also served as his gardener at Rydal Mount.[6] A further deduction was the annual pension paid to his predecessor.[7]

A letter from Wordsworth to Viscount Lowther on 28 March 1821 outlined his responsibility to receive Stamps from Head Office and distribute them to his deputies. 'At the close of every quarter, an account is sent to the Head Office in London of the Stamps on Hand, and at the same time Money is remitted to the amount of those sold.

'The Collection of Legacy Duty which is naturally attached to this Office is performed by supplying to Executors and Administrators certain papers called Forms to be then filled up according to the directions contained in them and returned to the Distributor. These papers are forwarded by him once a month to the Head Office where ... they are stamped, then returned to the Distributor, and from him forwarded through his Subdistributors to the Executors, who in these papers receive a Discharge for the Duty due under the Will.'[8] The letter complained of the large stock he had to hold, the preservation of which from the rigours of robbery, fire or other accidents was a great anxiety, and of the amount of time he had to spend on his work. The poundage (commission) was at the rate of four percent, subject to deductions to pay the subdistributors, his clerk and the pension.

In his first year, ended 5 January 1814, Wordsworth collected more than £33,000 in duty.[9] Over the last three years of his term, to mid-1842, the average receipts were slightly lower. The poundage by then had dropped to 1.15 percent on the overall sales for Wordsworth, and 1.1 percent to be divided among the subdistributors for their share: Wordsworth received an emolument of £561–6s–3d.[10] The money, when collected, was placed on deposit at Wakefield and Sons, a Kendal bank.[11] But much of the fees were paid in Scotch notes which the bank required to hold for six weeks before giving any interest.[12] From 1822 the money was remitted monthly to Head Office, so no interest accrued.[13] In the face of all this Wordsworth was compelled to try and widen his district and his field of activities. At the end of 1820 Workington, Cockermouth and Maryport were added,[14] joined by the sizeable Carlisle District in 1831.[15] In 1834, when the Board of Stamps was combined with Taxes, his income and workload correspondingly increased. On 20 October 1831 his son William was appointed as resident subdistributor at Carlisle.[16] Some of the subdistributors were not honest, others were threatened with bankruptcy in

The resignation of William Wordsworth as Distributor of Stamps for Cumberland and Westmorland on 3 June 1842 was followed by the appointment of his son William as his successor on 13 June, with the recommendation that he live at Carlisle, where the collection was biggest. IR13/67 no 62

The warrant dated 6 April 1843 for the swearing in and admission of William Wordsworth as Poet Laureate in place of his deceased near neighbour, Robert Southey. He was succeeded by Alfred Tennyson after his own death in April 1850. LC3/71 p230

the management of their own affairs and Wordsworth was forced to take steps to protect the Board's finances.[17] It was far from the comfortable position he had anticipated.

On 3 June 1842 he submitted his resignation to the Board and was succeeded by his son, William Wordsworth.[18] Whereas the poet had kept his stock at his Rydal home, although the head station was more than fifty miles to the north, at Penrith, the Board now stipulated that his son should live in

Diagram 5: An elaborate Strict Settlement of the Sockbridge estate in Westmorland, made under the poet's will, 1847

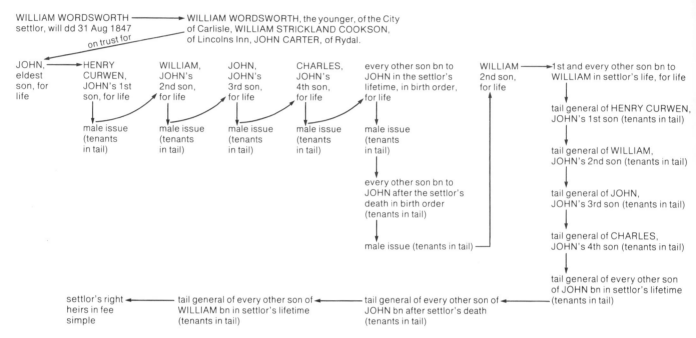

Settlement Trustees

WILLIAM WORDSWORTH → WILLIAM WORDSWORTH, the younger, of the City
settlor, will dd 31 Aug 1847   of Carlisle, WILLIAM STRICKLAND COOKSON,
       on trust for   of Lincolns Inn, JOHN CARTER, of Rydal.

JOHN, → HENRY | WILLIAM, | JOHN, | CHARLES, | every other son bn to | | WILLIAM → 1st and every other son bn to
eldest | CURWEN, | JOHN's | JOHN's | JOHN's | JOHN in the settlor's | | 2nd son, | WILLIAM in settlor's life, for life
son, for | JOHN's 1st | 2nd son, | 3rd son, | 4th son, | lifetime, in birth order, | | for life
life | son, for life | for life | for life | for life | for life

male issue | male issue | male issue | male issue | male issue
(tenants | (tenants | (tenants | (tenants | (tenants
in tail) | in tail) | in tail) | in tail) | in tail)

tail general of HENRY CURWEN,
JOHN's 1st son (tenants in tail)

tail general of WILLIAM,
JOHN's 2nd son (tenants in tail)

every other son bn to
JOHN after the settlor's
death in birth order
(tenants in tail)

tail general of JOHN,
JOHN's 3rd son (tenants in tail)

male issue (tenants in tail)

tail general of CHARLES,
JOHN's 4th son (tenants in tail)

tail general of every other son
of JOHN bn in settlor's lifetime
(tenants in tail)

settlor's right ← tail general of every other son of ← tail general of every other son of ←
heirs in fee   WILLIAM bn in settlor's lifetime   JOHN bn after settlor's death
simple   (tenants in tail)   (tenants in tail)

Carlisle, which was by far the biggest source of collection. An increase of his commission to two percent was recommended, in view of his extra personal workload.

William Wordsworth was subsequently nominated Poet Laureate by a Royal Warrant of 6 April 1843, in the place of his late near neighbour, Robert Southey, of Keswick in Cumberland.[19] The salary it brought him was £72 a year, payable in quarterly instalments.[20] After his death he was succeeded by Alfred Tennyson on 19 November 1850.

William Wordsworth's will was made on 31 August 1847.[21] In it he set up a strict settlement of the freehold and customary land in the parish of Barton in Westmorland, to which he was entitled under the will of his nephew, John Wordsworth, a surgeon at Ambleside in the same county, subject to a life annuity of £150 for Jane, the widow of the poet's brother Richard, and now wife of John Lightfoot. A life estate was given to his eldest son Rev. John Wordsworth, then to John's eldest son, Henry Curwen Wordsworth, with remainders to the first and every other son of the latter as tenants in tail in succession. The diagram sets out the settlement and the final provision for the reversion of the fee simple estate to the poet's heir at law, and if there was more than

Portrait of William Wordsworth by B. R. Haydon. National Portrait Gallery, London.

one, they were to hold the land as joint tenants. One of the conditions for possession was that the person entitled should apply within twelve calendar months for a royal licence to acquire and use the name and arms of Wordsworth, unless already doing so.

He bequeathed a carved oak almery (*sic*) or chest in his dining room at Rydal Mount to his son William for life and thereafter to his grandson William (son of Rev. John), which, with the sword once belonging to the poet's late brother, Captain John Wordsworth, were to pass as heirlooms to whomever was entitled to the land. The chest's inscription read 'Hoc op' fiebat Ao Dni MCCCCCXXV ex sūptu Willmi Wordesworth filii W. fil Joh: fil W. fil Nich: viri Elizabeth filia et hered W. P'ctor de Penystō qorū anīabus prpicietur De' ' [translated: this work was made in the year of Our Lord 1525 at the expense of William Wordesworth son of W. son of John son of W. son of Nicholas husband of Elizabeth daughter and heiress of W. Proctor of Penystone on whose souls may God have mercy]. Apparently it was owned by the Wordsworths of Penistone in Yorkshire until the last decades of the eighteenth century when it was sold, but was given to the poet in 1840. It now sits in Dove Cottage Museum at Grasmere in Westmorland.[22]

William Wordsworth also held land in Applethwaite in Cumberland, which he gave to Edward Quillinan, the widower of his daughter Dorothy, for life, and then to his son William, the Distributor of Stamps. The residue of his estate, not mentioned in the will, was to be put on trust for sale at the best price and the proceeds used to settle his debts, funeral and probate expenses, while the balance was to be invested in the names of his trustees, the annual income passing to his widow Mary, with sufficient money set aside to effect a life annuity of £100 for his sister Dorothy, to commence payment on his widow's demise, the trustees withholding what they deemed appropriate to maintain and support her in comfort. Unfortunately for her, she died on 25 January 1855, four years before her sister-in-law. The trust capital was to be held for the two sons equally.

The executors and trustees included Wordsworth's faithful clerk, John Carter, and his son, William, and it was proved in the Prerogative Court of Canterbury on 27 May 1850, after his death on 23 April.

The Death Duty Register[23] records that another probate was granted in the Prerogative Court of York on 30 July, relating to his property in that province, amounting to under £9,000. His literary works were valued at £2,000 and upgraded his estate in P.C.C. from below £9,000 to under £12,000. An abstract

for Legacy Duty purposes would have been compiled by his son William as one of the executors, who in his other role also arranged for the collection of the duty and its transmission to London. The rates of payment under the Stamp Act of 1815 were £5 at one percent on the legacy of £500 to the poet's granddaughter, Jane Stanley Wordsworth, made on 19 February 1859, and £212–9s–6d being one percent of the residue of £21,247–18s–1d shared by his two sons, paid on 19 July 1859. The Register also notes that the widow died on 17 January 1859, his son John on 25 July 1875, and the granddaughter on 9 January 1912, and it provides the dates of death of two grandsons, William on 7 March 1917, and John on 30 January 1927.

The residuary account[24] of his estate shows that the manuscript of 'The Prelude' was worth £750, the

---

Part of the Death Duty Accounts filed in February 1859, of the estate in the provinces of York and Canterbury of William Wordsworth, after the death of his widow on 17 January. This extract relates to moneys and debentures in the province of York, including heirlooms valued at £15 (probably the sword and oak almery), the manuscript of 'The Prelude', worth £750, and railway debentures for the life of his son-in-law, an ironic investment considering his violent opposition to extending the line from Windermere to Grasmere. IR59/42

two heirlooms £15 and his books at Rydal Mount £241–18s–3d. There was £25 in cash in the house, he had debts of 2s 1d in Income Tax, 2s 8d in Church rates, and owed the washerwoman five guineas and £25–15s in wages to servants. Among his investments were five shares in the Australian Agricultural Company, valued at £75 in 1850 and £350 when his wife died. Duty was based on the difference.

The Field Book prepared for the Valuation Office under the Finance Act of 1909 for the purposes of assessing Increment Value Duty on the value of the site,[25] reckoned Rydal Mount and its garden to be worth £1,730 gross market value for the fee simple, and the site itself, minus the buildings, was calculated at £200. The freehold was owned in 1910 by Stanley Hughes le Fleming who lived close by in Rydal Hall, and the occupier was John Fisher Wordsworth on a tenancy of fourteen years from 11 November 1897, at an annual rent of £105. He was also responsible for the rates and taxes and for insurance. The Field Book tells us that the house contained a wine cellar and two larders, a dining room, drawing room, morning room, kitchen, scullery and pantry on the ground floor, on the first floor were seven bedrooms and a bathroom and wc, and on the second another bedroom and two boxrooms. There were two coachhouses, greenhouses, a heating chamber, stick-houses, a potting shed and tool sheds in the grounds, and the overall condition of the buildings was described as fair.

William Wordsworth's father, John, was an attorney, and acted for the first Earl of Lonsdale. Registers of affidavits of due execution of articles of clerkship of attorneys in the Court of King's Bench show that on 2 September 1760 he was at Penrith in Cumberland when attached for five years to Andrew Whelpdale, who practised there.[26] Unfortunately, the original affidavits to 1775 do not survive, so these are the only available particulars, but we know that the articles were transferred to a London attorney, John Baynes Garforth, of St Marylebone, for the completion of the term, and that on 17 December 1761, threepence Apprenticeship duty was paid on the five shilling premium.[27] Once admitted as a lawyer, he returned to Cumberland and set up at Cockermouth. Attorneys specialized in common law, but had no right of appearance in the superior courts, briefing a barrister to do this for their clients. On 21 May 1768, Richard Wordsworth, described as John's son, of Cockermouth, was articled to him for five years,[28] a penny-halfpenny being levied in duty.[29] Like John, his articles were transferred to a London-based lawyer, Anthony Parkin, at a premium of £7–10s, in 1772.[30] John took on other trainees, paying duty on the premiums in 1772,[31] 1773[32] and 1779,[33] while Richard did likewise in 1780,[34] when he was in business at Whitehaven in Cumberland. He moved to Branthwaite, in the same county, and as an attorney of the Court of King's Bench took on Richard

Apprenticeship Book recording moneys received by the Commissioners of Stamp Duties. Duty of 1½d was paid on 31 May 1768 on the five shilling premium for the five years' articles of clerkship entered by Richard Wordsworth with John Wordsworth, an attorney, at Cockermouth, Cumberland. In 1772 the remainder of the term was transferred to a London attorney and a further Duty of 3s 9d paid. IR 1/25 p165 no 15

Wordsworth as his clerk under an indenture of 18 February 1786,[35] the other parties being Richard Wordsworth of Whitehaven and Christopher Crackanthorpe Cookson of Penrith (the boy's guardians). His articles were to prepare him to be both an attorney and solicitor allowing him to deal with cases for the Equity Courts. A further indenture of 31 December 1790[36] assigned the remainder of his five-year period to Anthony Parkin of Holborn Court, Gray's Inn, Middlesex, who was an attorney in the General Post Office and was his principal's London agent.[37] Richard was sworn in and admitted in the Court of Common Pleas, as of Staple Inn, on 10 February 1794. The printed *Law List* for 1799 reveals that he ran his practice from 11 Staple Inn, dealing with work for both the King's Bench and Court of Common Pleas. By 1811 he was in partnership with Richard Addison and continued from 9 Staple Inn until he died in 1816.

The poet's uncle, Richard Wordsworth, the guardian of the above attorney's clerk in the 1786 indenture, was engaged as an Additional Waiter for the Board of Customs at the Port of Whitehaven under a Treasury Warrant of 16 July 1761;[38] by 1 September he was promoted a Landwaiter.[39] A letter from the Commissioners of the Board of Customs to the Collector there gave instructions for his training in 'the discharging of foreign and Coast Goods and to learn the gauge and if after six months attendance you find him sufficiently qualified you are to join with the rest of the principal officers in a cert. thereof and transmit the same to us'.[40]

Wordsworth was directed by the Board in June 1764 to go to Berwick-upon-Tweed to deal with two loads of tobacco due to arrive shortly, as none had ever been landed there before and an experienced officer was necessary to help weigh the goods and exact the relevant duty.[41] For this he was to take a third of the sum for himself 'as an Encouragement to the Officers who make the Seizure'. He was to hasten back, but first settle with the Collector for horse hire, riding charges in either direction, and

the number of days' attendance, plus any reasonable allowance. If he was diligent and careful, five shillings a day would not be thought too much.

The Board was notified on 22 August 1768 that he had a relation who had recently died in South Yorkshire and 'has left him some Business of Consequence to transact, that Obliges him to Crave your Honrs leave for six weeks absence to attend the same'.[42] Leave was granted for a month, with a loss of two-thirds of his salary. The Board was more magnanimous on 23 July 1772 when a Treasury Warrant gave consent for three months' absence to attend to his private affairs, as no penalty was imposed.[43]

The affidavit of due execution of articles of clerkship of Richard Wordsworth, sworn by a witness, William Arnot, on 5 March 1786, and filed in the Court of King's Bench (Plea Side). Richard Wordsworth, of Whitehaven, and Christopher Crackanthorpe Cookson, of Penrith, were the clerk's guardians and the attorney, Richard Wordsworth, was his cousin. Note that Stamp Duty of eightpence was paid. KB105/3 no 6015

Pedigree of the Wordsworths of Cumberland and Westmorland

RICHARD WORDSWORTH =
purchaser of the Sockbridge estate,
parish of Barton, Westmorland, died 1760

RICHARD WORDSWORTH = *ELIZABETH FAVELL*
of Whitehaven, Cumberland, bn c. 1731, additional
waiter at the Port of Whitehaven from 16 July 1761,
acting Land Surveyor, 4 May 1775, and 1777,
Landwaiter 6 June 1776, appointed Collector
18 Mch 1778, aged 41 in 1772, died 18 June 1794

JOHN WORDSWORTH = *ANN COOKSON*
of Sockbridge, 1758, Penrith, Cumberland, 1760, and *marr 5 Feb 1766, at*
Cockermouth, Cumberland, attorney, 1768, articled as *St Andrew, Penrith*
a clerk to JOHN RICHARDSON, of Penrith 7 Nov 1758,
to ANDREW WHELPDALE, 2 Sept 1760, and to JOHN
BAYNES GARFORTH, of London, 5 Nov 1761. *died 1783*

RICHARD WORDSWORTH
of Branthwaite, Cumberland,
attorney, 1786, articled as a
clerk to his 'father' JOHN
WORDSWORTH, 21 May
1768, articles assigned to
ANTHONY PARKIN, of the
General Post Office,
London, 2 June 1772

RICHARD WORDSWORTH =
of Staple Inn, London,
attorney, articled as a clerk to
RICHARD WORDSWORTH,
18 Feb 1786, articles
assigned to ANTHONY
PARKIN, 31 Dec 1790, held
land at Sockbridge, named in
brother's will, 1847, as
deceased, *died 1816*

JANE
named in
brother-in-
law's will,
1847

= JOHN
LIGHTFOOT
named in will of
WILLIAM
WORDSWORTH,
1847

WILLIAM WORDSWORTH =
of Rydal Mount, Rydal,
Westmorland, Stamp
Distributor for Cumberland
and Westmorland, 1813–42,
Poet Laureate 6 Apr 1843
until his death, devised land
at Sockbridge under his
nephew JOHN's will, held
land at Applethwaite,
Cumberland, died 23 Apr
1850, will dd 31 Aug 1847,
codicil dd 30 Dec 1848, pr
27 May 1850. Death Duty
paid 1859

MARY
HUTCHINSON
named in
husband's will,
1847, died
17 Jan 1859

JOHN
WORDSWORTH
Captain, Hon.
East India
Company
Service, named
in brother's will,
1847, as
deceased, *died*
1805

DOROTHY
named in
brother's will,
1847, died
25 Jan 1855

JOHN WORDSWORTH =
of Ambleside, Westmorland,
surgeon, held land at Sockbridge,
died 1846, having made a will,
named in uncle WILLIAM's will,
1847, as deceased

JOHN WORDSWORTH =
Clerk in Holy Orders,
named in father's will,
1847, to have land at
Sockbridge, died
25 July 1875

WILLIAM WORDSWORTH =
of the City of Carlisle, Cumberland,
gent, 1850, Stamp Distributor for
Cumberland and Westmorland,
13 June 1842, named in father's
will, 1847, to have an oak almery,
executor 1850

EDWARD QUILLINAN = DOROTHY
named in father-in-law's   named in father's
will, 1847, to have land at will, 1847, as
Applethwaite, aged 58 in   deceased, died
1847, died — July 1852   9 July 1847

HENRY CURWEN WORDSWORTH
named in grandfather's will, 1847,
as eldest son

WILLIAM WORDSWORTH
named in grandfather's will,
1847, as 2nd son, died
7 Mch 1917

JOHN WORDSWORTH
named in grandfather's
will, 1847, as 3rd son,
died 30 Jan 1927

CHARLES WORDSWORTH
named in grandfather's will,
1847, as 4th son

JANE STANLEY
named in grandfather's
will, 1847, under 21,
died 9 Jan 1912

The details in italics refer to sources held outside the Public Record Office

Richard Wordsworth became Land Surveyor on 4 May 1775, with an allowance of £10 awarded him to make his income up to £50 a year.[44] This promotion came about because of the age and infirmity of Daniel Fleming, the existing Surveyor, who was to continue with Wordsworth's assistance.

But affairs had reached crisis-point at Whitehaven, for on 6 June 1776 the Surveyor General reported to the Board on an information received that there was an accounting deficiency, false weights having been recorded for tobacco landed there, thus committing a fraud on the Revenue.[45] Wordsworth and four of the Landwaiters were not dismissed, but were strictly warned to be extremely careful in the execution of their duty. This was only the tip of the iceberg. The trouble appears to have stemmed from the appointment of George Harrington as Collector on 29 December 1774.[46] One of the officers was dismissed by him for neglect of duty, bad conduct, smuggling and drunkenness in early 1777;[47] another was reported for not having appeared once during the three weeks after his engagement;[48] Wordsworth himself brought the Board's attention, accused in December 1776 of impertinently refusing to give the Collector access to the Landwaiters' Book of ships importing tobacco, but this complaint was thrown out after further investigation by the Board,[49] along with a charge against other officers for embezzling tea.[50]

On 27 March 1777, the Board Commissioners wrote to the County Surveyor General that many of the papers relative to the Port of Whitehaven seemed to be running into great confusion 'through the very extraordinary and irregular Conduct of the Collector'.[51] For example, a new set of beams was sent to replace the old, decayed ones used for weighing goods, but was not put into use for eighteen months in spite of repeated and urgent pressure from Richard Wordsworth.[52] The Collector had also openly refused to accept Wordsworth's elevation to Acting Land Surveyor in 1775, and challenged him for some offence taken in the discharge of his duty.[53] 'How little knowledge soever he may have had of the Nature and duty of his Office on his first Entrance upon it, We nevertheless hoped that by a calm and steady Attention to every part of his Duty he would by degrees make himself Master of it . . . we had but too soon Cause to apprehend the contrary, for in May last, we found our selves under the Necessity of Mulcting the Collector three Months salary.'[54] After consideration of his answer to the myriad charges, the Board dismissed Harrington on 24 May; on 5

Ages and Capacities of Customs Officers at the Port of Whitehaven, Cumberland, for the year ended Christmas 1776. No 3 on the list, Richard Wordsworth, Waiter and Assistant Searcher, is described as 'an officer whos [sic] behaviour has been very Improper.' In March 1777 he was reported to the Commissioners in London for being impertinent to the Collector. The Collector was later dismissed and in 1777 the annual report gave Wordsworth as 'A very good officer now acting Land Surveyor.' CUST82/178

June it issued a threat of legal action if he continued to withhold his papers and refused to sign the Abstract of account up to 28 May to show what money was in his hands when dismissed.[55]

A Treasury Warrant of 17 March 1778 appointed Richard Wordsworth as the new Collector and he was awarded £640 to defray the necessary expenses of the Port.[56] First, he was asked to nominate to the Examiners of Officers two sufficient persons in the sum of £4,000 as security for his post, and to certify that they had enough money to answer the sum.[57] In return he was to be given all the books, bonds, papers, seals, stamps and other relevant material to the position.

On his appointment Wordsworth's salary increased to £90 a year, with an additional allowance for a clerk.[58] The returns of Officers, Stations, ages, qualifications, residence and places appointed, survive for Whitehaven from 1771.[59] From this we see the descending order of staff down to the boatmen who were paid £5 a quarter. The County Surveyor General, Charles Lutwidge, received £30 each quarter. In the year ended at Christmas 1772, Richard Wordsworth was described as aged forty-one, living at Whitehaven, and working there as an Additional Waiter and Searcher. His conduct then and in 1773 and 1774 was described as good and very good; but the return

made on 5 January 1777 recorded that he was 'An Officer whose behaviour has been very Improper' (exacerbated by Harrington's presence as Collector, no doubt), but his reputation was restored by the next year.

During his time as Collector, various local deputies were appointed for the absentee Patent Comptroller, Peter Garrick, the brother of the actor, David Garrick. The last, John Smith, took over as Comptroller on 15 April 1797, after Garrick's death at Lichfield.[60] It is likely that he and Wordsworth were in business correspondence from time to time.

On 18 June 1794 the Board's Commissioners were informed that 'About Four o'clock this Morning Mr Richard Wordsworth Collector here departed this life the Deputy Customer has taken the charge of the Collector ...'.[61] According to the published letters of William and Dorothy Wordsworth, the cause of his demise was jaundice, a cough, and swelling of the legs, all symptoms of dropsy.[62]

In this example we are fortunate that published private correspondence can illuminate what the public records contain about offices of profit and the professions, the responsibilities and problems which went with them, and their holders' attitudes towards their careers.

11

THE GARRICK AND MARX FAMILIES

Here are two contrasting immigrant families. First we have the Huguenot grandparents of the actor David Garrick, arriving in the penultimate decade of the seventeenth century, settling in the City of London and worshipping in the French Protestant Church in Threadneedle Street. They were granted letters of denization giving them rights as British subjects, and a son took a commission in the Army where he remained for the rest of his life. Among his sons, living in Lichfield in Staffordshire, one became an attorney's articled clerk, another obtained a Customs Office sinecure, and the third shared the patent of the Drury Lane Theatre in London. Two centuries after their arrival, a descendant on the female line changed his name by deed poll as a reminder of his famous connections.

The second family belongs to Karl Marx, whose arrival at the Port of London in 1849 is plotted among the Home Office records, along with his failed memorial for a certificate of naturalization.

The Pulman Collection, at the College of Arms in London, contains Peter Fermignac's English translation of the Journal compiled by a Huguenot immigrant, David Garric, covering family events between 1685 and 1701.[1] It has been published.[2] He writes 'The 4th Oct. 1685 – I Garric, arrived at London, having come from Bourdeaux the 31st August of the same year, running away from the persecution of our Holy Religion. I passed to Xaintonge, Poitou and Brittany. I embarked at St. Malo for Guernsey, where I remained for the space of a month, leaving thing [*sic*], even my wife and a little boy four months old, called Peter Garric, who was then out at nurse at the Bastide, near Bourdeaux.' This was a recognized Huguenot escape route, along the Atlantic coastline, taken by many of the refugees fleeing from the steady restrictions imposed on their civil and religious liberties in the years leading up to the Revocation of the Edict of Nantes on 22 October 1685. Two months later, on 5 December, his wife arrived in London.

Garric wrote '. . . she embarked from Bourdeaux the 19th November, from whence she saved herself the Fourth, and in a Bark of 14 ton, being hid in a hole, and was a month upon sea with strong tempests, and at great peril of being lost and taken by our persecutors, who were very inveterate'. Fermignac identified the Master of the vessel as a Guernseyman but failed to name the bark itself.

A succession of children were born to the couple in London. The first, a daughter, born on 6 September 1686, was given her mother's name of Jane at her baptism at the English parish church, St Andrew's Mary-Hill, 'in our street, Philpot Lane'. This Church was St Andrew Hubbard and Philpot Lane still exists, running north from Eastcheap to Fenchurch Street, in the heart of the City. On 5 September 1687 a boy arrived, baptized Stephen on 14 September at the Walloon Church. His godparents were Stephen Pigon, a merchant described as being a native of the city of Amiens in Picardy, and Madame Mary Perin of Paris, wife of another merchant, Stephen Soulhard, of London. The Walloon church he referred to was the one situated in Threadneedle Street, not far from Philpot Lane. The church was originally granted to the Walloons in 1550, but was closed by Queen Mary in 1553, and restored to them in 1560. The church was shared with the French Protestants until 1842 and came to be known as L'Eglise de Londres. The congregation then moved to a new site in St Martin's le Grand, and finally in 1893 to Soho Square. The registers of baptisms, 1599–1840, and of marriages, 1599–1753, have been deposited in the Public Record Office,[3] and published by the Huguenot Society.[4] The entries are written in French, the first Garric to be recorded being the boy Estienne (Stephen). There are no burial registers, but the Journal tells us that he died on Sunday 28 April 1689 at seven o'clock in the morning, and was buried at the Post House the next day. The Journal then notes that on 22 May 1687 'Little Peter arrived at London by the grace of God in the ship John White, with a

Part of the register of Threadneedle Street Church, London, including the baptism of David, son of David Garric and his wife, sponsors Pierre Noval and Madame Soullard, 30 January 1688/9. The entries are written in French, the columns on the right mark out the numbers of males and females. R G4/4643

servant, Mary Mougnier, and I paid for their passage 22 guineas'.

A Royal Warrant dated at Whitehall on 5 March 1685/6 authorized the Attorney or Solicitor General to prepare a grant of free denization to a number of alien born Protestants, including David Garrie (*sic*).[5] They had already received the Sacraments according to the Church of England, and the conditions of the grant were that they should remain in the King's realm or Dominions and that within twelve months those aged sixteen and more should take the oaths of allegiance and supremacy at Quarter Sessions, and the rest do so within twelve months of reaching sixteen. Certificates to that effect were to be filed in the Petty Bag Office within three months of the oaths

being sworn. A copy of the grant of letters patent dated 20 March 1685/6 was enrolled on the Patent Roll.[6] A similar warrant was issued on 19 August 1688[7] and a grant of denization enrolled on the Patent Roll on 10 October 1688 for Jane Gario (*sic*) and Peter her son.[8] In spite of the spelling of the names there is little doubt that these people are to be identified with the author of the Journal and his wife and son.

A bill for an Act of Parliament granting naturalization to David Garric was first presented in the House of Lords on 21 January 1689/90,[9] but after its second reading, it lapsed, and a further bill was read in the House of Lords on 11 February 1695/6 and received the royal assent on 7 March 1695/6.[10] In the bills David Garric's birthplace was given as Montpelliers, in Languedoc, France, and his parents as Peter and Madalena or Anna Garric. By this time David Garric was living in the parish of St Bartholomew by the Exchange, in the City of London. A published index of names of London inhabitants within the Walls on 1 May 1695, based on parish lists drawn up for taxation purposes, shows him to have shared his house with his sons Peter and David, and daughters Mary and Jane.[11] Being so close to the banking and commercial nucleus of London, he may have had connections in that field. Many Huguenot refugees' wealth lay in capital rather than real estate and thus they had money for investment, and were successful merchants.

The Journal records details of the dates of birth and baptism of the further children of David and his wife Jane. One, Jean, was born on 26 August 1690 and baptized five days later, only to die on 18 January 1691/2. He was buried in Putney churchyard on 20 January. A marginal note tots up the cost of the funeral which came to 52 shillings: there was 10s for the coffin, 3s for gloves, 8s for a coach, 4s for three bottles, 17s for the minister and 10s for the sexton. This was 18 shillings more than the cost of the obsequies for Stephen, another son, who died on 4 July 1693, and was buried a day later in the New Churchyard at Wandsworth. On Sunday 2 December 1694, at ten o'clock at night, Garric's wife died, and she was interred in Bartholomew Lane, behind the Royal Exchange. The Journal states that they married in April 1682. From the pages of the Threadneedle Street Church registers we know that she was called Jeanne Sarrazin. Her children, with one exception, appear to have been named after one of the

Part of the letters patent of 19 August 1688 granting denization to a list of named aliens organized without any apparent order and giving family relationships where appropriate, including Jane Gario and her son Peter. There are some Jewish people among them. Enrolment took place on 10 October 1688. C66/3310 no 27

godparents, and by using the registers in conjunction with the entries in the Journal it is possible to discern the kinships among them, the intervals elapsing between birth and baptism, and the incidence of infant mortality, as well as where they were conveyed for burial, twice to the western outskirts of London, and latterly close to where they lived.

The Journal concludes with references to the arrival in England of David Garric's brother Peter, from Rotterdam, in July 1696, in company with their eldest sister Magdalen, aged sixty-three. Peter fell sick and after three weeks of illness 'having suffered like a martyr with a retention of urine' he died on 4 August and was buried alongside David's wife Jane. On 16 May 1701 Magdalen died of dropsy and was buried next to them. There the Journal ends and we do not know what subsequently happened to David.

David and Jane Garric's eldest son, Peter, was commissioned as an ensign in Sir Roger Bradshaigh's newly raised Regiment of Foot on 12 April 1706,[12] and was sent to Ireland, where he was commissioned in Tyrrell's Foot Regiment as a lieutenant, on 23 November 1708.[13] When the regiment was disbanded in 1712 he was placed on half-pay on the English Establishment, and received 2s 4d a day (or £42–11s–8d a year) from 8 August 1712 until 22 July 1715,[14] when he was appointed a lieutenant in Tyrrell's new Regiment of Dragoons,[15] raised to repel the Old Pretender's Invasion. He obtained a commission as Captain Lieutenant on 7 December 1717, but when the regiment was disbanded in November the next year, he was again in receipt of half-pay.[16]

Under a Royal Warrant of 16 November 1716, all reduced officers of His Majesty's Land Forces and Marines on half-pay were to be examined by a Board of General Officers, at such times as it thought fit, each regiment being summoned in turn to the Great Room at the Horse Guards in Whitehall.[17] This was designed to prevent frauds and abuses whether by concealment of death or by other means whereby allowances were paid out, thereby increasing the burden on the public. As well as notifying the Colonels, the Board announced the appointed dates for examination in *The London Gazette*. Each officer was required to appear in person bringing his commissions, have his Colonel identify him and certify the commissions as relating to him. The Board sought to find out when the regiment had been disbanded, whether the officer had been dismissed for any offence or misbehaviour, had been court-martialled, or had lent support to the Jacobite Rebellion, and whether he had found another active service in another regiment. Peter Garrick presented himself to the board on 23

August 1722[18] and again on 6 May 1726.[19] He was found qualified to receive half-pay, with no other provision. The observations in the Board's register for 1726 note his age as forty, with twenty-two years of Army service behind him, some of it spent in Spain and Portugal. He signed the entry. The twelve other commissioned officers in Tyrrell's Dragoons also came before the Board, with the four quartermasters and the surgeon. From the information supplied about them we can see that their ages ranged between a quartermaster of twenty-six with eight years in the Army, to a Captain of sixty-four with thirty-eight years of service. The average age was thirty-nine with twenty-one years' service.

Peter Garrick did not have long to wait before another commission came his way. This time it was as Captain of a Company in the Princess of Wales's Own Regiment of Foot, under the command of

The signature of Captain-Lieutenant Peter Garrick graces this entry of officers on half-pay of the British Establishment examined by a Board of General Officers at Horse Guards, Whitehall, on 6 May 1726. He was then 40, had been 22 years in the Army, and had served in Spain and Portugal. WO25/2986 p151

Major General Piercy Kirke. The commission was dated 26 December 1726,[20] and on 22 July 1731 he was given a further Company to command.[21]

From the published letters of his son David, written from the family home in the City of Lichfield, we know that Captain Garrick was stationed at Gibraltar by January 1732/3, and did not return to England until the Spring of 1736.[22] On 11 May 1735 the Chancellor of the diocese of Lichfield and Coventry travelled to London and gained Kirke's permission for him to come home.[23] On 1 January 1736/7, while in the City of London, Peter Garrick composed and wrote his own will.[24] He was dead by 31 March, the day on which two of his longstanding London friends went to Doctors' Commons and under oath acknowledged the handwriting and signature as his, for the will had not been witnessed.[25] These formalities dispensed with, the will was proved in the Prerogative Court of Canterbury on 7 April 1737, on the oath of his widow, Arabella Garrick, one of the two executors, with power reserved to make a similar grant to the other executor, his brother-in-law, Lewis Laconde, when he so applied.

The will gave legacies of £500 each to his eldest son Peter, his eldest daughters Magdelaine and Jane, £400 to his son William, £300 each to son George and daughter Merrial, while his son David was left one shilling. All the rest of his personal estate was left to their mother Arabella for life, and after her death was for the benefit of the younger children, to make their fortunes equal with those of their older siblings. Any overplus was to be disposed of by her as she thought proper.

Peter's widow did not survive him long, for on 19 September 1740 she had her will drawn up following her husband's wishes.[26] She was living in the City of Lichfield. David's seemingly churlish legacy of a shilling from his father was explained as being 'because he was otherwise provided for', but without going into any more details. She earnestly hoped that her children would keep house together and share her household goods for as long as was convenient, and whenever they parted or lived separately they were to be sold and the proceeds applied to increasing their fortunes. Her son Peter was made sole executor and probate was granted to him in the Prerogative Court of Canterbury on 11 March 1740/1.

The source of young David Garrick's provision was his uncle of the same name, who was a merchant living in Lisbon in the Kingdom of Portugal, but at the time he wrote his will on 16 December 1736 was at Carshalton in Surrey, and 'weak in body'.[27] The accompanying affidavit stated that he died on 19

December, and the will was proved five days later in the Prerogative Court of Canterbury. Large sums of money were left to his sisters Laconde and ffermignac, and the £1,000 given to his nephew David was 'to be put out at Interest by the Executors Jointly with my Brother to such time he is of age or to be paid before in case there is a good place that offers in given money', with the proviso that if he was disobedient to his parents before he came of age, the money was to be given to his father to do as he thought most convenient. His cousin Cazalet was given £100, 'she may give to her husband what she pleases', Mr Laconde his horse and wine, and his sister ffermignac all the clothes he had at Mr Laconde's, while his brother, Captain Garric, was to have the residue of his estate. This presumably explains why Peter was able to leave sums of money in his own will, made less than a fortnight after David's death, having benefited from the wealthy merchant. Other monetary gifts were given to the two executors and to the French Church in Threadneedle Street towards the relief of poor French refugees.

Lewis Laconde, one of his executors, was also at Carshalton to write his will on 22 November 1737, in which everything was left to his wife Jane.[28] Like his two brothers-in-law he seems to have seen no need to employ a lawyer to draft it for him and like them he did not have it witnessed. Peter Fermignac, of Throgmorton Street, London, gentleman, was one of the two people who identified the handwriting and signature, and the will was proved on 18 March 1746 in the Prerogative Court of Canterbury on the oath of his widow. On 24 September 1747 letters of administration with will annexed of his goods and chattels left unadministered by the executrix, who was now also dead, were granted to the attorney of one of his creditors, Susanna Poilblanc, in the Kingdom of Prussia. Jane had died intestate, and Mary ffermignac, widow, her sister, and David, George, Peter, Maryall and Magdalen Garrick, and William Garrick, her nephews and nieces and only next of kin, although first cited had failed to appear to have a grant made to them. Their reluctance is our gain, for we know which of Peter's children were still alive in 1747, and which of Jane's own generation.

One of David Garrick's letters, sent to his father at Gibraltar on 10 April 1735, outlined the birthdates of his seven children.[29] The I.G.I. of Staffordshire contains information on the baptisms of six of Peter and Arabella's progeny, at Lichfield Cathedral from 1710 until 1726. Published biographies of David Garrick assert that he was born at the Angel Inn at Hereford, where his father was recruiting for his regiment in 1717.[30] The I.G.I. of Herefordshire shows that he was baptized on 28 February 1716, at Hereford All Saints Church. The date is given under the old, Julian Calendar, in force until 31 December 1751, so in the new style of the Gregorian Calendar is actually 1717, usually rendered as 1716/17 for the hiatus months of January and February and up until 24 March to make it clear that the date has been modernized.

David Garrick apparently visited his uncle in Lisbon with a view to a career as a wine merchant,[31] but on 9 March 1736/7, two days before his father's burial at Lichfield, he was admitted as a student at Lincolns Inn to train for the legal profession.[32] Then he made a second abortive attempt at the wine business, in partnership with his elder brother Peter in premises in Durham Yard, between the Strand and the River Thames.[33] He began to perform as an amateur actor, and then professionally, at the theatre in Goodman's Fields, London. In 1742 he was a member of the Drury Lane Company of actors under the management of the patentee, Charles Fleetwood. A year later he and the other players were complaining to the Lord Chamberlain that Fleetwood had failed to pay their salaries.[34] Apparently he had gambled away the profits. Fleetwood was succeeded as manager and patentee by James Lacy,[35] and on 14 May 1747 he and Garrick obtained the King's Warrant to form 'Our Royal Company of Comedians' to perform tragedies, plays, operas and other performances of the stage at Drury Lane Theatre and elsewhere.[36] The patent was for twenty-one years and was to run from 2 September 1753, and was enrolled on the Patent Roll on 4 June 1747.[37] This was renewed for a further twenty-one years by a Royal Warrant on 2 September 1774.[38] No representations on the stage were allowed under the patent whereby 'the Christian Religion in General or the Church of England may in any manner suffer Reproach strictly inhibiting every Degree of Abuse or Misrepresentation of sacred characters tending to expose Religion itself and to bring it in contempt ...'. Garrick later sold his share in the patent in 1776 to Richard Brinsley Sheridan and two others, while retaining a mortgage on Lacy's half.[39]

During the years ending 5 April 1751 and 5 April 1755 until 5 April 1762, Garrick was paying duty of £4 a year on a four-wheeled chariot, and between 1755 and 1757 £2 a year for his two-wheeled chaise.[40] His address was given as Southampton Street, Covent Garden. He was also paying duty of £2 a year on silver plate weighing 800oz during the years ending 5 July 1757 until 1762.[41] His brother Peter, at Lichfield, paid five shillings on 100oz of silver plate during

257

King's Warrant to James Lacy & David Garrick Esq for the Term of Twenty one Years to form a Comp. of Comedians &c.

George R.

Our Will and Pleasure

that you forthwith prepare a Bill fit for Our Royal Signature for a Patent to be granted to James Lacy and David Garrick Esqrs their Executors Administrators and Assigns for the Term of Twenty one Years to commence from the 2 day of September One Thousand Seven Hundred & Fifty Three with full Power Licence and Authority to gather together, form entertain, govern privilege and keep a Comp.y of Comedians for our Service to exercise and act Tragedies Plays Operas and other Performances on the Stage within the House in Drury Lane wherein the same are now exercised or within any other House built or to be built where they can best be fitted for that Purpose within the City of Westminster or within the Liberties thereof & within such Places where We Our Heirs & Successors shall reside and during such Residence only such House or Houses so to be built if Occasion shall require to be assigned & allotted out by the Surveyor of Our Works for a Theatre or Play House with necessary Tiring and retiring rooms and other Places convenient for such Extent and Dimension as the said James Lacy and David Garrick their Ex.rs adm.rs or assigns shall think fitting wherein Tragedies Comedies Plays Operas Musick, Scenes and all other Entertainm.ts of the Stage whatsoever may be shewed and presented. To be styled Our Royal

and china ware, his carriages, horses and stock in his cellars for her own use, and £1,000 was to be paid her immediately after his death, with a further £5,000 twelve months later with interest added at four percent. A life annuity of £1,500 was to be paid to her quarterly free of any intermeddling or debts of any future husband. But his widow was required to remain in England and make Hampton and the Adelphi her chief places of residence otherwise all the gifts were rescinded and she was only to receive a clear annuity of £1,000 for life. The other condition imposed was that the gifts were to be in lieu of the dividends, interests and profits on the sum of £10,000 agreed to be invested in stock or securities under the terms of their marriage settlement, and to replace her rights of dower at common law. She was to signify

LEFT *The royal warrant granting a 12-year patent from 2 September 1753 to James Lacy and David Garrick to form a Company of Comedians to perform at the House in Drury Lane and elsewhere. LC5/161 p257*

BELOW *Portrait of David Garrick by Thomas Gainsborough. National Portrait Gallery, London.*

the same period, but was not listed as owning any wheeled vehicles.

David Garrick's will, made on seven sheets of paper, was drawn up on 24 September 1778 and proved in the Prerogative Court of Canterbury on 5 February 1779.[42] An endorsement on the original will described him as late of the parish of St Martin in the Fields, Middlesex, and as having died the previous month. By the time of his death he owned houses at the Adelphi in the Strand, and at Hampton in Middlesex, as well as two islands in the Thames. These, with the pictures, household goods and furniture in both houses, and a statue of Shakespeare, were to be held on trust by his executors for the use of his wife Eva Maria Garrick during her lifetime, on condition that she kept the premises in good repair and paid all the outgoings on them. Besides these, she was to have all his household linen, silver plate

her consent to this in writing to the executors within three calendar months of her husband's demise, or the legacies and annuities would become void and the houses and their contents sold and the proceeds invested. The statue of Shakespeare was excluded from any sale.

A nephew, David Garrick, was to have the messuage and garden which he occupied at Hampton, with its contents, plus all other land in the parish not given to Eva Maria Garrick. The manor of Hendon and the advowson of the church there, and all other lands, were to be sold and the clear profits invested in the names of his executors as trustees. However, his houses in Drury Lane, which he had bought from the Fund for decayed Actors, which he had set up by Private Act of Parliament in 1776, were to be restored to the Fund.

After his widow's death, Garrick instructed that the statue of Shakespeare and all his collection of old English plays were to be given to the trustees of the British Museum for the use of the public. His books (after his wife had selected some to the value of £100) were designated for his nephew Carrington Garrick. The rest of the personal estate was to be sold and invested to pay out the legacies and annuities for his wife. His brothers George and Peter Garrick, his sister Meriel Doxey, nephews Carrington and David Garrick, nieces Catherine Garrick and Arabella, wife of Captain Schaw, were to have money given them, David's £5,000 being 'besides what I agreed to give him on his marriage', and Arabella's £6,000 was to be held on trust for her to be paid out as she should direct in writing. In all the legacies totalled £46,000, and his estate was to bear the annuity of £1,500 for the remainder of his widow's life, which, as circumstances turned out, was a long one, for she did not die until 1822, forty-three years after her spouse![43] Mindful of the sums involved, David Garrick made provision for the legacies to be abated if there were insufficient funds to meet them and the balance paid on the sale of the house at Hampton and the release of capital on his widow's death. If there was an overplus after his instructions had been carried out and all his debts and expenses paid, then this was to be divided among his next of kin as if he had died intestate.

Shakespeare's statue, of which he was so proud, was commissioned by him from the sculptor Roubiliac for the Jubilee celebrations which he organized at Stratford-upon-Avon between 6 and 8 September 1769. By all accounts they were a fiasco, not helped by foul weather.[44]

The house at the Adelphi was one of a group of terraced properties designed by Robert Adam in Durham Yard, scene of David Garrick's earlier attempts in the wine trade. The house overlooked the river and Robert Adam was his next-door neighbour.[45] Eva Maria Garrick continued to occupy this and the house at Hampton. In 1780 she paid tax on four male servants in each of them.[46] David Garrick, her husband's nephew, had a similar number employed at Hampton, while Rev. Mr Garrick was paying tax on two male servants at Hendon.

Eva Maria Garrick's will was made on 28 January 1819, and with two codicils, was proved in the Prerogative Court of Canterbury on 30 October 1822.[47] She requested interment as near as possible to the remains of her husband in Westminster Abbey. As she and her husband had no children of their own it was her numerous friends, her servants and various charities who benefited from her will. The Theatrical Fund of Drury Lane Theatre attracted £200, her mantua maker £50, and Mrs Siddons was left 'a pair of gloves which were Shakespeare's and were presented to my late husband during the Jubilee at Stratford on Avon'. There was money left to her husband's niece, Mrs Catherine Payne, to her own niece, Elizabeth de Saur, wife of Peter de Saur of Vienna, while her husband's nephew, Christopher Garrick, was to have the gold snuff box set with diamonds, the gift of the King of Denmark, and another nephew, Nathan Egerton Garrick, the gold enamelled snuff box presented by the Duke of Parma. Christopher and his wife were left the silver plate bought when Eva Maria married his uncle on 22 June 1749 (presumably forming the bulk of the silver plate on which her husband had paid duty). There was a tea kettle and lamp, a coffee pot, two ladles for cream, a complete tea chest, three pairs of candlesticks, two dozen knives and forks, and two dozen dessert knives, two dozen table- and dessert-spoons, a soup ladle, two salters with spoons, two sauce boats with ladles, six wine labels, a lemon squeezer and a crane, a chocolate pot and a plated night candlestick. More mundanely Christopher was also bequeathed the table service of pewter used by David Garrick as a bachelor and which she requested should always remain in the family bearing the surname of Garrick, and a painting of the actor as Richard III which she had bought after his death. Nathan Egerton Garrick was to have a similarly purchased portrait of her husband by Zoffany, in which he was represented without a wig.

When calculations were made for Death Duty, Mrs Siddons' bequest was thought to be 'An old pair of Gloves – not worth £1.'[48]

The I.G.I. of London contains many entries of Garrick baptisms and marriages. Carrington and

Articles of clerkship for the training in the law of George Garrick, to commence on 25 March 1741 for five years. John Leake, the younger, an attorney of Wellington in Shropshire, undertook to take him to London for the last three years of the term. George's eldest brother, Peter, was one of the parties to the agreement, both their parents being then deceased. CP5/38 p4

David Garrick were the sons of the actor's brother George and his wife Catherine. George Garrick was articled for five years as a clerk to John Leake, the younger, of Wellington in Shropshire, gentleman and an attorney in the Court of Common Pleas, by an indenture of 16 March 1740/1.[49] Peter Garrick, of the City of London, wine merchant, and George himself, of the City of Lichfield, were the other parties to the agreement with Leake. George undertook to live with the attorney throughout the period of his clerkship which was to commence on 25 March 1741, for which £105 was paid towards his maintenance and instruction. He covenanted not to embezzle, misspend or purloin any of the estate, money, goods, writings or chattels of the attorney or his clients, which he might receive or have under his care or charge, nor would be absent himself without consent, or disclose any of his master's or clients' secrets to their prejudice, 'but shall in all things behave Himself as a true and faithfull Servant and Clerk ought to do'.

Leake undertook to inform and instruct his pupil in the profession of the law and practice of an attorney, and to go with him to London at his own expense in the last three years of the term, and to find and provide him with competent and sufficient meat, drink and lodging. The indentures were countersigned. A memorandum on the dorse states that on 1 July 1741 duty of £5–10s was received by the Shropshire Collector by way of the levy of one shilling in the pound imposed on indentures where the premium was £50 or more. The washing was valued at £5. On 22 November 1749, George Garrick, of Orange Street, Westminster, swore on oath at Serjeants' Inn, Norfolk Street, London, that the articles had been duly executed and that he had served the full term of five years. He was sworn in and enrolled as an attorney of the Court of Common Pleas at Westminster on the same day. However, on 16 January 1753, he was sworn in and admitted as Stable Keeper at Somerset House, and as His Majesty's Riding Surveyor in Ordinary and was to have, receive and enjoy the salaries allowed for both by the Establishment of His Majesty's Stables, with all other fees and allowances as usual, starting from 15 October 1752;[50] this post was apparently obtained for him using the influence of his father-in-law, Nathan Carrington, a King's Messenger.[51]

George's will was dated 30 January 1779, when he was living in Great Russell Street, in the parish of St Paul Covent Garden, in the Liberty of Westminster.[52] As his children by his first marriage were deemed to be amply provided for, he ignored them altogether, and made provision for his present wife Elizabeth, and any issue that they should have. On 23 March 1779, the Treasurer, and the Office Keeper of Drury Lane Theatre authenticated the signature on the will.[53] A day later one of the executors, William Ward, of Hatton Street in the parish of St Andrew Holborn, testified that he had been closely acquainted with the deceased for many years until his demise on Wednesday 3 February. On Friday 29 January he received a message that Garrick wished to see him. He went round that evening to Garrick's lodgings in Great Russell Street, where Garrick gave him oral instructions about the general disposition of his estate and asked Ward to prepare the will. On his return home he drew up a draft which he read out to Garrick the following day and asked him to appoint an executor, which he did, as well as order some alterations and additions to the draft, with which Ward complied. He read out the final draft which Garrick approved and asked if it 'would stand good without being written fairly'. His maidservant (given £100 in

the will) was then called into the room and Garrick signed each of the four corners and the margin of the paper containing the draft, and affixed a wax seal on one corner, the maidservant making a mark as the witness. Ward said that though ill and weak in body he had found Garrick of sound mind and memory and capable of giving instructions. Ward was then entrusted with the will and asked to put it in a cover and deliver it to Garrick's wife, telling her what it was but not revealing the contents. On the day of Garrick's death, Ward went to collect the will from his widow, broke open the seal and read the will to her. On 26 March probate was granted to Ward as

Appointment of George Garrick as Stable Keeper at Somerset House and His Majesty's Riding Surveyor in Ordinary, as from 15 October 1752. This was in the nature of a sinecure for his main interest lay with his brother's theatre in Drury Lane. LS13/202 p8

one of the two executors. On 14 November 1801, a grant of letters of administration with will annexed of the goods left unadministered by Ward and by the other executor, both of whom were now deceased, was made to the residuary legatee, George Garrick, son of the testator, an earlier similar grant having been made to his mother Elizabeth, as his guardian, when he was under twenty-one.

Of the issue of George's first marriage, Carrington Garrick, born in 1752, was educated at Eton and St John's College, Cambridge, before being ordained a deacon in 1776 and a priest later the same year.[54] He was instituted as Vicar of Hendon on 10 January 1777 on the presentation of his uncle, David Garrick, its patron.[55] When he made his will on 3 July 1785,[56] he was heavily in debt. He wanted a private burial in his vault in Hendon churchyard and his executor was to burn and destroy all his written sermons and private papers. He had entered a trust deed with his executor, John Bond, of Hendon, gentleman, and two others, on 30 November 1782 for the benefit of his creditors. Bond was to have the residue of his estate on trust to sell and dispose of it to the best advantage, and after payment of his debts and funeral expenses, was to invest it and apply the dividends, interests and profits to pay an annuity of £50 clear to his wife for life, payable in quarterly instalments. If she were to remarry then the annuity was to be used for the maintenance and education of his son Christopher

---

Enrolment of the change of name by deed poll of Frederick Stephen Trevor to that of Trevor-Garrick, effected on 26 April 1886. He was the great-great-great-grandson of George Garrick, the actor's younger brother. C54/19056 m33 no 107

PETER GARRIC = MADALENA or ANNA

PETER GARRIC
arrived at London from Rotterdam, Holland, 16–27 Jly 1696, died 4, bur 6 Aug 1696, in Bartholomew Lane, behind the Royal Exchange, City of London

PETER GARRICK = ARABELLA
of the City of London 1736/7, late of the City of Lichfield, Staffs, *bn c. May/June 1685, arrived London 22 May 1687, from Bordeaux, letters of denization dd 19 Aug 1688,* Ensign in Bradshaigh's Regt of Foot, 12 Apr 1706, rising to Captain in Kirke's Regt of Foot, 26 Dec 1726, served in Spain, Portugal and at Gibraltar, named in brother's will, 1736, own will dd 1 Jan 1736/7, pr 7 Apr 1737

ARABELLA
of the City of Lichfield, 1740, named in husband's will, executrix 1737, will dd 19 Sept 1740, pr 11 Mch 1740/1

LEWIS LACONDE
of Carshalton, Surrey 1736–1746/7, named in brother-in-law's will, executor 1736, will dd 17 Mch 1746/7 pr 18 Mch 1746/7 Admon with will annexed 24 Sept 174[]

PETER GARRICK
of the City of London, 1749, City of Lichfield, 1756–62, wine merchant, 1749, Patent Comptroller of the Port of Carlisle, Cumberland, 8 Apr 1761 until his death, *bn 24 bp 29 June 1710, at Lichfield Cathedral,* named in father's will, 1736/7, mother's will, executor, 1740/1, next of kin of JANE LACONDE, 1747, named in brother's will, 1778, paid tax on silver plate 1756–62, will dd 23 Feb 1791, pr 20 May 1796

MAGDALAINE
bn 29 Apr 1715, named in father's will, 1736/7, mother's will, 1740, next of kin of JANE LACONDE, 1747

DAVID GARRICK =
of Southampton Street, Covent Garden, Middx, 1751–62, and the Adelphi and Hampton, Middx, 1778, actor and manager, *bn 19 bp 28 Feb 1716/17, at Hereford All Saints, Herefs,* held manor and advowson of Hendon, Middx, granted a 21-year patent for a Company of Comedians at Drury Lane Theatre, London, and elsewhere, from 2 Sept 1753 and 2 Sept 1774, paid tax on a chariot 1751–62 and a chaise 1755–62, named in uncle's will, 1736, father's will, 1736/7, mother's will, 1740, next of kin of JANE LACONDE, 1747, died Jan 1779, bur in Westminster Abbey, will dd 24 Sept 1778, pr 5 Feb 1779

EVA MARIA
of Adelphi Terrace and Hampton, 1[] marr 22 June 17[] paid tax on male servants at Adelphi and Hampton, 1780, named in husband's will, 1778, died 15 C[] 1822, will dd 28 1819, codicils d[] 28 Nov 1821, 15 Aug 1822, p[] 30 Oct 1822

CHARLES TREVOR =
of Bridgwater, Somerset,
Officer of Customs

The details in italics refer to sources held outside the Public Record Office

Pedigree of Garrick of Languedoc, France, Lichfield, Staffs, and London

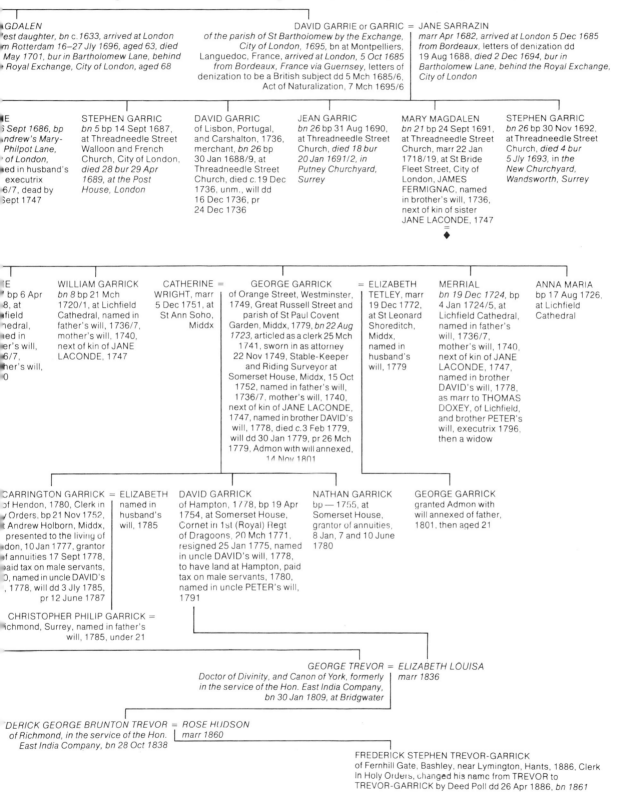

GDALEN
est daughter, bn c.1633, arrived at London
m Rotterdam 16–27 Jly 1696, aged 63, died
May 1701, bur in Bartholomew Lane, behind
Royal Exchange, City of London, aged 68

DAVID GARRIE or GARRIC = JANE SARRAZIN
of the parish of St Bartholomew by the Exchange, | marr Apr 1682, arrived at London 5 Dec 1685
City of London, 1695, bn at Montpelliers, | from Bordeaux, letters of denization dd
Languedoc, France, arrived at London, 5 Oct 1685 | 19 Aug 1688, died 2 Dec 1694, bur in
from Bordeaux, France via Guernsey, letters of | Bartholomew Lane, behind the Royal Exchange,
denization to be a British subject dd 5 Mch 1685/6, | City of London
Act of Naturalization, 7 Mch 1695/6

NE
Sept 1686, bp
ndrew's Mary-
Philpot Lane,
of London,
ied in husband's
executrix
6/7, dead by
Sept 1747

STEPHEN GARRIC
bn 5 bp 14 Sept 1687,
at Threadneedle Street
Walloon and French
Church, City of London,
died 28 bur 29 Apr
1689, at the Post
House, London

DAVID GARRIC
of Lisbon, Portugal,
and Carshalton, 1736,
merchant, bn 26 bp
30 Jan 1688/9, at
Threadneedle Street
Church, died c.19 Dec
1736, unm., will dd
16 Dec 1736, pr
24 Dec 1736

JEAN GARRIC
bn 26 bp 31 Aug 1690,
at Threadneedle Street
Church, died 18 bur
20 Jan 1691/2, in
Putney Churchyard,
Surrey

MARY MAGDALEN
bn 21 bp 24 Sept 1691,
at Threadneedle Street
Church, marr 22 Jan
1718/19, at St Bride
Fleet Street, City of
London, JAMES
FERMIGNAC, named
in brother's will, 1736,
next of kin of sister
JANE LACONDE, 1747
=
♦

STEPHEN GARRIC
bn 26 bp 30 Nov 1692,
at Threadneedle Street
Church, died 4 bur
5 Jly 1693, in the
New Churchyard,
Wandsworth, Surrey

E
bp 6 Apr
8, at
field
hedral,
ied in
er's will,
6/7,
her's will,
0

WILLIAM GARRICK
bn 8 bp 21 Mch
1720/1, at Lichfield
Cathedral, named in
father's will, 1736/7,
mother's will, 1740,
next of kin of JANE
LACONDE, 1747

CATHERINE =
WRIGHT, marr
5 Dec 1751, at
St Ann Soho,
Middx

GEORGE GARRICK
of Orange Street, Westminster,
1749, Great Russell Street and
parish of St Paul Covent
Garden, Middx, 1779, bn 22 Aug
1723, articled as a clerk 25 Mch
1741, sworn in as attorney
22 Nov 1749, Stable-Keeper
and Riding Surveyor at
Somerset House, Middx, 15 Oct
1752, named in father's will,
1736/7, mother's will, 1740,
next of kin of JANE LACONDE,
1747, named in brother DAVID's
will, 1778, died c.3 Feb 1779,
will dd 30 Jan 1779, pr 26 Mch
1779, Admon with will annexed,
14 Nov 1801

= ELIZABETH
TETLEY, marr
19 Dec 1772,
at St Leonard
Shoreditch,
Middx,
named in
husband's
will, 1779

MERRIAL
bn 19 Dec 1724, bp
4 Jan 1724/5, at
Lichfield Cathedral,
named in father's
will, 1736/7,
mother's will, 1740,
next of kin of JANE
LACONDE, 1747,
named in brother
DAVID's will, 1778,
as marr to THOMAS
DOXEY, of Lichfield,
and brother PETER's
will, executrix 1796,
then a widow

ANNA MARIA
bp 17 Aug 1726,
at Lichfield
Cathedral

CARRINGTON GARRICK =
of Hendon, 1780, Clerk in
Orders, bp 21 Nov 1752,
Andrew Holborn, Middx,
presented to the living of
don, 10 Jan 1777, grantor
f annuities 17 Sept 1778,
aid tax on male servants,
0, named in uncle DAVID's
, 1778, will dd 3 Jly 1785,
pr 12 June 1787

ELIZABETH
named in
husband's
will, 1785

DAVID GARRICK
of Hampton, 1778, bp 19 Apr
1754, at Somerset House,
Cornet in 1st (Royal) Regt
of Dragoons, 20 Mch 1771,
resigned 25 Jan 1775, named
in uncle DAVID's will, 1778,
to have land at Hampton, paid
tax on male servants, 1780,
named in uncle PETER's will,
1791

NATHAN GARRICK
bp — 1755, at
Somerset House,
grantor of annuities,
8 Jan, 7 and 10 June
1780

GEORGE GARRICK
granted Admon with
will annexed of father,
1801, then aged 21

CHRISTOPHER PHILIP GARRICK =
ichmond, Surrey, named in father's
will, 1785, under 21

GEORGE TREVOR = ELIZABETH LOUISA
Doctor of Divinity, and Canon of York, formerly | marr 1836
in the service of the Hon. East India Company,
bn 30 Jan 1809, at Bridgwater

DERICK GEORGE BRUNTON TREVOR = ROSE HUDSON
of Richmond, in the service of the Hon. | marr 1860
East India Company, bn 28 Oct 1838

FREDERICK STEPHEN TREVOR-GARRICK
of Fernhill Gate, Bashley, near Lymington, Hants, 1886, Clerk
In Holy Orders, changed his name from TREVOR to
TREVOR-GARRICK by Deed Poll dd 26 Apr 1886, bn 1861

Philip Garrick, and any other child alive at his death, in equal parts. Bond was to be guardian of his children, and given a gold watch and chain, with its seals and trinkets, usually worn by Garrick. His wife was left a choice of his furniture and books to the value of £30 over and above those he had given her during his lifetime, and all her own plate and linen which came to him by their marriage. Bond, as patron, presented the new vicar to Hendon in 1790.[57]

Carrington Garrick and his brother Nathan granted several annuities.[58] The memorial of an indenture dated 17 September 1778 was enrolled on the Close Roll on 28 September.[59] By this, Carrington Garrick, in consideration of £300 paid with his consent by James Purcell to John Reeves to secure an annuity of £50, and a further consideration of five shillings paid to Garrick by Purcell before the sealing of the agreement, now sold to Purcell and his executors for the natural lives of Garrick and Reeves the above annuity, payable quarterly out of a messuage called Chesterfield Arms, at the north corner of the east side of Little Carrington street, in the parish of St George Hanover Square, and rented out at £60 a year. Garrick leased the premises to Charles Hayes and his executors for 500 years at a peppercorn rent subject to the above trusts. It was signed and sealed by Garrick and Reeves, and a bond was entered in the penal sum of £600 conditioned for payment of the annuity. In other words Carrington needed to raise money and did so by guaranteeing an annuity out of the rent received from a property which he leased out at a nominal rent for 500 years. If the annuity failed to be paid then £600 was forfeit by himself and Reeves.

Another brother, David, was commissioned as a cornet in the First (Royal) Regiment of Dragoons on 20 March 1771,[60] but served in the Army only a few years before selling his commission on grounds of ill-health.[61]

George and David Garrick's elder brother Peter, once a midshipman in the Royal Navy,[62] then a wine merchant,[63] was granted a patent to be Patent Comptroller of His Majesty's Customs at the Port of Carlisle, on 8 April 1761, but he was never resident, preferring to operate via a deputy.[64] The last, John Smith, was appointed on 17 April 1790 and succeeded him as Comptroller on 15 April 1797 after Garrick's death.[65] Peter Garrick remained in the City of Lichfield, and was there when he made his will on 23 February 1791, and this was proved on 20 May 1796 in the Prerogative Court of Canterbury.[66] His sister Merrial, wife of Thomas Docksey of Lichfield, was given land there as well as his dwelling house and was to share the £3,000 and claim to the residue in the estate left him by their brother David with their nephew David Garrick, and nieces Arabella Schaw, Catherine wife of John Payne, and Merrial wife of James Susanna Patten, as tenants in common. His last-named niece was to have his messuage called the Beacons Farm in the parish of St Lawrence, in Essex. By the time the will was proved, his sister Merrial Docksey, one of the two executors, was a widow.

Towards the end of the nineteenth century, Rev. Frederick Stephen Trevor, of Fernhill Gate, Bashley, near Lymington in Hampshire, changed his name to Trevor-Garrick. The deed poll was enrolled in the Chancery Division of the High Court of Justice on 30 April 1886.[67] Research into the Trevor ancestry, using printed sources, established that he was the grandson of George Trevor who in 1836 married Elizabeth Garrick, daughter of Christopher Philip Garrick and granddaughter of the Vicar of Hendon.[68]

This change of name poses another dilemma for the genealogist, for the names we start out with may not be those with which we ultimately die. A search of the paternal line's surname may not always be the one we expected.

Unlike David Garric, Karl Marx's attempt to become a naturalized British subject was a failure. The memorial in which he applied for a certificate of naturalization on 1 August 1874, was addressed to the Right Honourable Richard Assheton Cross, Esquire, MP, His Majesty's Principal Secretary of State for the Home Department.[69] He swore and signed an affidavit to the veracity of the statements it contained, and described himself as Carl Marx, of No. 1 Maitland Park Road, Haverstock Hill, Middlesex, Doctor of Philosophy. The memorial asserted that he was a natural-born subject of the Emperor of Germany, and had emigrated by permission of the Prussian Government in 1846 at which point he ceased to be a Prussian subject, and had not since been naturalized in any other country. By 1874 he was fifty-six, having been born on 5 May 1818, at Trèves in Rhenish Prussia, and was an author by profession. He was married with one daughter under full age, Eleanor, nineteen, who lived with him. During the past eight years Marx had lived for five of them or more in the United Kingdom at his present address, and intended to continue in Great Britain, and so wished to obtain the rights and capacities of a natural-born British subject on the grounds that 'your Memorialist has so long resided in England that he has become attached to the United Kingdom and its Government'.

There were four supporting statutory declarations, made by William Frederick Adcock of 6 Southampton Road, Maitland Park, Robert William Seton, of 18 Southampton Road, both described as gentlemen, Julius Augustus Manning, a merchant, of 55 Fellowes Road, Haverstock Hill, and Farquhar Matheson, of 11 Soho Square, Doctor of Medicine. All attested that they had known the applicant for ten years or more (Seton for twenty), and were able 'to vouch for the respectability and loyality of the said Carl Marx'. None was acting as his attorney or agent in the

application nor was employed by him professionally, and all declared that the particulars given in the memorial were true. But then, on 17 August 1874, came a report from Sergeant W. Reimers of the Metropolitan Police Office, Scotland Yard, which scotched Marx's aspirations. Reimers disclosed that 'he is the notorious German agitator, the head of the International Society, and an advocate of Communistic principles. This man has not been loyal to his own King and Country.' The referees, however, were considered respectable householders and their statements about knowing Marx correct. The application was refused on 26 August 1874. There was no appeal available. Robert Willis endeavoured to find out the reasons for refusal on behalf of his client, but the recommendation of the Home Office was to decline to do so. There the matter rested.

Marx continued to live in London. The 1881 census of Maitland Park Road shows him aged sixty-two, living at number 41 with his wife Jenny, sixty-six, like him a native of Germany, their unmarried daughter Eleanor, twenty-six, born in the parish of St Pancras in Middlesex, and their general servant,

RIGHT *The memorial of Carl Marx to the Secretary of State at the Home Office for a certificate of naturalization, 1 August 1874, supported by the testimonials of four of his neighbours. His date and place of birth, marital status and the name and age of his unmarried daughter living with him at number 1 Maitland Park Road are also supplied. HO45/9366/36228*

LEFT *The report of Sgt Reimers of the Metropolitan Police Office, 17 August 1874, describing Carl Marx as 'the notorious German agitator ...'. The application for naturalization was accordingly turned down. HO45/9366/36228*

TOP *The 1881 census of Maitland Park Road, Haverstock Hill, includes in schedule 272, at no 41, the household of Karl Marx, then aged 62, lodged between those of an organ builder and a doorkeeper at the House of Lords. Note also that Robert Scott, a shipping and passenger agent, lived in the same road, presumably booking berths for people like the Marx family emigrating or going on business trips abroad. RG11/211 f59 p48*

ABOVE *The 1851 census of St Ann Soho, Westminster, where Charles Mark and his family rented an apartment at 28 Dean Street with three other households. Note that those of foreign extraction gave only country of birth. In accordance with enumerators' instructions only the first forename was recorded, followed by initials for other names, hence the four Jenny Mark entries. Their birthplaces are a useful pointer to approximate stays in France and Belgium. HO107/1510 f261 p11*

Helen Demuth, from Germany.[70] Karl Marx gave his occupation as 'Author Political Economy', which is interesting because he lived next door to Henry Goddard, the eighty-year-old doorkeeper of the House of Lords, on one side, and Edwin Willis, an Organ Builder, on the other!

The first census in which the Marx family featured was that of 1851. Then they were living at 28 Dean Street in the parish of St Ann Soho, a property which seems to have been divided up into four apartments, one occupied by John Marengo, a cook (born in Italy, but a British subject), another by Morgan Kavanagh, a Dublin-born teacher of languages, the third by Peter Pepigni, a confectioner from Italy, and finally the Marks household.[71] Charles Mark, Doctor (Philosophical author) was then thirty-two, and his wife Jenny thirty. There were four children and because it was a requirement that only the first names be recorded with the initials of any further forenames it seems that all three daughters, aged six, five and one month, were named after their mother. The son, Henry E. Mark, was four. The two oldest children were scholars at home. Their birthplaces demonstrate the family's movements from *c.* 1845: Jenny C. Mark was born about that year in France, her brother and sister Jenny L. between 1846 and 1847 in Belgium, and Jenny E. in February 1851 in the parish of St Ann's, Middlesex. Their parents emanated from Prussia, like the house servant, Helena Demuth. The family employed a nurse, Elizabeth Moss, a widow of forty-six, and born in Bethnal Green, Middlesex. The community in which they lived was very cosmopolitan and would form an excellent and worthwhile basis for a social history study.

In 1864 Johan Friedrich Wilhelm Wolff, of Chorlton-upon-Medlock, Manchester, a teacher of languages, died leaving Frederick Engels and Karl Marx as two of his three executors and beneficiaries. The Death Duty Register for that year reveals that Karl Marx was to have a legacy of £100 and was appointed his residuary legatee.[72] The residue amounted to £909–16s–7d, on which duty of £90–19s–8d was paid on 19 December 1869, the will having been proved on 1 June 1864. Karl Marx himself merited 'No Entry' in the index to the Registers for 1883, the year of his death.[73]

Marx's appearance in this country can be traced among the lists of aliens furnished by Masters of ships arriving at the Port of London in 1849. A return made to the Chief Officer of Customs on 27 August, for the *City of Boulogne*, which sailed from Boulogne, includes his name among those of seven aliens coming from Poland, France, Buenos Ayres and Greece.[74]

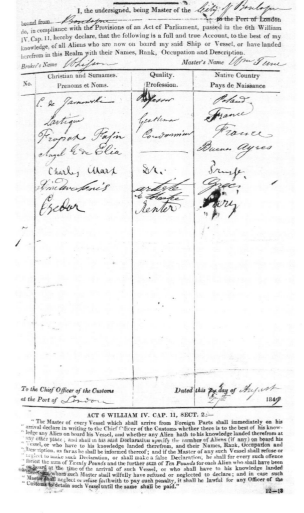

A list of aliens arrived at the Port of London by 27 August 1849 on board the City of Boulogne, *from Boulogne. Judging by the different styles of handwriting the signatures are probably those of the passengers including Dr Charles Marx, a native of Prussia. HO3/53*

His name was given as Charles Marx, his occupation as doctor, and his native country as Prussia. It seems that he also signed the entry. Less than a month later, on 19 September, a similar List notes Jenny Marx as having come from Boulogne on board the *Albion* with a number of unspecified persons (their children).[75] So it seems that Garric and Marx had at least one thing in common: the husband went on ahead and sent for his family later; this must have been a pattern repeated many times by other settlers.

12

THE DYER, BRENTON AND WALKER FAMILIES

We now glimpse three emigrant families, two in the seventeenth century to Massachusetts, and the third in the mid-nineteenth century to New Zealand. The Dyers of Boston can be linked back to their origins in London and Lincolnshire via the Poll Tax of 1640, while their near neighbours, the Brentons, moved to Rhode Island, and suffered heavy loss for their loyalty to the British Crown at the time of the American War of Independence. A strong Royal Naval connection was maintained over two generations, several members becoming distinguished officers. The Walkers of Keswick, in Cumberland, were assisted to emigrate to New Zealand in 1842 by the Colonial Land and Emigration Office. Papers belonging to the New Zealand Company include the family's application for a free passage, and the passenger list showing their embarkation.

Governor John Winthrop of Massachusetts was the author of a graphic account of a monstrous birth at Boston in October 1637.[1] Mary Dyer, wife of William Dyer, sometime a milliner of the New Exchange in London 'both young and very comely persons', was delivered of a premature stillborn female child. Its size was normal but 'The face of it stood soe low into the breast, as the Eares (wch were like an Apes) grewe upon the Shoulders, the Eyes and Mouth stood more out then other Childrens, the Nose grew hookeing upwards, the face had noe parte of head behinde, but a hollowe place, yet unbroaken, Itt had noe fforehead, but in the place thereof were fower perfect hornes, whereof two were above an Inch long, Thother two somewhat shorter. The Breast and Shoulders were full of Scales, and sharpe pricks, like a Thornebacke; the Navell and all the belly with the distinction of the Sex, were behinde, under the Shoulders, and the backparte, were before the Armes and leggs were as other Childrens, But instead of toes it had on each foote 3 Clawes with sharpe Talents like a fowle, In the upper parts of the backe behinde, yt had two great Mouthes, and in each a peece of redd flesh

stickeing out.' Winthrop actually saw the child for himself.

William and Mary were in Boston by 1635, for a son was baptised Samuel there on 20 December.[2] William was a freeman in 1636, but on 15 November 1637 was disenfranchised and disarmed five days later for supporting John Wheelwright, convicted of seditious preaching.[3] Dyer was driven out to the Island of Acquidneck (Rhode Island) in 1638[4] and he was one of the founders of the settlement at Newport, where he served as Clerk.[5] His wife bore him four more sons, before returning to Boston in 1659 to preach as a Quaker, and was hanged a year later for her beliefs.[6]

The will of their son, Major William Dyre, of the County of Sussex in the territories of the Province of Pennsylvania, was dated 20 February 1687/8 and proved in the Prerogative Court of Canterbury on 4 September 1690, on the oath of his son William Dyre, with power reserved to his widow, Mary, when she should apply for probate.[7] From the will it is clear that he had amassed large tracts of land there and in Newcastle County, as well as in the Pequit of Narragansett Country in New England 'with all my right and title of inheritance to the estate of my late father William Dyre deceased upon Rhode Island, within the Province of Providence Plantation'. His property was in all probability acquired under patent from the Governor and Council of the Colony.

Genealogies of Rhode Island Families, vol. 1, 1983, contains an article on the emigrant William Dyer's ancestry by W.A. Dyer.[8] According to Boston Town Records he was allotted forty-two acres to the north and north-east of Boston, at Rumney Marsh and Pullens Point, sometime between 1635 and 1637. As he was said by Winthrop to be a milliner in London the names of officers, liverymen and freemen returned by various London Livery Companies assessed for a Poll Tax on 19 August 1641 were examined.[9] The file included a return made by the Fishmongers Company in which William Dyer was listed as a milliner in New England. The apprenticeship bindings books of this Company revealed that he was put to Walter Blackborne for nine years on 20 June 1625. His father was William Dier, a yeoman of 'Kerkbie' in Lincolnshire. The place was identified as Kirkby la Thorpe and William's baptism took place there on 19 September 1609, making him almost fifteen at the start of his apprenticeship. He was made free of the Company in 1633. A milliner sold small wares and was so called because most of his goods were originally imported from Milan, such as pouches, gloves, brooches, textiles, daggers, swords and knives.

His master was a haberdasher, but does not himself appear to have been apprenticed in the Company;

The Poll Tax returns for the Fishmongers Company, one of the first twelve in the City of London, under the Act of 16 Charles I c9 (1640). Freemen were to contribute a shilling, yeomen (non-liverymen) three pounds, and liverymen five pounds. Included are several freemen of other buying and selling trades, among them the milliner William Dyer of New England. E179/251/22

perhaps he purchased his freedom. Other taxpayers in the Company were goldsmiths, scriveners and linendrapers, and Dyer was not the only one overseas. Possibly membership of it conferred special trading privileges and concessions with the new colony of New England. Certainly it gave intending migrants ready access to the sailing dates and routes of vessels chartered or owned by freemen or officers of the Company to fish regularly along the North American coastline. As experienced navigators with sea-worthy ships and a sound knowledge of the best landing-places, they offered a good investment for passengers. The masters were happy to carry paying passengers to America and later to bring them goods and raw material with which to trade, and to supply and improve the new settlements, in return for timber and materials to effect repairs to their vessels, and for safe harbours in which to shelter. Dyer probably travelled in a group with others of similar status, but we do not know exactly when, for no extant ship's passenger list has his name on it. We know that his former master was in New England with a wife in 1640, but was gone back home in 1641,[10] so the migration was by no means one-way. Dyer probably retailed some of the very arms of which he was deprived in 1637.

The International Genealogical Index of London and Middlesex (1988 edition) records that William Diar, son of William and Mary, was baptised on 24 October 1634, at St Martin's in the Fields, Westminster. The published registers of this parish show that he was buried three days later, and that Gulielmus Dyer and Maria Barret were married there by licence on 27 October 1633.[11] No trace has been found of the groom's application for the licence, which would have told us more about him, but it may well be that this was the 'young and very comely' couple described by Governor Winthrop, for by then his apprenticeship was over, leaving him free to marry and set up his own home.

One of the Dyers' near neighbours in Boston under the Great Allotment of 1635-7, was William Brenton, apportioned 164 acres.[12] C.E. Banks alleged that he was a merchant from Hammersmith in Middlesex, and had arrived in Boston by October 1633.[13] Later he removed to Providence, Rhode Island, and was party to a compact for the settlement of Newport with William Dyer, Clerk, and other Elders.[14] He was elected President of the Colony in 1660, became Deputy Governor in 1663, Governor from 1666 until 1669, and died in 1673/4.[15]

Like William Dyer, Brenton owned land in Narragansett Country and his farm estate at Newport was called Hammersmith.[16] This passed to his grandson, Jahleel Brenton, who died in March 1767. According to J.O. Austin's *Genealogical Dictionary of Rhode Island*, 1978, his eighth child, born on 22 October 1729, was named Jahleel after his father.[17]

On 1 September 1783, Jahleel Brenton, Post-Captain in His Majesty's Navy, and then aged fifty-four, petitioned the Commissioners considering the claims of American Loyalists for losses sustained during the Revolutionary War.[18] He had lived on Rhode Island at the time the troubles began and was now on half-pay in the Navy, in which he had served for many years. He had been forced to abandon his home, estate and family in 1775, and seek asylum on board HMS *Rose* then in Rhode Island harbour. He fled to Boston where he read a proclamation calling on the King's subjects to help suppress the insurgents, and made his way to England to volunteer his assistance. He had to borrow money to underwrite the cost of his voyage, on which there was an annual interest of £50. He was declared an enemy and a traitor to the Liberties of America under an Act of Resolves passed by the General Assembly on 9 December 1775, and his estates and effects were sequestrated and sold for the public benefit.[19] Brenton had supplied fresh provisions to the King's troops and the inhabitants of Boston, after the Battle of Bunkers Hill in June that year,[20] which was the direct cause of his proscription, while a house in Rhode Island owned by him had been used as a naval hospital and the stocks and crops taken to service it.[21] A list of items removed by the rebels from the house and farm in June, October and December 1775 was valued at £5,344–14s–6d.[22] One of his negro slaves, worth £45, was compelled to enlist in the Rebel Army. From this inventory we can see what type of husbandry was conducted on his plantation. He grew Indian corn, barley, oats, potatoes, flax and turnips and had planted three hundred young fruit trees of different sorts. Ten large full-grown apple trees had been demolished by the German Regiment. The livestock numbered dairy cows, pigs, a boar, sheep, turkeys, geese, ducks, chickens, barn doves and horses. While in England he learnt that the rebels had destroyed his outhouses, rendered his house unfit for habitation, and had utterly despoiled his plantation.[23] At the start of the rebellion the 200-acre Hammersmith estate was worth more than £4,000, and he had land in Newport belonging to his wife, valued at £337–10s, and 1,600 acres in Maine left to him by his father (though the documents relating to this were lost when he made his escape).[24] A schedule of his

Part of the Memorial of Jahleel Brenton, Post Captain in the Royal Navy, sent on 1 September 1783 to the Commissioners for considering the claims of American Loyalists. He and his family were driven from their large estate in Rhode Island by the rebels. His wife and eight children remained in New York while he went to England. Other supporting documents include leases, title deeds, and an inventory of stock, crops and household goods. Their negro slave, worth £45, was forced to enlist in the rebel army. The total claim came to £4,988–17s–6d, based on 4s 6d to the dollar. AO13/68 pt 1 no 79 papers included a partition deed of 5 August 1767 between himself, Samuel and Benjamin Brenton, all of Newport, and James Brenton, of Halifax, Nova Scotia, of 1,100 acres of land at Hammersmith, late the property of their father, Jahleel Brenton, of Newport, deceased, left to the first three as tenants in common under his will.[25] They agreed to divide it into four parts, Jahleel's share being 100 acres of the farm and $77\frac{1}{2}$ acres of pasture, and each man was to have free access through the others' land to reach his own. There were also several counterparts of ten-year leases made by Jahleel and his wife Henrietta in 1774, relating to land fronting on Thames Street in the town of Newport.[26]

On 5 January 1777 the Lords of the Treasury voted him a pension of £100 a year, to support his burgeoning family, but it was stopped a year later, as by then he was back in His Majesty's Navy.[27] The 1783 petition asserted that when interviewed by the examining board he had failed to disclose full details of his case owing to an ignorance of what was required of him and he now wished to rectify this. His wife and six children were driven to New York during the evacuation of Rhode Island by the King's troops,[28] at great expense, for he then had no constant employment, staying there until 23 May 1780, and paying exorbitant wartime prices.[29] The cost of their passage to England and of taking a furnished house in London necessitated two more loans of £482 and £600.[30] He then outlined his more recent Naval career.[31]

Brenton's first command was of His Majesty's Storeship *Pembroke*, when he also acted as Purser. The vessel apparently sailed from London to Halifax, Nova Scotia, between June and November 1776, when he was discharged and returned to England. He had employed a clerk to make up for his own deficiency as purser and when £50 was unaccounted for it was deducted from his own wages as was customary. He received lieutenant's half-pay from December 1776 until June 1777 and on 23 August was commissioned to command His Majesty's Storeship *Tortoise*, with the rank of Master and Commander, and was sent with clothing for the Army at New York. He was not entitled to any growing wages on the ship until he had served in her a whole year, had submitted his accounts and been properly certified. His attorney meanwhile continued to lend him money to enable him to sail appropriately equipped. He remained on the *Tortoise* for almost two years before transferring to the *Strombolo* Fireship, at New York, to be more immediately in the line of service. From June until September 1780 he was again on half-pay, but on 19 September he was appointed

Commander of His Majesty's Ship *Queen* Armed Vessel, and was commissioned as Post-Captain ten days afterwards. The muster for this ship for the period 7 October to 30 November 1780 shows that it was based at North Shields and carried a complement of 120 men.[32] In May 1782 it was found to be too small for this class and was reduced to a Sloop. He was then superseded and placed on half-pay, and that was his position at the time of the petition.[33]

Meanwhile, the July 1780 Session of the General Assembly in Rhode Island, passed an Act for his apprehension and transportation if he returned as he had left the State and joined the enemy. If transported and found to have returned again the penalty would be death.[34] It was just as well his last ship was based in home waters.

On 22 June 1782 he wrote to the Commissioners from Ranelagh Street, Buckingham Gate, London, urging them to pay him a pension for the time he was Master and Commander of the *Tortoise*, as he understood others to have been in similar circumstances.[35] He had been paid eight shillings a day, or £146 a year as his salary, but now he was receiving half-pay of six shillings a day as Post-Captain.[36] He had been in the Royal Navy for thirty-seven years or more and was 'far too advanced in Life to procure Bread in any other Line, for his wife and eight children'.[37] Two of these must have been born after the flight to New York. He had debts of £146 owing to him, and he estimated his total loss as £4,500. The Treasury awarded him £50 a year, to start from 5 July 1782 as 'His case however appears to us so very meritorious and his family so large that we think his Half Pay as a Post Captn not sufficient to support him'.[38] On 30 October 1783 he asked that the interest payments of £53–7s–6d on the loans from his friend be taken into consideration, as he only had £104 clear to maintain himself and his family, so a further £50 was forthcoming, to date from Michaelmas 1783,[39] but was reduced to £90 a year from 21 December 1785.[40] He was also paid a lump sum of £646–12s by Parliament in compensation for his loss of property, out of a total of £1,616 allowed him. A deduction of £16–10s was made on account of his pension, leaving an outstanding balance of £952–18s.[41]

In February 1784 the General Assembly passed a resolution to drop any more rights or claims against Brenton's estates, and to allow his creditors to pursue their own demands.[42]

In 1778 his brother, Benjamin Brenton, pressed an uncorroborated claim for losses incurred at Newport for freighting hay and cattle to the King's troops at Boston in October 1775. He was captured

The passing certificate as lieutenant in the Royal Navy issued by the Navy Board to Jahleel Brenton on 6 December 1752. He had been at sea for more than six years, some of it in the merchant service, and was now more than 23 years of age. Note the names and lengths of time spent on board the various Royal Naval vessels, from which he produced Journals and testimonials from the Captains. ADM107/4

by the rebels and his family left destitute after the estate was sequestrated and his personal goods sold. The Treasury appears not to have considered his appeal any further.[43]

Jahleel Brenton passed the examination to be a Royal Naval lieutenant on 6 December 1752, having produced an affidavit to show he was more than twenty-three years of age, and had been at sea over six years (part of which was in the Merchant Service). The longest time spent in any vessel was on His Majesty's Ship *Vigilant* for four years seven months two weeks and five days, first as an ableseaman and then as midshipman.[44] From the lengths of service it is possible to estimate approximately when he was on board, between 1748 and 1752: the weekly ships' musters would confirm the date and port of entry.

In pursuance of an Order in Council made on 24 March 1802, in consideration of the distressed circumstances of Henrietta Brenton, widow of Rear Admiral of the Blue Jahleel Brenton, and her five daughters, an annual pension of £100 was granted to her, with £20 a year each to her daughters until marriage, to commence from the day of his death on 30 January 1802.[45] The first payment was made on 24 June 1802 to Misses Elizabeth, Mary, Martha, Henrietta and Frances Brenton, and to their mother,

and thereafter in regular half-yearly instalments at Christmas and Midsummer. The register for the years 1801–5 reveals that Frances Brenton was paid up to 26 March 1805, the day preceding her marriage.[46] On 29 March 1814 a certificate was sent to the Secretary of the Admiralty supporting the widow's renewed appeal for help, on the grounds that she did not have a clear annual income of double £120 and was therefore entitled to benefit from the Charity to relieve poor widows of Commissioned and Warrant Officers.[47] A certification of the marriage accompanied her application, asserting that her wedding took place on 29 December 1765, at Newport, Rhode Island, when her husband was in or about his 35th year. She had not subsequently remarried and was currently residing in Paddington, in London. Her late husband had contributed the usual allowance of 3*d* in the pound towards widows' pensions and one was duly given her, backdated to 1 January 1814.

The weekly musters of HM Storeship *Tortoise*, between 1 November and 31 December 1777, show that four Brentons were on board among a crew of 160 officers and men, in addition to the Master and Commander, Jahleel Brenton.[48] It was in dock at Deptford in June when he first entered the ship, then

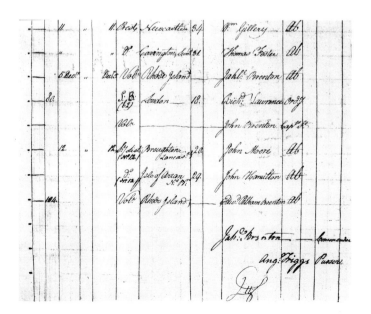

Brenton, both joining on 15 October; ableseaman John Brenton on 6 February 1781, and James Wallace Brenton, the Captain's servant, on 8 April 1781, completed the complement. On 25 September Captain Brenton moved to HMS *Termagant* taking all except John Brenton with him.[49] Who were they?

According to J. Marshall's *Royal Naval Biography*, vol. 2, part 1, 1824, his son, Jahleel Brenton, was born on 22 August 1770 and was commissioned as a lieutenant in 1790, having previously served at that rank in the Swedish Navy, so when he was present on board his father's ship he was aged only seven. The list of Flag Officers, 1844, confirms this improbable situation.[50] His seniority as lieutenant was dated 20 November 1790, and he rose to the rank of Com-

---

LEFT *Part of the sworn signed application of 29 March 1814 for a pension from the Charity for the Relief of Poor Widows of Commissioned and Warrant Officers of the Royal Navy, made by Henrietta, widow of Rear Admiral Jahleel Brenton, who died on 30 January 1802, giving their date and place of marriage. ADM6/352*

BELOW *The Ship's Muster of HM Storeship* Tortoise, *1 January–28 February 1778, signed by its Commander, Jahleel Brenton; conveyed on board were Jahleel's sons Edward Pelham Brenton and Jahleel Brenton, both born on Rhode Island, and volunteers as ableseamen. The Captain's servant, John Brenton, cannot be attributed as their brother with any certainty. ADM36/7889*

sailed for New York on 15 September, reaching port on 29 November, and on the return journey it called at Rhode Island on 21 December, began the voyage home on 21 February 1778, put in at Falmouth on 20 March and arrived at Woolwich on 30 May. Jahleel Brenton volunteered as an ableseaman on 5 December, giving his birthplace as Rhode Island, and from 11 January 1778 he was employed as a clerk; John Brenton also joined the ship in December as the Captain's servant, while on 25 December Benjamin Brenton volunteered as a coxswain. Edward Pelham Brenton came on board in February 1778, as an ableseaman and transferred to HMS *Dromedary* on 14 April, returning to the *Tortoise* on 8 September. His age was given then as twenty-two.

Some of them followed the Commander onto HMS *Queen*, for the muster between 7 October and 30 November 1780 contained the names of ableseamen Jahleel Brenton and Edward Pelham

mander on 3 July 1799, Captain on 24 April 1800, Rear Admiral of the Blue on 22 July 1830, of the Red on 10 January 1836, was Vice-Admiral of the Blue on 1 July 1840, and of the White on 23 November 1841. On 1 April 1844 he was aged seventy-four. *The Commissioned Sea Officers of the Royal Navy 1660–1815*, 3 vols, 1954, gives his date of death as 21 April the same year.

Captains' letters record his activities with the two tenders, *Polly* and *Peggy*, based at Greenock during late 1792 and 1793.[51] It appears that he was engaged in recruiting and impressment, for in January he was writing to the Admiralty that the Glasgow magistrates were offering him some seafarers arrested and jailed for rioting in the streets. A lieutenant was dispatched to collect them. Another lieutenant was sent to Plymouth with 103 volunteers on board the Tender *Polly*

including some who had deserted to spend their Bounty money. These were intended for HMS *Queen* and HMS *Victory*. A runaway Irish boy turned up, under an assumed name, and was restored to his anguished father; six American seamen volunteered for the British Navy; a sailor taken on with the rank of midshipman in December 1792 had proved himself perpetually intoxicated and unfit for service once he had been paid. Enquiries revealed that he had been sent ashore to sick quarters from another ship and was still on her payroll as ableseaman! He was arrested in Glasgow in February for toasting the health of Tom Paine, and for threatening to knock a lieutenant's brains out and put a pair of bullets through him. Brenton had to pay his prison expenses for he had no money of his own, and thus wanted reimbursement for this strain on his resources.

In 1798 he was in command of His Majesty's Sloop *Speedy*. The Captain's logs give vivid descriptions of two encounters with the Spanish on 4 October and 7 November 1799.[52] On the second occasion the vessel was stationed off Europa Point, Gibraltar. A schooner was spotted bound for Gibraltar from Newfoundland and conditions were breezy and cloudy. At three in the afternoon despatches were sent on shore. Half-an-hour later he 'observed 15 Spanish Gun Boats bearing down on us, soon after engaged them very close: the Brig bore up to the Ptwd [portward] at 6 perceiving they endeavoured to cut off the Ship wore and broke their Line, and engaged them on both sides, at 7 the Enemy pulled off'. Three of his men were killed or wounded and the Sloop damaged. He put in to Tertiran Bay where the carpenters were employed in stopping the leaks and the men in repairing the rigging.

On 2 July 1803 his frigate, *La Minerve*, hit the French coast near Cherbourg in thick fog. The ship was seized and he was captured and later exchanged for a French prisoner taken at the battle of Trafalgar.[53] He and his crew faced a court martial on 7 February 1807 for her loss, but were honourably acquitted.[54]

Part of a Captain's letter to the Lords Commissioners of the Admiralty sent by Jahleel Brenton on board HMS Spartan, Malta, 14 December 1809, itemising his expenditure on entertaining the English and Spanish Ambassadors and their entourages in April. The total amount came to over 523 dollars, which Brenton paid on 16 April; the person on whose account the refund was to be settled had since died, leaving Brenton inconvenienced. ADM1/1548 no 56

He next commanded HMS *Spartan* in the Mediterranean. A missive sent by him to the Admiralty from Malta on 14 December 1809 details his expenses incurred in transporting and feeding the English and Spanish Ambassadors and their entourages from Malta to Trieste that April.[55] 'In consequence of my having a family and very limited income my own habits of living are very economical, and that my table was only provided for the number which the custom of the Service renders indispensably necessary and I in general make use of the common and cheap wines of the Country.' He had jut come back from a long cruise off the coast of Egypt and was in quarantine, so he was obliged to buy an entirely new set of table linen from the impossibility of getting his own washed. His accounts list the 12 tablecloths, 24 napkins, the coffee, tea, Madeira, Porter, almonds,

mustard, pickles, cheese, pigeons, fowl, turkeys, geese, sheep, goats, tongues, beef, vegetables, 92 dozen oranges, ten dozen eggs, and four chamber pots, six pencils, 100 quills and three log books which he purchased in Malta so that he could entertain his eminent passengers.

Part of the Captain's Log of HMS Spartan, *written by Edward Pelham Brenton, who took over from his brother, Captain Jahleel Brenton, when he was dangerously wounded by grape shot in the hip on 3 May 1810, while engaging the French in the Bay of Naples. A list of the ten killed and 17 wounded accompanies the entry. Captain Brenton survived to take up other commands, and died in 1844. ADM51/2807*

The Captain's log of this vessel for Thursday, 3 May 1810, when it was standing in the Bay of Naples, catalogues the action taken against a French squadron.[56] Brenton started firing at 7.58 in the morning and at 9 o'clock he fell severely wounded by grape shot in the hip. Firing ceased an hour later as the enemy was out of gun shot, but the brig was captured and taken in tow. Ten of his crew were killed and seventeen wounded, his own injury being considered dangerous. For this he was given a pension of £300 a year, was voted a sword worth 100 guineas from the Patriotic Fund at Lloyds, and awarded the Grand Cross of the Neapolitan Order of St Ferdinand and of Merit by the King of the Two Sicilies.[57] His agent complained that Brenton should have continued to draw full pay to 17 October 1810, when the pension commenced, but his wages had been curtailed on 26 September when he ceased to command the ship. The Admiralty's retort was that it did not interfere in the Navy Board's affairs.[58]

On 20 February 1812 Captain Brenton was at 2 Church Street, Paddington (presumably where his mother lived), when a letter was directed to him appointing him Captain of HMS *Stirling Castle*.[59] In March he went on board at Chatham and found her without Warrant Officers, the boatswain and gunner being reported unfit for service, and there was no carpenter.[60] He then issued a string of requests for the transfer to his new ship of officers and men with whom he had previously sailed, selecting the gunner from HMS *Spartan*, now in HMS *Canopus*, a chaplain, and a lieutenant from two earlier ships.[61]

His stock was high, for on 3 November 1812 he was created a baronet.[62]

Marshall tells us that he was brother to Edward Pelham Brenton and to a lieutenant mortally wounded whilst commanding an attack from His Majesty's Sloop *Peterell*, near Barcelona, in 1799.

Edward Pelham Brenton was commissioned as a lieutenant on 27 May 1795.[63] A signed memorandum of his services was filed on 15 August 1817.[64] The first vessel in which he recorded himself as ableseaman was HMS *Crown* in 1788, yet we know that he was on board his father's Storeship *Tortoise* in 1778, when his age was given as twenty-two. It seems likely that this was a ruse, to effect his escape from America, to have his passage paid for and his father's income boosted by claiming his wages at that rank, along with those of his brother Jahleel, and the other two Brentons. We cannot even be sure whether they actually sailed with him in later ships or that their father continued to enter their names on his muster and to draw the money. It certainly appears suspicious.

The 1817 memorandum outlines length of service, stations, capacities and names of commanders of the ships in which Brenton was crew member. He twice served in different ships under the same captains, before taking command of his own ship, HMS *Lark*, stationed in the West Indies for two months from June 1802. On 25 September 1810 he is recorded as having succeeded his wounded brother Jahleel on HMS *Spartan*, remaining with her off America until 15 November 1813.

Captains' letters to the Admiralty include a number from Edward Pelham Brenton.[65] It seems he actually commanded the *Spartan* from 3 May 1810, the date his brother was dangerously hurt, but was not appointed Captain until 27 September.[66] The ship was off Belle Isle on 24 March 1811, when he wrote to recover £14–14s–3½d paid to a ship and house-painter in Leith the previous November for works done there on HMS *Amaranthe*, an earlier command. The labour costs were four shillings a day, double pay on Sunday.[67]

James Wallace Brenton was given seniority as a lieutenant on 1 January 1798.[68] He joined HMS *Peterell* and paid the Navy Board five shillings for slops (clothes).[69] The Muster Book noted him as being discharged dead on 19 November 1799, having been taken to Mahon Hospital on 27 October, while the ship was anchored in Port Mahon, Spain. The Captain's log reports on 27 October that the first lieutenant (unnamed) was sent out in command of the Pinnace with a Jolly boat to entice the enemy away from the beach.[70] They came under heavy musketry fire and at 1.45 the Captain made a signal for them to return. The lieutenant and four of his men were wounded, two of whom died the same day and their bodies were taken ashore next day for burial. The others were transferred to hospital. This date is at variance with the muster because until October 1805 24-hour naval log book entries began at noon the day before. On his death Brenton's clothes and effects were auctioned, as was customary, and the proceeds of £1–11s credited to his wages.[71]

W.R. O'Byrne's *A Naval Biographical Dictionary*, 1849, contains particulars about commissioned officers alive in 1845. John Brenton was born on 28 August 1782 and was married on 28 September 1815 to Henrietta, one of the five daughters of Rear Admiral Jahleel Brenton, the Crown Loyalist, who died in 1802, and sister of Sir Jahleel Brenton, Baronet, and Captain Edward Pelham Brenton (born on 19 July 1774 and died on 6 April 1839, making him a very precocious ableseaman at the age of four). John first entered the Royal Navy on 28 August 1798,

MEMORANDUM of the Services of *Captain Edward Pelham Brenton*

Several Bearings, or Ranks.	Names of the several Ships.	Names of the several Admirals, Captains, and Commanders.	Stations on which the Ship was chiefly employed.	Date of Entry.	Date of Discharge.
A.B.		Hon: Wm Cornwallis Com:			
"	Crown	Capt: James Cornwallis			
"	"	Capt: Isaac Schomberg	East Indies	Nov: 12th 1788	June 1792
Mid.	"	Capt: Monice Belgiano			
"	"	Capt: Robt M Sutton			
Mid.	Bellona	Capt: George Wilson	Channel Fleet	August 1793	August 1794
Mid.	Queen Charlotte	Adm: Earl Howe. Rear Adm: Sir Roger Curtis Capt: Sir A. S. Douglas	Channel	August 1794	May 29th 1795
Lieut:	Venus	Capt: L. W. Halstead	North Seas	June 1795	Feby 1796
Lieut:	Phænix	Capt: L. W. Halstead	North Seas	Feby 1796	Sept 1796
Lieut:	Agamemnon	Capt: R. D. Fancourt	North Seas	Oct: 1796	Nov: 1797
Lieut:	Raven	Capt: J. W. T. Dixon	North Seas	Nov: 1797	Feby 1798 Ship wrecked
"	Agincourt	Hon: Vice Adm: Wm Waldegrave. Capt: John Bligh	Newfoundland	March 1798	June 1801
Lieut:	Agincourt	Vice Adm: Sir Cha: Pole Capt: G. F. Ryves	Newfoundland		
"	"	Hon: Vice Adm: Wm Waldegrave Capt: John Bligh	Channel and West Indies	June 1801	June 1802
Lieut:	Theseus				
Commander	Lark	Self.	West Indies	June 1802	Augt 1802
Commander	Merlin	Self.	North Seas	Augt 1803	Feby 1805
Commander	Amaranthe	Self.	North Seas and West Indies	Feby 1805	Feby 1809
Post Capt: for Rank				Dec 13th 1808	
" Capt:	Belleisle	Commodore Jno d burn	West Indies	March 1809	June 1809
" Capt:	Donegal	acting for Capt: Malcolm	Cadiz	July 1809	Nov: 1809
" Capt:	Cyane	Self.	Western Ocean	April 1810	Sept: 1810
" Capt:	Spartan	Self.	America	Sept: 25 1810	Nov: 15 1813
" Capt:	R: Sovereign	Rear Adm: Sir B Hollowell	Plymouth	April 16th 1815	June 5th 1815
Captain	Tonnant	Do Do Do	Do	June 6th 1815	Nov: 1815

Edward Pelham Brenton
4 Park Lane August 15th 1817

Return of the services of Captain Edward Pelham Brenton, Royal Navy, signed by him at 4 Park Lane, London, on 15 August 1817. He was son of the American Loyalist Jahleel Brenton, and first went to sea in January 1778 as an ableseaman on board HM Storeship Tortoise *under his father's command. ADM9/3*

his sixteenth birthday,[72] and passed lieutenant on 5 June 1806,[73] rising to the rank of Commander on 12 November 1812, and to Captain on 26 December 1822. His application to the Commissioners of the Board of Admiralty for a lieutenancy vouched for his having been six years at sea, two of which were as midshipman, and he produced regular journals and good certificates from his Commanders as to his sobriety, diligence and qualification as an ableseaman. On examination he proved his knowledge of the practice and theory of navigation. The attached baptism certificate gave his christening at Halifax, Nova Scotia, on 28 August 1783, the son of William and Mary Brenton.[74]

A signed return of his services, made in 1817, shows that in 1801 and 1802 he was in turn midshipman, Master's mate and acting lieutenant on HMS *Caesar*, commanded by Jahleel Brenton, off Cadiz, Gibraltar and Minorca. Altogether he sailed in seventeen ships until 14 November 1815, when he was paid off from HMS *Hasty*, apparently his last command.[75] A further return, made from Ryde, on the Isle of Wight, on 2 April 1846, added that while his actual employment at sea of about fifteen years ten months might appear sparse, his answer would be 'that I have now by me, 13 letters from the Board from February 1813 to December 1818 in answer to my applications as Commander, and 11 letters in answer to mine as Captain from 1824 to 1831 for an Employment in any part of the World'.[76] Why he was not taken up on his offers is not clear, for in 1817 he was still only thirty-five. *The Commissioned Sea Officers of the Royal Navy, 1660–1815* reveals that he attained the rank of retired Vice-Admiral on 5 January 1858, a year before his death on 17 September 1859.

As John Brenton was born in 1782, he cannot be the person acting as Captain's servant on the Storeship *Tortoise* in 1777 and 1778. This may have been another of the Commander's children spirited away from America, and similarly the coxswain, Benjamin Brenton, or they could have been his nephews, the offspring of Benjamin Brenton of Newport.

A much later emigrant, to the new British colonies in the Antipodes, was born in the Lake District. The General Vestry Meeting of ratepayers, held at Grasmere in Westmorland on 5 May 1842, resolved to raise £7 from the Poor Rates to defray the necessary expenses of John Walker, his wife and five children to London, 'who are going to Imigrate to New Zealand'.[77] No trace of John Walker's name was found in the correspondence to the Poor Law Commissioners in London from the Board of Guardians of Kendal Poor Law Union, which covered Grasmere, nor in the adjacent Cumberland Cockermouth Union.

The alphabetical list of candidates for employment in New Zealand yielded no reference to the Walkers, but the Application Register of emigrant labourers asking for a free passage to the Colony, from 1839 until 1850, had two entries of John Walkers. Entry number 5411 related to an application made on 28 March 1842.[78] This John Walker was a thirty-eight-year old quarryman living at Keswick, in Cumberland, thirteen miles of rugged ground away from Grasmere. His wife Sarah was aged thirty-three and they had three sons of ten, seven and two, and two daughters aged nine and four. Their embarkation number was recorded, but not the ship, nor of any charge imposed for the voyage, so we must assume Walker's wish was granted.

As the family must have made their way down to London soon after 5 May, a search was undertaken of the indexes of ships sailing from the ports closest to London in May and June that year.[79] Only three

---

Application Register of Emigrant Labourers for a free passage to New Zealand. Entry no 5411 is that of John Walker, a quarryman of Keswick in Cumberland, his wife Sarah and their five children, all of whose ages are recorded. Application was made through an agent, Dr Briggs, and they were allotted embarkation number 2377. The date of entry was 28 March 1842. CO208/273

194

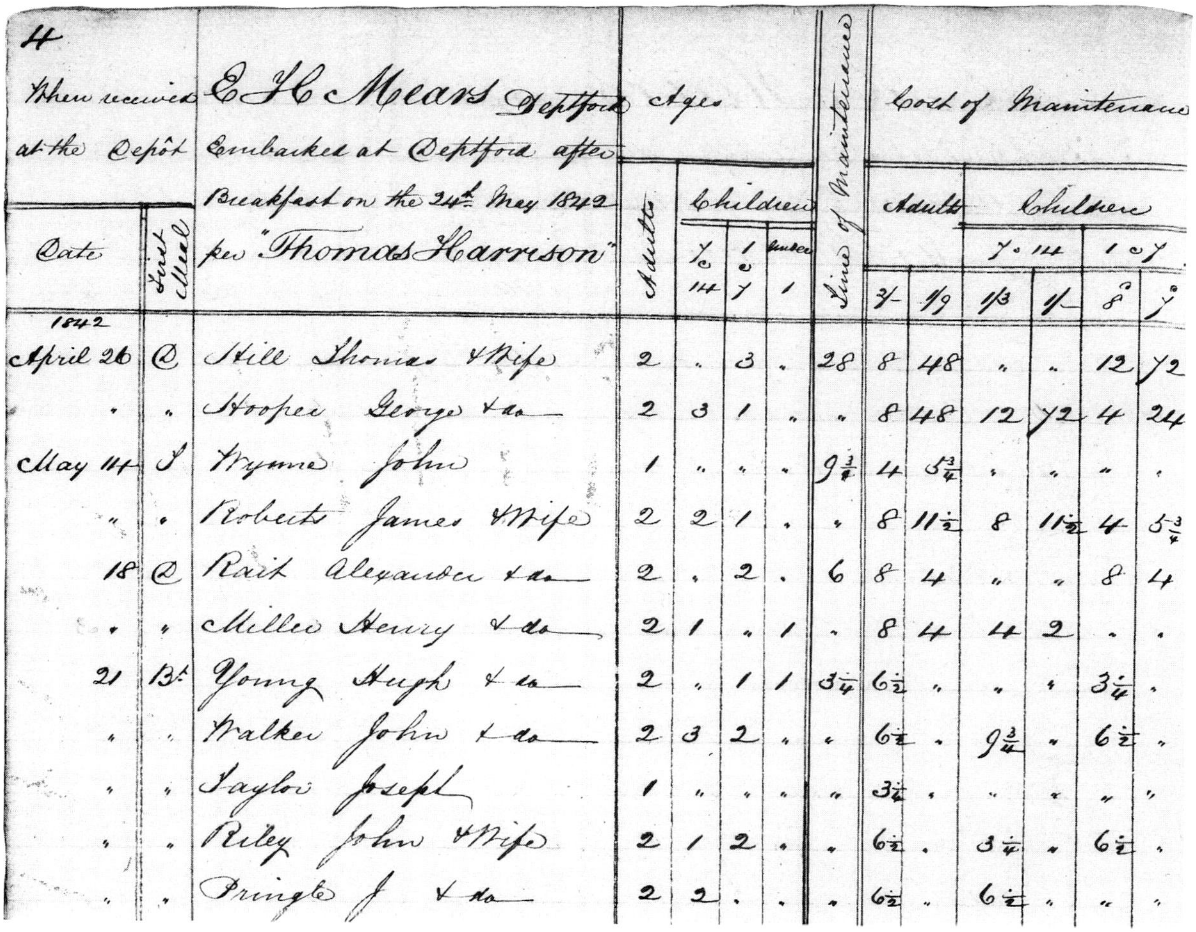

4

When received at the Depôt		E & C Mears Deptford. Embarked at Deptford after Breakfast on the 24th May 1842 per "Thomas Harrison"	Ages				Line of Maintenance	Cost of Maintenance					
			Adults	Children				Adults		Children			
				7 to 14	1 to 7	under 1				7 to 14		1 to 7	
Date	First Meal							3/-	1/9	1/3	1/-	8d	7d
1842													
April 26	D	Hill Thomas & Wife	2	.	3	.	28	8	48	"	"	12	72
.	"	Hooper George & do	2	3	1	"	"	8	48	12	72	4	24
May 14	T	Wynne John	1	"	"	.	9¾	4	5¾	,	"	"	.
"	.	Roberts James & Wife	2	2	1	.	.	8	11½	8	11½	4	5¾
18	D	Rait Alexander & do	2	.	2	.	6	8	4	"	"	8	4
.	.	Miller Henry & do	2	1	"	1	.	8	4	4	2	.	.
21	Bt	Young Hugh & do	2	"	1	1	3¾	6½	"	"	.	3¾	.
.	.	Walker John & do	2	3	2	.	.	6½	.	9¾	.	6½	.
.	.	Taylor Joseph	1	"	.	"	"	3¼	.	.	.	"	"
.	.	Riley John & Wife	2	1	2	.	.	6½	.	3¼	.	6½	.
.	.	Pringle J & do	2	2	.	.	.	6½	.	6½	.	"	.

The embarkation list of the Thomas Harrison, *of maintained emigrants to New Zealand, boarding at Deptford after breakfast on 24 May 1842. John Walker, his wife and five children took breakfast on 21 May as their first meal. CO208/278 p4*

were commissioned: the *Thomas Harrison* left Gravesend on 26 May, the *George Fyfe* on 16 June, and the *Olympus* the same day. The *Thomas Harrison* took 105 adults and 80 children aged 14 and under. The passengers embarked at Deptford after breakfast, on 24 May 1842.[80] John Walker and his wife were among their number, and they and their children were given subsistence of $3\frac{1}{4}d$ a day apiece. As the voyage took about four months, we would not expect to find any record of the family at its chosen destination before the end of September. We do not know what happened to them, if indeed they all survived the journey, but records in New Zealand would tell us more about their origins and where they settled. It is interesting to note that Otago Settlement, on South Island, had as a resident one David Garrick, who paid £120–10*s* for $70\frac{3}{4}$ acres in and around the town sometime between 1847 and 1851.[81]

The 1841 census of the township of Keswick, in the parish of Crosthwaite, showed that John Walker lived at Harrimanfield.[82] He was described as a slater journeyman, aged about thirty-five, and born out of the county. His wife Sarah, aged about thirty, and John, ten, Mary, seven, Isaac, five, Sarah, three, and George, aged one, were all native to Cumberland. Being so close to the border with Westmorland, it is likely that John came from there.

Also residing in Keswick was the Poet Laureate, Robert Southey, whom William Wordsworth succeeded two years later.[83] Wordsworth lived at Rydal Mount and attended Grasmere Church, and may well have contributed towards the Walkers' fare to London.

13

THE LYONS, EVANS, MASSY AND ATKINSON FAMILIES

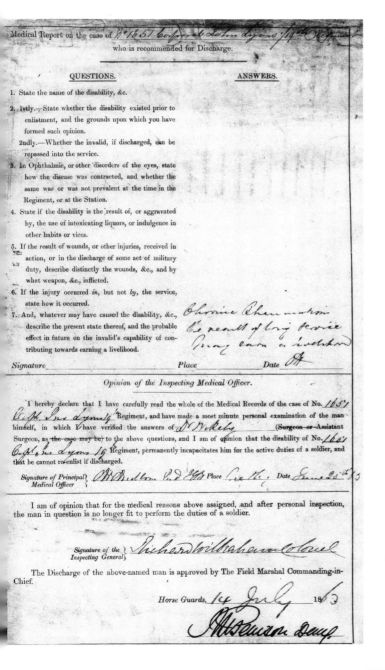

For the last example of the sources at work, I have chosen the careers of four military men in the 19th Regiment of Foot, three of whom received the Victoria Cross, two for outstanding bravery during the Crimean War, 1854–6, and the other being the first soldier awarded the Cross posthumously after his death in the Boer War, 1899–1902. The fourth was an Irish officer serving in the Crimea, whose family had a long tradition of Army service, most suffering injury or death, not least Lieutenant 'Redan' Massy, severely wounded at Sebastopol in 1855, but nonetheless rising to the rank of Lieutenant-General by the end of the century.

John Lyons, native of Carlow, county Carlow, in Ireland, enlisted in the 19th Regiment of Foot (The Green Howards) at Carlow on 11 July 1842. He was eighteen-and-a-half years old, by trade a painter. The attestation and discharge papers of this soldier, dated 6 December 1862, show that he never rose above the rank of corporal during his twenty years in the army, three-quarters of which was spent abroad in the Mediterranean, the West Indies, North America, Turkey, the Crimea and India.[1] He was allotted regimental number 1651, and a careful record kept of his appearance, his service, conduct and medical history. From this we know that he was five feet ten-and-a-half inches tall, had a fair complexion, blue eyes and brown hair, and was aged thirty-nine years and seven months on his discharge from the Royal Victoria Hospital at

Part of the Attestation and Discharge Papers of Corporal John Lyons, of the 19th Regiment of Foot. He was discharged as unfit for further service on 14 July 1863, but deemed capable of earning a livelihood. When he enlisted at 18 in 1842, his trade was given as painter. Much of his 20 years' service was spent abroad, latterly in the Crimea and India, and he intended to retire to Ireland. WO97/1453

Netley on 14 July 1862, when he was found to be unfit for further military service on the grounds of his chronic rheumatism, attributed to exposure and long service. The Medical Board ascribed his disability to causes other than any constitutional infirmity or predisposition, vice or other intemperance while in the Army, which would have affected his pension rights. He drew a shilling and a halfpenny from 14 July 1863 as his daily pension, paid to his home at Carlow, having put in another period of service from 6 December, although most of it was spent in convalescence.

A further medical examination on 25 June 1863 judged Lyons to be capable of earning a livelihood: obviously retirement agreed with him.

His service record indicates that he was in the regiment for twelve years before being promoted to corporal on 13 November 1854. This was short-lived, for he was reduced a private on 19 April 1855, having spent three days in confinement in the Guard Room, but was restored a corporal on 19 June, reduced to private on 11 October after more time in the Guard Room, and was not promoted again until 15 September 1860. He was court martialled on three occasions, but the discharge papers do not tell us why. From 10 August 1858 he was awarded Good Conduct Pay of a penny a day, raised to twopence in 1860 and to threepence in 1862. At the time of discharge his conduct was described as very good; more than this, he had been decorated with the Victoria Cross for having distinguished himself in the trenches before Sebastopol 'in having moved a live shell from the place where it had fallen', and was also honoured as a Knight of the Legion of Honour by the French.

The London Gazette published on 24 February 1857 announced the British decoration for his act of valour on 10 June 1855.[2] The Victoria Cross was instituted under a Royal Warrant of 29 January 1856, and made retrospective to the Autumn of 1854 so that it could include the Crimean War, as a recognition of very outstanding deeds of gallantry in the presence of the enemy, and the Cross itself was said to have been manufactured from the metal of one of the Russian guns captured at Sebastopol. Altogether 111 officers and men were honoured for their conduct during the Crimean War. Lyons was one of the first to be nominated, and with sixty-one others (including Private Samuel Evans of the same regiment) went to Hyde Park, in London, on 26 June 1857, to receive it from the Queen. All holders below the commissioned ranks were entitled to an annual pension of £10 backdated to the action.[3]

Part of a letter from Lieutenant Colonel Lysons of the Royal Welsh Fusiliers to the General of the Day, Right Attack, 11 June 1855, at the Camp before Sebastopol, reporting on the day's action against the Russians, and drawing attention to the gallant conduct of Private John Lyons. Lyons was awarded the Victoria Cross. WO28/188 Part 1

We have an account of the events on 10 June 1855 from the Siege Papers written by the Colonel in command at the camp before Sebastopol to the General of the Day.[4] About four hours after daylight, the enemy began hurling 13-inch shell grape shot and round shot. The Colonel scattered his men, but sustained heavy casualties. A very brisk musketry fire was kept up on the enemy's battery, with good effect.

Lyons was singled out for having seized a live shell which had fallen amongst the men and thrown it over the parapet. For this act he seems to have been promoted nine days later.

The Registers of the Regimental Courts Martial report that on 20 March 1855 he was tried for being drunk on duty, on 18 April and 10 October for being drunk in camp. On the first occasion he was forgiven, but was reduced in rank the second and third times.[5]

Private Samuel Evans, the other VC from the regiment, was invalided out to his home at Paisley in Lanarkshire as a result of a gunshot wound to the chest on 8 September 1855 at the siege of the Redan, one of the enemy strongholds.[6] Injured with him that day were 2,030 officers and men, another 153 were killed and 176 reported missing.[7] The Journal of Operations for the day[8] recorded that the English troops 'rushed with a most determined courage towards the Salient of the Redan, a distance of about 240 yards; – to cross the ditch, scale the Parapet, and leap into the Redan was the work of a minute, and then commenced a most terrific conflict. The heavy casualty list will show with what fierce courage and determined will the fight was sustained, – but owing to the terrible fire which mowed down our Supports before even they could come to the assistance of the foremost few: – after one hour and half severe fighting

ABOVE *The first list of people recommended to receive the Order of the Victoria Cross, outlining the act of valour of each and signed and approved by the Queen. The Order was made retrospective to Autumn 1854 to embrace the Crimean War. At the first investiture in Hyde Park on 26 June 1857, the Queen presented sixty-two VCs. WO32/7304*

BELOW *Examination Board for Invalid Soldiers, 13 May 1856, giving regiment, age, rank, period of service, pension rate, foreign service, character, disability or cause of discharge, the medical report, and details of birthplace, trade and physical attributes. Private Samuel Evans of the 19th Regiment of Foot, aged 34, had served in the Army for more than 16 years. On 8 September 1855 he sustained a gunshot wound to the chest, giving rise to his discharge. In April the same year he had earned himself the Victoria Cross. WO116/66*

and after a great loss of Officers, the men were compelled to return to their Trenches.'

Caught up in the mêlée was William Godfrey Dunham Massy, a young lieutenant in the 19th Regiment, and not yet seventeen years old. *The London Gazette* (Extraordinary edition) of 22 September 1855 contained a Despatch from Sebastopol stating that a second onslaught on the Redan had proved impossible because the trenches were so full of troops.[9] The enemy evacuated the Redan overnight, and early the following day the British moved in to rescue the wounded, including Lieutenant Massy, whose injuries were considered dangerous.

From the Commander-in-Chief's Memoranda it is possible to construct a fascinating picture of 'Redan' Massy's career and family background. On 1 October 1853, his uncle, Henry William Massy, applied on his behalf for a commission as an ensign.[10] The youth was his adopted son, his own father, William Godfrey Massy, having died, leaving him as the eldest son. Apparently commissions in the 19th Regiment had already been granted to the writer's two younger brothers and he was anxious that his nephew should join them. On 6 May 1854, he wrote again to the Military Secretary of the War Office, from his home at Rosanna, Tipperary, in Ireland. He hoped that his nephew's name might be considered at the pending nominations and that he might be summoned to attend the usual preparatory examination for that

ABOVE *Part of the Attestation and Discharge Papers of Private Samuel Evans, 13 May 1856, giving his physical description. The discharge was caused by a gunshot wound to his chest, before the Redan, near Sebastopol, on 8 September 1855. He died in 1898.* WO97/1452

LEFT *Part of a letter from 15-year-old William Godfrey Dunham Massy from his uncle's residence at Rosanna, Tipperary, on 12 June 1854, while waiting for a Commission in the 19th Regiment of Foot. Because of the infrequency of local Confirmations he had not yet taken the Anglican rites but promised to forward testimonials from his priest in Dublin and his University tutor as to his religious instruction and attendance.* WO31/1061

purpose. He was now highly proficient in science, especially mathematics, and was a 'handsome well grown lad'. Another effusion was sent on 27 May setting out the family's history of service in the Army. Both Henry William Massy's brothers were captains in the regiment, now based in Turkey. Their uncle, Godfrey Massy, had lost his life while a Captain of Marines on the coast of one of the West Indian Islands; another uncle, Eyre Massy, had earlier fought in Holland under the Duke of York, only to return home wounded with a sabre-cut to the head, which had rendered him helplessly insane, and the writer and his father had to support him for more than forty years. General Massy, later Lord Clarina, was a grand-uncle, and his son, Major General Lord Clarina, died during duty in the West Indies. A final missive was sent from the United Service Club in Dublin on 11 October 1854. This reported that Captain Godfrey Massy, his brother, had recently gone through much sickness in Bulgaria 'where my first cousin of the 77th Regiment died in his arms', while his own financial circumstances had suffered a down turn owing to a sale of property in Ireland at a loss of many thousands of pounds below its estimated value. The nephew was now excelling in Classics and science at the University 'and is reading for extra prizes in Modern Languages. He passed the Sandhurst Examination on the 1 July last, and has learned a good deal of military Drill in Dublin, which will quickly make him an effective officer.' His wish was granted, for on 23 October he obtained an ensigncy in his chosen regiment on the death of the holder.

The *Army List* of 1855 lists W.G.D. Massy as a lieutenant, commissioned on 9 February that year, and his uncles, Captain Godfrey William Hugh Massy and Captain Hugh Francis Massy, in the same regiment.

After the catastrophe of 8 September 1855, a confidential report on the nature of Massy's injuries was furnished by the Medical Board on 21 February 1856 at Camp Sebastopol.[11] He suffered a gunshot wound, the ball entering the top of the thigh posteriorly, passing this and making its exist anteriorly lower down and fracturing the femur at about the junction of the upper and middle third of the bone. The injury was classed as most severe and dangerous, and would require six months to heal. The regimental surgeon opined that the fracture was now firmly united but 'as there is serious oozing, although very slight, from the site of the anterior wound, it is not improbable that a fragment of necrosed bone remains within. There is about $1\frac{1}{2}$ inch of shortening, and the patient is thereby rendered lame for life.' What the report omits to mention is which was the affected leg!

A claim for six months' pay at the rank of lieutenant was approved, but the officer himself wrote respectfully from the United Service Club in Dublin on 31 March 1856,[12] to the Deputy Secretary at War about the £59–6s-3d gratuity sent to him, 'I cannot avoid believing that some mistake exists in this, as from the Surgeons in the Crimea, and in this Country, I understood that the largest sum allowed would be awarded me.... Indeed with one exception, I am the only man of the Army who has survived a similar wound without amputation. . . . With my broken limb twisted under me, bleeding, amongst other injuries from a Gun Shot wound ... I lay for fourteen hours in the power of the Russians. After six weeks my agony was renewed by the necessity of having my limb disunited and reset. For nearly six months I lay in Camp in my bed enduring sufferings well known to the Army. I find myself now at home disabled and helpless, already at a considerable expense for Surgical advice, the continuance of which alone will cost me more than the sum awarded me.... If I gained nothing but my wounds by my honorable place, it scarcely seems to be justice.' He explained that he had been put in charge of a Grenadier Company and drew a field allowance and forage as Captain from 5 August 1855, succeeding Captain Hugh Massy, who was about to go to Scutari on leave of absence.[13] (The musters show that his uncle was placed on the sick list and departed for England on 13 August,[14] joining his brother Godfrey, already on sick leave from 22 June.) His promotion had been rapid, for he only arrived at Sebastopol on 12 July, having set sail from Malta ten days before.[15] Another Medical Board, at Dublin on 12 April 1856, concluded that the thigh, leg and foot were now greatly wasted and completely useless, the thigh having shrunk by three inches.[16] One of the colonels tried to exert his influence: '. . . it does not seem right that "Redan Massy" when had [*sic*] more than a dozen Lieutenants above him, but who was named in General Orders to take charge of a Company ... in consequence of his superior activity and intelligence should have his claim "set aside on any technical objections". It is almost a miracle that he has survived to make any claim at all.'[17] The War Office relented as a special act of grace for his distinguished conduct, even suggesting his nomination for the Victoria Cross.[18] His gratuity was topped up by £46–7s–8d, with another sum of £105–13s–11d awarded him as captain for a further six months from 24 May.[19]

On 5 January 1857 Lieutenant Massy corresponded with the Military Secretary at the War

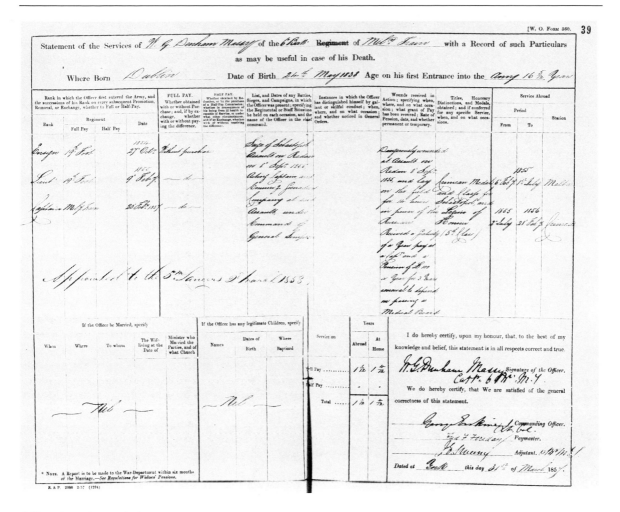

Signed statement of services of Captain W. G. Dunham Massy, of the 6th Battalion the Military Train, 31 March 1857. His date of birth is wrongly given as May rather than November 1838. The entry notes his transfer to the 5th Lancers on 2 March 1858. Details of his injury sustained at the Redan are incorporated, together with a record of his pension, later made permanent. WO25/582 f39r

Office about his wish for promotion to captain, as he had heard that one of the captains in his Regiment wanted to retire by sale of his commission.[20] Massy regretted that he was unable to attend Headquarters for the requisite examination as 'a large portion of bone is now coming away from one of my wounds'. On 10 January he stoically apologized for not acknowledging the Secretary's reply as he had been confined to bed. It would be financially inconvenient to have to buy a commission, and he considered his lameness a grave handicap in an infantry corps, so he asked that his name be withdrawn by the Regiment's agents, pending his promotion in the newly formed Military Train. This appointment was approved on 10 February. The Military Train was organized under a warrant of 24 January 1855 to be a more permanent formation of a Land Transport Corps for the Army both at home and in the field, and took precedence after the cavalry, artillery and engineers.[21]

Captain Massy appeared before another Medical Board on 13 September 1859 for a decision on whether his wounds were commensurate with the loss of a limb.[22] His annual pension of £100 granted him on 8 September 1856 was renewed, and on 8 September 1861 it was made permanent.[23]

His record of service, signed and dated by him at York on 31 March 1857, shows that he was in the 6th Battalion of the Military Train.[24] 'Particulars as may be useful in case of his Death' noted his birth at Dublin on 24 May 1838, and his age on entry to the Army on 27 October 1854 as $15\frac{11}{12}$ years. An attached note gave his transfer to the 5th (Royal Irish) Regiment of Light Dragoons (Lancers) on 2 March 1858. He was in receipt of the Crimean Medal with a Clasp for Sebastopol, the Turkish Medal, and the Legion of Honour (5th Class). Half his time had been spent abroad, in Malta and then the Crimea, which he left on 28 February 1856. A further return, made on 31 March 1870, when he was a major in the 5th Lancers, shows that he was at home from 1 March 1856 until 16 November 1863, and was then posted to the East Indies, acting as Assistant Adjutant General at Peshawur from 1 November 1867.[25] On 29 November 1869 he married Elizabeth Jane Seaton, at Calcutta Anglican Cathedral, and the next return, on 31 March 1872, recorded the birth of their daughter, Gertrude Annette Seaton Massy, on 28 August 1870, baptized at the Station Church at Murree. On 31 October 1871 he purchased a commission as lieutenant colonel.[26]

The *Army List*, 1900, sets out details of his date of birth, his Army appointments, war service, mentions in Despatches (three times), and finally his

retirement on half-pay, with the rank of lieutenant-general, on 1 April 1898. From this we know that he served in the Afghan War from 13 July 1879 until 1 March 1880, commanding a cavalry brigade at the battle of Charasiab and in subsequent operations culminating in the fall of Kabul, the capture of Sherpur, and the final pursuit of the enemy, before returning to Bengal. The last stage of his career was spent in Ceylon. On 21 June 1887, in celebration of the Golden Jubilee of Queen Victoria's reign, he was nominated a Companion of the Most Honourable Order of the Bath (Military Division), 3rd Class.[27]

From *The London Gazette* of 16 January 1880 we know that he sent a Despatch from Camp Kabul on 11 October 1879, where he was stationed as Brigadier General.[28] At 9.30 on the morning of 8 October he received orders to attack an enemy village. The cavalry brigade set out an hour-and-a-half later, without the expediency of organizing any rations. They were without food for two days, and many horses died or became non-effective through privation and fatigue on the treacherous mountain terrain. Worse – the enemy escaped under cover of night without any significant engagement. This seems to have been an awful prelude to the next published Despatch on 4 May 1880, and dated 9 February, for it seems to reflect a man out of kilter with the times and in decline.[29] On 11 December Massy had been instructed to transport the guns of the Field and Royal Horse Artillery along the road from Kabul to Ghazni, but instead struck out across country, and was forced into a skirmish with the enemy, hiding in the hills near Killa Kazi. His 'operations in continually advancing arms of precision and long range, such as the guns of the present day are, and thus losing their fire for the time, and in afterwards dismounting 30 lancers with carbines to stop the advance of 10,000 men, show him to have been quite unable to cope with the difficulties of the position to which he had committed himself'. His conduct was described as quite incomprehensible when he had such a small force of guns and cavalry and no infantry. He was ordered to slowly retreat and at once find a road to

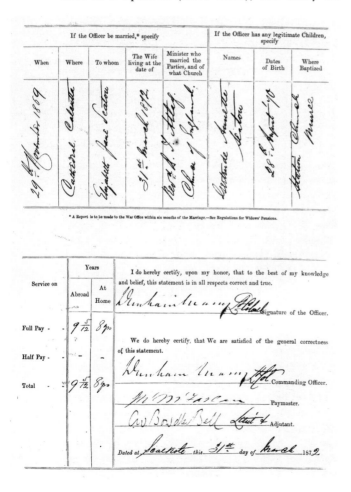

Part of the Return of Army Officers' Services made on 31 March 1872, and signed by Lieutenant Colonel (W. G.) Dunham Massy, also the Commanding Officer of the 5th (Royal Irish) Lancers. He became a lieutenant colonel by purchase on 31 October 1871, and had been in the East Indies since 17 November 1863. The Return sets out his marriage in India in 1869, and the birth there of his daughter. WO25/856/1

which the guns could be brought to safety. But the artillery's way was checked by a deep and narrow channel, and the enemy pressed its advance, out-flanking Massy's men on both sides. The guns had to be spiked and abandoned, and altogether, 51 horses, 278 officers and men were lost, and a further 25 men and 16 horses injured. It seems a sad end for one who had suffered so much at the very outset of his selected career.

William Godfrey Dunham Massy's half-pay as a lieutenant general of cavalry was £650 a year, paid quarterly to him, with deductions for Income Tax, at his home at Grantstown in Tipperary, from 1 July 1896.[30] On 1 April 1898 the sum was increased to £780 on his retirement.[31] The Paymaster General's register records that he died on 20 September 1906, and pension arrears of £165−2s−4d were assigned to his estate. Probate of his will was granted to his brother, Lieutenant-Colonel Charles Francis Massy, and to his daughter, Mrs Gertrude Annette Seaton Massey, of 18 Connaught Square, Hyde Park, in London.[32]

Commander-in-Chief's memoranda contained still more genealogical gems about the Massy family, thanks to Henry William Massy's predilection for the Army as a profession for others than himself and for keeping the War Office informed of his family's movements. On 27 September 1845, he wrote to the War Office from his residence at Rosanna reminding the Secretary that his brother, Godfrey William Hugh Massy, had been listed for an ensigncy since 1842, had now been to university and hoped that this would not be ruined by idleness at the most precious period of his life.[33] The young man was eager to set his mind at rest or seek another post. In July, J. Massy had also tried to advance his cause. He or she wrote from Mitchelstown in county Cork, 'I have been left by a late uncle (who was for over 40 years a clergyman for the established church and brother to two Military officers who lost their lives in the Service) as manager of the affairs of his infant children, and for many years I have endeavoured to discharge the trust and promote their Talent as far as lay in my power. One of the youngest boys of his family namely "Godfrey Hugh Massy" is anxious to get into the army... and is nearly 21 years of age... I have the money ready

A Retired Full Pay Register of the Army recording the three addresses of Lieutenant General William Godfrey Dunham Massy, his date of birth (24 November 1838) and death (20 September 1906) and the names of his two executors. On his death pension arrears of £165 24s were due to him out of the quarterly instalments. PMG3/94

ARMY.	NON-EFFECTIVE SERVICES.							
	Establish'ᵗ No.	Name and Address.	Rank.	Authorities, Attorneys, &c.	Date of Warrant.	Date of Commencement.	Rate.	Full Sum due for each Quarter.

for the purchase of his commission.' On 13 October £450 was lodged with Messrs Cox and Co, agents for the 19th Regiment of Foot and the ensigncy was his. The *Alumni Dublinienses, 1593–1860*, shows that he was admitted as a university student on 7 June 1841, aged seventeen, the son of William Massy, 'clericus', and was a native of county Tipperary. He graduated in the summer term of 1845.

Once in the Regiment, Massy appears to have been on a good deal of sick leave: he was sick on board ship between 17 November 1854 and 1 January 1855, on 22 June he was sent back to England on sick leave and was still there in September when his nephew was wounded.[34]

Another £450 was paid to the Regiment's agents by 29 July 1847 for an ensigncy for his brother, Hugh Francis Massy. A letter to the War Office from his brother Henry William Massy, on 18 June 1845, had advised that yet another brother, Charles William Massy, had been waiting for a commission since 1842.[35] He had given up and had now advanced himself in another line of life and wished to have his name withdrawn and that of his youngest brother substituted. Hugh Francis would be seventeen on 12 August. Their widowed mother, Elizabeth Massy, also wrote from Rosanna, on 12 February 1846, to plead his case with the Duke of Wellington, the Commander-in-Chief. Her son was 'fortunate enough to have a handsome pecuniary provision'. His father had died nearly sixteen years ago, leaving her with the care of six very young children, the youngest of whom had little set aside because of the suddenness of the last illness. The eldest son was a resident landowner and magistrate for two counties, two others had raised and commanded yeomanry corps, and Hugh Francis, who was now nearly eighteen, had left school in England where he had been sent to have the best possible education in Classics and modern languages, and had learned the skills of horsemanship. Her late husband's eldest brother, Captain Godfrey Massy, lost his life at an early age in the West Indies, while the youngest, Eyre Massy, served in the 49th Foot with the Duke of York in Holland, and had received a frightful sabre wound to his head causing periodic bouts of insanity. Without consulting his friends, he had sold his commission, spent the money, and returned home penniless. He was placed in an asylum to which her husband contributed £60 a year for over thirty years for his upkeep and care. She also referred to her husband's connection with the first two Lords Clarina, and finally to his first cousin, Major George Massy, who was twice dangerously wounded while serving in the 1st Foot under the

Duke at Waterloo. Mrs Massy's own family had a tradition of Army service, her father having commanded the Tipperary Regiment of Yeomanry Infantry, and his nephew, the late Lieutenant-Colonel Evans of the 38th Regiment, had a long Army career. Even this, and two more begging letters were ineffective, for it was not until 7 August 1847 that her son was granted his request for a vacant ensigncy.

The 19th Regiment's third Victoria Cross was awarded to regimental number 2364 Sergeant Alfred Atkinson, of the 1st Battalion, for gallantry he dis-

---

On 24 April 1902 Field Marshal Lord Roberts added his voice to the call for the VC to be awarded posthumously to Sergeant A[lfred] Atkinson, 1st Battalion the Yorkshire Regiment, who was mortally wounded during the Battle of Paardeberg, South Africa, on 18 February 1900. After a lot of correspondence, including a letter from his elderly mother, the Award was gazetted on 8 August 1902. WO32/7478

Pedigree of the Massys

HUGH MASSY = ELIZABETH
of Duntrileague, Co. Limerick

MASSY =

EYRE (MASSEY) = CATHERINE
created Baron Clarina of Elm Park, Co Limerick, 28 Dec 1800, General, the British Army, 1796, wounded at Culloden 1746, served with General Wolfe in North America, Colonel, the 27th Foot, 1773 until his death, 17 May 1804

NATHANIEL WILLIAM (MASSEY) succeeded his father as Lord Clarina, 1804, Major General, the British Army, 1808, died Jan 1810, at Barbados, West Indies
=
◆

EYRE MASSY
youngest son, served in Holland, in the 49th Foot, and severely wounded to the head, insane for 30 years, from c.1800

WILLIAM MASSY =
Clerk in Holy Orders c.1790, died c.1830/1

ELIZABETH
of Rosanna, Tipperary, 1846, daughter of —, commander of Tipperary Regt of Yeomanry

HUGH FRANCIS MASSY
bn 12 Aug 1828, educated in England, Ensign in the 19th Regt of Foot, 7 Aug 1847, Lieutenant, 9 Jly 1850, Captain, 3 Feb 1854, served in Turkey

GODFREY WILLIAM HUGH MASSY
bn c.1824, Ensign in the 19th Regt of Foot, 24 Oct 1845, when about 21, Lieutenant, 2 Feb 1849, Captain, 21 May 1852, served in Turkey and Bulgaria, 1854, BA of the University of Dublin, 1845

CHARLES FRANCIS MASSY
Ensign, 92nd (Gordon Highlanders) Regt of Foot, 26 May 1865, rose to Lieutenant-Colonel, Indian Staff Corps, 26 May 1891, served in the Abyssinian Campaign, 1868, and the Afghan War, 1879, executor of his brother's will, 1906

GEORGE MASSY
Major, 1st Regt of Foot, dangerously wounded 16 and 18 June 1815, at the battle of Waterloo

GODFREY MASSY
eldest son, Captain, the Royal Marines, killed in the West Indies before 1854

MASSY
raised and commanded a Yeomanry Corps in Ireland before 1846

MASSY
raised and commanded a Yeomanry Corps in Ireland before 1846

HENRY WILLIAM MASSY
of Rosanna, Tipperary, 1845–54

CHARLES WILLIAM MASSY
listed for an Ensigncy Sept 1842–5

WILLIAM GODFREY MASSY =
dead by 1 Oct 1853

ELIZABETH JANE SEATON
m arr 29 Nov 1869, at Calcutta Cathedral, India

MASSY
eldest son, a resident landowner and magistrate for two counties in Ireland, by 1846

WILLIAM GODFREY DUNHAM MASSY =
of Grantstown Hall, Tipperary, CB (1887), DL and JP for Tipperary, eldest son, bn 24 Nov 1838, at Dublin, LLB and LLD of the University of Dublin, 1873, Ensign, 19th Regt of Foot, 27 Oct 1854, Lieutenant, 9 Feb 1855, dangerously wounded during the assault on the Redan, by Sebastapol, in the Crimea, 8 Sept 1855 (Despatches), awarded Legion of Honour (5th class), Captain, the Military Train, 20 Feb 1857, 5th Lancers 2 Mch 1858, Major, 23 Jan 1863, rising to Lieutenant-General, 21 Jan 1893, served in Bengal and Ceylon and in the Afghan War, 1879 (Despatches), placed on retired list 1 Apr 1898, died 20 Sept 1906, will pr 15 Dec 1906

MASSEY = GERTRUDE ANNETTE SEATON
of Connaught Square, Hyde Park, Middx, 1906, bn 28 Aug 1870, bp at the Station Church, Murree, India, executrix of father's will, 1906, then marr

The details in italics refer to sources held outside the Public Record Office

played during the battle of Paardeberg, South Africa, on 18 February 1900. His was one of the first posthumous awards, gazetted on 8 August 1902,[36] and a gratuity of £50 was credited to his estate.[37] A series of correspondence surrounding the nomination shows that the Distinguished Conduct Medal with a gratuity of £20 was originally thought appropriate.[38] Lord Kitchener submitted his recommendation for the vc on 17 February 1901, almost a year after the sergeant's death on 21 February, but it was dismissed as there was no precedent for it. A posthumous promotion was similarly turned down, which would have given a higher rate of pension to his dependants.

A letter sent on 7 August 1901 to his father, James Atkinson, late Farrier Serjeant of the Royal Artillery, by the Lieutenant Adjutant, related how he met his death.[39] His battalion was the first to advance in an attack on the Boer trenches and remained in the firing line from dawn to dark, at very close range. In the morning, when his Company was near the Modder River, he had rescued a wounded lieutenant from another regiment, carried him to safety and bound up his wounds. He went down to the river seven times to fetch water for the casualties, until he fell mortally wounded in the head. The water's edge was only fifty yards from the enemy, with no cover, so his actions meant almost certain death, and indeed, four or five of his battalion had already been killed while trying to collect water at the same point. The heat was intense, making the need for water urgent. The wounded lieutenant recommended him for the Victoria Cross and said he was the bravest man he had

ever seen and that he undoubtedly owed his life to him. The letter ended on a bureaucratic note, reporting that the War Office would not waive the rule that nomination had to come during the person's lifetime, but the adjutant concluded, 'it is a consolation to know that no man could have died a more glorious death'. He was barely twenty-six years old and his grieving mother forwarded a copy of this letter to the War Office in January 1902, asking that the matter be reconsidered, 'for my husband is turned seventy years and a cripple and I assure you we are greatly in need of help'.

Alfred Atkinson was born on 6 February 1874, at Leeds, in Yorkshire,[40] after his father's discharge from the Royal Artillery at Aldershot on 2 October 1873, on the termination of his second period of limited engagement.[41] By then James was aged forty-three, and had put in twenty-one years of service, some of it in the Crimea and Canada. The Roll of the Married Establishment gave his wife's name as Margaret, placed on the establishment on 4 June 1855.[42] At the time of his discharge there were four children on the Roll, aged nine, seven, five and one. At the end of his career he was being paid 3s 5¾d a day with Good Conduct Pay of 4d. He was given passage money of 8s 3d for the journey from Aldershot to London, plus an allowance of £1. His intended destination was Bay Horse Head, Leeds, where he may have resumed his trade as a shoeing smith. His attestation and discharge papers reveal that his birthplace was Kirkby Malyard [Malzeard], near Ripon, in Yorkshire,[43] not far from the 19th Regiment's base at Richmond.

Roll of the Married Establishment of H. Battery, the 4th Brigade of the Royal Artillery, 1 October–31 December 1873. Sgt Farrier James Atkinson's wife Margaret is listed with their four children, aged between just under two years up to nine, she having been first placed on the Establishment on 4 June 1855. Their son Alfred was born on 6 February 1874, after his father's discharge on 2 October 1873. WO10/2517

NOTES

The following abbreviations represented in the notes apply to groups of records emanating from a variety of legal and government departments:

A	Alienation Office	HCA	High Court of Admiralty	PCAP	Judicial Committee of the Privy Council
ADM	Admiralty	HO	Home Office		
AIR	Air Ministry	IND	Index	PCOM	Prison Commission
AO	Exchequer and Audit Department	IR	Board of Inland Revenue	PEV	Court of the Honour of Peveril
ASSI	Clerks of Assize	J	Supreme Court of Judicature	PL	Palatinate of Lancaster
AST	National Assistance Board	JUST	Justices Itinerant	PMG	Paymaster General's Office
B	Court of Bankruptcy	KB	Court of King's Bench	PRIS	King's Bench Prison
BT	Board of Trade	LC	Lord Chamberlain's Department	PROB	Prerogative Court of Canterbury
C	Chancery	LR	Exchequer Auditors of Land Revenue	RG	General Register Office
CHES	Palatinate of Chester			REQ	Court of Requests
CO	Colonial Office	LS	Lord Steward's Department	SC	Special Collections
CP	Court of Common Pleas	MAF	Ministry of Agriculture, Fisheries and Food	SO	Signet Office
CRES	Crown Estate Commissioners			SP	State Paper Office
CUST	Board of Customs and Excise	MEPO	Metropolitan Police Office	STAC	Court of Star Chamber
DEL	Court of Delegates	MH	Ministry of Health	T	Treasury
DL	Duchy of Lancaster	MT	Ministry of Transport	TS	Treasury Solicitor
DURH	Palatinate of Durham	NDO	National Debt Office	WO	War Office
E	Exchequer	PALA	Palace Court	ZJ	*London Gazette*
FO	Foreign Office	PC	Privy Council Office		

1 The Legal System

1. E13, 20 Henry III, 1235/6–1875
2. Calendar of Tithe-suits enrolled in the Exchequer of Pleas, temp. Edward IV – George III, *Deputy Keeper's Report, 11, App. 11,* pp 249–72
3. CP40, 1 Edward I, 1272 – 38 Victoria 1875
4. CP43, Easter 25 Elizabeth, 1583 – 1837
5. Series I, CP41, 1573–1834, Series II, CP42, 1830–52
6. KB27, 1 Edward I, 1272 – 13 William III, 1700
7. KB122, 1702–1875
8. KB125, 1603–1877
9. KB28, 1 Anne, 1702 – 1911
10. KB26, 1 Richard I, 1289 – 56 Henry III, 1271
11. KB29, 3 Edward III, 1329 – 1843
12. C206, temp. Elizabeth – Victoria
13. C44, temp. Edward I – Richard III
14. C43, temp. Henry VII – James I
15. KB122, see n. 7
16. KB25, 1875–1906
17. J69, 1918–59
18. J70, 1907–26
19. JUST1, 1201–1348, Eyre Rolls
20. ASSI1–84, see PRO Information Leaflet, 'Assizes Records' for class arrangements of material under Circuit
21. KB20, 1664–1839
22. JUST1, 1248–1482
23. City of London and county of Middlesex, extended from 1834 to take in parts of Essex, Kent and Surrey
24. PCOM1, 1801–1904
25. HO26
26. HO27
27. HO140, 1868–1909
28. J89, 1875–1930 (King's Bench Division), 1875–80 (Common Pleas Division), 1875–80 (Exchequer Division), C78, 1875–1903 (Chancery Division Decree Rolls)
29. J89, 'Indexes' for King's Bench Division, 1879–1930, Common Pleas Division, 1875–80, and Exchequer Division, 1879–80; C32, 1875–80, J89, 1880–1940 for Chancery Division
30. KB20, see n. 21
31. see PRO Information Leaflet, 'Metropolitan Police Records of Service'. The chief classes are HO65/26, 1829–36, alphabetical register of the Force; MEPO4/333–8, September 1830–April 1857, July 1878–1933; MEPO3/2883–927, 1858–1933, joining papers and particulars of service of distinguished officers (closed 75 years); MEPO4/361–477, January 1889–November 1909, certificates of service records; MEPO4/339–51, March 1889–January 1947, registers of leavers; MEPO4/2, 1829–89, registers of deaths while serving; MEPO5/1–90, 1829–59, pensions and gratuities
32. see n. 20
33. Walker and Walker, *The English Legal System,* 4th ed., R. J. Walker, 1976, p. 16
34. HO23, 1847–66
35. HO77, 1782–1853
36. HO24, 1838–75
37. HO8, 1824–76, HO9, 1802–49
38. HO11, 1787–1870
39. HO10, 1788–1859
40. T53, 1716–44, T1, 1747–72
41. principally by P. W. Coldham, in *The Complete Book of Emigrants in Bondage, 1614–1775,* 1987
42. PC1/67/92, HO12, 1849–71, CO386/154, 1848–73
43. C88, 1277–1628, CP38, 1821–69, E159, 1217–1926, KB17, 1739–1834; enrolments of extents of lands and goods are in E172, 1602–Victoria, E173, 1639–1884, and KB140, temp. George III–Victoria
44. C1–C13, temp. Richard II – 1842
45. C14–C16, 1842–75
46. C21, temp. Elizabeth – Charles I, C22, 1649–1714; later Depositions are filed with the proceedings in C11–C16

47. C24, 26 Henry VIII, 1534 – 1853
48. C103–C116, various dates from the twelfth to mid-nineteenth century
49. C33, 36 Henry VIII, 1544 – 1875, Entry Books of Decrees and Orders, and C78, 26 Henry VIII, 1534 – 1903, Decree Rolls; C79, Supplementary Series
50. C33 above, the yearly indexes to them are on open access
51. C1–C3, temp. Richard II – Commonwealth
52. C5–C10, temp. James I – 1714, C11, 1714–58, C12, 1758–1800, C13, 1800–42
53. IND1/16820–53, temp. Elizabeth – Victoria
54. E111, temp. Henry VII – Elizabeth I, E112, Elizabeth – Victoria
55. REQ2, temp. Henry VII – Charles I
56. STAC1–STAC9, temp. Henry VII – Charles I
57. HCA1, 1535–1834
58. HCA5, 1746–67, HCA6, 1767–1810, HCA7, 1810–64 (Instance Court), with indexes to HCA6 and HCA7 in HCA56; HCA8, 1718–1840 (Prize Court); HCA43, 1689–1801, HCA44, 1793–1832 (Prize Appeal Court)
59. HCA27, 1860–1924 (Instance Court); HCA28, 1777–1842 (Prize Court)
60. HCA15–HCA20, 1629–1943 (Instance Court); from 1860 to 1918 access is via HCA27; indexes to HCA16, HCA17 and HCA27 are in HCA56
61. HCA49, 1636–1875
62. DEL1, 1609–1834, indexed in DEL11
63. DEL4, 1538–44, 1601–1756
64. DEL6, 1650–1829
65. DEL7, 1796–1834
66. PCAP1, 1834–79, Processes, PCAP2, 1833–78, Assignation Books, PCAP3, 1834–70, Case Books
67. PROB29, 1536–1819
68. PROB30, 1740–1858
69. PROB8, 1526–1858, PROB9, 1781–1858 (Limited Probates)
70. PROB6, 1559–1858, PROB7, 1810–58 (Limited Administrations)
71. PROB12, 1383–1858
72. PROB18, 1665–1858, Allegations, PROB25, 1664–1854, Answers
73. PROB24, 1657–1809, PROB26, 1826–57
74. PROB35, 1529–86, PROB36, 1658–1722, PROB31, 1722–1858
75. PROB48, 1666–1857, PROB53 for some sixteenth-century material
76. PROB28, 1642–1733, Cause Papers, PROB37, 1783–1858
77. British Record Society, Index Volume 85
78. *The Genealogist*, vol. 11, A–N, vol. 12, O–Z
79. with effect from 12 January 1858, under the Court of Probate Act, 20 and 21 Victoria c.77

80. E321, temp. Henry VIII – Philip and Mary
81. E315, temp. Henry VIII – Philip and Mary
82. Duchy of Lancaster, Equity proceedings: DL1, pleadings temp. Henry VII – 1835, DL49 papers in law suits, 1502–1853, DL3, depositions and examinations, temp. Henry VII – Philip and Mary, DL4, Elizabeth – 1818, DL48, sealed depositions, 1695–1739, DL9, affidavits, orders and petitions, 1560–1857, DL5, decrees and Orders, 1472–1872; Forest proceedings, DL39, Henry III – Victoria, DL50 estreats of fines and amercements, Henry V, Elizabeth – Victoria, DL46, coroners' inquests and returns, 1804–96; Palatinate of Chester: Exchequer Court, papers in causes CHES9, 1501–1830, CHES13, decrees and orders, 1559–1790, CHES14, Entry Books, 1562–1830, CHES12, depositions, Elizabeth – Victoria, CHES11, Exhibits, Henry III – Charles II; CHES15, pleadings, Equity side, Henry VIII – George IV, CHES16, pleadings, 1559–1762; The Great Session, Gaol Files, CHES24, 1341–1830; Chester and North Wales Assize Circuit, ASSI61, Crown Minute Books, 1831–1938, ASSI57, Civil Minute Books, 1843–78, ASSI62, Crown Books, 1835–83, ASSI64, indictments, 1831–91, 1908–45, ASSI65, depositions, 1831–91, 1909–44, ASSI59, pleadings, 1840–1927, ASSI66, coroners' inquisitions, 1798–1891; Wales and Chester Assize Circuit, ASSI79, Crown Minute Books, 1945, ASSI78, Civil Minute Books, 1945–6, ASSI83, indictments, 1945–57, ASSI84, depositions and case papers, 1945; Palatinate of Lancaster, Equity proceedings: PL6, bills, 1485–1853, PL7, answers, 1474–1858, PL8, replications, rejoinders etc, 1601–1856, PL10, depositions, 1581–1854, PL9, affidavits, 1610–1836, PL12, Exhibits, 1795–1860, PL11, decrees and orders, 1524–1848, PL14, miscellanea, Richard II – Victoria; common law: PL15, plea rolls, 1400–1845, PL16, dockets, 1362–1848, PL21, sessional papers, including pleadings, Henry VIII – 1848, PL19, jury panels and verdicts of suits, 1811–48; PL25/6–317, Assize Rolls, 1524–1843, PL28/1–12, Minute Books, 1687–1877, PL26, indictments, 1424–1868, PL27, depositions, 1663–1867, PL28, miscellanea, Richard II – Victoria; Palatinate of Durham: DURH2, Chancery bills and answers and other pleadings, 1576–1840, DURH7, interrogatories and depositions, 1557–1804, DURH1, affidavits, 1657–1812, DURH4, Entry Books

of decrees and orders, 1633–1958, DURH5, original decrees and orders, 1613–1775; Court of Pleas, DURH13, Judgment Rolls, 1344–1844, DURH14, jury panels, James I – Victoria; Assizes, DURH15, Minute Books, 1770–1876, DURH16, Crown Books, 1753–1876, DURH17, indictments, 1582–1876, DURH18, depositions, 1843–76, DURH19, miscellanea, 1472–1815, DURH3, coroners' inquisitions, temp. James I; from 1876 the Palatinate formed part of the North Eastern Assize Circuit, whose records are in ASSI41–47; Principality of Wales: South Wales Assize Circuit, ASSI76, Crown Minute Books, 1844–1942, ASSI75, Civil Minute Books, 1846–1943, ASSI77, Miscellaneous Books, 1837–84, ASSI71, indictments, 1834–92, 1920–45, ASSI72, depositions, 1837–1942, ASSI73, miscellanea, 1839–1937, ASSI74, *nisi prius*, pleadings and Judgment Rolls, 1841–2; records of the Chester and North Wales Assize Circuit are described above, and similarly of the Wales and Chester Assize Circuit under the Palatinate of Chester; Palace Court: PALA3, Docket Books, 1802–49, PALA6, Plea Rolls, 1630–1849, PALA5, Plaint Books, 1680–1849, PALA4, Habeas Corpus Books, 1700–1849, LS13, proceedings, 1673–1762, petitions and orders, 1684–1800, PALA1, Bail Books, 1692–1836, PALA2, Custody Books, 1754–1842; Court of the Honour of Peveril: PEV1, Action Books, 1682–1790, pleadings books, 1682–1761, and pleas, 1847–9
83. B4, 1710–1849
84. B5, 1710–1859
85. B3, 1759–1911
86. B1, 1710–1877
87. B6, 1733–1925
88. C32, 1875–80, J89, 1880–1940
89. J15, 1876–1955
90. KB30, 1848–88, Pleadings, KB31, 1853–6, Orders (Court for Crown Cases Reserved), J69, 1918–59, J70, 1907–26 (Court of Appeal), J81, 1908–72 (Court of Criminal Appeal)
91. J78, 1858–1958
92. J77, 1858–1937 (most closed 75 years)
93. J89, see n. 28
94. C78, see n. 28
95. C32, J89, see n. 29
96. J54, 1876–1942
97. J16, 1876–80, J17, 1880–1977 (Chancery and King's Bench Divisions)
98. J4, 1876–1945
99. J55, 1875–80
100. J54, see n. 96
101. J5, 1876–82 (Queen's Bench Division), J6, 1876–81 (Common Pleas Division), J7, 1876–80 (Exchequer Division)

102. KB28/127, Michaelmas 7 George II, 1733, m. 2
103. KB29/393, Michaelmas 7 George II
104. E331/Coventry/37/7: John Fletcher was instituted to the living on 20 December 1758

2 The Holding and Transfer of Land

1. PEV1, 1662–1850
2. SC2, thirteenth- to nineteenth-century Court Rolls, SC11 and SC12, temp. Henry III – William IV, Rentals and Surveys
3. CRES5, 1441–1950, Court Rolls etc.
4. LR3, 1286–1837 (Court Rolls), LR11, temp. Edward I – George III (Estreats of Court Rolls), LR13, 1568–1834 (Rentals etc)
5. DL30, temp. Edward I – Victoria (listed in SC2) for the Duchy of Lancaster; DURH3, 1381–1494 Court Rolls, and Halmote Court Books 1348–1619 of the Palatinate of Durham
6. MAF9, 1841–1925
7. MAF13, 1926–44, MAF27, 1936–57
8. Married Womens Property Act, 56 and 57 Victoria c.63
9. *viz* 1 January 1926
10. Ancient Deeds may be found enrolled on the Close Rolls, C54, as well as surviving in the following classes: C146, Series C, 1100–1627, C147, Series CC, *c.* 1100, C148, Series CS, Edward I – Elizabeth; E40, Series A, *c.* 1100–1603, E41, Series AA, *c.* 1100–1603, E42, *c.* 1100–1603, E43, Series WS, *c.* 1100–1603, E210, Series D, *c.* 1150, E211, Series DD, 1101–1645, E212, Series DS, 1228, E213, Series RS, Edward I; deeds once belonging to religious houses are in E326, Series B, *c.* 1200–1592, E327, Series BX, temp. Stephen, E328, Series BB, *c.* 1250–1569, E329, Series BS, 1148; Augmentation Office, E315, twelfth century–1730; Pipe Office, E354, Series P, 1524–1608, E355, Series PP, *c.* 1500–*c.* 1600; Crown lands, LR14, Series E, Henry III – Elizabeth, LR15, Series EE, *c.* 1400–*c.* 1700; Palatinate of Chester, and Wales, WALE29, Series F, Edward I – Elizabeth, WALE30, Series FF, *c.* 1507–1633; Modern Deeds, *c.* 149 temp. James I, E44, *c.* 1600–*c.* 1700, E214, 1672–1851, E330, Series B, temp. James I; Crown lands, LR16, Series E, seventeenth and eighteenth centuries; Palatinate of Lancaster, PL29, Series H, *c.* 1550–*c.* 1850; Welsh deeds including the Palatinate of Chester, WALE31, James II – nineteenth century
11. PROB11, 1383–1858
12. C53, 1199–1517, Charter Rolls; C66, 1201–1962, Patent Rolls; C54, 1204–1903, Close Rolls
13. DL36, temp. Henry I – James I, Duchy of Lancaster, and DL37, temp. Edward III – Henry VII; CHES2 1

Edward II, 1307 – 11 George IV, 1830, Palatinate of Chester
14. C143, temp. Henry III – Richard III, C142, temp. Henry VII – Charles II, C202, 1603 – Charles II; E151, temp. Henry III – Henry VI
15. C66, see n. 12
16. C60, 1199–1648
17. *Calendar of Patent Rolls*, to 1585, *Calendar of Fine Rolls*, to 1509
18. A4, 1571–1650, Entry Books of licences and pardons
19. C132–C142, temp. Henry III – Charles II
20. E149–E150, temp. Henry III – James I
21. *Calendar of Inquisitions Post Mortem*
22. *Calendar of Inquisitions Post Mortem of the reign of Henry VII*
23. Duchy of Lancaster, DL7, temp. Henry III – Charles I; Duchy of Cornwall, E306, 1438–1493; Palatinate of Chester, CHES3, Edward I – Charles I; Palatinate of Durham, DURH3, abstracts and registers, 1318–1567, originals, 1438–1637; Palatinate of Lancaster, PL4, Henry IV – Henry VIII
24. C60, see n. 16
25. C54, see n. 12
26. C54
27. J18, 1903–83
28. CP40, 1 Edward I, 1272 – Hilary 25 Elizabeth I, 1582/3, CP43, Easter 25 Elizabeth, 1583 – 1837
29. Law of Property Act 1925
30. 32 Henry VIII C.28
31. CP25, temp. Henry II – 1839
32. CP40 and CP43, see n. 28
33. CP50, temp. Henry III – 1660
34. A7, 1576–1661, A6, 1759–94
35. CP34, 3 Elizabeth, 1560/1–4 William IV, 1833, CP35, temp. Edward VI – William III
36. A6, see n. 34
37. C54, see n. 12
38. J18, see n. 27
39. C54, see n. 12
40. J18, see n. 27
41. SP44, 1661–1781
42. HO38, 1782–1868, HO142, 1868–78
43. ZJ1, 1665–1986
44. C103–C114, of various dates up to the mid-nineteenth century
45. IR26, indexed in IR27
46. E307 and E308, temp. Commonwealth, E351, temp. Charles II, LR1, 1670–1833
47. Duchy of Lancaster, DL37, 1440–1478, abstracts Henry VII, DL42, registers of leases, twelfth century–1835, DL14, drafts and particulars of leases, Henry VIII – George III, DL15, counterparts of leases, Edward VI–1875; Duchy of Cornwall, E306, Henry VIII – Charles II; Palatinate of Durham, DURH3, enrolments of leases, fourteenth–eighteenth centuries
48. see PRO Information Leaflet 'Enclosure Awards'; the main classes of enrolments of awards are C54,

CP40, CP43, E141, E159, CHES38, DURH4, DURH26 and DURH41
49. C54, 1756–7, CP43, 1762–1849, E13, 1771–1832, E159, 1817–51, KB122, 1760–1842, all listed in *Deputy Keeper's Report*, XXVII, App. pp 1–29, DL45, 1775–1872, CRES2, 1740–1867, CRES6, 1660–1918
50. MAF1, 1847–1936, MAF2, 1845–1963
51. IR30
52. IR29
53. IR23, 1798–1801
54. C1–C16, Chancery Pleadings, temp. Richard II – 1875, Exhibits of material dating from the thirteenth to nineteenth century are in C103–C114, Depositions, Country, in C21, temp. Elizabeth – Charles I, C22, 1649–1714, and Town, C24, 1534–1853; later Depositions are filed with the Pleadings in C11–C16. E111, Exchequer Pleadings, temp. Henry VII – Elizabeth, E112, temp. Elizabeth – Victoria, Exhibits *c.*1650–*c.*1850 are in E140, and some from the seventeenth until nineteenth century in E219; Depositions by Commission, temp. Elizabeth – Victoria are in E134, and before the Barons, for the same period in E133. See PRO Information Leaflets 'Chancery Proceedings (Equity Suits)', and 'Equity Proceedings in the Court of Exchequer'.

3 Tax and Other Sources of Revenue

1. Initially £4,000, the sum was later increased to £6,000 from each of the borough and shire quotas
2. E179, temp. Henry II – William and Mary
3. E179/161/9
4. P. Ziegler, *The Black Death*, 1969, pp 138–40
5. 14 and 15 Henry VIII c.16, in *Statutes of the Realm, 1509–1546*
6. E115
7. E179/161/198, E179/161/196
8. 13 Elizabeth c.27, in *Statutes of the Realm, 1547–1585*
9. E376, 1591–1691 (Chancellor's Series), E377 (Pipe Office Series)
10. 1 Charles I c.6, *Statutes of the Realm, 1625–1680*
11. 16 Charles I c.2, *Statutes of the Realm, 1625–1680*
12. SP16, 1634–40, listed in *Calendar of State Papers (Domestic Series) of the reign of Charles I*
13. PC2, 1633–40
14. 16 Charles I c.2
15. 16 Charles I c.4
16. 16 Charles I c.9
17. 16 Charles I c.30
18. 16 Charles I c.32, all the above are included in *Statutes of the Realm, 1625–1680*
19. E179/251/22
20. E179, and SP28/191–5
21. SP63/288–302, indexed in SP63/302

22. SP19, in *Calendar of the Committee for Advance of Money, 1642–1656*
23. SP20, 1643–53 (Committee for Sequestration); SP23 in *Calendar of Proceedings of the Committee for Compounding, 1643–1660*
24. SP25, 1649–60, SP27, same period, printed in *Calendar of State Papers (Domestic Series) of the Commonwealth*
25. SP21, 1644–50, Committee for Both Kingdoms; SP22, 1642–53, Committee for Plundered Ministers; SP24, 1647–56, Committee and Commissioners for Indemnity; SP28, 1642–60, Commonwealth Exchequer Papers
26. SP28/196–204, 1642–60
27. C54
28. 13 Charles II c.4, in *Statutes of the Realm, 1625–1680*
29. E179/255/5
30. 12 Charles II c.9
31. 12 Charles II c.20, c.21, c.27, c.29, all five of the foregoing are published in *Statutes of the Realm, 1625–1680*
32. 15 Charles II c.9
33. 14 Charles II c.10
34. 15 Charles II c.13
35. 16 Charles II c.3, all four are in *Statutes of the Realm, 1625–1680*
36. 1 William and Mary c.10, in *Statutes of the Realm, 1685–1694*
37. LS13/231
38. 8 and 9 William III c.6, in *Statutes of the Realm, 1695–1701*
39. 38 George III c.60
40. IR23
41. IR24/48 no. 36, 573
42. E174, temp. George I
43. IR23
44. E182, 1689–1830
45. LC3/36, 1854–69, LC3/35, 1759–98
46. T47/2–4
47. T47/5–7
48. T47/8
49. T47/2
50. IR84/6, 1848–53, IR83/17, 1853–6
51. IR12
52. AO3
53. IR72
54. IR49, 1800–33, IR13, 1799–1900
55. IR1
56. IR26, 1796–1903
57. AO3/370–1
58. CO5, 1730–1838
59. IR1
60. IR17
61. IR1/50/30, and CP5/38/4
62. IR1/25/165
63. IR1/27/123
64. IR27, 1796–1903
65. IR26
66. IR59, 1805–1981 (most closed 75 years)
67. IR67, 1853–66, IR6, 1812–36, IR19, 1796–1903 (specimens only), IR62, relating to delayed assessments and payment of Duty where gifts to the Nation or material of national

importance were involved, IR7, 1839–41, Scottish papers
68. C114/9–23, 153, C46
69. C114/16
70. C114/23
71. C114/23
72. C114/22
73. e.g. E403/2362–2370, 1558–74, 1600–28, 1697–8 registers of fees, annuities and pensions, E401/2591–2, contributors to Loans 1696 and 1698, E401/2598, contributors to a Loan in 1757, E401/2567, and in 1847, E351/53, purchasers of annuities, 1704
74. e.g. AO3/947–8, 1780–1852, list of contributors to the Scottish Fund, and their wives
75. E401/2600, E401/2599
76. E403/2379, 1698 annuity
77. NDO2/1
78. NDO2/2
79. NDO2/10–14
80. NDO2/15
81. ZJ1
82. NDO1/11
83. NDO1/13, 107
84. NDO2/46–51
85. NDO1/128–50
86. NDO2/53–8
87. NDO3/32, all are bound together
88. NDO1/1–3
89. *Blackmansbury*, vol. 5, nos 1 and 2 (April and June 1968)
90. NDO1/2 and 2A
91. NDO1/3
92. F. Leeson, *A Guide to the records of the British State Tontines and Life Annuities of the seventeenth and eighteenth centuries*, 1968, p. 7
93. NDO2/4
94. NDO2/6
95. NDO1/4
96. see n. 89
97. NDO1/128–50
98. NDO2/8
99. E403/2371/1–5
100. E403/2372–2378
101. AO3/370–1
102. C238
103. 7 Edward VI c.5, 1553
104. E176
105. C265
106. E180, temp. Elizabeth – Charles II, C203, James I – Charles I
107. AO3/1194–1242
108. AO3/1230, pp. 142, 195
109. IR121, IR124–IR135, arranged by Region
110. IR58, *c.*1910–*c.*1914
111. IR91, 1910
112. IR30, 1836–*c.*1846
113. IR29, 1836–*c.*1846
114. IR29/33/266
115. IR90, 1936–77
116. IR94, 1936–77
117. E331–E344, E347
118. C54
119. J18
120. E331
121. E334, 1535–1794, E335, 1688–1783, E338, 1540–1822

122. see p. 30
123. E331/Coventry/37/7

4 Strangers and Settlers
1. HO107 for 1841 and 1851, RG9 for 1861, RG10 for 1871, RG11 for 1881
2. RG12
3. RG18
4. RG10/4698, f62, p. 56 (kindly drawn to the author's attention by Mrs Susan Lumas)
5. RG11/1833, Pt. 1, f23
6. HO107/417, Book 7, f9 (cited by E. J. Higgs, *Making Sense of the Census, 1989*)
7. RG4, 1567–1858 (authenticated registers), RG8, 1646–1951 (unauthenticated registers)
8. RG6, 1613–1841, authenticated records of the Society of Friends
9. 26 George II c.33
10. RG7, 1667–*c.*1777
11. RG8/62–6
12. RG8/52–61
13. RG4/4658–65 (registers), RG5, 1742–1837 (certificates)
14. RG4/4666–76
15. RG4/4677–9, 1773–1838, indexed in RG4/4680
16. PROB11, 1383–1858, registered copy wills, PROB10, 1484–1858, original wills, both listed in PROB12
17. PROB18, 1665–1858 (Allegations), PROB25, 1664–1854 (Answers), PROB28, 1642–1733, PROB37, 1783–1858 (Cause Papers)
18. PROB24, 1657–1809, PROB26, 1826–57, PROB31, 1783–1858
19. PROB35, 1529–86, PROB36, 1653–1721, PROB31, 1722–1858 indexed in PROB33, 1683–1858
20. PROB24
21. PROB26
22. DEL1, 1609–1834, indexed in DEL11
23. DEL9, 1652–1859, indexed in DEL11
24. C1–C16, temp. Richard II – 1875
25. C21, Country Depositions, temp. Elizabeth – Charles I, C22, 1649–1714, C24, Town Depositions, 1534–1853. Later Country Depositions are filed with the Pleadings in C11–C16
26. see pp. 24–5
27. C110/135 and C110/136
28. E111, Pleadings, temp. Henry VII – Elizabeth I, E112, temp. Elizabeth – Victoria, located via the Bill Books, IND1/16820–53, temp. Elizabeth – Victoria, Depositions before the Barons, temp. Elizabeth – Victoria in E133, Depositions by Commission, same period, E134, all for the Court of Exchequer; REQ2, temp. Henry VII – Charles I, Pleadings and Depositions in the Court of Requests
29. E115
30. IR1
31. IR24, 1799–1963, access through IR22, 1799–1953 and IR23

32. C132–C142, E149–E150
33. MH12
34. MH15
35. ZJ1
36. SP44
37. HO38, 1782–1868, HO142, 1868–78
38. HO54
39. see n. 37
40. C65, 1327–1986
41. indexed in HO1, 1509–1935
42. Elias Daubeny, 23 Edward I on the Rolls of Parliament, I, 135, cited in Huguenot Society, vol. XVIII, p. iii
43. 25 Edward III
44. Statute of Westminster, 42 Edward III, 1368
45. 21 Henry VIII c.16
46. 7 James I c.2
47. 29 Charles II c.6
48. 9 William III c.20
49. 7 Anne c.5
50. Huguenot Society, vol. XXVII, pp 78–107 for KB24 and vol. XXXV, Section II for E169/86 and E196/10
51. KB24, 1708–12, E169/86; E196/10 are Sacrament Certificates
52. 13 George II c.3
53. 20 George III c.20
54. 13 George II c.7 and 20 George II c.44
55. 1740–72, Huguenot Society, vol. XXIV
56. 7 and 8 Victoria c.66
57. 33 and 34 Victoria c.14
58. HO334
59. SP44, 1661–1782
60. HO1, 1789–1871, HO5, 1794–1909
61. SO3, 1584–1851, indexed in SO4
62. SP39, 1609–61, SO7, 1661–1851
63. C66
64. SP44/67
65. SP44/67, pp. 9–10
66. SP44/67, pp. 15–16
67. Huguenot Society, vols VIII covering 1509–1603, XVIII 1603–1700, XXVII 1701–1800, and XXXV Supplement 1603–1800
68. C54
69. HO45, 1872–8, HO144, 1879–1949 (closed 100 years)
70. HO1
71. HO1, on open access
72. HO107/1510, Book 13, f 11
73. RG10 for 1871, RG11 for 1881 (and in 1992 RG12 for 1891)
74. BT26
75. BT32
76. HO2, indexed in HO5/25–32
77. HO3
78. HO1/1–5
79. HO69
80. FO95
81. PC1
82. WO1
83. T93
84. T50
85. T50
86. PMG53
87. RG4
88. RG8

89. KB101/26
90. R. E. G. Kirk, ed., *Returns of Aliens in London, 1523–1625*, Huguenot Society, vol. x
91. SP1 and SP2, Letters and Papers of Henry VIII, 1509–47, SP10–SP18, 1547–1660, SP29–SP37, 1660–1782, thereafter in HO42
92. SP68–SP70, 1547–77, thereafter in SP71–SP99 as far as 1782, and arranged under country. Later material is in FO (Foreign Office) records
93. E101, temp. Henry III – Charles I
94. E157, 1573–1677, E190, 1565–1798
95. PC1 and PC2
96. CO1, CO5
97. J. C. Hotten, *Original Lists of Persons Emigrating to America, 1600–1700*, 1874, and P. W. Filby and M. K. Meyer, eds, *Passenger and Immigration Lists Index*, 1981, with annual *Supplements*
98. G. Fothergill, *Emigrant Ministers to America, 1690–1811*, 1904, drawing on E407/82, T1, T29, T52, T53 and T60
99. E157
100. PC2
101. T53
102. P. W. Coldham, *The Complete Book of Emigrants in Bondage, 1614–1775*, 1987
103. T1, 1747–72
104. PC1
105. SP44
106. C66
107. see PRO Information Leaflet 'Assizes Records' for the arrangement of material by Circuit
108. T47/9–11 (England and Wales), T47/12 (Scotland)
109. B. Bailyn, *Voyagers to the West*, 1986, and D. Dobson, *Directory of Scottish settlers in North America, 1625–1825*, 1984
110. T47/9
111. PC2, PC1, PC5/1–16 included in *The Acts of the Privy Council of England, Colonial Series, 1613–1783*
112. CO5, in *Calendar of State Papers, America and West Indies, 1574–1738*
113. CO323, 1689–1952, Correspondence, CO324, 1662–1872, Entry Books, CO381, 1740, 1791–1872
114. C66 (Patent Rolls), C103–C114 (Chancery Masters' Exhibits)
115. TS12, 1658–1921
116. PROB11/401, q. 136
117. P. W. Coldham, *English Estates of American Colonists: American Wills and Administrations in the Prerogative Court of Canterbury, 1610–1858*, 3 vols, 1980, 1981
118. AO12, Series I, 1776–1831, AO13, Series II, 1780–1835
119. T50 and T79
120. T79

121. AO1/458/6–AO1/465/43
122. T77
123. FO4/1
124. FO566, 1817–1911, card index 1906–20, FO409, 1920–47
125. FO5/49
126. BT27
127. BT32, 1906–51
128. BT27/780B
129. BT27/780B
130. MT9/290/201
131. MT9/290 and BT100/260
132. BT158, BT165, BT159 (deaths at sea of British Nationals, 1875–88), BT160 (births at sea of British Nationals, 1875–91)
133. RG33/156, 1842–89, marriages on Royal Naval Ships, indexed in RG43/7
134. RG35/16, 1836–71, deaths on French vessels, RG35/17, 1839–71, deaths on Dutch ships, both indexed in RG43
135. RG32–RG36, indexed in RG43
136. E157
137. SP44/411
138. FO366
139. FO610, and samples of different types of passport from 1802 in FO655, with an index to places of issue on open access
140. FO611
141. FO612
142. CO323/97–104
143. e.g. T78, claims against France, 1815–55, and Denmark, 1834–55; FO316, claims against Spain made under the Peace of 1808, and Conventions of 1823 and 1828; WO148, South African War claims, 1902–3
144. FO304, FO303
145. FO305
146. WO148
147. T71
148. FO308
149. FO314
150. Cape Town, FO312, 1843–70, Havana, FO313, 1819–69, Sierra Leone, FO315, 1819–68; registers of slaves and slavers in the West Indies, Cape of Good Hope and Ceylon at various dates from 1813–34, with an index of claimants, 1835–46, T71
151. HCA30
152. AO14
153. NDO4
154. T70
155. all are in T71
156. FO313
157. FO312
158. CO267/111
159. FO315
160. CO278
161. HO10/21–7
162. M. R. Sainty and K. A. Johnson, eds, *New South Wales: Census … November 1828*, 1980
163. HO10, 1788–1859
164. HO16, 1815–49 (committals for trial), PCOM1, 1801–1904 (Old Bailey Sessions Papers)

165. HO26, 1791–1849, London and Middlesex only, HO27, 1805–92, England and Wales, and including London and Middlesex from 1850
166. HO10/27
167. HO27/10
168. ASSI5/134 Pt. 1
169. HO11
170. HO17, 1819–40, HO18, 1839–54
171. HO19
172. HO9, 1802–49, HO8, 1824–76
173. ADM101, 1817–53, MT32, 1858–67
174. ADM51, ADM52, ADM53
175. BT107, 1786–1854, BT108, 1855–9
176. PC1/67–92
177. CO386/154, 1848–73
178. HO12, 1849–71, indexed in HO14
179. CO384
180. CO201, 1784–1903
181. CO386
182. CO386/155/53
183. CO580
184. CO208/254
185. CO208/255, 267
186. CO208/285–9
187. CO386/29
188. CO208/272–3
189. CO208/275
190. ADM101
191. CO386/170, 1847–54, registers of births and deaths of emigrants at sea, CO386/171–2, registers of deaths of emigrants at sea, 1854–69; and ADM104, 1893–1950
192. CO386/171
193. CO386/186–7, 1854–92 (registers of particulars), 1891–4 (appointments)
194. CO208/269–70; application registers, 1839, are in CO208/268
195. CO208/279
196. CO208/240
197. MH12
198. MH15
199. MH19/22
200. MH13/252
201. see PRO Information Leaflets 'British Army Records as Sources for Biography and Genealogy', 'Royal Marines Records in the PRO', and 'Admiralty Sources for Biography and Genealogy'
202. ADM36–ADM41, 1688–1878
203. see n. 201
204. WO43/542–3
205. CO384/51
206. PROB14, 1666–1858
207. ADM44, indexed in ADM141
208. ADM45
209. ADM48, ADM142, 1786–1909, forming an index to this class
210. T64
211. ADM103
212. ADM103, 1755–1831, with a general index to prisons and prison ships in Britain in ADM103/524–48
213. AIR1/892/204/5/696–8
214. ADM1/8420/124
215. FO383
216. RG35

217. AIR49/383–5
218. AIR20/2336
219. ADM201/111
220. ADM116, Code 79
221. FO916
222. RG32, indexed in RG43
223. WO208/3999
224. WO308/54
225. AO3/873
226. ADM97/98–107, 114–25, 127, 131 and ADM105/42–3, 58
227. AO11/1–4, AO3/875–6
228. ADM103
229. WO28/182, 1854–6
230. ADM102, 1740–1860
231. RG8/180, 1854–7, Russian prisoners in Britain
232. WO900/45–6
233. MH106
234. WO94/105
235. HO214
236. MH8/39–92
237. WO315, 1939–50
238. AST18, 1947–68

5   The Turner and Plenderleath Families
1. HO107/1790, ED9A, f 175
2. HO107/1011, ED11, f 5
3. HO107/1790, ED9A, f 178
4. RG9/1134, ED12, f 24
5. RG9/1134, ED12, f 26
6. RG10/1721, ED12, f 5
7. RG11/1833, ED12, f 36
8. HO107/1011, ED12, f 45
9. Transcript compiled by L. H. Haydon Whitehead, baptisms 1558–1881, 4 vols (at the Library of the Society of Genealogists, London)
10. I. G. I. Suffolk, February 1988 ed.
11. Ibid
12. Whitehead Transcripts, see n. 9, plus marriages 1558–1837, in vol. 5, and burials 1558–1924 in vols 6–8
13. J599/3, p. 336, Registered Wills, Suffolk Record Office, Bury St Edmunds Branch
14. IR26/2395, f 409
15. IR26/2112, f 592
16. IR127/9/329, Suffolk West LXIV.13
17. IR127/9/658, Suffolk West LXIV 13NE
18. IR58/15839, ref. nos 401–500
19. IR30/33/266
20. IR29/33/266, Tithe Apportionment
21. HO107/1011, ED11, f 6
22. IR18/9858
23. IR29/33/266
24. IR23/82, ffs 139–42
25. ASSI45/69
26. ASSI41/16
27. ASSI44/168, Pt. 1
28. ASSI45/69
29. HO107/2428, ED5C, f 242
30. Ibid, ED5A, f 179
31. Ibid, ED5A, f 181
32. Ibid, ED5A, f 182
33. Ibid, ED5A, f 183
34. HO107/167, ED1, f 10
35. HO107/167
36. MH12/1675, Longtown Union Correspondence, 1834–42

37. M. Nissel, People Count, 1987, p. 59
38. E. J. Higgs, Making Sense of the Census, 1989, p. 12
39. HO107/1531, f 193. I am grateful to Mrs Susan Lumas for drawing my attention to this
40. HO107/2428, ED9A, f 316
41. Ibid, ED6, f 276

6   The Gainsborough Family
1. RG4/1861, births and baptisms, 1707–1837
2. SP44/38B
3. 1739–1858
4. ZJ1/31, no. 7208
5. B4/7, p. 245, no. 2465
6. B1/12, Order Books
7. ZJ1/31, no. 7240
8. PROB11/695, q. 80
9. SP44/265, pp. 355–6
10. G. H. Peters, Humphrey Gainsborough, 1948, p. 21
11. H. Belsey, Gainsborough's Family, 1988, p. 23
12. PROB11/1022, q. 358
13. G. T. Armytage, ed., The Register of Baptisms and Marriages at St. George's Chapel, May Fair, Harleian Society, vol. 15, 1889, p. 66
14. Ibid, p. viii
15. KB28/165, m. 7, listed in IND1/6658
16. Ibid
17. PRISI/9, no. 861, Fleet Prison Commitment Books, 1741–2
18. IND1/6658, Easter 16 George II
19. Ibid, Trinity 16 and 17 George II
20. Harleian Society, vol. 15, pp. ix and v (see also n. 13)
21. RG7/99, 178, 221, 239, 248, 272, 273
22. Dictionary of National Biography, vol. 7, p. 363
23. In Gainsborough's House Museum, Sudbury, Suffolk, lent by the Trustees of Gainsborough's House Society
24. T47/8, p. 459. There is a transcript of the list in the Library of the Society of Genealogists, London
25. DNB, vol. 7, p. 364
26. PROB1/20, original will
27. PROB11/987, q. 160. The will was proved on 7 April 1773, and again on 10 April 1773, the first probate being declared null and void on the grounds that the name of one of the executors, Samuel Gainsborough, was wrongly given as John Gainsborough in the earlier grant
28. T47/3, 1756–62, T47/4, 1764–6
29. T47/2, 1754–6
30. T47/5, 1756–62, T47/4, 1764–6
31. PROB11/1210, q. 515. The will was proved with a codicil of 1 January 1790 on 17 November 1791
32. RG4/1861

7   The Walter Family
1. PROB11/158, q. 93
2. C142/500/36
3. E179/163/435
4. E115/409/62

5. C54/3445, no. 2
6. C54/3485, no. 2
7. e.g. C54/5242, no. 8, 16 January, 10 George I, 1723/4
8. E331
9. *op. cit.*, p. 142, quoting from *Statutes*, iii, Jesus College, 92
10. *Records of the Society of Lincolns Inn, 1420–1799*, vol. 1, 1896
11. E173/1, Michaelmas 15 Charles I – Michaelmas 10 William III, Outlawry Books
12. SP19/A125, pp. 192, 195–7
13. 15 Charles II c.9, in *Statutes of the Realm, 1625–1680*
14. C66/2896, no. 9
15. SP23/183, p. 22, with other documentation relating to the various petitions between pp. 1 and 56
16. SP23/183, p. 15
17. SP23/183, pp. 1–2
18. *Ibid*, pp. 49–52
19. *Ibid*, p. 24
20. *Ibid*, pp. 1–2
21. *Ibid*, p. 2
22. *Ibid*, p. 17
23. SP19/A125, pp. 151, 156d
24. *Ibid*, p. 193
25. *Ibid*, p. 195
26. *Ibid*, p. 197
27. *Ibid*, p. 192
28. *Ibid*, p. 196
29. *Ibid*, p. 197
30. *Ibid*, p. 198
31. E179/255/4, Pt. 2, m. 157
32. E179/164/513, m. 51r
33. C110/136, Book 5 'Abstract of Sir Robert Walter's title to his manors of Sarsedon, Churchill, Lyneham etc in com Oxon 4 November 1729'
34. CP25(2)/710, Michaelmas 32 Charles II
35. see n. 33
36. see n. 33
37. see n. 33, and CP43/449. The Abstract has the advantage of summarizing the Common Recovery in English, whereas the enrolled copy is in Latin, in a heavy italicized hand, making it difficult to read.
38. PROB11/590, q. 64. The will was proved on 9 March 1722/3
39. *G.E.C.'s Complete Baronetage, 1611–1800*, vol. 2, 1902, p. 142
40. C110/135, Chancery Master's Exhibits
41. E331/Oxford/19
42. Institution Books, Series C, 1700–1838, Oxford diocese
43. C110/136, Book 7 'An Abstract of ye Preceeding Accounts and off the Method agreed upon and taken for payment of ye Debts Legacys and ffunerall Expences and ye Charge of Proving ye Will Remaining unsatisfied after applying ye Personall Estate not Specifically Devised as for the same would extend'
44. C110/136, copy of a tripartite Indenture of Settlement, 18 January 1723/4
45. *Ibid*, Book 7

46. *Ibid*
47. *G.E.C.'s Complete Baronetage*, vol. 2
48. C110/136, Book 2, p. 3 'Draft case on the Settlement and Sir Robert Walter's will'
49. PROB11/648, q. 318. Administration with Will and codicil dated 16 November 1731 was granted on 22 June 1748 of the goods and chattels left unadministered by the widow, now deceased
50. C33/391, Pt. 1, ff 74, 239; Pt. 2, ff 353, 357, 497–8. The case was in connection with a loan of £250 made to Dame Mary and Daniel Rich on 20 May 1735 and another on 2 April 1736 for £500
51. C110/186, Pt. 1, Walter v. Mander
52. C110/136 'A Catalogue of the Goods of the Honourable Sir Robert Walter late of Saresdon in Oxfordshire Bart. Being a very choice collection. And will be sold some Time in June next, by Lots: Printed by R. Raikes, Gloucester, 1732'
53. C110/136 and C110/186, Pt. 1
54. C110/136, Bundle FF, no. 62
55. C110/135, C110/136 and C110/186, Pt. 1
56. C110/135, no. 10
57. *Ibid*, no. 34
58. *Ibid*, no. 59
59. *Ibid*, no. 11, John Peisley to Mr Mander, 21 August 1746
60. *Ibid*, no. 57, Rev. Nathaniel Sturges to Mr Mander, 19 November 1746
61. *Ibid*, no. 57, and no. 50, 27 November 1746, no. 49, 11 December 1746
62. *Ibid*, no. 30, 15 February 1746/7
63. *Ibid*, no. 48, 11 March 1746/7
64. *Ibid*, no. 27, 27 August 1751, Thomas Bulley to Thomas Mander
65. C110/136, Book 5

8   The Statham Family
1. REQ2/26/48
2. *Ibid*
3. C3/169/28
4. C33/26, f 30d
5. C3/169/28
6. C33/26, f 76d
7. *Ibid*, f 106r
8. *Ibid*, f 201d
9. *Ibid*, f 351r
10. C33/28, f 54r
11. *Ibid*, f 67d
12. *Ibid*, f 273d and C78/21, no. 30
13. Feet of Fines Ms Index, 5–10 Elizabeth, under Derbyshire
14. PROB11/61, q. 7
15. PROB11/6, q. 1
16. E149/244/8
17. E326/B3360
18. PROB11/20, q. 26
19. PROB11/21, q. 32

9   The Fardon Family
1. RG6/35, p. 27
2. RG6/34, p. 5
3. RG6/8, p. 6

4. *Ibid*, p. 16
5. RG6/1332, Monthly Meeting, Banbury: births 1632–1776, burials 1665–1776, marriages 1737–69; RG6/1220, marriages 1662–1737; RG6/1569, births 1776–94, burials 1776–94, marriages 1776–92; RG6/34, births 1795–1837; RG6/8, marriages 1798–1836; RG6/35, burials 1795–1837
6. *Victoria County History of Oxfordshire*, vol. 9, 1969, Bloxham Hundred, pp. 86–112
7. *Ibid*, vol. 9, pp. 93–4
8. *Ibid*, vol. 9, p. 101
9. RG6/1332
10. *Ibid*, pp. 259–60
11. RG6/1220, 16th day 9th month 1713
12. *Ibid*, 29 May 1725 (*sic*)
13. *Ibid*, 10th day 3rd month (May) 1708
14. *Ibid*, 20th day 9th month 1733
15. *Ibid*, 17th day 6th month 1732
16. *Ibid*, 8th day 9th month 1685, James Gilks and Mary Lamb
17. *Ibid*, 1st day 8th month 1720, William Gilkes and Anne Harris
18. 1708 Thomas ffardon and Mary ffowler, 1713 John Smith and Elizabeth Farden, 1720 John Tutty and Hannah ffardon, and on the same day (20th of the 3rd month) Thomas ffardon and Mary Prestage, 1725 Richard Fardon and Mary Archer, and 1731 John Fardon and Elizabeth Pottinger
19. RG6/1220
20. PROB11/355, q. 115
21. RG6/1332, p. 3
22. RG6/1220, p. 105
23. RG6/1332, p. 142
24. *Ibid*, p 146
25. *Ibid*, p. 167
26. *op. cit.*, vol. 1, p. 574
27. *Ibid*, p. 576
28. RG6/1220, p. 313, Thomas ffardon, married in 1720
29. RG6/1332, p. 113, Jonathan Fardon, whose son, Thomas, was born on 30 May 1771
30. RG6/8, p. 16, Richard Fardon, married in 1805
31. RG6/35, p. 19, Jonathan Fardon, died 14 September 1823
32. *Victoria County History of Oxfordshire*, vol. 9, p. 101, based on information in Quaker registers
33. E179/161/198, m30d, 24 December 15 Henry VIII, 1523 and E179/161/96, 4 January 16 Henry VIII, 1524/5
34. E179/162/226, first instalment, 34 and 35 Henry VIII [?September]
35. E179/162/331, second instalment, 8 and 9 Elizabeth [?February] 1566/7
36. E179/162/345, m6, 23 Elizabeth, 1580/1
37. E179/238/144, third Subsidy, 1 March 22 James I, 1624/5
38. E179/164/493, first instalment, 31 May 18 Charles I, 1642
39. E179/255/5, Return, 15 November 1661

40. E179/255/4, Book 2, p. 179, 11 October 1662
41. E179/164/507, 29 October 15 Charles II, 1663
42. E179/164/509, 17 March 16 Charles II, 1663/4
43. E179/164/513, 17 Charles II, 1665/6
44. T47/2, year ended 5 April 1754 – 5 April 1756
45. T47/3, year ended 5 April 1757 – 5 July 1762
46. IR23/69, f 139d
47. *Ibid*, f 120d
48. IR24/48, no. 36,573
49. RG6/35, p. 8
50. RG6/1332, p. 74, son of Richard and Mary ffardon, born 15th day 11th month 1732
51. IR23/69, f 460r
52. C213/206

10   The Wordsworth Family

1. *The Letters of William and Dorothy Wordsworth, III The Middle Years, Pt. 2, 1812–1820,* arranged and ed. by E. de Selincourt, 2nd ed., revised by M. Moorman and A. G. Hill, 1970, p. 88, letter from Dorothy Wordsworth to Catherine Cookson, 6 April [1813]
2. *Ibid*, p. 93, letter from William Wordsworth to Lord Lonsdale, 19 April 1813
3. *Ibid*, p. 93n. The original is at the Wordsworth Library, Grasmere
4. *Ibid*, pp. 56–8, letter from William Wordsworth to Lord Lonsdale, 27 December 1812
5. *Ibid*, p. 89, letter from Dorothy Wordsworth to Catherine Cookson, 6 April [1813]
6. *Ibid*, p. 88
7. *Ibid*, p. 86, letter from William Wordsworth to Lord Lonsdale, 14 March 1813
8. *The Letters of William and Dorothy Wordsworth, III The Later Years, Pt. 1, 1821–1828,* revised, arranged and ed by A. G. Hill, 1978, pp. 56–7
9. AO3/1003. £33,205–14s–5¾d was collected
10. IR13/67, no. 68
11. *The Letters of William and Dorothy Wordsworth, V The Later Years, Pt. 2, 1829–1834,* 2nd enlarged ed. revised, arranged and ed. by A. G. Hill, 1979, p. 586, letter from William Wordsworth to John Spedding, 2 February [1833]
12. *The Letters of William and Dorothy Wordsworth, II The Later Years, Pt. 1,* p. 58, letter from William Wordsworth to Viscount Lowther, 30 March [1821]
13. *Ibid*, p. 171, letter from William Wordsworth to Lord Lonsdale, 29 November 1822
14. *The Letters of William and Dorothy Wordsworth, III The Middle Years, Pt. 2,* p. 612, letter from Dorothy Wordsworth to Dora Wordsworth, [23 June 1820]

15. *The Letters of William and Dorothy Wordsworth, V The Later Years, Pt. 2,* p. 370n. The District was added on 26 February 1831, after the sudden death of the previous Distributor for Cumberland
16. *Ibid*, p. 428, letter from Dorothy Wordsworth to Catherine Cookson, 9 September [1831]
17. *The Letters of William and Dorothy Wordsworth, III The Later Years, Pt. 1,* p. 25, letter from William Wordsworth to Viscount Lowther, 7 February 1821: Richard Bateman, stationer, recently recommended as Subdistributor for Appleby, was found to have expensive habits and was liable to succumb to temptation; *The Letters of William and Dorothy Wordsworth, III The Middle Years, Pt. 2,* pp 356–7, letter from William Wordsworth to Henry Parry, 17 January 1817: John Hall, Subdistributor for Kirkby Lonsdale, was arrested on a debt of £100, while owing £300 due to the Government, and in danger of being declared a bankrupt. p. 366, by 17 February 1817 William Wordsworth had arranged for a Bill of Sale in the sum to be issued by Hall and an Extent made, which thereby overrode any action a creditor might take
18. IR13/67, no. 62
19. LC3/71, p. 230
20. LC3/51
21. PROB1/90, original will
22. *The Letters of William and Dorothy Wordsworth, V The Later Years, Pt. 2,* p. 445 and n., letter from William Wordsworth to Joseph Hunter, 31 October 1831
23. IR26/1886, f 289
24. IR59/42
25. IR58/46594, no. 18
26. IND1/4596, no. 119
27. IND1/4568, no. 27
28. IR1/23/37
29. IND1/4568, no. 1777
30. IR1/25/165
31. IR1/27/123
32. *Ibid*. On 26 June 1722 £3–11s was paid on Edward Grave's premium of £71
33. IR1/28/11. On 22 December 1773 £3–11s–6d was paid on Joseph Steel's premium of £71–10s
34. IR1/30/53. On 18 March 1779 £4–12s–6d was paid on James Garnett's premium of £92–10s
35. IR1/30/151. On 18 April 1780 £2–10s–6d was paid on Jonathan Winder's premium of £50–10s
36. KB105/3, no. 6015
37. KB105/5, no. 7881
38. *The Letters of William and Dorothy Wordsworth, The Early Years, 1787–1805,* 2nd ed. revised by C. L. Shaver, 1967, pp. 25–6n.
39. CUST82/19, p. 81, no. 325
40. *Ibid*, p. 84, no. 338

41. CUST82/147, f 106, no. 263, 16 June 1764
42. CUST82/11, no. 3
43. *Ibid*, no. 8, 30 August 1768
44. *Ibid*, no. 435
45. CUST82/12, f 89, no. 49
46. *Ibid*, f 126, no. 68
47. *Ibid*, f 75, no. 111
48. *Ibid*, letter from the Board of Customs to the Collector, 27 March 1777
49. *Ibid*, report from Richard Wordsworth on Thomas Raine, Landwaiter at Workington, 12 May 1777
50. *Ibid*, no. 37, Board of Customs to the Collector, 27 March 1777. On 16 December 1776 the Collector went to view tobacco on the coastal trade from London to ensure it was properly marked with Importation numbers, and called on Richard Wordsworth for the Landwaiter's Book to the ships importing it. Wordsworth refused, was charged about it, and his answers considered by the Board Commissioners with the report of the Surveyor General, Mr Lutwidge, and the complaint was dismissed; likewise an accusation made against the Collector, Deputy Customer and Comptroller at Workington by Harrington for having embezzled 24lb of tea, part of a large quantity seized by them
51. *Ibid*, no. 37; a further letter was also sent to Harrington on the same day, outlining the charges
52. *Ibid*
53. *Ibid*
54. CUST82/59, f 26, no. 22, 18 March 1778, f 29, no. 32, 7 April 1778
55. *Ibid*, f 34, no. 52, 21 May 1778
56. *Ibid*, f 26, no. 22
57. *Ibid*, f 29, no. 32, 7 April 1778
58. CUST18/371, p. 67: an annual allowance of £70 was made for clerks
59. CUST82/178
60. CUST82/159, p. 70
61. CUST82/16, no. 78
62. *The Letters of William and Dorothy Wordsworth, The Early Years, 1787–1805,* p. 123, letter from Dorothy Wordsworth to Richard Wordsworth, 28 May [1794]

11   The Garrick and Marx Families

1. Pulman Collection, 63, V, ff 412–25
2. Rev. D. C. A. Agnew, *Protestant Exiles from France in the reign of Louis XIV,* 3 vols, 1874
3. RG4
4. in 4 vols, ed T. C. Colyer-Ferguson
5. SP44/67, p. 9
6. C66/3286, no. 4
7. SP44/67, pp. 15–16
8. C66/3310, no. 27
9. *Letters of Denization and Acts of Naturalization for Aliens in England and Ireland 1603–1700,* Huguenot Society, vol. xviii, 1911, p. 217
10. *Ibid*, p. 240

11. *London Inhabitants within the Walls 1695*, London Record Society, vol. 2, 1966
12. C. Dalton, ed., *English Army Lists and Commission Registers*, vol. 5, *1702–7*, 1960, p. 200
13. WO25/2984
14. WO25/2979
15. WO25/13, p. 132
16. C. Dalton, *George I's Army 1714–1727*, 1910, p. 277
17. WO25/2985, pp. 1–3
18. WO25/2985, p. 154
19. WO25/2986, p. 151
20. WO25/16, p. 89
21. SP44/181, p. 114
22. D. M. Little and G. M. Kahrl, eds, *The Letters of David Garrick*, 3 vols, 1963, vol. 1, p. 2, n. 1 and p. 23, n. 6: grant of leave was signed at Lichfield on 31 May 1736
23. *Ibid*, p. 22, letter 11: David Garrick to Captain Peter Garrick, May 1735. Richard Rider replaced the former Chancellor, who died on 30 October 1734, on the nomination of Richard Smalbroke, Bishop of Coventry and Lichfield between 1731 and 1749
24. PROB10/1847, original will
25. PROB11/682, q. 85
26. PROB11/708, q. 65
27. PROB11/680, q. 268; original will PROB10/1841
28. PROB11/753, q. 76
29. *The Letters of David Garrick*, vol. 1, pp. 16–17
30. A. Kendall, *David Garrick*, 1985, p. 13
31. *Dictionary of National Biography*
32. *Lincolns Inn Admission Registers, 1800–1893*
33. *Dictionary of National Biography*
34. September 1743, listed in *Theatrical References in the Lord Chamberlain's Office*, 2 vols, as being in The Precedent Book, no. 3, f 63
35. *Dictionary of National Biography*
36. LC5/161, pp. 257–8
37. *Ibid*, quoted on p. 261
38. LC7/9, pp. 120–2
39. *Dictionary of National Biography*
40. T47/2, 1751–6, T47/3, 1757–62
41. T47/5, 1756–62
42. PROB1/16, original will
43. *Dictionary of National Biography*
44. A. Kendall, *David Garrick*, pp. 130–42
45. *Ibid*, p. 153
46. T47/8, pp. 426–7, 459
47. PROB11/1662, q. 526
48. IR26/907, f 1097 *et seq.*
49. CP5/38/4
50. LS13/202, p. 8
51. D. M. Little and G. M. Kahrl, eds, *The Letters of David Garrick*, vol. 1, pp. 185–6, n. 5: Nathan Carrington, the father of George Garrick's first wife, was a King's Messenger for almost 50 years; at the time of his death in 1777 he was a Poor Knight of Windsor
52. PROB11/1051, q. 104
53. Thomas Evans, of Bow Street, parish of St Paul Covent Garden, was the Treasurer of Drury Lane Theatre, and Thomas Watson, of Little Russell Street, parish of St Martin's in the Fields, the Office-Keeper
54. J. A. Venn, ed., *Alumni Cantabrigienses 1752–1900*, 1947
55. Institution Books, 1700–1838, Series C, London diocese
56. PROB11/1154, q. 269; probate was granted on 12 June 1787
57. Institution Books, 1700–1838, Series C, London diocese
58. IND1/1296, 1777–83. Nathan Garrick granted an annuity of £100 on £600 capital to Welbore Ellis Agar on 8 January 1780, assigned on 7 June 1780 to Thomas Gordon; he granted an annuity to Gordon of £300 on £1,800 capital on 7, 8 and 10 June 1780, and with another, granted an annuity of £50 on capital of £350 to Sarah Prescott on 10 June 1780
59. C54/6525, no. 85
60. *Army List*, 1775. [1776 annotated in ink 'Ret'. His successor William Payne was commissioned on 25 January 1776]
61. WO12/454. He resigned on 25 January 1776. D. M. Little and G. M. Kahrl, *The Letters of David Garrick*, vol. 1, p. xxviii ascribe the cause as being asthma and obesity
62. D. M. Little and G. M. Kahrl, *The Letters of David Garrick*, vol. 1, p. 3, n. 8. In January 1732/3 he was apparently in the West Indies under the command of Sir Chaloner Ogle
63. *Dictionary of National Biography*
64. T42/1 for the appointment, and CUST82/15, letter no. 1, 1789, for an example of appointment of a deputy
65. CUST82/159, p. 70
66. PROB11/1275, q. 248
67. C54/19056, no. 107
68. J. A. Venn, ed., *Alumni Cantabrigienses 1752–1900, Kelly's Handbook to the Titled, Landed and Official Classes*, 1925, *Who's Who*, 1902, J. Foster, ed., *Alumni Oxonienses 1715–1886*, F. Boase, *Modern English Biography, 1851–1900*, 1965, *The Times*, 20 June 1888, p. 11
69. HO45/9366/36228 for the failed naturalization attempt, HO5/43, p. 290 for the refusal
70. RG11/211, ED8, f 59, p. 48
71. HO107/1510, ED9, f 11, p. 260
72. IR26/2403, f 606
73. IR27/442, 1883
74. HO3/53
75. *Ibid*

12 The Dyer, Brenton and Walker Families

1. CO1/9, p. 197
2. J. Savage, *Genealogical Dictionary of the First Settlers of New England*, vol. 2, 1977, p. 89
3. *Genealogies of Rhode Island Families*, vol. 1, 1983, p. 286
4. J. Savage, *ibid*, p. 89
5. *Genealogies of Rhode Island Families*, vol. 1, p. 282
6. J. Savage, *ibid*, p. 89
7. PROB11/401, q. 136
8. *op. cit.*, pp. 280–97
9. E179/251/22
10. *Genealogies of Rhode Island Families*, vol. 1, p. 296
11. *The Register of St. Martin in the Fields, London, baptisms, marriages and burials 1619–1638*, Harleian Society, vol. LXVI, 1936
12. *Genealogies of Rhode Island Families*, vol. 1, p. 283
13. C. E. Banks, *The Winthrop Fleet*, 1930, p. 61
14. *Genealogies of Rhode Island Families*, vol. 1, pp. 288–9
15. J. O. Austin, *Genealogical Dictionary of Rhode Island*, 1978, p. 254
16. *Ibid*
17. *Ibid*, pp. 254–5
18. AO13/68, Pt. 1, nos 78 and 79
19. *Ibid*, no. 84
20. *Ibid*, no. 85 and AO13/68, Pt. 2
21. AO13/100, no. 26
22. AO13/68, Pt. 1, no. 87
23. AO13/68, Pt. 2
24. AO13/68, Pt. 1, nos 78 and 79
25. *Ibid*, nos 82 and 90
26. *Ibid*, nos 82, 93, 94, 114
27. AO13/68, Pt. 2
28. AO13/68, Pt. 1, no. 78
29. AO13/68, Pt. 2
30. AO13/68, Pt. 1, no. 80
31. AO13/68, Pt. 2
32. ADM36/8924
33. AO13/68, Pt. 2
34. AO12/84, 2/72
35. AO13/68, Pt. 2
36. AO12/99, no. 28
37. AO13/68, Pt.1, nos 78 and 79
38. AO12/99, 28
39. AO12/100, 10
40. AO12/101, 278
41. AO12/109
42. AO12/84, 2/86
43. AO13/68, Pt. 2
44. ADM107/4, p. 246
45. ADM22/19, p. 61
46. *Ibid*, p. 312
47. ADM6/352
48. ADM36/7889
49. ADM36/8924
50. ADM11/64
51. ADM1/1508, B189, B190, B192, B193, B198, B203a, B218
52. ADM51/1310
53. J. Marshall, *Royal Naval Biography*, vol. 2, Pt. 1, 1824, pp. 261–70
54. ADM13/103
55. ADM1/1548, 56
56. ADM51/2807
57. Marshall, *ibid*
58. ADM1/1550, 805
59. ADM1/1552, 94
60. *Ibid*, 117
61. *Ibid*, 117, 118, 212
62. Marshall, *ibid*
63. *The Commissioned Sea Officers of the Royal Navy 1660–1815*, vol. 1, 1954

64. ADM9/3, no. 453
65. e.g. ADM1/1529, 631–50 for 1803,
    ADM1/1532, 613–19 for 1804,
    ADM1/1539, 448–54 for 1806, and
    ADM1/1550, 687, 732 for 1810
66. ADM37/2457
67. ADM1/1550, 732
68. *The Commissioned Sea Officers of the
    Royal Navy*, vol. 1
69. ADM36/15128
70. ADM51/1305
71. ADM36/15128
72. ADM9/4, no. 1196
73. ADM107/34, p. 547
74. *Ibid*, p. 549
75. ADM9/4, no. 1196
76. ADM9/22, no. 427
77. WPR/91/V1, p. 47, Cumbria Record
    Office (Kendal)
78. CO208/275 (index), CO208/273
    (register)
79. CO208/269, pp. 64–70
80. CO208/278, pp. 4–5
81. CO208/242, CO208/255
82. HO107/161/24, ED3, f 11, p. 17
83. *Ibid*, ED2, f 1, p. 1

**13   The Lyons, Evans, Massy and
Atkinson Families**
1. WO97/1453
2. ZJ1/295
3. Sir John Smyth, *The Story of the
   Victoria Cross*, 1963
4. WO28/188, Pt. 1
5. WO28/126, pp. 87, 127, 128
6. WO97/1452, WO116/66
7. ZJ1/289
8. WO28/188, Pt. 2
9. ZJ1/289
10. WO31/1061
11. WO43/1057, ff 432–3
12. *Ibid*, f 439
13. *Ibid*, ff 442, 448
14. WO12/3632
15. *Ibid*
16. WO43/1057, f 453
17. *Ibid*, f 446
18. *Ibid*, f 447
19. *Ibid*, f 456
20. WO31/1135
21. *Ibid*
22. WO43/1057, f 464
23. WO23/83
24. WO25/582
25. WO25/826/1/3
26. WO25/856/1
27. ZJ1/429
28. ZJ1/393
29. ZJ1/394
30. PMG4/261, no. 700
31. PMG3/86, no. 3755
32. PMG3/94, no. 4405
33. WO31/893
34. WO12/3632
35. WO31/927
36. ZJ1/512
37. Sir John Smyth, *op. cit.*
38. WO32/7478
39. *Ibid*
40. *The Register of the Victoria Cross*, This
    England Books, 1981
41. WO97/1765
42. WO10/2517
43. WO97/1765

BIBLIOGRAPHY

Introduction

Baxter, J. H. and Johnson, C., *Medieval Latin Word-List*, 1934

Bevan, A. and Duncan, A., *Tracing Your Ancestors in the Public Record Office*, 1990

Cantwell, J. D., *The Public Record Office, 1838–1958*, 1991

Cox, J., *The Nation's Memory*, 1988

Fitzhugh, T. V. H., *The Dictionary of Genealogy*, rev. ed. 1988

Fryde, E. B., Greenway, D. E., Porter, S. and Roy, I., *Handbook of British Chronology*, 1986

Galbraith, V. H., *An Introduction to the Use of the Public Records*, 1963

Hector, L. C., *The Handwriting of English Documents*, 1966

HMSO, *Government Publications, Sectional List 24, British National Archives*, 1984

Latham, R. E., ed., *Revised Medieval Latin Word List*, 1965

Martin, C. T., *The Record Interpreter*, 1976

Martin, G. H. and Spufford, P., eds, *The Records of the Nation*, 1990

Mullins, E. L. C., *Texts and Calendars, an Analytical Guide to Serial Publications*, 1958, repr. 1978

Mullins, E. L. C., *Texts and Calendars, 1957–1982*, 1983

Munby, L., *Reading Tudor and Stuart Handwriting*, 1988

Newton, K. C., *Medieval Local Records: A Reading Aid*, 1986

PRO, *Current Guide to the Contents of the Public Record Office*, 9 parts, in progress

PRO, Family Fact Sheet 1. How to Obtain a Document Reference

PRO Information Leaflets:
  Births, Marriages and Deaths
  Family History in England and Wales: Guidance for Beginners
  Genealogy before the Parish Registers
  How to Read Roman Numerals

Richardson, J., *The Local Historian's Encyclopedia*, 2nd ed., 1986

Riden, P., *Record Sources for Local History*, 1987

Steinberg, S. H. and Evans, I. H., *Steinberg's Dictionary of British History*, 1974

1: The Legal System

Bailey, V., ed., *Policing and Punishment in nineteenth century Britain*, 1981

Baker, J. H., *The Order of Serjeants at Law*, 1984 (Selden Society Supplementary Series, vol. V)

Bateson, C., *The Convict Ships 1788–1868*, 1974

Beattie, J. M., *Crime and the Courts in England 1660–1800*, 1986

Bell, H. E., *An Introduction to the History and Records of the Court of Wards and Liveries*, 1953

Bernau Index (a selective index of defendants and deponents in the Equity Courts of Chancery and Exchequer, the Court of Requests and Court of Star Chamber; see Garrett, below, who describes its format)

Birkett, Lord, ed., *The New Newgate Calendar*, 1960

Blatcher, M., *The Court of King's Bench 1450–1550; A Study in Self-Help*, 1978

British Record Society Index Library, *Administrations in the Prerogative Court of Canterbury 1581–1595*, vol. LXXVI, *1596–1608*, vol. LXXXI, *1609–1619*, vol. LXXXIII, *1631–1648*, vol. C, *1649–1654*, vol. LXVIII, *1655–1660*, vols LXXII, LXXIV, LXXV; *Prerogative Court of Canterbury Wills 1383–1558*, vols X, XI, *1558–1583*, vol. XVIII, *1584–1604*, vol. XXV, *1605–1619*, vol. XLIII, *1620–1629*, vol. XLIV, *1653–1656*, vol. LIV, *1657–1660*, vol. LXII, *1671–1675*, vol. LXVII, *1676–1685*, vol. LXXI, *1686–1693*, vol. LXXVII, *1694–1700*, vol. LXXX.

Burke, J., ed., *Osborn's Concise Law Dictionary*, 6th ed., 1976

Butlin, N. G., Cromwell, C. W., and Suthern, K. L., *General Return of Convicts in New South Wales 1837*, 1987

Cheney, C. R., *Handbook of Dates for Students of English History*, 1981

Cockburn, J. S., *A History of English Assizes 1558–1714*, 1972

Cockburn, J. S., *Crime in England 1500–1800*, 1977

Coldham, P. W., *English Adventurers and Emigrants 1609–1660, Abstracts of Examinations in the High Court of Admiralty, with Reference to Colonial America*, 1984

Coldham, P. W., *The Complete Book of Emigrants in Bondage 1614–1775*, 1987

Cox, J., *Wills, Inventories and Death Duties, a Provisional Guide*, 1988

Crook, D. *Records of the General Eyre*, PRO Handbook no. 20, 1982

Duncan, G. I. O., *The High Court of Delegates*, 1971

Elton, G. R., *Star Chamber Stories*, 1958

Emsley, C., *Crime and Society in England 1750–1900*, 1987

Flower, C., *Introduction to the Curia Regis Rolls, 1199–1230* (Selden Society, vol. 62), 1943

Garrett, R. E. F., *Chancery and Other Legal Proceedings*, 1968

Gibson, J. S. W. and Rogers, C. D., *Coroners' Records in England and Wales*, 1989

Glencross, C. M., ed., *Administrations in the Prerogative Court of Canterbury 1559–1580*, 2 vols, 1912–17

Guy, J. A., *The Court of Star Chamber and its records to the reign of Elizabeth I*, PRO Handbook no. 21, 1985

Harding, A., *The Law Courts of Medieval England*, 1977

Hastings, M., *The Court of Common Pleas in fifteenth-century England*, 1947

HMSO, *Chronological Table of the Statutes 1235–1975*, 1976

HMSO, *Curia Regis Rolls, temp. Richard I–1242*, 1923–79

Howell, P. A., *The Judicial Committee of the Privy Council 1833–1876, Origins, Structure and Development*, 1979

Hunnisett, R. F. and Post, J., *Medieval Legal Records*, 1978

Johnson, W. B., *The English Prison Hulks*, rev. ed., 1970

Jones, W. J., *The Elizabethan Court of Chancery*, 1967

Lists and Indexes: vol. IX *List of Sheriffs for England and Wales from the Earliest Times to AD 1831*, 1898; vol. XII *List of Early Chancery Proceedings, Richard II–Edward IV*, 1901; vol. XVI *1467–1485*, 1903; vol. XX, *1485–1500*, 1906; vol. XXIX, *1500–1515*, 1908; vol. XXXVIII, *1515–1529*, 1912; vol. XLVIII, *1529–1538*, 1922; vol. L, *1533–1538*, 1927; vol. LI, *1538–1544*, 1929; vol. LIV, *1544–1553*, 1933; vol. LV, *1553–1558*, 1936; vol. VII, *Index of Chancery Proceedings, Series II, 1558–1579*, 1896; vol. XXIV, *1579–1621*, 1908; vol. XXX, *1621–1660*, 1909; vol. XIII *List of Star Chamber Proceedings 1485–1558*, 1910; vol. XIV *List of Records of the Duchy of Lancaster*, 1901; vol. XXXIX, *Index of Chancery Proceedings, Bridges' Division, 1613–1714, A–C*, 1913, vol. XLII *D–H*, 1914, vol. XLIV *I–Q*, 1915, vol. XLV *R–Z*, 1917; vol. XL *List of Records of the Palatinates of Chester, Durham and Lancaster, Honour of Peveril and Principality of Wales*, 1914; vol. XLVII *Index of Chancery Proceedings, Series 1, James I, vol. I, A–K*, 1922

Supplementary Lists and Indexes, vol. IV, *Index (of Persons) to Proceedings in the Court of Star Chamber 1485–Elizabeth* vol. VII, *Index to Proceedings in the Court of Requests Henry VII–James I*

Marriner, S., 'English Bankruptcy records and Statistics before 1850' in *Economic History Review*, 2nd series, vol. 33, pp. 351–66, 1980

Matthews, J. and G. F., eds, *Abstract of Probate Acts in the Prerogative Court of Canterbury 1630–1655*, 7 vols, 1903–14

Matthews, J. and G. F., eds, *Abstract of Probates and Sentences in the Prerogative Court of Canterbury 1620–1624*, 1911

Matthews, J. and G. F., eds, *Sentences and Complete Index Nominum (Probate and Sentences 1630–1639)*, 1907

Moir, E., *The Justice of the Peace*, 1969

Morrison, J. H., ed., *Prerogative Court of Canterbury: Letters of Administration 1620–1630*, 1935

Morrison, J. H., ed., *Prerogative Court of Canterbury: Wills, Sentences and Probate Acts 1661–1670*, 1935

Osborne, B., *Justices of the Peace 1361–1848. A History of the Justices of the Peace for the Counties of England*, 1960

PRO, Family Fact Sheet 8. Tracing an Ancestor in the Metropolitan Police

PRO Handbook no. 12, *Records of the Forfeited Estates Commission*, 1968

PRO Information Leaflets:
    Assizes Records
    Australian Convicts: Sources in the Public Record Office
    Chancery Proceedings (Equity Suits)
    Equity Proceedings in the Court of Exchequer
    Metropolitan Police Records of Service
    Probate Records
    Records of Attorneys and Solicitors
    Records of the Royal Irish Constabulary
    Registration of Companies and Businesses

PRO Records Information: Dormant Funds in Court

Pugh, R. B., *Imprisonment in Medieval England*, 1981

Pugh, R. B., *Itinerant Justices in English History*, 1967

Richardson, W. C., *History of the Court of Augmentations 1536–1554*, 1961

Robson, R., *The Attorney in the eighteenth century*, 1959

Sainty, J. C., *List of Lieutenants of Counties of England and Wales 1660–1974*, 1979 (List and Index Society Special Series, vol. 12)

Society of Genealogists, *Bankrupt Directory 1744–1786, 1820–1843*

Somerville, R., *History of the Duchy of Lancaster*, vol. I, 1953

Somerville, R., *Office-Holders in the Duchy and County Palatine of Lancaster from 1603*, 1972

Squibb, G. D., *Doctors' Commons*, 1977

Statutes of the Realm, 1235/6–1713, 11 vols, 1810–28

Steedman, C., *Policing the Victorian Community. The Formation of English Provincial Police Forces 1856–1880*, 1984

Stephens, E., *The Clerks of the Counties 1360–1960*, 1961

Stephens, W. B., *Sources for English Local History*, 1981

Sutherland, D. W., *Quo Warranto Proceedings in the Reign of Edward I 1278–1294*, 1963

Turner, E. R., *The Privy Council of England in the sixteenth and seventeenth centuries 1603–1784 [sic]*, 1927

Walker, R. J., ed., *The English Legal System*, 4th ed., 1976

Whitmore, R., *Victorian and Edwardian Crime and Punishment*, 1978

Williams., W. R., *The History of the Great Sessions in Wales 1542–1830*, 1899

Wrottesley, G., *Pedigrees from the Plea Rolls 1200–1500*, c. 1906

2: The Holding and Transfer of Land

Addleshaw, G. W. O., *Rectors, Vicars and Patrons*, 1956

Barber, R., *The Knight and Chivalry*, 1974

Camp, A. J., ed., *An Index to Wills Proved in the Prerogative Court of Canterbury, 1750–1800, A–Sh*, 5-vols, 1976–91

Dibben, A. A., *Title Deeds*, 1990

English, B. and Saville, J., *Strict Settlement: A Guide for Historians*, 1983

Gibson, J. S. W. and Rogers, C. D., *Electoral Registers since 1832*, 2nd ed., 1990

Hargreaves, A. D., *Introduction to the Principles of Land Law*, 1963

Harley, J. B., *Maps for the local historian*, 1971

Harvey, P. D. A., *Manorial Records*, 1984

HMSO, *Calendar of Charter Rolls 1226–1516*, 1903–27

HMSO, *Calendar of Close Rolls, 1204–1509*, 1833–1975

HMSO, *Calendar of Fine Rolls 1272–1509*, 1911–63

HMSO, *Calendar of Inquisitions Miscellaneous temp. Henry III–Henri VII*, 1916–68

HMSO, *Calendar of Inquisitions Post Mortem temp. Henry III–1405*, 1904–89, *Henry VII*, 1898–1956

HMSO, *Calendar of Patent Rolls 1216–1509, 1547–1580*, 1901–89 (vol. 5 includes Fine Rolls 1547–53)

HMSO, *Calendar of State Papers, Domestic 1547–1704*, 1856–1972

HMSO, *Descriptive Catalogues of Ancient Deeds*, 6 vols, Series A, B, C and D, 1890–1915

HMSO, *Home Office Papers, George III 1760–1775*, 1878–99

HMSO, *Letters and Papers, Foreign and Domestic, Henry VIII 1509–1547*, 1864–1932 (includes Patent Rolls)

HMSO, *Maps and Plans in the Public Record Office*, vol. 1: *British Isles*, 1964, vol. 2: *North America and West Indies*, 1974

Josling, J. F., *Change of Name*, 1974

List and Index Society, vols 151, 152, *Ancient Deeds, Series A*, vol. 158, *Series AS and WS*, vols 95, 101, 113, 124, *Series B*, vol. 137, *Series BB*, vol. 200, *Series DD*, vol. 181, *Series E*

Lists and Indexes, vol. VI *List and Index of Court Rolls*, Pt. I, 1896, vol. XVII *List of Inquisitions ad quod Damnum 28 Henry III–18 Edward III*, 1904, vol. XXII *19 Edward III–2 Richard III*, 1906 vol. XXIII *Index of Inquisitions Post Mortem, Henry VIII–Philip and Mary*, 1907, vol. XXVI *Elizabeth*, 1908, vol. XXXI *James I*, 1909, vol. XXXIII *Charles I and later*, 1909, vol. XXV *List of Rentals and Surveys and other analogous Documents*, 1908, vol. XLIII *List of State Papers, Domestic 1547–1792, and Home Office Records 1782–1837*, 1914

McGuinness, M., 'Inquisitions Post Mortem' in *Amateur Historian*, vol. VI, no. 7, pp. 235–42, Spring 1965

Megarry, R. C. and Wade, H. W. R., *The Law of Real Property*, 1984

Milward, R., *A Glossary of Household, Farming and Trade Terms from Probate Inventories*, 1982

Munby, L. M., ed., *Short Guides to Records*, 1972

NCSS, *The Historian's Guide to Ordnance Survey Maps*, 1964

Park, P. B., *My Ancestors were Manorial Tenants: how can I find out more about them?* 1990

Phillimore, W. P. W. and Fry, E. A., *Index to Changes of Name 1760–1901*, 1986

PRO Information Leaflets:
 Change of Name
 Enclosure Awards
 Maps in the Public Record Office
 Private Conveyances in the Public Record Office
 Records of the Ordnance Survey
 Records relating to the Dissolution of the Monasteries
 Sources for the History of the Jacobite Risings of 1715 and 1745
 Valuation Office Records created under the 1910 Finance Act

Riddall, J. G., *Introduction to Land Law*, 1979

Seymour, W. A., ed., *A History of the Ordnance Survey*, 1980

Tate, W. E. (Turner, M. E., ed.), *A Domesday of English Enclosure Acts and Awards*, 1978

Thirsk, J., *Tudor Enclosures*, rev. ed., 1989

Turner, M. E., *Enclosure in Britain 1750–1830*, 1984

Youings, J., *The Dissolution of the Monasteries*, 1971

3: Tax and other Sources of Revenue

Aylmer, G. E., *The Personal Rule of Charles I*, 1990

Aylmer, G. E. and Morrill, J. S., *The Civil War and Interregnum*, 1979

Beresford, M. W., *Lay Subsidies and Poll Taxes*, 1963

Best, G. F. A., *Temporal Pillars, Queen Anne's Bounty, the Ecclesiastical Commissioners, and the Church of England*, 1964

Bossy, J., *The English Catholic Community 1570–1850*, 1975

Evans, E. J., *The Contentious Tithe 1750–1850*, 1976

Evans, E. J., *Tithes and the Tithe Commutation Act 1836*, 1978

Gibson, J. S. W. *The Hearth Tax, other later Stuart tax lists and the Association Oath Rolls*, repr. 1990

Gibson, J. S. W. and Mills, D., *Land Tax Assessments c. 1690–c. 1950*, 1987

Harvey, W. J., ed., *List of the Principal Inhabitants of the City of London 1640*, 1969

HMSO, *Acts of the Privy Council of England 1542–1631*, 1890–1964

HMSO, *Calendar of Proceedings of the Committee for Compounding 1643–1660*, 5 vols, 1889–93

HMSO, *Calendars of the Committee for Advance of Money 1642–1656*, 3 vols, 1888

HMSO, *Feudal Aids 1284–1431*, 6 vols, 1899–1921

Hoon, E. E., *The Organisation of the English Customs System 1696–1786*, 1968

Hope-Jones, A., *Income Tax in the Napoleonic Wars*, 1939

Jarvis, R. C., *Collected Papers on the Jacobite Risings*, 2 vols, 1971–2

Kain, R. J. P., *An Atlas and Index of Tithe Files of mid-nineteenth century England and Wales*, 1980

Kain, R. J. P. and Prince, H. C., *The Tithe Surveys of England and Wales*, 1985

Leeson, F., *A Guide to the records of the British State Tontines and Life Annuities of the seventeenth and eighteenth centuries*, 1968

Lewis, S., *Topographical Dictionary of England*, 4 vols, 1848–9

Lewis, S., *Topographical Dictionary of Ireland*, 2 vols, 2nd ed., 1846

Lewis, S., *Topographical Dictionary of Scotland*, 2 vols, 2nd ed., 1846

Lewis, S., *Topographical Dictionary of Wales*, 2 vols, 3rd ed., 1845

Magee, B., *The English Recusants*, 1938

McKinley, R. A., *A History of British Surnames*, 1990

Prendergast, J. P., *The Cromwellian Settlement of Ireland*, 3rd ed., 1922

PRO Information Leaflets:
Apprenticeship Records
Confiscations, Sales and Restoration of Crown and Loyalist Lands, 1642–1660: Sources in the Public Record Office
Customs and Excise Records as Sources for Biography and Family History
Death Duty Registers
Tax Records as a Source for Local and Family History
Tithe Records in the Public Record Office

Reaney, P. H., *A Dictionary of British Surnames*, 1983

Sabine, B. E. V., *A History of Income Tax*, 1966

Short, B., *Geography of England and Wales in 1910*, 1990

Smith, G., *Something to Declare! 1000 years of Customs and Excise*, 1980

Ward, W. R., *The English Land Tax in the eighteenth century*, 1953

Willard, J. F., *Parliamentary Taxes on Personal Property 1290–1334*, 1934

4: Strangers and Settlers

Agnew, D. C. A., *Protestant Exiles from France, before and after 1681*, 2 vols, 3rd ed., 1886

Andrews, C. M., *Guide to Materials for American History in the Public Record Office of Great Britain*, 2 vols, 1912, 1914

Army List, 1754 onwards

Bailyn, B., *Voyagers to the West*, 1986

Banks, C. E., *The Planters of the Commonwealth*, 1967

Banks, C. E., *The Winthrop Fleet*, 1930

Bardsley, C. W., *A Dictionary of English and Welsh Surnames, with Special American Instances*, 1988

Barnett, C., *Britain and Her Army 1509–1970*, 1970

Boynton, L., *The Elizabethan Militia 1558–1638*, 1967

Bridenbaugh, C., *Vexed and Troubled Englishmen 1590–1642*, 1976

Bridenbaugh, C. and R., *No Peace beyond the Lines: The English in the Caribbean 1624–1690*, 1972

Burn, J. S., *The History of the French, Walloon, Dutch and other Foreign Protestant Refugees Settled in England*, 1846

Burns, P. and Richardson, H., *Fatal Success: A History of the New Zealand Company*, 1989

Camp, A. J., *My Ancestor was a Migrant (in England and Wales): how can I trace where he came from?* 1987

Coldham, P. W., *American Loyalist Claims*, 1980

Coldham, P. W., *American Wills and Administrations in the Prerogative Court of Canterbury 1610–1857*, 1989

Coldham, P. W., *Emigrants from England to the American Colonies 1773–1776*, 1988

Coldham, P. W., *English Estates of American Colonists 1610–1858*, 3 vols, 1980, 1981

Coleman, T., *Passage to America*, 1972

Cresswell, D., *Early New Zealand Families*, 1956

Currer-Briggs, N. and Gambier, R., *Huguenot Ancestry*, 1985

Dickson, R. J., *Ulster Emigration to Colonial America 1718–1775*, 1966

Dobson, D., *Directory of Scottish settlers in North America 1625–1825*, 1984

Fidlon, P. G. and Ryan, R. J., eds, *The First Fleeters*, 1981

Filby, P. W., *Passenger and Immigration Lists Bibliography 1538–1900*, 2nd ed., 1988

Filby, P. W. and Meyer, M. K., *Passenger and Immigration Lists Index*, 3 vols, 1981, with Annual Supplements thereafter

Gandy, M. J., ed., *My Ancestor was Jewish: How can I find out more about him?* 1983

Gibson, J. S. W., *Census Returns 1841–1881 on Microfilm: A Directory to local holdings*, 5th ed., repr. 1990

Gibson, J. S. W., *General Register Office and International Genealogical Indexes: Where to find them*, 1988

Gibson, J. S. W., *Marriage, Census, and other Indexes for Family Historians*, 3rd ed., 1988

Gibson, J. S. W. and Dell, A., *Tudor and Stuart Muster Rolls*, 1989

Gibson, J. S. W. and Medlycott, M., *Militia Lists and Musters 1757–1876*, 2nd ed., 1990

Gillen, M., *The Founders of Australia, a Biographical Dictionary of the First Fleet*, 1989

Gwynn, R. D., *Huguenot Heritage: The history and contribution of the Huguenots in Britain*, 1985

Hawkings, D. T., *Bound for Australia*, 1987

Higgs, E. J., *Making Sense of the Census, The Manuscript Returns for England and Wales 1801–1901*, 1989

HMSO, *Acts of the Privy Council, Colonial Series, 1613–1783*, 1908–12, *Unbound Papers 1676–1783*, 1912

HMSO, *Calendar of State Papers, Colonial: America and West Indies 1574–1738*, 1860–1969, *East Indies, China and Japan 1513–1624*, 1862–78, *East Indies, China and Persia 1625—1629*, 1884, *East Indies and Persia 1630–1634*, 1892

HMSO, *Calendar of State Papers relating to Ireland 1509–1670*, 1860–1912

HMSO, *Calendar of State Papers relating to Scotland 1509–1603*, 1858

HMSO, *Calendar of Treasury Books 1660–1718*, 1904–62

HMSO, *Calendar of Treasury Books and Papers 1729–1745*, 1898–1903

HMSO, *Calendar of Treasury Papers 1557–1728*, 1868–89

HMSO, *Journals of the Board of Trade and Plantations 1704–1782*, 1920–38

HMSO, *The Records of the Colonial and Dominions Offices*, PRO Handbook no. 3, 1964

Hockly, H. E., *The Story of the British Settlers of 1820 in South Africa*, 1949

Holding, N. W., *Location of British Army Records – World War I Sources*, 1985

Holding, N. W., *More Sources of World War I Army Ancestry*, 1986

Holding, N. W., *World War I Army Ancestry*, 1982

Huggett, F. E., *Slaves and Slavery*, 1975

Hughes, R., *The Fatal Shore: A History of Transportation of Convicts to Australia 1787–1868*, 1987

Huguenot Society vol. VIII *Letters of Denization and Acts of Naturalization for Aliens in England and Ireland 1509–1603*, ed. W. Page; 1893; vol. XVIII *1603–1700*, ed. W. A. Shaw, 1911; vol. XXVII *1701–1800*, ed. W. A. Shaw, 1923; vol. XXXV *Supplement, 1603–1800*, ed. W. A. Shaw, 1932; vol. XXIV *Naturalizations in the American Colonies 1740–1772*, ed. M. S. Giuseppi, 1921

International Genealogical Index, latest edition

Johnson, S. C., *A History of Emigration from the United Kingdom to North America 1763–1912*, 1913

Kirk, R. E. G. and E. F., *Returns of Aliens in London 1523–1625*, Huguenot Society vol. X, 5 parts, 1900–08

Lawton, R., ed., *The Census and Social Structure. An Interpretative Guide to nineteenth century Censuses for England and Wales*, 1978

Lloyd, C., *The British Seaman 1200–1860, a Social Survey*, 1968

Longmate, N., *The Workhouse*, 1974

Mercantile Navy List, 1857 onwards

Nissel, M., *People Count, A history of the General Register Office*, 1987

Norton, M. B., *The British Americans: The Loyalist Exiles in England 1774–1789*, 1974

Philip, B., *British Residents at the Cape 1795–1819*, 1981

PRO, Family Fact Sheet 2. Tracing an Ancestor in the Army: Soldiers

  3. Tracing an Ancestor in the Army: Officers

  4. Tracing an Ancestor in the Royal Navy: Ratings

  5. Tracing an Ancestor in the Royal Navy: Officers

  6. Tracing an Ancestor in the Merchant Navy: Seamen

  7. Tracing an Ancestor in the Merchant Navy: Masters and Mates

  9. Tracing an Ancestor who was an Immigrant

  10. Tracing an Ancestor who was an Emigrant

PRO Information Leaflets:

  Admiralty Records as Sources for Biography and Genealogy

  American Land Grants

  British Army Records as Sources for Biography and Genealogy

  Censuses of Population 1801–1881

  Emigrants: Documents in the Public Record Office

  Immigrants: Documents in the Public Record Office

  Militia Muster Rolls 1522–1640

  Passport Records

  Prisoners of War and Displaced Persons 1939–1953

  Prisoners of War: Documents in the Public Record Office

  Records of Courts Martial: Army

  Records of Medals

  Records of the American and West Indian Colonies before 1782

  Records of the Board of Ordnance

  Records of the Colonial and Dominions Offices from 1782

  Records of the Registrar General of Shipping and Seamen

  Records Relating to Shipwrecks

  Records relating to the SS Titanic

  Royal Marines Records in the Public Record Office

  Service Medal and Award Rolls: First World War (WO329)

  The American Revolution

PRO, *Records of Officers and Soldiers who have served in the British Army*, 1985

Richardson, P., *Empire and Slavery*, 1968

Robson, L. L., *The Convict Settlers of Australia*, 1965

Rodger, N. A. M., *Naval Records for Genealogists*, PRO Handbook no. 22, 1988

Rose, M. E., *The Relief of Poverty 1834–1914*, 1972

Ryan, R. J., *The Second Fleet Convicts*, 1982

Sainty, M. R. and Johnson, K. A., eds, *New South Wales Census … November 1828*, 1980

Savage, J., *Genealogical Dictionary of the First Settlers of New England*, 4 vols, 1977

Simmons, R. C., *The American Colonies from Settlement to Independence*, 1976

Smiles, S., *The Huguenots*, 1868

Smith, J. M., ed., *Seventeenth Century America: Essays in Colonial History*, 1959

Smith, P. C., *Per Mare Per Terram: A History of the Royal Marines*, 1974

Society of Genealogists, *Census Indexes in The Library of the Society of Genealogists*, 1987

Steel, D. J., ed., *National Index of Parish Registers*, vol. 2, *Sources for Nonconformist Genealogy and Family History*, repr. 1981

Steel, D. J., ed., *National Index of Parish Registers*, vol. 3, *Sources for Roman Catholic and Jewish Genealogy and Family History*, repr. 1986

Thirsk, J., *Sources of Information on Population 1500–1760*, 1965

Waters, H. F., *Genealogical Gleanings in England*, 2 vols, 1969

Watts, C. T. and M. J., *My Ancestor was a Merchant Seaman: How can I find out more about him?* repr. with addenda 1991

Western, J. R., *The English Militia in the eighteenth century. The Story of a Political Issue 1600–1832*, 1965

Woolcock, H., *Rights of Passage: Emigration to Australia in the nineteenth century*, 1986

Yeo, G., *The British Overseas*, 2nd ed., 1988

6:   The Gainsborough Family

Belsey, H., *Gainsborough's Family*, 1988

Breed, G. R., *My Ancestors were Baptists: how can I find out more about them?* rev. ed., 1988

Fulcher, G. W., *Life of Thomas Gainsborough*, 1856

Gomme, A. A., *Patents of Invention*, 1946

Hayes, J., *Gainsborough*, 1975

Leary, W., *My Ancestors were Methodists: how can I find out more about them?* 1990

Leonard, J. N., *The World of Gainsborough 1727–1788*, 1969

Lindsey, J., *Thomas Gainsborough: His Life and Art*, 1981

Peters, G. H., *Humphrey Gainsborough*, 1948

PRO Information Leaflet: Patents and Specifications for Inventions, and Patent Policy: Sources in the Public Record Office

Waterhouse, E., *Gainsborough*, 1966

Woodall, M., ed., *The Letters of Thomas Gainsborough*, 1963

7:   The Walter Family

Foster, J., *Alumni Oxonienses 1500–1886*, 1891

G. E. C., *Complete Baronetage 1611–1800*, 6 vols, 1902

Groene, B. H., *Tracing your Civil War Ancestor*, 1977

Shaw, W. A., *The Knights of England*, 2 vols, 1906

Stone, L., *The Crisis of the Aristocracy 1558–1641*, repr. 1971

8:   The Statham Family

Jeayes, I. H., *Derbyshire charters in Public and Private Libraries and Muniment Rooms*, 1906

9:   The Fardon Family

Besse, J., *Sufferings of the Quakers*, vol. I, *c. 1654–1688*, 1753

Milligan, E. H. and Thomas, M. J., *My Ancestors were Quakers: How can I find out more about them?* 1983

10:   The Wordsworth Family

de Selincourt, E. arr. and ed., *The Letters of William and Dorothy Wordsworth: I The Early Years 1787–1805*, 2nd ed. rev. by C. L. Shaver, 1967, *II The Middle Years 1806–1811*, 2nd ed. rev. by M. Moorman, 1969, *The Middle Years 1812–1820*, 2nd ed. rev. by M. Moorman and A. G. Hill, 1970, *III The Later Years Pt I 1821–1828*, 2nd ed. A. G. Hill, 1978, *V The Later Years Pt. II 1829–1834*, 2nd enl. ed. rev. arr. and ed. by A. G. Hill, 1979

Law List, 1775 onwards

11: The Garrick and Marx Families

Crockford's Clerical Directory, 1858 onwards

Dalton, C., *English Army Lists and Commission Registers 1661–1714*, 6 vols, 1960

Dalton, C., *George I's Army 1714–1727*, 1910

Kendall, A., *David Garrick*, 1985

Little, D. M. and Kahrl, G. M., eds, *The Letters of David Garrick*, 3 vols, 1963

Oman, C., *David Garrick*, 1958

PRO Information Leaflet: Royal Warrant Holders and Household Servants

Russell, A., *The Clerical Profession*, 1980

Venn, J. and J. A., *Alumni Cantabrigienses, from the Earliest Times to 1900*, 1922–7

12:   The Dyer, Brenton and Walker Families

Austin, J. O., *Genealogical Dictionary of Rhode Island*, 1978

Genealogies of Rhode Island Families, 2 vols, 1983

Marshall, J., *Royal Navy Biography*, 6 vols, 1823–30; *Commissioned Sea Officers of the Royal Navy 1660–1815*, 3 vols, 1954

Navy List, 1814 onwards

O'Byrne, W. R., *A Naval Biographical Dictionary*, 1849

Rutman, D. B., *Winthrop's Boston*, 1975

Steel's Navy List, 1782–1817

13:   The Lyons, Evans, Massy and Atkinson Families

Cannon, R., *Historical Record of the 19th Foot*, 1848

Hieronymussen, P., *Orders, Medals and Decorations of Britain and Europe*, 1967

Powell, G., *The Green Howards*, 1968

Smyth, Sir John, *The Story of the Victoria Cross*, 1963

This England Books, *The Register of the Victoria Cross*, 1981

Wehrlich, R., *Orders and Decorations of All Nations*, 1965

INDEX

Page numbers in *italic* refer to information in the captions

Act for the better preventing of
  Clandestine Marriages (1753),
  121
Adam, Robert, 175
Adcock, William Frederick, 181
Adderbury West, 63, 153, 157, *157*
Addison, Richard, 165
Administration of Estates Act (1925),
  32, 34
Admiralty, 11, 29, 92, 95, 99, 100, 188,
  190, 191, *191*, 192, 194
  High Court of *see* courts
Adventurers for Lands in Ireland, *4*, 57
Afghan War, 202–3
Agriculture, Board of, 34
Agriculture, Fisheries and Food,
  Ministry of, 34, 47
Aids, levying of, 32, 49
Air Department, 100
Albion, 183
Alcock, Hannah, 151
Alcock, Sarah, 152
Alienation Office, 36, 41
aliens, 52, 54, 78–83, 183
  returns of, 83
Alsop, 140, 141, *144*, 145
Alsop, Thomas, 141, 142
Alumni Dublinienses, 204
Amaranthe, HMS, 192
America/United States
  emigration to, 84, 85, 86, 87, 95, 99
    see also Brenton family;
    Dyer family
  Loyalists, 86, 186
  refugees, 83
  transportation to, 19
  War of Independence, 86, 184, 186
American Loyalists Claims Commission:
  Minute Books 1784–1804, 86
Ancient and Modern Deeds, 35, 145,
  147
Anglican Church, 75, 79
Anne, Queen, 79
Annual Criminal Registers, 15, 31, 91
annuities, 44, 47, 54, 55, 63, 67–71,
  72, 83, 135, 162, 163, 174, 178,
  180, *180*

Appeal, Courts of *see* courts
Applethwaite, 163
apprenticeship, 65–6, 77, 122, 185
Apprenticeship Books, 65–6, *164*
Archdeacons' Visitation Records, 55
Archer, Hannah, 151
Archer (later ffardon), Mary, 151
Arches, Court of *see* courts
Armed Services, 95, 99 *see also* name of
  service
Army, 74, 95, *96,* 99, 169, 171–2, *172,*
  178, 180, 196–206
Army List, 200, 202
Arthuret, 114, *114,* 115, 116
Assessed Tax cases, 64
Assheton, Richard, 181
Assize Courts *see* courts
Assize of Clarendon (1166), 17
Association Oath Rolls, 157
Atkinson, Alfred, 204, 206, *206*
Attorney General, 25, 119, 120, 170
Audit Office, 65, 68, 71, 86, 90, 100,
  160
Augmentations of the Revenues of the
  Crown, Court of *see* courts
Austin, J. O., 186
Australia, 19, 91, 92, *92,* 93, 95, 99
  see also New South Wales

Bacon, Sir Nicholas, *143*
Ball, Hannah, 152, *153*
Ball, Nathaniel, 150, 152, 153, *153*
Baltimore, 87
Banbury, 150, *151,* 153, *153,* 154, 157
Bank of England, 70
bankruptcy, 28–9, 39, 119–20, 161
Bankruptcy, Court of *see* courts
Banks, C. E., 185
Bantock, William, 71, 109
baptism records, 7, 75, 76, 83, 102,
  105, 116, 118, 169, 173
Baptists, 76
Barbados, 84
Baring Island, 91
Barret, Maria, 185
Barton, 162
Bath, 122

Beaumont, Sir George, 160
Belgian refugees, 100
benefit of clergy, 19, 21
Bermuda, 84
Bernau Index, 24–5, 31, 77
Besse, Joseph, 152
Bill Books, 22, 24, 25
birth records, 7, 75, 76, *76,* 83, 89, 115,
  150
Bishops' Certificates of Institutions to
  Benefices, 30
Blackborne, Walter, 185
Black Death, 32, 52
Black Lion Hotel, Lavenham, 71–2,
  102, 103, 105, *108,* 109
Bleasby, 149
Blount, Michael Henry, *63*
Bodicote, 152
Boer War, 90, 99, 196, 206
Bloxham, hundred of, *51,* 52, 54, *54,*
  154, *155*
Bond, John, 180
boroughs, taxation of, 49
Boston, 184, 185, 186, 187
Bouillon Papers, 82
Bradshaigh, Sir Roger, 171
Brenton family, 184, 185–94
Brereton, Mr, 132
Bristol, 75
British and Portuguese Slave Trade
  Commission, 90
British Lying-In Hospital, 76
British Museum, 175
Broughton, *51,* 52, *54,* 150, 152, 153,
  154, *155,* 156
Bruce, Lady Mary, *22,* 133, 139
Bruern, 46, 125, 127
Brydges, Elizabeth Louisa, 135
  see also Walter family
Bulley, Abraham, 42
burgage tenure, 32
burial records, 83, 102, 118–9, 150,
  152
Burma Independence Act (1947),
  81
Burr, Margaret, 75, 121
Bury and Norwich Post, 112

Bury St Edmunds, 71, 108, 109, 119
Bush Inn, Longtown, 112–3, 115

Caesar, HMS, 194
Calendar of Prisoners, 15
Canada, 86, *95, 96*
Canavan family, *99*
Cape Colony, 95
Cape of Good Hope, 91
Cape Town, 90, 91
Capital Transfer Tax, 67
Carlisle, 161, 162
Carlow, 196, 197
Carrington, Nathan, 177
Carter, John, 160, 163
carucage, 49
census, 6, 48, 72, 73–5, 81, 88, 102,
    103, *103,* 104, *104,* 105, *106,* 110,
    112, 114, *114,* 115–6, 181, *182,*
    183, 195
    in New South Wales, 91
    of convicts overseas, 20
Central Criminal Court *see* courts
certificates
    of arrival of aliens, 81, *82*
    of conformity, 28
    of naturalization, 80, 81, 169, 181,
    181
    of residence, 53, 54, 77, 127, 154
Ceylon, 91
Chamberlain, Sir Thomas, 132
Chamberleyn, Cecily le, *41*
Chancery, Court of
    Bernau Index, 24–5, 31, 77
    Bill Books, 22, 24
    Country depositions, 22, 23, 24–5
    Entry Books of decrees and orders,
        24, 29, 30, *143*
    and land, 35, 36, 37, 44, 46, 47, 77,
        127, 133, 143–5
    and licences, 71
    and lotteries, 67
    Masters' exhibits, 22, *22,* 31, 44, 67,
        68, 77, 86, *136,* 138
    officers, 22–3, *23*
    problems with records, 22–6, 30–1,
        77
    Proceedings, 21–5, 30, 31
    Reynardson's Series, 31
    Six Clerks series, 24, 31
    and Statham family, 77, 143–5
    Town depositions, 24–5
    and Walter family, 22, 125, 127, 133,
        136, 138
    and wills, 27, 77, 133, *136*
    work of, 13, 21–5, 27, 28
    mentioned, 29, 86, 121
Chancery Division *see* High Court of
    Justice
Channel Islands, refugees in, 82
Chapman, Dr Clarence, 95

Charles I, King, 24, 25, 39, 46, 52, 55,
    59, 125, 128, 130, 131, 132
Charles II, King, 54, 55, 59, 62, 79, 84
Charter Rolls, 35
Cheney, C. R., 48
Chester, Palatinate of, *see* Palatinates
children's portions, 44
chivalry, 32
Christie family, *35*
Churchill, *43, 45,* 125, 127, 128, 130,
    131, 134, 139
City of Boulogne, 82, 183, *183*
civil procedure, 15–16
Civil Procedure Act (1833), 15
Clapham, John, 41
Clarina, Lords, 200, 204
Classis Lottery, 68, *68*
clergy, 11, 52, 84, 120
Close Rolls, 38, 39, 41, 44, 45, 47, 59,
    72, 79, 81, 128, 180
Cockermouth, 161, 164
Cockfield, 71, *108,* 109
College of Arms, 6, 44, 79, 127, 169
Colonial Land and Emigration
    Commission, 92
Colonial Land and Emigration Office,
    93, 184
Colonial Office records, 84, 90, 91, 92,
    95, 99
    General Correspondence, 90
colonies, 19, 20, 26, 31, 88–9, 90, 91,
    92–5, 184–95
Colwell, Edwin, *96*
Commission of Bankruptcy, 28
*Commissioned Sea Officers of the Royal
    Navy 1660–1815,* 190, 194
Commissioners, tax, 53, 55
Committee/Commissioners for
    Advance of Money, *56,* 57–8, 131,
    132
Committee for Compounding for the
    Estates of Royalists and
    Delinquents, 57, 58–9, 128, 130,
    130, 131
Committee for Removing Obstructions
    in the Sale of Delinquents' Land,
    57
Committee for the Sale of Fee-Farm
    Rents or Crown Rents, 57
Committee for Scottish Affairs, 58
Committee for Sequestration, 57
Common Law courts *see* courts
Common Law Procedure Acts (between
    1852 and 1860), 15
Common Pleas, Court of *see* courts
Common Pleas Division *see* High Court
    of Justice
common recoveries, 40, *40,* 41, 48
common socage *see* socage
Commonwealth Exchequer Papers, 59
commutation, 72

compensation claims, 90–1, 186, 187
Complete Baronetage, 1611–1800
    (G.E.C.), 132
composition, 58–9
compurgation, 15–16, 21
constables
    Hundredal, 53
    parish, 18
    petty, 61
contingent interests, 39, 44
contingent remainders, 39
Contribution, Act of, 56–8, *57*
Controlment Rolls, 13, 30
convicts, 19, 20, 84–5, 91–2
Cookson, Christopher Crackanthorpe,
    165, *165*
co-ownership, 34
co-parceny, 13, 34
Cope, Lady Anne, 127
Copyhold Acts, 34
copyhold tenure, 32, 33, 34, 150
    enfranchisement of, 34
Coram Rege Rolls, 13
Cornwall, Duchy of, 37
coroner's inquests, 17, 18, 113, 114
Correspondence and Entry Books,
    Colonies, General, 1662–1782,
    86
County courts *see* courts
County Police Act (1839), 18
county record offices, 34, 62
courts
    in action, 15–19
    of Appeal, 13, 16, 25, 29
    of Appeal for Prizes, 26
    of Appeal in Chancery, 25
    of Arches, 27
    of Assize, 13–15, 16, 18, 31, 85, 91,
        102, 113–4
    of Augmentations of the Revenues of
        the Crown, 27, 46
    of Bankruptcy, 28–9, 119
    of Chancery *see* Chancery, Court of
    Central Criminal, 15, 19, 26, 91, 114
    civil procedure, 15–16
    Common Law, 11–13, 29, 30 *see also*
        names of common law courts
    of Common Pleas, 11, 12, 29, 39,
        40, 41, *41,* 113, 132, 135, *146,*
        165, 176, 177
    County, 28, 29
    of Criminal Appeal, 29
    Criminal Law, 13–15 *see also* names
        of criminal law courts
    criminal procedure, 16–19
    Crown, 15, 29
    for Crown Cases Reserved, 29
    for Divorce and Matrimonial Causes,
        30
    of Doctors' Commons, 25, 121, 172
    ecclesiastical, 13, 19, 21, 26, 27, 29

courts – *cont*
of Equity, 11, 21–5, 27, 29, 31, 38, 44, 77 *see also* names of courts of equity
of Exchequer *see* Exchequer
of Exchequer Chamber, 13, 16
of Exchequer of Pleas, 11, 12 *see* Walter family feudal, 11
of the General Surveyors of the King's Lands, 27
of Great Sessions, 27
High Court of Admiralty, 25–6, 29, 90
High Court of Delegates, 26, 27, 77
High Court of Justice, 11, 12, 13, 15, 25, 26, 27, 28, 29, 30, 38, 39, 180
of the Honour of Peveril, 27, 33
hundredal, 11
inferior, 13, 29
of King's Bench, 11, 12–13, 15, 16, 28, 29, 30, *31*, 72, 83, 119, *119, 121,* 121, *122,* 131, 164, 165
Leet, 17, 33–4
local, 11
manorial, 17, 33, 48
Old Bailey Sessions, 15, 25–6, 91, 114
Palace, 27
petty or possessory assizes, 14–15
petty sessions, 17
Prerogative Court of Canterbury, 27, 35, 76, 86, 99, 120, 122, *124,* 127, 133, *136,* 138, 145, 172, 173, 174, 175, 178, 184
Prerogative Court of York, 163
Prize, 26
of Probate, 27
of Protection, 29
of Queen's Bench, 29
of Requests, 21, 25, 77, 140–3, 144
of Review, 28, 29
shire, 11, 13
of Star Chamber, 17, 25, *26,* 31
Supreme Court of Judicature, 13, 29–30
of Upper Bench, 12
Vice-Admiralty, 26
Courts Act (1971), 15
Cox, Josiah, 156, *157*
Crimean War, 99, 196, 197–9, 200, 202
Criminal Appeal, Court of *see* courts
Criminal Justice Act (1948), 18
Criminal Law Courts *see* courts
criminal procedure, 16–19
Crispe, John, 132, 139
Crispe, William, 132, 139
Crow, John, *84*
Crown, HMS, 192
Crown Cases Reserved, Court for *see* courts

Crown Commissions, 18
Crown Courts *see* courts
Crown Estate commissioners, 34
Crown Minute Books, 85
Crown Rolls, 13, 30
Crusades, 49
Cumberland Assizes (1851), *17,* 19, 113–4
Curia Regis, 11, 12 Rolls, 13
customary tenants, 32, 33
Customs, Board of, 160, 165, 167, *167, 168*
Cutslow, 125, 127

Darcy, William, *40*
darrein presentment, 14
de aetate probanda writ, 37
Death Duty Registers, 44, 48, 67, 102, 108, 109, 163, 183
Residuary Accounts, 67
death records, 89, 95, 99, 100, 115, 117
de Banco Rolls, 12
Decimation Tax, 59
Declaration of Indulgence (1671/2), 118
Declarations of Alienage, 81
Declarations of British Nationality, 81
Declarations of Nationality, 81
Deddington, 153, 154, 157
deed poll, change of name by, 78–9, *178*
deeds, 22, *24,* 29, 31, 35, 37, 38, 39, 41, 127, 141, 145, 157, 178
Deeds, Ancient, 35
Deeds, Modern, 35
Deeds Registries, 46, 47
Deeks, Susan, 105
delinquents, 39, 46, 58–9, 128, 130
Demuth, Helen, 183
denization, 79–81, 169, 170, *171*
depositions, 15, 22, 25, 27, 28, 29, 30, 31, 76–7, 114, 144
Country, 22, 23, 24–5
Town, 24–5
Dictionary of National Biography, 127
Dissenters, 55
Dissolution of the Monasteries, 27, 46
District Apportionments, 72
District Registrar, 73, 74, 102, 112, 115, 116
Divisional Cause Books, 15, 30
divorce, 11, 29–30
Divorce and Matrimonial Causes, Court for *see* courts
Docksey, Merrial, 175, 178, 180
Doctors' Commons, Courts of *see* courts
Dr Williams' Library, 76, *76*
Domesday Survey (1086), 32
double vouchers, 40
Dove Cottage Museum, 163

Dovey, Richard, 121, *121*
Dromedary, HMS, 189
Drury Lane Company, 173
Drury Lane Theatre, *20,* 169, 173, 175, 177
Dunch, Walter, *56,* 131, 132
Dupont family, 66, 122
Durham, Palatinate of, *see* Palatinates
Dyer family, 55, 57, 86, 184–5, *185*

East Florida Claims Commission, 86
ecclesiastical courts, 13, 19, 21, 26, 27, 29
disputes, 25
Edward i, King, 13, 14, 15
Edward iii, King, 25, 52, 53
Edward vi, King, 52, 54
Elizabeth, 85
Elizabeth i, Queen, 24, 25, 31, 53, 54, 71
emigrants, 84–100 *see also* Brenton family; Dyer family; Walker family
emigration, assisted, 20, 93–5
Emigration Commissioners, 95
Emigration Office Regulations, 93
enclosure, land, 11, 25, 44, 47
Enclosure Awards, 47
Engels, Frederick, 183
Enrolment Books (High Court of Justice), 38, 41, 44, 45, 72, 79
entail *see* fee tail estate
Entry Books of decrees and orders (Chancery), 24, 30, *143*
Entry Books of Rules (King's Bench), 13
enumerators, census, 73, 112, 115, 116
equity courts *see* courts
Estate Duty, 66–7, *107 see also* Death Duty
Estate Duty Office, 71
estates, forfeits of, *16,* 19, 20, 27, 33, *33,* 46
estates in land, 35–46
fee simple, 34, 35–9
fee tail, 35, 39–41, 125, 132, 140–5, 162
leasehold, 45–6
life, 35
Euxine, 95
Evans, Samuel, 197, *198,* 198–9, *199*
Exchequer
Accounts, 83
Bernau Index, 25
Bill Books, 25
and emigrants, 84, 86, 89
and land, 37, 46, 47
Land Revenue Office, 34, 46
Orders, Entry Books of, 27
Outlawry Books, 20
of Pleas, *see* courts

Port Books, 84
taxation and revenue, 49, 51, 52, 53, 55, 57, 60, 61, 62, 63, 64, 68, 70, 71, 72
work of court, 11, *12*, 25
mentioned, 13, *24*, 27, 31, 77, 113, 127
Exchequer Chamber, Court of *see* courts
Exchequer Division, *see* High Court of Justice

Family Disputes, 76–7
Family Division *see* High Court of Justice
Fardon family (also known as ffardon or Vardon), 54, *54*, 59, 63, 150–9
fee-farm rents, 46, 59
Fee-Farm Rents effected by Trustees, 59
fee simple estate, 35–9, 44
fee tail estate, 39–41
Feet of Fines, 41, *41*, 47, 48, 145, *146*
felony, 17, 19
feoffment, deed of, 35, 37–8
feudal tenure, 32–3, 36, 49
ffenys, Richard, *155*
ffermignac family, 83, 169, 173
fford, Mary, 121
Field Books (Valuation Office), 71, 109, 164
Fiennes, Richard, 156
Fiennes, William, 150
Fillongley, 30, 72
Final and Interlocutory Appeals, Motions, 13
Final Interlocutory Orders, Order Books, 13
Finance Act (1909), 164
Fine Rolls, 36, 37
fines
for alienation, 36
for delinquents, 58
and fee tail estate, 40, 41
for non-attendance at church, 55
Fines and Recoveries Act (1833), 41
First Fruits and Tenths, 72
Fishmongers Company, 55, 184–5, *185*
Fleet Prison, 29, 75, 121, 122, *122*
Fleetwood, Charles, 173
Fleming, Daniel, 167
Fleming, Stanley Hughes le, 164
Foreign Office, 82, 86, 87, 89, 90, 91, 99, 100
foreign Protestant churches, 83
see also Threadneedle Street Church
Forfeiture Act (1870), 19, 33
Foster, Jonathan, 113, 115
Founders' Kin, Privilege and Pedigree (Squibb), 128
Fowler family, 151
frankalmoign, 32
frankpledge, 17
freehold, 18, 19, 32, 35, 63 *see also* fee

simple estate; fee tail estate; life estate
free settlers, 92–3
French
church *see* Threadneedle Street church
prisoners of war, 100
refugees, 82–3 *see also* Huguenots
French Refugees Relief Committee, 83
Frith, James, 122

Gainsborough, John, 28
Gainsborough, Thomas (artist), *35*, 66, 75, 118, 119, *119*, 120, 121, 122, 124, *124*, portraits by, *119, 174*
Gainsborough family, 118–24
see also Gainsborough, Thomas
Gaol Books, 15
gaol delivery, commissions of, 14, 29
sessions of, 25–6, 113
gaols *see* prisons
Garforth, John Baynes, 164
Garrick, David (actor), 30, *35, 63,* 64, 83, *165,* 168, 169, *170,* 172, 173–5, *175*
Garrick family, 30, 47, 66, *80,* 81, 83, 168, 169–80 *see also* Garrick, David
Gate, Thomas, *129*
Geelhand, Alida Catharina, 68
Genealogical Dictionary of Rhode Island (Austin), 186
Genealogies of Rhode Island Families Vol I, 184
General Assembly, 186, 187
General Board of Health, 95
General Enclosure Acts, 47
General Eyre, 13–14, 17
Rolls, 13
General Register Office, 6
General Surveyors of the King's Lands, Court of *see* courts
George I, King, 83
George Fyfe, 195
German internees, 100
Gilkes family, 151
Goddard, Henry, 183
Godstow, 46, 127
Goodwin, Frederick, *88*
Gore, Ralph, *96*
Graham, John, 112
Grand Jury, 18
Grasmere, 93, 163, 194
Gravesend, 84
Great Session, Court of, *see* courts
Gregory, Thomas, *40*

Hall, James, 131
Halmote rolls, 33
Handbook of Dates for Students of English History (Cheney), 48
Harcourt, Simon, Lord Viscount, 135
Harrington, George, *167,* 167–8

Hasted, William, 138
Hasty, HMS, 194
Havana, 90, 91
Hayes, Charles, 180
Health, Ministry of, 95, 100
Hearth Tax, 53, *60,* 60–2, 64, *132, 156*
heir at law, 34, 35, 37
heir, minority of, 33
Hendon, 175, 180
Henry I, King, 11
Henry II, King, 11, 14, 19, 49
Henry III, King, 12, 37
Henry IV, King, 52
Henry VI, King, 52, 53
Henry VII, King, 25, 37, 47, 52
Henry VIII, King, 19, 26, 27, 37, 72
taxation, 52, 53–4
Hereford, 173
hidage, 49
High Collector, 53
High Constable, 61
High Court of Admiralty *see* courts
High Court of Delegates *see* courts
High Court of Justice
Chancery Division, 11, 25, 27, 28, 29, 30, 39, 180
Divisional Cause Books, 30
Enrolment Books, 38, 41, 44, 45
Family Division, 27, 29–30
Judgment Books, 15, 30
Probate, Divorce and Admiralty Division, 26, 27, 29
Queen's Bench Division, 11, 12, 13, 26, 29
record-keeping, 30, 38
took over work of other courts, 11, 12, 13, 25, 26, 27
work of, 29–30
Hiorne, Elizabeth, 151
Home Office, 15, 20, 44, 79, 80, 81, *82,* 82, 91, 92, 100, 169, *181,* 183
Warrant Books, 44, 79
Home Secretary, 79, 80
Honour of Peveril, 33
House of Commons, 11, 53, 130
House of Lords, 11, 13, 16, 25, 28, 170
Record Office, 47
Huguenots, 80, *80,* 81, 83 *see also* Garrick family
Huguenot Society, 81, 83, 169
Hume, Robert, 121
Hyde, Sir Edward, 132

idiocy, 13, 37
immigrants and migrants, 60, 73–83
Income Tax, 64, *64*
Increment Value Duty, 164
Independents, 76, 118
indictment
bill of, 18
trial on, 17

infants, protection over, 21, 29
informations, 25
inheritance of land, 34–5
Inheritance Act (1833), 34
Inland Revenue, 63, 64, 65, 67, 72, 109
inquisitions post mortem, 13, *33*, 36–7, *38*, 47, 77, 127, 145, 146, 147
Instance Court (High Court of Admiralty), 25, 26
Institution Books, 72, 128
interlocutory injunctions, 21
International Genealogical Index (I.G.I.), 75, 76, 77, 84, 116, 117, 122, 173, 175, 185
intestates, 34, 35, 46
invention, patents of, 118, 120–1
Izard family (also known as Shillingford), *37*

Jacobites, 13, 171
Jamaica, 90, 91
James I, King, 24, 77, 79, 127
Jamestown, 84
Jeffery, Thomas, *12*
Jenden, Ann, 91
Jervys, Richard, 142, 149
Jesus College, Oxford, 125, 128
joint tenancy, 34
jointures, 44
judges, 11, 12, 13, 14, 16, 25, 26
Judgment Books, 15, 30
judicial separation, decree of, 34
juries, 14, 15, 16, 17–18, 19, 25, 113
justices itinerant in eyre, 14, *17*
justices of the peace, 11, 15, 18, 61

Kart, Gustave, 183
Kavanagh, Morgan, 183
Keith, Rev. Alexander, *121*, 121–2, *122*
Kendal, *78*
Keswick, 184, 194, 195
Kilburn, Edward, *18*
kin, next of, 34, 35, 46, 66
King, 11, 12, 22, 25, 26, 35, 36, 37, 40, 49, 53, 79 *see also* names of kings
King, Gregory, 62
King's Bench, Court of *see* courts
King's Bench Prison, 13, 29, 75
King's Bills, 81
King's Cofferer, 49
King's Council (Curia Regis), 11, 12, 25
King's Silver, 40
Kirkby la Thorpe, 185
Kirke, Piercy, Maj. Gen., 172
Kirkpatrick, William, *17*, 18–19, 112, 113, 114, 115, 116
Kitchener, Lord, 206
Kneller, Sir Godfrey, 133
Knight service, 32

Knights of England, The (ed. Shaw), 127
Kynaston, Thomas, 138

Laconde, Lewis, 172, 173
Lacy, James, 173, *174*
Lamb family, 150, 151, 157
Lambeth Palace Library, 27
La Minerve, 190
Lancaster, Duchy of, 27, 29, 33, 34, 36, 37, 46
  Palatinate of, *see* Palatinates
land
  alteration to settlements, 11
  contracts for sale of, 29
  Crown, 27
  enclosure, 11, 47
  escheat of, 20, 27, 29, 33, 34, 37
  estates, 35–46
  holding and transfer of, 7, 32–48
  in colonies, 85–6, 93
  inheritance, 34–5
  mortgages and annuities, 46–7
  problems of using records, 47–8, 13, 21
  strict settlement, 41–5, 135, 162
  tenure, 32–4
  title to, 14
  see also Statham family; Walter family
Land and Emigration Board Regulations, 93
Landells, John, *76*
Land Registration Acts, 39, 46
Land Registry, 46
Land Revenue Office of the Exchequer, 34, 46
Land Tax, 48, *63*, 63–4, 71, 72, 77, 112, 157, *157*
Lark, HMS, 192
Latimer, Jane, 116
Laurent family, *90*
Lavenham, 71, 72, 75, 102, 103, *103*, *104*, 105, *106*, 108, *108*, 109, *109*, 110, *110*, 112
Law List (1799), 165
Law of Property Act (1922), 32, 34 (1925), 34, 39, 41, 47
Lay Subsidies, 49–52, 53, 54, 55, 57, 59, 60, 127, *127*, 154, *155*
Leake, John, 176, 177, *177*
lease and release, 38
leasehold, 45–6
leases, 39, 45, 46
Legacy Duty, 66, 160, 163
Legacy Duty Act (1805), 66
Legacy Duty Office, 66
legal system, 7, 11–31
legitimacy cases, 26
Leicester, Earl of, 36
Lenten Certificates, 71
letters close, 35
  patent, 13, *24*, *33*, 35, 128, 131, 170

licences
  royal, 78, 79
  to go abroad, 84, 89
  to sell land, 36
  to sell wine, flesh, 65, 71
Lichfield, 169, 172, 173, 178
Lichfield, Bishop of, 30, *31*
life estate, 35
Lightfoot family, 162
Lists of Immigrants, 81–2
Little, Robert, 115, 116
Littleton, William, *129*
Livery Companies, 57, 145, 184
Lloyd, John, *129*
loans, 57, 59, 131
local courts, 11
Local Land Charges Registers, 46
London, 4, 14, 22, 25, 27, 28, 29, 73, 75, 76, 77, 82, 83, 85, 89, 115, 130, 131, 149, 153, 164, 169, 170, 171, 172, 177, 183, 184, 187, 188, 194
London Gazette, The, 28, 44, 69, 79, 99, 119, 120, 171, 197, 199, 202
Long Parliament, 55
Longtown, *17*, 102, 112, *114*, 115
Lonsdale, Earl of, 160, 164
Lonsdale, Henry, 113
Lord Chamberlain's Department, 64, 160
Lord Chancellor, 13, 21, 22, 25, 28, 29, 31, 53, 119, *119*, 120, 140, 143
Lord Chief Justice of England, 12
Lord Steward's Department, 62
Lord Treasurer, 13, 25
lotteries, 67–71, 83
Lowther, Viscount, 160
Lucas, Louis Stephen, *82*
lunacy, 13, 21, 37
Lutwidge, Charles, 168
Lyneham, *43*, 125, 127, 130, 132, 134, 135, 138
Lyons, John, *196*, 196–8
Lysons, Lieut. Col., *197*

Magna Carta, 12, 14, 32, 49
Mander, Thomas, *136*, 138, 139
Manning, Julius Augustus, 181
manorial courts *see* courts
manorial (or customary) tenants, 32–4
manors, Crown, 33–4
  Palatinates, 33
Marengo, John, 183
Maritime Counties of England and Wales, 26
Marloe, John (alias John Smith), 87, *87*
marriage, 7, 37, 44, 75, 83, 86, 89, 93, 102, 116, 121, 122, 150–1, 169, 188
Married Women's Property Act (1882), 34
Marshall, J., 189

Marshalsea, 29
Marx, Karl, 81, 169, 181, *181,* 183
Marx family, 81, 169, 181–3
Mary I, Queen, 169
Mary II, Queen, 61, 62, 63
Maryland, 84, 85
Maryport, 161
Massachusetts, 184
Massy, William Godfrey Dunham, 99, 196, 199–203
Massy family, 99, 196, 199–203
Masters of Requests, 25
Matheson, Farquhar, 181
Matrimonial Causes Act (1857), 30, 34
Mattham, William, 105, *106*
Matthers, Robert, *12*
Maulden and Son, 71
Mayfair Chapel, 75, 121
Medical Journals, 92, 95
mental patients, 29
mercantile disputes, 25
merchant seamen, 74, *94*
Merydale, Thomas, *141,* 142
Metropolitan Police Act (1829), 18
Metropolitan Police Force, 18, *18*
Middlesex, 13, 15, 20, 46
Middlesex, Bill of, 13
Middlesex, Sheriff of, 13, 121, *122*
migrants and immigrants, 7, 73–83
Military Train, 201
Millbank Prison, 20
Million Bank, 67–8, *68*
Million Lottery, 67
Mint, the, 75
Mitchelhill, Mary, 116
mitigation, 19
Money Books of the Treasury, 84–5
Morley, 140, 141, 146, 147
mort d'ancestor assizes, 14
mortgages, 21, 29, 46–7, 48
Moss, Elizabeth, 183

name, changes of, 11, 44, 48, 78–9, 135, 169, *178,* 180
National Assistance Board, records of, 100
National Covenant, 58, 130
National Debt Office, 69, 90
Nationality and Status of Aliens Act (1914), 81
naturalization, 11, 79–81, 169, 170, 181
   and Patents of Denization, Acts and Certificates of, 79
   Act of (private), 81
Naturalization Act (1870), 80
Naval Biographical Dictionary (O'Byrne), 192
Navy Board, 192
Negative Oath, 58, 130
Nevis, 84
New England, 84, 86, 184, 185

Newgate Prison, 20
New Jersey, 86
Newport, Rhode Island, 184, 185, 186, 187, 188
New South Wales, 91, *91,* 92, 93
New Zealand, 92, 93, 94, 95, 99, 184, 194, *194,* 195, *195*
New Zealand Company, 93, 184
   Original Correspondence, 94–5
New Zealand Journal, 92
Nicolson, Mary, 116
19th Regiment of Foot *see* Evans, Samuel; Lyons, John; Massy family
non-Anglican, marriages of, 29
non-jurors, *16*
non-parochial records, 75–6
Norbury, 145
Norfolk Island, 91
North East Frontier, 90
North Newington (Newton), 52, 54, 59, 150, 152, 153, 154, *155,* 156
Nova Scotia, 86
novel desseisin assizes, 14

oath
   of abjuration, *16*
   of allegiance, *16,* 79, 80, 84, 89, 170
   of succession, 80
   of supremacy, 79, 170
O'Byrne, W. R., 192
official receiver, 29
Okover, Thomas, *146*
Old Bailey Sessions, 15, 25–6, 91, 114
Olympus, 195
Ordnance Survey maps, 71, 73, *108,* 109
ordeal, trial by, 18
Orders, Entry Books of, 24, 25, 27, 29, 30
   Final Interlocutory, 13
   Interlocutory, 21
   of discharge, 29
   protection, 34
Original Correspondence, America and West Indies, 1606–1807, 86
Orthodox Churches, 83, 100
outlawry, 20, 128, 131
Outlawry Books, 20
Owen, George, *24*
Oxford, 127, 130, 131, 132, 159
   diocese of, 128
Oyer and terminer, commissions of, 14, 29
   sessions, 6
   Books, 26

Paardeberg, battle of, 206
Paisley, 198
Palace Court, 27
Palatinates (Chester, Durham, Lancaster), 29, 33, 34, 36, 37, 38, 46
Papists' Estates, registration of, 63

Pardon and Oblivion, Act of (1651), 59
pardons, 19, 20, *33*
Parish, John, 118
parish registers, 60, 62, 102, 105, 110, 117, 145, 185
Parker, Agnes, 141, 142
Parkhurst Prison Register, *21*
Parkin, Anthony, 164, 165
Parliament, 11, 14, 47, 80, 81, 125, 128, 130, 132, 187
   Private Acts of, 44, 47, 79
   Rolls, 79
   and tax, 49, 52, 53, 55, 57–9
   see also House of Commons; House of Lords
passes and passports, 82, 89–90
Patent Rolls, 36, 81, 85, 86, 170, 173
patents of invention, 118, 120–1
Paymaster General's Office, 83, 99, 203
Payne, Catherine, 175, 180
peace, breaches of, 13
Peasants' Revolt (1381), 52
Pedigrees from the Plea Rolls, 1200–1500 (Wrottesley), 31
peerage claims, 11
Peggy, 190
Pembroke, HM Storeship, 187
Pennsylvania, 86, 184
Pensions, Ministry of, 99
Pentonville Prison, 20
Pepigni, Peter, 183
Perin, Mary, 169
Perpetuities and Accumulations Act (1964), 39
Perrot, Henry, 138
Perry, Henry, 138
Peterell, 192
petitions, 28, 29
petty Assizes *see* courts
Petty Bag Office, 13, 170
petty constable, 61
petty jury, 14, 16, 17–18, 113
Pigon, Stephen, 169
Pipe Office, 55
piracy, 25–6
Placita Coram Rege Rolls, 13
Placita de Banco Rolls, 12
Plantation Books, 85
planters, 85–6
Plea Rolls, 11, 12, 13, 15, 30, 31
Plenderleath family, *17,* 19, 102, 112–7
Poilblanc, Susanna, 173
Polish refugees, 83, 100
Poll Books, 64
Poll Taxes, 52–3, 54, 55, 59, 60, 62, *62,* 83, 184, *185*
Polly, 190
Poor Law Commissioners, 77, 194
Poor Law Unions, 74, 77, *78,* 95, 115, 194
possessory Assizes, *see* courts

Posteas, 12, 15
Prerogative Court of Canterbury *see* courts
Prerogative Court of York *see* courts
Presbyterians, 76, 118
Preston, William and Agnes de, *41*
Princess Carolina, 85
Prison Commission, 20
prisoners of war, 99–100
prisons
 census returns, 74
 debtors', 29
 records, *19,* 19–20, *20, 21,* 92, *122*
Private Acts of Parliament, 44, 47, 79
Privy Council, 11, 26, 28, 80, 83, 84, 92
 Appeals records, 26
 Papers, 85
 Registers, 55, 85
Privy Seal, 25
Prize Court (High Court of Admiralty), 26
Probate, Court of *see* courts
Probate, Divorce and Admiralty Division *see* High Court of Justice
Probate Act (1881), 60, 66
probate inventories, 86, 154
Probate Literary Department, 6
Protestants, 75, 79, 80, 83, 169, 170
Public Service Lists, 93
Pulman Collection, 169
Purcell, James, 180
Puritans, 84

Quakers, 55, 80, 184 *see also* Fardon family; Society of Friends
Quarter Sessions, 15, *16,* 18, 60, 84, 153, 159
 Rolls, 55
Queen, HMS, 187, 189, 190
Queen Anne's Bounty, 72
Queen's Bench, Court of *see* courts
Queen's Bench Division *see* High Court of Justice
Queen's Prison, 29
Quillinan, Edward, 163

Ray, John Mead, 124
Reading Gaol, *19*
Real Property Limitation Act (1833), 15
recognizances, 13
Recovery Rolls, 12
Recusant Rolls, 55
recusants, Popish, convict, 16, 55, 58
Reeves, John, 178, 180
refugees, 82–3, 86, 100 *see also* Garrick family
Regimental Courts Martial Registers, 198
Registrar General, 73, 75, 83, 89, 99, 100, 115, 116

Registration Districts, 73, 74
regnal year, 30, 34, 37
Reimers, Sgt, 181, *181*
Requests, Court of *see* courts
Resolves, Act of (1775), 186
revenue *see* taxation/revenue
Review, Court of *see* courts
Reynardson's Series, 31
Rhode Island, 86, 184, 185, 186, *186,* 187, 188, 189
Rich, Daniel, 138
Rich, Dame Mary, *22,* 133, 139
Rich, Sir Robert, *22,* 133, 139
Richard II, King, 52
Roanoake, 84
Roberts, Lord, Field Marshal, *206*
Rock, Samuel, 42
Rolle, Isabella Charlotte, 42, 135
Rolle (later known as Walter), John, 138, 139
Rolls Chapel Series (pleadings, Court of Chancery), 13
Roman Catholics, *16,* 25, 39, 42, 48, 55, 60, 63, 75, 84
Roos, Robert de, *33*
Rose, HMS, 186
Rosenthal, Michael, *82*
Roston, 140, *144,* 145
Roubiliac, 175
Royal African Company, 90
Royal Air Force, 99
Royal Bounty, 84
Royal Household, 64, 177
 Marshalsea of, 29
Royalist Composition Papers, 58
Royalists, 57, 59
royal licence, change of name by, 78, 79
Royal Marines, 95, 99, 100
Royal Naval Biography (Marshall), 189
Royal Navy, 74, 95, *96,* 99, 100, 180, 184, 186, *186,* 187, 188, *188,* 189–90, 192, *193*
Royal prerogative, 22
Royal Proclamations, 25
Rushworth, John, 30, *31,* 72
Rydal Mount, 160, 163, 164, 195

Sacheverell family, 140, *140,* 141, *141,* 142, 143, *143, 144,* 147, 149
Sage family, 88, *88,* 89, *89*
St Christopher, 84
St George's Chapel *see* Mayfair Chapel
Saladin Tithe, 49
Sales of the King's Goods and Lands, 59
Salveyn family, *33, 36, 38, 41*
Sarrazin, Jeanne, 171
Sarsden, *22, 43, 45, 60,* 125, 127, *127,* 128, 130, *132,* 133, *133,* 134, 135, 136, *136,* 138, 139
Saur, Elizabeth de, 175

Schaw, Arabella, 175, 180
Scott, Robert, *182*
scutage, 32, 49
Seaton, Elizabeth Jane, 202
Sebastopol, 196, 197, 200
seisen, 14
 livery of, 35, 37
sequestration, 59
serjeants at law, 12, 14
serjeanty, 32
servants, emigration of, 85–6
Seton, Robert William, 181
Settled Land Acts (1882 and 1925), 44
settlements, 21, 35
 marriage, 21, 31, 127, 135, 174
Sewell, Thomas, 85
Shaw, W. A., 127
Sheridan, Richard Brinsley, 173
sheriff, 18, 49, 55, 61
Shillingford (also known as Izard) family, 37
Ship Money, 55
ships' passenger lists, 81–2, 84–5, 87–9, 184
ships, convict, 31
 damage to, 25
 salvage of, 25
shires, 49
Shutford, 154
Sibford Ferris, 150, 153, 157
Sibford Gower, 150, 154
Siddons, Mrs, 175
Sierra Leone, 90, 91
Signet Office Docquet Books, 81
single voucher, 40
Six Clerks, 22, 23, *23,* 24, 60
Six Clerks Series, 24, 31
Sixty Clerks, 22
Slave Compensation Commission, 90, *90*
slave trade, 84, 90–1
Smalley, 147, *147*
Smith, John, 168
Smith, John (alias John Marloe), 87, *87*
Smith family of Lavenham, 104, 105
Smith family of Oxfordshire, 151
Snelston, 140, 141, *144,* 145
socage, 32, 33, 34
Society of Friends: Minutes of Meetings, 75, 150
Society of Genealogists, 6, 25, 70
Solicitor General, 119, 120, 121, 170
Soulhard, Stephen, 169
South Africa, 90, 206
Southampton, 75, 88
South Carolina, 90
Southey, Robert, 162, 195
Spanish refugees, 83
Spartan, HMS, *190,* 191, *191,* 192, *192*
Speedy, 190
Springett, G., 71, 109

Squibb, G. D., 128
Stamp Act (1815), 66, 163
Stamp Duty, 65–7, 70, 160, *164*
Stamp Office, 71
Stamps, Board of, 65, 161
Stanyford, Henry, 120
Star Chamber, Court of *see* courts
State Paper Office, 125
State Papers, 59, 89
State Papers, Domestic, 44, 55, 57, 58, 59, 79, 81, 83, 85
State Papers, Foreign, 83
State Papers, Ireland, 57
State Papers of the Council of State, 59
Statham family, *26, 37,* 77, 140–9
Statute De Donis Conditionalibus (1285), 39
Statute for Charitable Uses (1601), 44–5
Statute of Enrolments (1536), 38
Statute Quia Emptores (1290), 32
Statute of Uses (1535), 38
Statute of Westminster (1285), 14
Statute of Wills (1540), 36, 125
Statutes of the Realm, 79
statutes, offences against, 25
Stevens family, 151
Stinton, Jane, 91
Stirling Castle, HMS, 192
Stratford-upon-Avon, 175
strict settlement, 41–5, 135, 162
Strombolo Fireship, 187
Sturges. Nathaniel, *133,* 133–4, *136,* 139
subinfeudation, 32
Succession Duty Act (1853), 66
Sudbury, 71, 118, *119,* 120, 122, 124
    Old Meeting House of the Independent Congregation, 109, 124
Sufferings of the Quakers (Besse), 152–3
Suffolk Record Office, 119
summary trials, 17
Superintendent Registrar, 73, 112, 115, 116
Supreme Court of Judicature, 13, 29–30
    Enrolment Books, 72, 79
    see also High Court of Justice
Supreme Court of Judicature Acts (1873 and 1875), 11, 15, 29
Surinam, 91
surveys, manorial, 33
sworn clerks, 22

tallage, 49
Tasmania (Van Diemen's Land), 91
taxation/revenue, 7, 35, 49–72, 77, 83, 109, 112, 124, 127–8, 132, 150, 154–5, *155,* 156, *165,* 173–4
    see also name of tax
Taxes, Board of, 65, 161

Taylor, Elizabeth, *56,* 131, 132
Taylor, Humphrey, *56,* 131, 132
tenants-in-chief, 32, 36, 77
tenants in common, 34
tenants in tail, 39, 40, 41, 42, 44, 48, 132
Tennyson, Alfred, 162
tenures, 32–4
    incidents of, 32–4
Tenures Abolition Act (1660), 32
Termagent, HMS, 189
Thomas Harrison, 195
Thompson, Joseph, 116
Threadneedle Street Church, 83, 169, *170,* 171, 173
Titanic, SS, *88,* 88–9, *89*
Tithe Act (1936), 72
Tithe Redemption Commission, 72, 102, 109
tithes, 48, 49, 72, 109, *109,* 110, *110,* 112
    disputes, 11, 21, 25, 26, 30
Toleration, Act of (1689), 75
tontines, 67–71
Tonypandy, 89
Tortoise, HM Storeship, 187, 188, 189, *189,* 192, *193,* 194
Tower of London, 13, 100
Trade, Board of, 81, 87, 89, 92, 100
trade disputes, 25
Transport, Ministry of, 88
transportation, 19, 20, 31, 84, 85, 91–2
Treasurer, 25
Treasury
    Board Papers, 85
    and Brenton family, 187, 188
    Commissioners, 36
    and emigrants, 84–5, 86, 90–1
    Money Books, 84–5
    records, 20, 64, 83, 84–5, 86, 90–1, 99, 157
    and refugees, 83
    and tontines, 69
    Warrants, 165, 168
Tredwell, Alexander, 151
Tregenna, Edward, 41
Trevor (later known as Trevor-Garrick), Frederick Stephen, *178,* 180
trials, 13, 15, 16–19, 31
tribunals, 29
trusts, 21, 29, 39, 44–5, *45,* 128, *129*
Tufton, Lady Mary, *43,* 133, 139
Turner family, 71, 102–12

United States *see* America/United States
Upper Bench, Court of, *see* courts
uses, 37–8

Valentine, Mathias, 131
Valuation Books (commonly called Domesday Books), 71

Valuation Office, 71–2, 102, 164
    Field Books, 71, 109, 164
Van Diemen's Land (Tasmania), 91
Van Praet, Anna Maria, 67–8
Van Praet, Joannes Baptista, 68
Varnan family, *156*
Vice-Admiralty Courts *see* courts
Vice Chancellors, 22, 28, 29
Victoria Cross, 196, 197, *198,* 200, 204, *205, 206*
Victory, HMS, 190
Victuallers' Recognizances, 71
Views of Frankpledge, 33
Vigilant, HMS, 188
villein tenure, 32, 33
Virginia, 84, 85, 90
Vital and Parish Listings, 116, 117

Wales, Principality of, 15, 26, 27, 29, 53, 63
Walker family, 93, 184, *194,* 194–5, *195*
Walloons, 169
Walter family, 20, 22, *22,* 41, 42, *42, 43,* 44, *45,* 46, *56,* 58–9, *60,* 77, 125–39
Ward, John, 112, 113, 115
Ward, William, 177, 180
wardship, 33, 37
Warehorne, *40*
War Office, 83, 90, 99, 100, 199, 200–1, 203, 204, 206
Warrant Books of the Home Office, 44, 79
Warron, John, 151
Watt, James, *120,* 120–1
Watts, George, *21*
Wellesley, Rev Gerald, *64*
Wellesley, William Pole Tilney Long, *20*
Wellington, Duke of, *20,* 204
Wesleyan Methodist Metropolitan Registry, 76
Western Australia, 91
West Indies, 84, 86, 90, 91, 95
    Original Correspondence, 86
Westminster, 12, 13, 15, 16
    Palace of, 27
West New Jersey Society, 86
Westrop family, 105, 112
Wheelwright, John, 184
Whelpdale, Andrew, 164
Whitehaven, 160, 164, 165, 167, 168, *168*
Wilde, Oscar, *19*
William I, King, 32
William III, King, 61, 62, 63, 83, 157
Williams, Mrs E., 89
Williams, Leslie, 88, 89
Willis, Robert, 183
wills, 7, 21, 31, 35, 44, 60
    and fee tail estate, 39, 125, 133, 145–9, 162, 172–3, 175
    and migrants, 76–7, 83, 86, 99

and taxation, 66, 67
and work of Prerogative Court of Canterbury, 27, 76, 120, 122, 127, 133, 138, 172–3, 174, 175, 184
disputes, 13, 21, 27, 76–7, 133
for wills of particular families *see* name of family
Wine Licence Office, 65, 71
Winston, Richard and family, *4*
Winthrop, John, 184, 185
Wisham, George, *26*
witnesses, trial of, 15, 16
Wolff, Johan Friedrick Wilhelm, 183
Wolvercote, 127
Woodrow, George Robert, 91
Wootton Wawen, 152
Worcester, 91, 153

Wordsworth, William (poet), 65, 67, 160–4, 195
Wordsworth family, 65, 66, 67, 160–8
    see also Wordsworth, William
Workington, 161
World War II, 34
Wright, Lawrence, 145
writ system, abolition of, 15
writs,
    de aetate probanda, 37
    of *capias excommunicatum*, 121
    of certiorari, 13
    of covenant, 40
    of entry, 41, 122
    of error, 13, 16, 131
    of extent, 131
    of habeas corpus, 13, 27

    of *latitat*, 13
    of *levanfacias*, 131
    of mandamus, 13, 30, *31*
    of nisi prius, 14–15
    of *praecipe quod reddat*, 40
    of prohibition, 13
    of quo warranto, 13
    of subpœna, 133
    of trespass and contempt, 121
Wrottesley, G., Maj. Gen. the Hon., 31

Yorkshire, 46

Zouche, Jane, 142
    William, 147, *147*